AMERICAN
SIGN LANGUAGE
AND SIGN SYSTEMS

American Sign Language and Sign Systems is a volume in the
PERSPECTIVES IN AUDIOLOGY SERIES—Lyle L. Lloyd, Ph.D., series
editor. Other volumes in this series include:

Published:

**Communicating with Deaf People: A Resource Manual for Teachers and
Students of American Sign Language** by Harry W. Hoemann, Ph.D.

Language Development and Intervention with the Hearing Impaired by
Richard R. Kretschmer, Jr., Ed.D., and Laura W. Kretschmer, Ed.D.

Noise and Audiology edited by David M. Lipscomb, Ph.D.

**Auditory Management of Hearing-Impaired Children: Principles and
Prerequisites for Intervention** edited by Mark Ross, Ph.D., and Thomas G.
Giolas, Ph.D.

Supervision in Audiology by Judith A. Rassi, M.A.

In preparation:

Aging Perception of Speech by Moe Bergman, Ed.D.

Rehabilitative Audiology (Part I: The Adult / Part II: The Elderly Client) edited
by Raymond H. Hull, Ph.D.

Acoustic Amplification: A Unified Treatment by Harry Levitt, Ph.D.

A Primer of Acoustic Phonetics by J. M. Pickett, Ph.D.

Hearing Assessment edited by William F. Rintelmann, Ph.D.

Introduction to Aural Rehabilitation edited by Ronald L. Schow, Ph.D., and
Michael A. Nerbonne, Ph.D.

Acoustical Factors Affecting Hearing Aid Performance edited by Gerald A.
Studebaker, Ph.D., and Irving Hochberg, Ph.D.

Publisher's Note

Perspectives in Audiology is a carefully planned series of clinically oriented,
topic-specific textbooks. The series is enriched by contributions from leading
specialists in audiology and allied disciplines. Because technical language and
terminology in these disciplines are constantly being refined and sometimes
vary, this series has been edited as far as possible for consistency of style in
conformity with current majority usage as set forth by the American Speech
and Hearing Association, the *Publication Manual of the American Psychological Association,* and *The University of Chicago Manual of Style.* University Park Press and the series editors and authors welcome readers' comments about individual volumes in the series or the series concept as a whole
in the interest of making **Perspectives in Audiology** as useful as possible to
students, teachers, clinicians, and scientists.

A Volume in the Perspectives in Audiology Series

AMERICAN SIGN LANGUAGE AND SIGN SYSTEMS

by
Ronnie Bring Wilbur, Ph.D.
Division of Reading and Language Development
Boston University

University Park Press
Baltimore

UNIVERSITY PARK PRESS
International Publishers in Science, Medicine, and Education
233 East Redwood Street
Baltimore, Maryland 21202

Typeset by Photo Graphics, Inc.

Manufactured in the United States of America by
The Maple Press Company

Library of Congress Cataloging in Publication Data

Wilbur, Ronnie Bring.
American sign language and sign systems.

(Perspectives in audiology series)
Bibliography: p.
Includes index.
1. Sign language. I. Title. II. Series.
HV2474.W54   419   78-21887
ISBN 0-8391-0994-6

to
All those people who kept asking
if you could really do linguistics on sign language
and to
All those people who asked about
using sign language in the education of deaf children
and to
my parents, Ira and Sylvia.

CONTENTS

TABLES

FIGURES

PREFACE TO PERSPECTIVES
IN AUDIOLOGY

Audiology is a young, vibrant, dynamic field. Its lineage can be traced to the fields of education, medicine, physics, and psychology in the nineteenth century and the emergence of speech pathology in the first half of this century. The term "audiology," meaning the science of hearing, was coined by Raymond Carhart in 1947. Since then, its definition has expanded to include its professional nature. Audiology is the profession that provides knowledge and service in the areas of human hearing and, more broadly, human communication and its disorders. As evidence of the growth of audiology as a major profession, in the 1940s there were no programs designed to prepare "audiologists," while now there are over 112 graduate training programs accredited by the Education and Training Board of the American Board of Examiners in Speech Pathology and Audiology for providing academic and clinical training designed to prepare clinically competent audiologists. Audiology is also a major area of study in the professional preparation of speech pathologists, speech and hearing scientists, and otologists.

Perspectives in Audiology is the first series of books designed to cover the major areas of study in audiology. The interdisciplinary nature of the field is reflected by the scope of the volumes in this series. The volumes currently in preparation (see p. ii) include both clinically oriented and basic science texts. The series consists of topic-specific textbooks designed to meet the needs of today's advanced level student. Each volume will also serve as a focal reference source for practicing audiologists and specialists in many related fields.

The **Perspectives in Audiology** series offers several advantages not usually found in other texts, but purposely featured in this series to increase the practical value of the books for practitioners and researchers, as well as for students and teachers.

1. Every volume includes thorough discussion of all relevant clinical and/or research papers on each topic.
2. Every volume is organized in an educational format to serve as the main text or as one of the main texts for graduate and advanced undergraduate students in courses on audiology and/or other studies concerned with human communication and its disorders.
3. Unlike ordinary texts, **Perspectives in Audiology** volumes will retain their professional reference value as focal reference sources for practitioners and researchers in career work long after completion of their studies.
4. Each volume serves as a rich source of authoritative, up-to-date information and valuable reviews for specialists in many fields, including administration, audiology, early childhood studies, linguistics, otology, psychology, pediatrics, public health, special education, speech pathology, and speech and hearing science.

American Sign Language (ASL) and the various contrived or pedagogical sign systems have become increasingly important in the education and habilitation of the hearing impaired. The use of manual signs has increased with severely hearing impaired and other severely communicatively impaired individuals. A thorough understanding of language and communication sign systems therefore is critical if audiologists and others concerned with research and service designed to meet the needs of hearing-impaired individuals are to meet their professional responsibilities.

During the past decade numerous articles and chapters have been written on the various pedagogical sign systems. In more recent years an increasing number of books and collections of papers on the topic have appeared and significant portions of texts on education of the hearing impaired and on communication disorders in general have been devoted to it. However, to date, there has not been a cohesive, single-author treatise that has examined and analyzed the linguistics of ASL, the pedagogical systems, and the application of manual sign.

Ronnie Wilbur's *American Sign Language and Sign Systems* is designed to meet this need. This volume provides a thorough linguistic perspective on ASL, considering the nature of the sign (the phonology or cherology); morphology, grammar, and syntax; psycholinguistic aspects; and sociolinguistic aspects. In addition to these research and theoretical perspectives on ASL, Wilbur considers other sign languages and various pedagogical systems used in English-speaking countries, and adds discussion of educational considerations with both hearing-impaired and other severely communicatively impaired populations.

This volume provides a comprehensive coverage of theory, research, and application of manual sign. It is intended to provide an up-to-date reference for those interested in basic research in the area and in clinical and educational applications. Through this book's contribution to research and service, it is hoped that we will be better able to provide improved educational and habilitative services to hearing-impaired persons and to others with severe communication disorders.

Lyle L. Lloyd, Ph.D.
Chairman and Professor of Special Education
Professor of Audiology and Speech Sciences
Purdue University

ACKNOWLEDGMENTS

Before writing this book, I never clearly understood how an author could acknowledge "all those people without whom this book would not have been possible." And then there are those "too numerous to mention." Now I understand.

I am fortunate in one way: the list of people to whom I am most clearly indebted, but who are "too numerous to mention" here, may be found in the reference section at the back of the book. The primary people "without whom this book would not have been possible" are the people who have conducted the basic research and who have shared their results in print. They have sent me copies of their papers, have helped me run up my long-distance phone bill, and referred me to otherwise missed articles. In many cases, they have read, commented, criticized, and helped revise sections of this book. Special thanks here go to Francois Grosjean, Robert Hoffmeister, Howard Poizner, Harry Hoemann, Ursula Bellugi, Rachel Mayberry, and members of the New England Sign Language Society, especially Mark Bernstein, Rebecca Kantor, Nancy Chinchor, Joan Cottle Poole, and Judy Kegl.

I also owe a tremendous personal debt to friends who literally clothed me, shopped for and cooked my food, did my laundry, and understood about my not answering the phone. Significant contributions in this respect came from Irma Rosenfield, Eric Wiseman, Robin Ault, Lise Menn, and George Carnevale. My thanks to Kattagarör for guarding the various stages of the manuscript.

Judy Kegl must be singled out for her enormous contribution to my perspective on sign language linguistics, her willingness to argue with me, to repeat until I understood, to forgive when I didn't, and her fantastic chocolates which kept me glued to the typewriter until I finished the first draft. To Lyle Lloyd, the series editor for **Perspectives in Audiology,** goes the blame for getting me started on this project in the first place, and my thanks to him for his receptive attitude toward my perennial delays and for his continuing encouragement.

AMERICAN SIGN LANGUAGE AND SIGN SYSTEMS

CHAPTER 1

INTRODUCTION

CONTENTS

American Sign Language (ASL or Ameslan) is, in the United States, the native language of many deaf people who have deaf parents and is the language used by many deaf adults among themselves. O'Rourke et al. (1975) suggest that nearly 500,000 deaf people and an unknown number of hearing people use ASL, making it the third most widely used non-English language in the United States (Spanish, 4.5 million; Italian, 600,000). American Sign Language differs from these other languages, however, because unlike English, Spanish, Italian, and others, ASL is primarily manual/visual rather than oral/auditory.

ASL (like other sign languages) is not derived from any spoken language, although its coexistence with English in a bilingual environment allows it to be influenced in a number of ways (borrowing through fingerspelling, Battison, 1978, see Chapter 2; initialization of signs, see Chapters 2 and 3; and influence of English word order, Chapter 4; Fischer, 1975; Liddell, 1977). ASL's nearest sign language relative is French Sign Language (FSL), a result of the intervention of Thomas Gallaudet and a deaf teacher from France, Laurent Clerc (Chapter 7). These educators brought FSL to the United States in 1817, while others spread FSL all over Europe, influencing such sign languages as Swedish, Latvian, Irish, Spanish, Dutch, Italian, Swiss, Austrian, Russian, and, eventually, Australian (Stokoe, 1972). ASL has been carried to Africa and India in recent years, where it will probably interact with the native sign languages. Woodward (1977b) identifies several language families based on hypothesized relationships between known sign languages. In the French sign language family are Old FSL, Modern FSL, Old ASL, Modern ASL, and Danish (recall again that these are *not* related to spoken French). In the British sign language family are British Sign Language, Formal Australian Sign Language, Informal Australian Sign Language, Old Catholic Scottish Sign Language, and Modern Scottish Sign Language. Notice that although English is spoken in both America and Britain, the sign languages of the two countries are not related, nor are they mutually intelligible. Other families identified by Woodward include Asian (Japanese, Taiwanese, and Hong Kong) and South American (Costa Rican, Colombian). Egyptian, Indian (now being studied extensively by Wilson, 1978, and Vasishta, Wilson, and Woodward, 1978), and Malaysian are of unknown affiliation. Others, such as Adamorobe (Ghana: Frishberg, in preparation) and Providence Island (Washabaugh, Woodward, and DeSantis, 1976) appear to be indigenous. In addition to these, several other sign languages are being investigated. This author has a film of Mainland Chinese Sign Language (graciously supplied by C. C. Cheng) to compare with a film of Taiwanese Sign Language (thanks to Fanny Yeh and Al Marotta). Poole (in preparation) examines the relationship of Martha's Vineyard Sign Language to ASL in a manner similar to Johnson's (1978) investigation of Oregon and British Columbia sawmill sign languages, which may be related to ASL. Mayberry (1978) looks at French-Canadian Sign Language, and of course the relationship between ASL and FSL has been extensively studied by Woodward and DeSantis (1977a,b) (further discussion in Chapter 6). Sign languages used by hearing people for primary purposes other than communication with deaf people have also been studied. Kegl and Nigrosh (1975) reported on Plains Indian Sign Language, which was used as an interlanguage among Indians of different spoken languages. Kegl and Nash (1976) described Warlpiri Sign Language, used for ceremonial purposes among the Warlpiri in Australia as well as for communication with deaf people.

Family relationships, such as those suggested by Woodward, do not imply mutual intelligibility. Jordan and Battison (1976) have demonstrated that Modern FSL, ASL, and Danish Sign Language, although related, are not mutually intelligible. The lack of mutual intelligibility does not rule out the possibility of establishing communication between signers of these different (or other) sign languages, which can be accomplished by spontaneously creating a hybrid or pidgin, or by resorting to mime.

Quite apart from the use of ASL in the United States is the use of a modified form, signed English. The fact that one can sign and speak at the same time has allowed educators to take advantage of the bilingual situation in which American deaf people exist. Taking the signs from ASL and the word order from English, sign language *systems* (cf. Bornstein, 1973, 1978; Caccamise, 1976; Wilbur, 1976) have been established artificially for teaching English syntax to deaf children. These systems are discussed in Chapter 7. In addition to deliberate modifications by educators, signed English also includes those modifications in signing that result from 1) hearing native speakers of English who are unfamiliar with ASL syntax but have learned ASL signs and 2) deaf signers' own modifications reflecting the influence of English syntax when in contact with hearing people (for details, see Chapter 6). The larger context in which ASL is used, surrounded by English speaking and English signing hearing people, and the bilingual nature of deaf people themselves must constantly be kept in mind.

BACKGROUND ON EARLY SIGN LANGUAGE RESEARCH

The early writings on sign language were concerned with its status as a language and its role in the education of deaf children. Later research on ASL and other sign languages was thus aimed at demonstrating 1) that it is indeed a language and 2) that it is beneficial in educating deaf children. More recent linguistic research has shifted away from proving that ASL is a language to concentrating on providing an adequate linguistic description, with the possible subsequent goal of constructing a grammar useful for teaching ASL to nonsigners. However, more recent educational research is still aiming at demonstrating utility of sign language in education. Efficient teaching techniques and maximum utilization of the available modalities remain to be investigated more carefully.

A review of the factors that led to the above two goals provides some perspective on both recent research and the earlier research. Negative attitudes toward sign languages in general have arisen from several sources. One is a lack of understanding of the nature of language itself, and the related failure to separate language from speech. The lack of a traditional orthography for sign language has also contributed, because it has led to the use of inadequate glosses (names of signs). Glosses do not indicate crucial information about the way a sign is made; for example, in the sentences "John hit Bill" and "Bill hit John," the verb would be glossed (with capital letters, see p. 11) as HIT for both sentences, even though in each sentence the verb would start and end at different points. Thus, the gloss obscures information about the formation of the sign that is critical to the understanding of the nature of sign language. The use of glosses allowed only crude analyses of the language, and indeed many people did little more than compare a glossed sentence to an English sentence. This resulted in conclusions that ASL consisted of unordered, mimetic gestures and was incomplete, inferior, situation-bound, and concrete. Such terms represent not only a lack of understanding of manual language, but an oral language bias, from which it is exceedingly difficult to escape. These negative attitudes and early linguistic descriptions provided the proponents of oral education for the deaf with the upper hand in the so-called "oral/manual controversy." It was their challenge to those interested in the use of sign language to first prove that sign language was both a language and useful in the education of deaf children (which meant, in addition, to prove that it did not harm deaf children's acquisition of speech; see Chapter 8). The oral language bias inherent in this entire situation is evidenced by the fact that the proponents of manual communication have responded unquestioningly to the challenge (Chapter 8) while, as Conrad (1975) pointed out, never issuing a similar challenge to the proponents of oral education to demonstrate the effectiveness of their methods for the total development of the deaf child.

The failure to make the initial separation of language from speech goes back far into history, and may be related to the fact that writing was a late innovation, and that even to this day, languages without writing systems still exist. The Bible tells us that at the Tower of Babel, the Lord went down and "did there confound their language, that they may not understand one another's speech" (Genesis 11:7). In sharp contrast to this view of oral supremacy, Hewes (1973) has suggested that gestures may have been the origin of language, and speech was a later development.

The education of deaf people has been profoundly affected by the failure to recognize the distinction between language and speech. Siegel (1969, p. 96) described the character of eighteenth-century educators of the deaf:

> The task of educating the deaf was undertaken mainly by charities often manned by fierce evangelical reformers. Filled with enthusiasm and caught up in the evangelical tide which was making deep eddies in English social philosophy, these men of good will and great piety saw their role in terms of Biblical text. The deaf to them were pitiable outcasts whose tongues were tied, and as Christ had opened the ears of the deaf man and had loosened his tongue, so must they try to do.

At the same time, "in France, the situation was quite different, and there was by the end of the XVIIIth century great concern for the total education of the deaf " (Siegel, 1969, p. 97). By 1790, the Abbé de l'Epée had founded his school for the deaf in Paris, and had developed a modified sign system, a form of signed French, which he called "methodical signs" (Markowicz, 1976).

Both France and England were influenced by John Locke's empirical philosophy, which maintained that the mind worked only on what the senses conveyed to it. Introspection on the part of some Englishmen revealed to them that they thought in words—they spoke to themselves—and they concluded that speech conveys information to the mind. Therefore, a person deprived of speech would necessarily be deprived of means by which to think. The French interpreted Locke's writings as implying that the mind would work on information conveyed to it by any sense and that deaf people should be able to profit from meaningful material in a visual mode. "That two such opposite philosophies could grow simultaneously in two countries [England—oral, France—manual] which shared so many other ideas certainly warrants an investigation of the historical and intellectual climates which produced these ideas" (Siegel, 1969, p. 98). Two rather extensive discussions of the historical events that surrounded the education of the deaf may be found in Lane (1976) and Moores (1977).

The conflict between these two diverse methods of educating the deaf continues to this day. However, in the United States, there has been a rapid increase in total communication (TC) usage (simultaneous use of signs and speechreading) in programs for deaf children. Jordan, Gustason, and Rosen (1976) found that 510 programs reported using total communication, some 333 of which (about 65%) had changed between 1968 and 1975. (This represents a significant increase in the number of deaf children who are learning a form of signed English, thus providing the potential for greater influences of English syntax on the structure of ASL.) This rise in total communication has been greeted with mixed reviews. On one hand, the establishment of effective communication with young deaf children is viewed to be essential to their socioemotional development as well as to their academic achievement (Chapter 8). On the other hand, there are unanswered questions concerning the potential for processing two modalities at the same time (Beckmeyer, 1976; Stokes and Menyuk, 1975; Wilbur and Flood, 1977), concern over the greater amount of processing time that signed English takes compared to ASL or to spoken English (Bellugi and Fischer, 1972), concern over the declining emphasis placed on specific speech skills training (Moores, 1978; Wilbur, in press b; Chapter 8), and the proliferation of language programs of any kind without considering the individual needs of each particular child (Moores, 1978; Wilbur, in press b).

LINGUISTIC INTEREST IN SIGN LANGUAGE

The existence of any unstudied language represents a great attraction to most linguists. For that language to be visual/spatial rather than commonplace auditory heightens their interest. Of primary concern among linguists is the extent to which languages used by humans have features in common and what might account for these universal characteristics. In this respect, sign languages represent a challenge to theories of linguistic universals, as well as to metalinguistic concepts of "possible grammar." If it were found that proposed constraints on, for example, what syntactic rules may or may not do (Ross, 1967) are valid also for a visual/manual language, confidence in a description of language that incorporates such constraints would be greatly strengthened.

The search for linguistic universals has traditionally included only oral languages (Chinchor et al., 1976; Greenberg, 1966). Many attempts to investigate linguistic universals with respect to manual languages thus displayed an oral language bias. In order to fully understand how this bias can affect manual language research, and to emphasize the need for caution when interpreting any research on sign languages, it is instructive to consider an early attempt by Schlesinger (1970) to study Israeli Sign Language (ISL) to see if manual languages expressed grammatical relations such as subject, object, and indirect object, which are claimed to be linguistically universal.

Schlesinger's experiment was designed to elicit sentences in ISL (which is not related to ASL) that contain three noun phrases ("arguments") in the function of subject, object, and indirect object, as illustrated by the English sentence "John gave the book to Mary," where "John" is the subject, "the book" is the direct object, and "Mary" is the indirect object. The same relations hold if the sentence is reworded as "John gave Mary the book." The sender had in front of him a picture that contained a man, a bear, and a girl, in which the man might be handing the bear to the girl, or handing the girl to the bear, etc. The receiver had six pictures in which each of the possible combinations was portrayed. The sender had to communicate in sign language to the receiver which picture to choose. Thirty subjects were used. They varied greatly in background; some had a good knowledge of Hebrew (and probably limited knowledge of ISL) whereas others had limited knowledge of Hebrew (and probably were users of ISL). It is also likely that those with good knowledge of Hebrew used signed Hebrew, which is to ISL as signed English is to ASL. The results of Schlesinger's experiment showed a high degree of misunderstanding between sender and receiver. Schlesinger concluded that ISL did not have a means for expressing grammatical relations, because the receivers would pick the wrong pictures and thus indicate that they were not receiving the grammatical information of who was doing what to whom. Therefore, he concluded that grammatical relations must not be linguistically universal.

The same experiment was conducted by Bode (1974) with American Sign Language and the results were very different. Bode used a group of native users of ASL and a hearing control group who used spoken English. She found 86% comprehension for the signers and 95% for the speakers, the difference being not significant. Schlesinger had an average of 52% comprehension for his signers. Why such a large difference? Bode screened her subjects to make sure that all of them were native users of the language, whereas Schlesinger did not. In Israel, this can be a great mistake, since the population is heterogeneous, including immigrants from all parts of the world, some of whom may have only recently arrived in Israel. Stokoe (personal communication) feels that Israeli Sign Language is in fact a convenient fiction for a lingua franca (a working language for people with different linguistic backgrounds) composed of sign languages that came together only shortly before the establishment of Tel Aviv. In such a situation, variables like age, education, and residency can be of critical importance. Schlesinger's subjects could not understand the messages sent, not because of a lack of grammatical relations in Israeli Sign Language, but because they were not all using the same language. "The comparable situation in the United States indicates that users of ASL often readily comprehend sentences from signed English, but that users of only signed English have great difficulty understanding ASL. This is primarily due to the fact that the education system insists on teaching English syntax to deaf children in school and that they are consequently familiar with the syntax of signed English. Educational institutions in the United States do not teach American Sign Language or its structure. The result is that deaf individuals may have a range of competency in ASL" (Chinchor et al., 1976). The same situation is probably true in Israel. In any event, the failure to investigate these factors may lead to a lack of validity for experimental conclusions.

Another problem inherent in Schlesinger's study, which will shed light on later reports as well, is his data analysis. He assumed that grammatical relations would be displayed in a linear sequence, thus he chose to analyze only "full sentences," those that contained separate signs for the subject, direct object, and indirect object in linear sequence with the verb. This excluded from analysis any utterances that used a sign language device of establishing positions in space for nouns and moving or orienting the verb sign between them (Chapter 3). The recognition of the importance of simultaneity of grammatical information in sign languages is a crucial step toward shaking oral language bias. The effects that these assumptions had on Schlesinger's overall analysis are discussed more fully in Chinchor et al. (1976). For present purposes, it is only the historical perspective this study provides that is of specific interest. Nor is Schlesinger alone. In Wilbur and Jones (1974), lack of understanding of the function of pointing in ASL (Chapters 3 and 4) led them to ignore certain signs used by hearing children of deaf parents; thus they missed important stages of development (Chapter 5). Others have framed their descriptions of ASL in terms of comparisons with English. Fant (1972a), for example, wrote that ASL has no passive voice, no sign for the verb "to be," and no determiners. By itself, this description is insufficient, because it fails to indicate how such information is communicated in ASL. In addition, further investigation into ASL itself (without comparison to English) reveals constructions that may be interpreted as passive (Kegl, 1978b; Chapter 4), head nods and other facial expressions which appear in constructions that in English would require "be" (Liddell, 1977; Chapter 4), and indicators of definite and indefinite nouns which in English would be marked with the determiners "the" and "a" (Chapter 3).

PROCEEDING WITH SIGN LANGUAGE RESEARCH

This review of the research on sign language and its educational applications is divided into two major parts. Part I concentrates on structural descriptions of ASL and psycholinguistic and sociolinguistic aspects of its usage. Of necessity, descriptions of sign language must begin with descriptions of the sign itself. Stokoe (1960) provided a description of sign formation, a "cherology" (coming from a Homeric Greek morpheme *cher* meaning "handy") parallel to oral language phonology, which has been built upon, refined, and modified in subsequent years by himself and others (Chapter 2). The term "phonology" has been retained in this book because it has become apparent that traditional notions of segment structures, their effects on surrounding segments, and their combination into larger units (spoken words or signs) are appropriate for sign structure as described so far (Chapters 2 and 3). "Alternate Descriptions" (Chapter 2) is not light reading, even for the most sophisticated of readers. Because of the diversity of this audience, and the need for all readers to obtain some familiarity with ways in which sign structure might parallel the sound structure we are familiar with, this author has reviewed competing descriptions of sign distinctive features because they are likely to appear in future works on sign language. Thus, even the most casual reader is urged to cover the section at least once, and by comparison, reading the rest of the book will seem easy.

The whole of Chapter 2 ("The Sign") concentrates on the sign as it appears in isolation (citation form). In Chapter 3, some of the statements made in Chapter 2 are modified as the sign is considered in the context of other signs. Phonological modifications may occur in the formation of particular signs (change of location, handshape, orientation, etc.), depending on the context in which they occur. Morphological modifications may also result in formational changes (Chapter 3). "Grammatical Modifications" (Chapter 3) is an introduction to the changes in formation that may be made for particular grammatical purposes. The distinction between this section and Chapter 4 is purely arbitrary. However, Chapter 3 serves as an introduction to sign behavior for those unfamiliar with sign language and as an introduction to linguistic description for those unfamiliar with current linguistic theory. With few exceptions, Chapter 4 assumes knowledge of grammatical modifications, and the total picture of ASL syntax cannot be gained by reading either chapter alone. Chapter 5 concentrates on psycholinguistic aspects of ASL usage, including discussion of iconicity, ASL acquisition, production and perception of signs, cerebral lateralization, and memory processes. Chapter 6 includes sociolinguistic aspects of ASL and its use in the deaf community, including theories of the history of ASL, variation in ASL, and modifications of ASL in contact with English. The role of ASL in defining an identifiable community is also discussed. The importance of this information for those who are responsible for education of the deaf and who still tend to view deafness as a handicap cannot be overstated.

Part II, Educational Considerations, contains three chapters. Chapter 7 is concerned with the artificial signed English systems, including the most commonly used of these, Signing Exact English (SEE 2) and Signed English (distinguished from signed English in the latter part of Chapter 7). Also included are fingerspelling, which is used very little in ASL but which may be used simultaneously with speech (and no signs) in the Rochester Method, and Cued Speech, which is not a sign system at all but an auxiliary system of manual gestures for assisting in comprehension of speech (see "Fingerspelling and Cued Speech," Chapter 7). Chapter 8 deals with the education of deaf children and the resulting influence of sign usage (ASL, signed English, or whatever) on the language development of deaf children (English and sign language), speech skills, socioemotional development, and attainment of adequate memory, perception, and reading skills. Chapter 9 focuses on recent reports of successful language intervention using signs with nondeaf populations. This has included autistic children, mentally retarded individuals, multiply handicapped students, individuals with cerebral palsy, and even a child with tracheostenosis. The surprising result of many of these intervention attempts has been that some of these individuals with normal vocalization mechanisms have eventually increased their vocalizations and improved their verbalizations to intelligible levels. "Why Does It Work?" (Chapter 9) contains speculations on the apparent success of sign language intervention, although explanations offered so far do not seem to be entirely satisfactory (see also Fristoe and Lloyd, in press).

The diversity of topics included in this book reflects the diversity of people who are concerned with deafness and sign language. The information presented here is not all there is to know about ASL or sign language research in general, nor is every paper from every researcher included (a result of time and space requirements). Rather than participating in the continual oral/manual controversy, this author has instead chosen to present available factual information. Where appropriate, the information presented has been questioned. The reader is advised to do the same. Do not assume that the summaries herein contain all of the original author's data, arguments, or intentions, or that you have understood all of the subtleties that may be involved. Finally, particular attention should be paid to the use of words like "seems," "could be," and "may," in which the author has avoided stating as fact those things that are still controversial, remain to be investigated, or are insufficiently documented. In many cases, the use of such terms are the original author's, and in no case should their usage be considered detrimental.

EXPLAINING THE NOTATION

The hardest thing to do with a dynamic, three-dimensional language is to reduce it to two-dimensional linear description. Transcriptions, illustrations, and photographs fall far short of the ideal representation. Several detailed transcriptions have been proposed for describing the formation of signs. The notation in Stokoe, Casterline, and Croneberg's (1965) *Dictionary of American Sign Language* has been retained here. Others (Newkirk, 1975; Sutton, 1976) suggest that a wider variety will be available in the future.

In addition to Stokoe notation, which is discussed early in Chapter 2, a few other conventions are necessary. The glosses (names) of all signs are written in capital letters, e.g., HIT. The English translation (or best approximation thereof) is presented in double quotation marks, e.g., "hit." Complex glosses are connected by hyphens, e.g., SIT-ON-IT "sit on it." Fingerspelled letters are indicated in single quotation marks, e.g., 's'. Fingerspelled sequences are written in lower case with hyphens between each letter, e.g., s-e-a-r-c-h-i-n-g "search-ing." Most transcriptions have been greatly simplified (e.g., in "Gram-matical Modifications," Chapter 3, Kegl's examples have been trans-lated into a simpler notation) with the exception of maintaining the exact transcription used in Liddell (1977) when discussing his thesis in Chapter 4). When formational information is necessary for syntactic discussions, the use of subscripts to indicate arbitrary points in space has been adopted from Kegl. Thus, PRO_1-HIT-PRO_2 indicates that a person previously established in space at point 1 (see "Morphological Modifications," Chapter 3) hit another person previously established in space at point 2, i.e., "He/she$_1$ hit him/her$_2$" (gender is not marked on these pronouns in ASL). When first person "I/me" is intended, PRO_{1p} is used, except for Liddell's notation, which is PRO.1. Simi-larly, for "you," PRO_{2p} is used (Liddell's PRO.2). The English trans-lation always attempts to clarify what the meaning is.

When necessary, descriptions of the formation of the sign are given in parentheses in awkward English. The reader may want to have the Stokoe, Casterline, and Croneberg (1965) *Dictionary of American Sign Language* or the O'Rourke (1973) *A Basic Course in Manual Communication,* or some other sign reference manual, avail-able to see what signs not illustrated here look like. Finally, an asterisk * before a sentence indicates ungrammaticality.

PART I

AMERICAN
SIGN LANGUAGE

CHAPTER 2

THE SIGN

CONTENTS

Traditional analyses of sign language have concentrated on the sign as the primary unit. Stokoe (1960) investigated sign formation, "cherology," treating it as analogous to the phonological system of oral languages. He defined three parameters that were realized simultaneously in the formation of a particular sign—DEZ (designator, handshape); TAB (tabulation, location); and SIG (signation, motion). A fourth parameter, ORIENTATION, which refers to the orientation of the palm, was added later by Battison (1973; Battison, Markowicz, and Woodward, 1975). These parameters are later considered in detail, along with conventions for writing signs in Stokoe notation. Constraints on the structure of signs, which separate signs from mime, are discussed, including visual constraints, linguistic constraints, and violations of these constraints for humorous purposes. Historical changes in signs have supported many of the hypothesized constraints, and are thus of interest when discussing sign formation. Recently, several distinctive feature systems have been proposed for signs. Many of the details remain to be worked out, but the concept of describing signs in terms of distinctive features is attractive for many purposes. Thus, as further work is done, the actual features and their descriptions may vary from those presented here, but the utilization of some set of distinctive features in describing signs seems to be with us to stay.

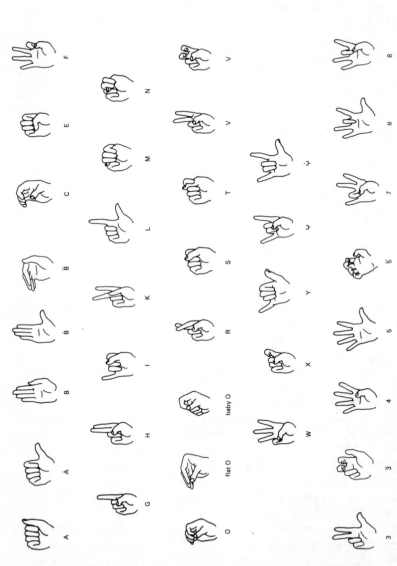

Figure 1.   ASL Handshapes (presented in an order allowing comparison with the Manual Alphabet in Figure 2).

HANDSHAPE

ASL handshapes are given in Figure 1, and the American manual alphabet is given in Figure 2. Table 1 contains the handshape symbols as defined by Stokoe, Casterline, and Croneberg (1965). The DEZ parameter has 19 values (although there are many more handshapes; see "Alternate Descriptions," this chapter). It is important to emphasize that although some of the handshapes are named with letter names

Table 1.   Symbols for writing the signs of the American Sign Language: DEZ symbols, some also used as TAB

Symbol	Description
A	Compact hand, fist; may be like 'a', 's', or 't' of manual alphabet
B	Flat hand
5	Spread hand; fingers and thumb spread like '5' of manual numeration
C	Curved hand; may be like 'c' or more open
E	Contracted hand; like 'e' or more claw-like
F	"Three-ring" hand; from spread hand, thumb and index finger touch or cross
G	Index hand; like 'g' or sometimes like 'd'; index finger points from fist
H	Index and second finger, side-by-side, extended
I	"Pinkie" hand; little finger extended from compact hand
K	Like G except that thumb touches middle phalanx of second finger; like 'k' and 'p' of manual alphabet
L	Angle hand; thumb, index finger in right angle, other fingers usually bent into palm
3	"Cock" hand; thumb and first two fingers spread, like '3' of manual numeration
O	Tapered hand; fingers curved and squeezed together over thumb; may be like 'o' of manual alphabet
R	"Warding off" hand; second finger crossed over index finger, like "r" of manual alphabet
V	"Victory" hand; index and second fingers extended and spread apart
W	Three-finger hand; thumb and little finger touch, others extended spread
X	Hook hand; index finger bent in hook from fist, thumb tip may touch fingertip
Y	"Horns" hand; thumb and little finger spread out extended from fist; or index finger and little finger extended, parallel
8	Allocheric variant of Y; second finger bent in from spread hand, thumb may touch fingertip

From Stokoe, Casterline, and Croneberg (1965) with permission.

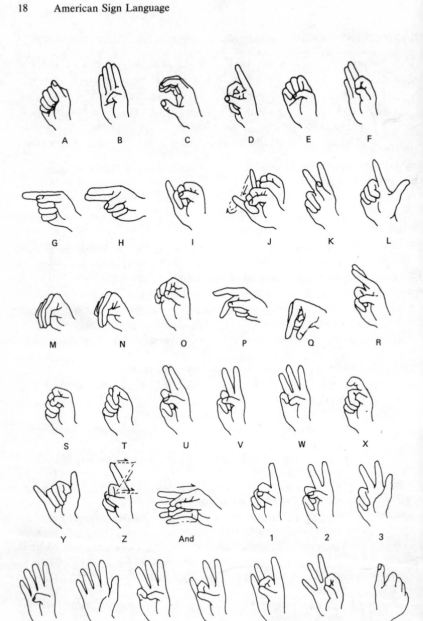

Figure 2.   The American manual alphabet.

(A, B, G, etc.), these handshapes are not necessarily identical in formation to the letters of the manual alphabet of the same name (compare, for example, G in Figures 1 and 2). Furthermore, the use of letter names for handshape configurations does not imply a connection between the formation of the sign and the letters of the English word that is used to translate that sign. There are some signs whose formation has been modified so that the handshape does correspond to the first letter of the English word (initialized signs), but these are discussed separately.

Notice in Table 1 that according to Stokoe, the manual letters 'a', 's', and 't' are not distinctive, but are considered variants of A. In American Sign Language before the introduction of initialized signs, a sign made with the handshape 'a' of the manual alphabet was not distinct in meaning from a similar sign made with the handshape 's' or 't'. Initialization has created several signs from one, by attaching distinctive meanings to the different handshapes borrowed from the manual alphabet. Thus, the sign made with the A handshape, which may be translated as "try, attempt, strive," has been split so that with the 'a' handshape from the manual alphabet it means "attempt," with the 's' manual letter it means "strive," and with the 't' manual letter it means "try." These borrowings are discussed in more detail later in this chapter, and in Chapter 3.

LOCATION

Table 2 lists the Stokoe symbols for the location of a sign. A basic distinction is made between those signs made on the body (including so-called "body anchor verbs") and those made in neutral space. All signs must be made within the "signing space" (Battison, 1973; Bellugi and Fischer, 1972; Frishberg, 1975), described by Lacy (1974) as extending from the top of the head to just below the waist (or hip area) on the vertical axis while horizontally and laterally forming a "bubble" in front of the speaker, extending from the signer's extreme right to the signer's extreme left (an arc of 180°). The signing space may be proportionately enlarged for signing to larger audiences ("louder") or confined for purposes of more rapid signing or to be secretive ("quieter") so as not to be "over-seen." Few signs are made over the head, behind the ear, or below the waist (Lacy, 1974). Bellugi (1972) reported that when signed English was compared to ASL, the signing that was intended to parallel English was produced in a more compact space in front of the signer's body, whereas when ASL was signed, a larger signing space was used. In addition to the locations listed in Table 2,

Table 2. Symbols for writing the signs of the American Sign Language: TAB symbols

Symbol	Description
$\emptyset$	Zero, the neutral place where the hands move, in contrast with all places below
$\cap\!\!\!\cup$	Face or whole head
$\cap$	Forehead or brow, upper face
$\sqcup$	Mid-face, the eye and nose region
$\cup$	Chin, lower face
$\}$	Cheek, temple, ear, side-face
π	Neck
[ ]	Trunk, body from shoulders to hips
$\diagdown$	Upper arm
$\diagup$	Elbow, forearm
α	Wrist, arm in supinated position (on its back)
$\mathcal{D}$	Wrist, arm in pronated position (face down)

From Stokoe, Casterline, and Croneberg (1965) by permission.

several of the handshapes listed in Table 1 may serve as place of formation for signs that involve two hands touching. Thus, the sign NAME involves the touching of one H hand to the other H hand, whereas the sign THAT involves a Y hand touching a 5 hand (Figure 3).

MOTION

Table 3 lists the Stokoe parameters for describing the motion of a sign. This is the most difficult area to transcribe. The first three symbols refer to vertical action, the next three to side-by-side motion, the next three to horizontal motion toward or away from the signer, the next three to rotary action, and the rest to complex motions involving either the fingers, the hands, or the lower arms and hands. Notice that two

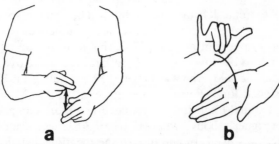

a　　　　　　　**b**

Figure 3. The sign NAME involves touching one H hand to the other H hand (a). The sign THAT involves a Y hand contacting a base 5 hand.

of the symbols refer to closing and opening action and require specification of a final handshape in addition to the initial handshape.

CONVENTIONS FOR USING STOKOE NOTATION

In addition to the three parameters, Stokoe, Casterline, and Croneberg (1965) provide a set of rules for writing the signs with the parameter notation. The place of formation, or location, is referred to as the TAB, herein T, which is written as the first symbol. The second parameter, handshape or DEZ, D, is written next, followed by a superscript indicating motion, or SIG, ^{s}, giving TD^s. Thus, "know" may be transcribed as $\cap B_T^x$ (Figure 4). It is also possible for a sign to have two movements

Table 3.   Symbols for writing the signs of the American Sign Language: SIG symbols

Symbol	Description	Action
∧	Upward movement	
∨	Downward movement	Vertical action
∾	Up-and-down movement	
>	Rightward movement	
<	Leftward movement	Sideways action
≷	Side-to-side movement	
T	Movement toward signer	
⊥	Movement away from signer	Horizontal action
I	To-and-fro movement	
ɑ	Supinating rotation (palm up)	
ɒ	Pronating rotation (palm down)	
ω	Twisting movement	Rotary action
ŋ	Nodding or bending action	
□	Opening action (final DEZ configuration shown in brackets)	
#	Closing action (final DEZ configuration shown in brackets)	
ℛ	Wriggling action of fingers	
e	Circular action	
)(	Convergent action, approach	
×	Contactual action, touch	
⊠	Linking action, grasp	
‡	Crossing action	Interaction
○	Entering action	
÷	Divergent action, separate	
‹›	Interchanging action	

From Stokoe, Casterline, and Croneberg (1965) by permission.

Figure 4.   The sign KNOW.

that are simultaneous, such as downward and to the right. This would be written TD^s. Also occurring are TD^{ss}, TDD^s (for two-handed signs, TDD$_s^s$, TDD^{ss}), TD(D)$_{ss}^s$ (the parentheses indicate that the second hand may or may not be involved), TD(D)^{sss}, and TD(D)$_{ss}^{ss}$. Some examples are given in Table 4.

Several modification symbols are also required, some indicating the relationship between two hands. Thus, if one hand is held below the other (touching or not), the lower hand is indicated with a line over its handshape symbol; thus, ĀA$^\times$ "coffee" (Figure 5) from Stokoe, Casterline, and Croneberg (1965). Conversely, the upper hand may be marked with an underline, as in A̲Ȧ$^\times$ "assistant" (Figure 6). (No regulations are given as to when the uppermost is marked and when the lower one is marked.) If the two hands are parallel to each other side-by-side, either close together or touching, it is indicated with a straight vertical line as in ∅A$^|$A$^\times$ "with" (Figure 7). If one hand is

Table 4.   Examples of various arrangements of TAB, DEZ, and SIG

Parameter notation	Sign	Meaning
TD^s	∩B$_\top^\times$	"Know"
TD$_s^s$	[]F$^{\sim}_\times$	"Pin"
TD^{ss}	[]C$_\top$ $^{\times\cdot}$	"Complain"
TDD^s	[]C$_\top$ C$_\top$ $^\perp$	"Fat, chubby"
TDD$_s^s$	∅A$_a$A$_a$ $_\perp^\square$	"Cause"
TDD^{ss}	∅B$_\top$ B$_\top$ $^{\times\cdot}$	"Jail, prison"
TDD$_{ss}^s$	∩BB$^{\wedge}_{\times\sim}$	Variant of "invent, invention"
TDD^{sss}	∅B$_a$B̈ $^{\times\perp\,\times}$	"Often," variant of "million"

Figure 5. The sign COFFEE.   Figure 6. The sign ASSISTANT.

behind the other, again with or without contact, it is indicated with the subscript ₉ on the first handshape symbol, as in $\emptyset A^{\perp}_{o}A^{\perp}$ "follow" (Figure 8). Also, the symbol ✝ , which indicates crossing movement, can be used after the first handshape symbol to indicate that the initial part of the sign is made with crossed forearms, wrists, hands, or fingers, e.g., $\emptyset B^{\ast}B^{\perp}_{p}$ "divide" (Figure 9). A dot over a handshape indicates that an otherwise unextended finger or thumb has been extended, e.g., $U\dot{A}^{\perp}$ "not" (Figure 10). Three dots over a handshape indicate that it is made with the fingers bent, e.g., $B_{a}\ddot{C}^{\perp}_{p}$ "rough" (Figure 11). A prominent forearm is indicated by the symbol ✓ , placed before the handshape symbol; thus, $\emptyset \checkmark C^{e}_{a}$ "always" (Figure 12). If the two hands are linked together initially, this is indicated by ⊼ , e.g., $F^{\pi}F^{e}$ "cooperate" (Figure 13). If one hand is interrupted by the other (through the fingers), a circle with a dot inside is placed after the first DEZ, as in $5^{\circ}G^{a}$ "begin, start" (Figure 14). The orientation of the palm, although not considered a separate parameter by Stokoe, Casterline, and Croneberg, is nonetheless partially indicated by two subscripts, ɑ and ᴅ, the last two symbols in Table 2. Thus SCHOOL and MONEY differ in that one hand faces the other in SCHOOL, whereas both face the same way in MONEY. Thus, SCHOOL $B_{a}B^{x}_{a}$ and MONEY $B_{a}B^{x}_{a}$ (Figure 15). A dot over a motion symbol indicates that the motion is short, sharp, tense, and checked (e.g., "strict" $\sqcap\ddot{V}^{x}$). A dot after the motion symbol indicates a single repetition of the entire motion, whereas two dots afterward indicate two repetitions. If the two hands alternate in their motion, rather than both alternating to-

Figure 7.   The sign WITH.

Figure 8.   The sign FOLLOW.

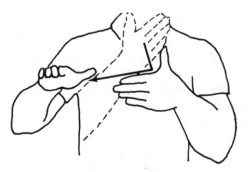

Figure 9.   The sign DIVIDE.

Figure 10.   The sign NOT/DENY.

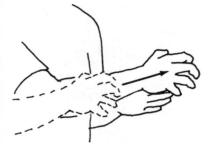
Figure 11.   The sign ROUGH.

Figure 12.   The sign ALWAYS.

Figure 13.   The sign COOPERATE/RELATE.

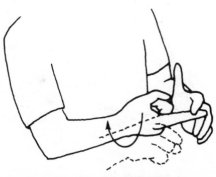
Figure 14.   The sign BEGIN/START.

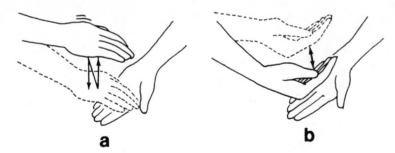

Figure 15.   The signs SCHOOL (a) and MONEY (b).

gether, a wavy sign is used, as in ∅FF^~ "if." Sometimes the hand-shape of a sign will change during its formation; this is indicated by the closing sign ⋕ (if it is a closing change) followed by a second (the new) handshape symbol in brackets, e.g., "and" 5_<>⋕ [O] (Figure 16). Finally, compound signs are indicated by a double row of vertical dots between the two parts, e.g., "lady" (GIRL + FINE))Ȧ×ː ː[ ]5×̌ (Figure 17).

The Stokoe notation was an innovative method for transcribing meaningful, constrained visual/manual information. Signs are listed in the *Dictionary* according to TAB, then DEZ, then SIG. A few words of caution on using the *Dictionary* are required. The *Dictionary* is a bilingual dictionary; that is, words are listed in ASL but glossed and defined in English. A true ASL dictionary would, of course, contain no English, just as an English dictionary contains no Swahili (except perhaps to mention the etymology of certain Swahili-derived English forms). Second, no dictionary is comprehensive, in the sense that it contains all the possible words, past and present, of a language. Thus, it is unreasonable to count the number of entries in the *Dictionary* and

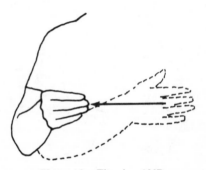

Figure 16.   The sign AND.

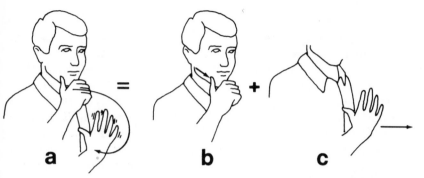

Figure 17.   The sign LADY (a) is originally a compound of the signs GIRL (b) and FINE (c).

then conclude that ASL only has X signs. It should also be remembered that dictionaries are lists of words and, consequently, do not indicate syntax, the order of elements in a sentence, or case markings, although Stokoe, Casterline, and Croneberg (1965) do provide a brief description of aspects of ASL syntax (Chapter 4). However, after reading the *Dictionary*, one cannot claim that one has learned ASL, or that one has learned all the possible signs. What a native user of a language knows greatly exceeds what can be entered into a dictionary.

CONSTRAINTS ON SIGN FORMATION

In oral language, distinctive features are simultaneously combined to produce consonantal and vocalic segments. Analogously, the four Stokoe parameters are produced simultaneously to form signs. In oral languages, physical constraints make certain combinations of divisions impossible. For example, a vowel cannot at the same time be both *high* and *low*. Other combinations are not possible on purely linguistic grounds. Many similar redundancy conditions have been described for combinations of sign parameters. Adherence to these conditions defines a possible sign, whereas violations are considered impossible or improbable signs. Just as English has actual words like "brick," possible but nonoccurring words like "blick," and nonoccurring and not possible words like "bnick," ASL also has "blick"-type signs, which are used creatively, as well as "bnick"-type signs, which are not used at all (see "Violations of Constraints and Art-sign, this chapter). Some of the conditions on allowable signs may be attributable to constraints placed on the visual mode by perceptual mechanisms whereas others may be linguistically arbitrary.

Visual Constraints

Siple (1978) indicates that optimal visual acuity for sign reception occurs in an area that encompasses two fixation points, one between the eyes and the other slightly lower, assuming a downward cast of the eyes, at about neck or chin. Within this high acuity area, it is easier to detect small differences in handshape (such as between X and babyO), in location (e.g., the small difference between APPLE on the lower cheek and ONION on the upper cheek by the bone), and in motion (e.g., the sweep downward of the sign GIRL contrasted with the sweep upward and outward of the sign TOMORROW, both made with the same handshape and in the same location on the cheek). In the areas of lesser acuity, discrimination becomes more difficult, and it is not surprising to find that signs made in this area do not utilize fine details of handshape or small distinction of location or motion, but instead maximize discriminability in a number of ways. These include grosser distinctions in handshape (e.g., open B or 5 and closed S, but not G and H, which differ only in the number of fingers extended), larger motions, and increased redundancy of sign formation (tendency to be two-handed symmetrical sign; utilization of reduplication).

Linguistic Constraints

Battison, Markowicz, and Woodward (1975) give several examples of linguistic constraints on sign formation. Some signs involve two sequential contacts with the body. If the body is divided into four major parts—head and neck, trunk, arm, and hand—then only the combinations summarized in Table 5 are permissible for the first and second contacts. In addition, the second contact is constrained to a centralized position in the major contact area, so that a sign may go from head to center chest, but not from head to either shoulder or to a corner or

Table 5.   Permissible contacts with the body for double-contact signs

First contact	Second contact			
	Head	Trunk	Arm	Hand
Head	+[a]	+	+	+
Trunk	−	+	−	+
Arm	−	−	+	−
Hand	+	−	−	+

Based on Battison, Markowicz, and Woodward, 1975.

[a] + indicates an acceptable sequence, − indicates an unacceptable sequence.

side of the trunk. A constraint such as this, which is not required by physical limitations although it is possibly an aid to perception, distinguishes signs from pantomime.

Battison (1974) described two further constraints related specifically to signs formed with both hands. Basically, there are three types of two-handed signs: 1) both hands move independently; 2) only one hand moves but both handshapes are identical; and 3) only one hand moves (the dominant one) and the handshape of the nondominant, nonmoving hand is restricted to one of a limited set of the possible handshapes. For the signs in which both hands move, a symmetry condition exists, specifying that the handshapes and movement for both hands must be identical and that the orientations and movements of both hands must be identical or opposites (mirror images). For two-handed signs in which the handshapes are not identical (3 above), a dominance condition exists, specifying that the nondominant hand must remain static while the moving dominant hand produces the sign. (The dominant hand is most often considered to be the hand that is used by the signer to make one-handed signs and the moving hand in two-handed signs where only one hand moves. Kegl and Wilbur, 1976, diverge from this practice by considering any moving hand to be dominant; thus if both hands are moving, they are both dominant, and if a signer first makes a one-handed sign with his right hand and then a different one-handed sign with his left hand, he has switched dominance.) Furthermore, the nondominant hand can assume only one of the six most unmarked handshapes, which include (see Figure 1):

1. S hand: a closed fist
2. B hand: the flat palm
3. 5 hand: the B hand with fingers spread apart
4. G hand: fist with index finger extended
5. C hand: hand formed in a semicircle
6. O hand: fingertips meet with thumb, forming a circle

Battison pointed out that these six handshapes are considered the least marked because they are found in all other sign languages studied to date, they are maximally distinct formationally and perceptually, and they are among the first acquired by children learning sign language (Boyes, 1973). Lane, Boyes-Braem, and Bellugi (1976) noted that these six handshapes constitute "69% of all the entries in the Stokoe et al. dictionary (1965) and 81% of all the entries in a 1-hr. corpus of the signing of a deaf two-and-a-half year old."

In summary, "signs with two active hands must be symmetrical and signs which have different handshapes can only have one active hand. In these cases, a relative complexity in one part of the sign (two hands vs. one hand moving; different handshapes vs. identical ones) is counteracted by a reduction in complexity somewhere else (symmetry; one hand remains still)" (Battison, 1974, p. 20).

It is important to emphasize that these conditions hold for the citation forms of signs. The citation form is the isolated answer that is given to the question "What is the sign for X?" In actual signing, grammatical modifications or creative use of signs may result in forms that appear to violate these conditions (Chapter 3).

Violations of Constraints and Art-sign

Some of the existing constraints on the formation of possible signs are linguistic and not physiological. Clearly it is possible for two hands to move along different paths simultaneously (although it is often difficult, e.g., rubbing your stomach while patting your head). The nonuse of all the possible formational combinations provides a reservoir from which puns, rhymes, and art-sign (poetry and song) may be made (Klima and Bellugi, 1975). Challenging Tervoort's (1961) claim that "the spontaneous use of signs in an ironical or metaphorical way is rare to non-existent," Klima and Bellugi investigated manipulation of signs for creative purposes. In addition to identifying sign puns, several types of sign-play were found (these are creative uses that do not depend on the structure of English). Three basic processes were reported: 1) the overlapping of two signs, 2) the blending of two signs, and 3) the substitution of one value of a regular formational parameter for another.

Overlapping   Overlapping of two signs is possible because there are two hands that can move independently, and although in "straight signing" the symmetry condition prohibits different simultaneous motions, this condition is lifted for creative purposes. For example, to indicate mixed feelings about taking a new job, Klima and Bellugi cite the signs EXCITED and DEPRESSED, produced simultaneously. Both signs are normally two-handed and are related formationally in that they differ only in the direction of motion, DEPRESSED moving down the chest, EXCITED moving up. Thus, to produce both at once, one hand moves down while the other simultaneously moves up. Another way to overlap signs is to form one with one hand and hold the hand in that position while the other hand forms another sign. A third possible way is to start with a two-handed sign, hold one hand in that position, and make another sign with the other hand. These combinations are most effective when the differences between the two signs are minimal, when they use the same handshape, or when the place of formation of the first is the starting point of the second.

Blending   Blending of signs can be accomplished by combining the hand configuration of one sign with the movement and location of another sign. This process occurs regularly as a grammatical device in "straight signing" (not sign-play) where the handshape of a noun, pronoun, or numeral is combined with the movement and location of a verb (see "Grammatical Modifications," Chapter 3). The creation of "name signs" (Meadow, 1977) is similar. Within the deaf community, each individual is given a name sign which is used in place of spelling out the whole name. A single individual may have several name signs, each one given by different groups within the community. The name sign is chosen to include some salient characteristic of the individual; thus if a particular person is the chief programmer at work, the worst player at bridge, and a loving husband at home, he may have three name signs, each of which reflects these different characteristics, although it is just as likely that because all these groups are in the same city, he may have the same sign in all three. Name signs ordinarily consist of the handshape corresponding to the fingerspelled first letter of the name and the movement and location of an appropriate verb, noun, or adjective. For example, Shelley Lawrence's eye winks frequently, and she has been given a name sign consisting of an S handshape and the movement and location of the sign WINK (two hands in front of eyes, one moves down quickly then up). My own name sign is less exciting—an R handshape made at the side of the chin where the signs GIRL, MOTHER, SISTER (a compound of GIRL and SAME) are made, indicating female. Name signs are a good example of signs which, although mentioned in the Appendix, are not listed in the *Dictionary of American Sign Language*. Since they are productively generated by rules, the list of name signs is seemingly infinite.

Systematic Substitution of Parameters   The systematic substitution of one of the parameters of a sign is a planned effort to change the meaning of the sign in a recognizable way. The results are signs that do not violate any of the constraints on signs, and thus are possible but not actual signs of the language. Klima and Bellugi illustrate several types, including 1) change in the hand configuration (using the little finger to make the sign UNDERSTAND instead of the normally used index finger; the little finger changes the meaning from "understand" to "understand a little") (Figure 18), 2) changes in orientation (signing NEW YORK (city) with the dominant hand underneath the nondominant hand to indicate "underhanded" New York) (Figure 19), 3) changes in movement (signing UNDERSTAND with the reverse motion—rather than snapping the index finger open from a closed fist, the index finger starts extended and shuts into a closed fist; to indicate

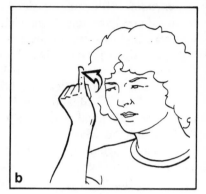

Figure 18.   The meaning of the sign UNDERSTAND (a) is changed to "understand a little" (b) by using the little finger in place of index finger. Copyright © U. Bellugi, The Salk Institute.

"don't understand" in straight signing one would sign NOT UNDER-STAND, two separate signs, as in Figure 20), and 4) changes in location (to indicate a bruised eye that was swollen shut, one signer signed "My eye is deaf" by moving the sign DEAF from its normal location across the cheek to a location across the eye).

HISTORICAL CHANGES

The general linguistic constraints discussed above are also reflected in historical changes that some signs have undergone. Descriptions of

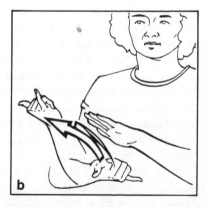

Figure 19.   The meaning of the sign NEW YORK "New York City" (a) is modified when the dominant hand moves underneath the nondominant hand, indicating "under-handed New York" (b). Copyright © U. Bellugi, The Salk Institute.

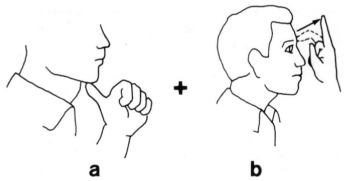

a   **b**

Figure 20.   The formal version of "don't understand" is indicated by signing NOT (a) and UNDERSTAND (b).

signs are available from as early as 1797 for Old French Sign Language and 1850 for American Sign Language. Significant changes can be seen in signs in the relatively short time since Long (1918). Frishberg (1975, 1976a) reports that changes in signs over time have tended to increase the symmetry of a sign, increase the fluidity between parts of a sign, move signs to a more centralized location, and modify the formation of some signs so that the hands are the main conveyor of the information rather than the facial expression or body or head movements.

Increase in Symmetry

Several modifications have occurred which result in increased symmetry. Signs that are made below the neck have tended to change from one-handed to two-handed (cf. modern version of DIE/DEAD, HURRY, ANGRY). Signs that are two-handed have tended toward identical handshapes, although, as mentioned before, two-handed signs in which only one hand moves may still have a different handshape on the nondominant hand. Frishberg (1976a) illustrated this tendency with several signs which indicate that it is usually the nondominant hand that changes to the handshape of the dominant hand. The old sign for DEPEND was made with a dominant G hand and a nondominant B hand. The new sign is made with two G hands. Similarly, the old sign for SHORT/BRIEF was made with a dominant H hand and a nondominant B hand and is now made with two H hands. The sign LAST/ FINAL provides an interesting counter-example to this trend, in that here it is the dominant hand that has changed. The old sign was made with a dominant G hand and a nondominant I hand. The current sign is made with two I hands. Two factors are possibly involved. One is the preservation of morphological information, the I hand being made with the fifth finger and the fifth finger being the *last* finger in most counting or listing. Thus to have given up the I hand to become two G hands would have been to lose this morphological information. The other possible factor is avoidance of homonymity. Two signs that are already made with two G hands in motions similar to that of LAST/FINAL are CAN'T and a recent version of TOMATO. This may have provided some resistance to the change to two G hands.

Fluidity

The term "fluidity" refers to the smoothness of the transition from one part of a sign to the next. In compound signs that are recently formed, an indication of compoundness may be the shortness of the interval between the formation of the two signs. As the compound becomes lexicalized, parts of the first and/or second sign may be lost and a tighter bond between the remaining parts may result. Movements, locations, and handshapes may be modified to create a smoother transition. The old sign FOR (as in "this is for you") was made as two separate movements, a G hand first pointing to the forehead then pointing to object (if present) or its established location in space (use of space for this purpose is discussed in greater detail in "Grammatical Modifications," Chapter 3). The current sign is made as a single smooth movement with the G hand from the forehead out. The sign INFORM is now made with two hands throughout, one slightly higher than the other, retaining the handshape change from BRING. One particularly illustrative example that Frishberg gives is the Toronto sign HOSPITAL. This sign originally was made as a compound, SICK + HOME. SICK is made with two open8 hands, one at the forehead, the other at the stomach. HOME is itself a compound, originally EAT + SLEEP (Figures 21, 22). (EAT is made with a flatO handshape at the mouth; SLEEP is made with a B hand at the cheek. HOME developed into a two-touch sign using the flatO

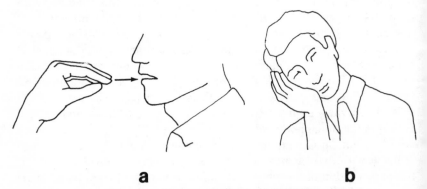

a   **b**

Figure 21.   The signs EAT (a) and SLEEP (b).

Figure 22. The sign HOME, a compound of EAT and SLEEP (see Figure 21).

handshape, touching first near the mouth and then at the cheek (modern versions include two touches both in the same place on the cheek,
midway between the two older contacts.)) Thus, HOSPITAL was
made as SICK with two open8 hands at the forehead and stomach
(Figure 23), followed by HOME made with the O handshape contacting
first near the mouth and then on the cheek. The first contact of HOME
dropped out, as did the lower hand of SICK, leaving HOSPITAL as
an open8 hand at the forehead, moving to the cheek and changing to
an O hand. Eventually the change to an O hand also dropped out,
leaving HOSPITAL as a two-touch sign with open8 hand, first at
forehead, then at cheek. Fluidity of formation increased as the movement changed from two contacts to a continuous contact, starting at
the forehead and moving down the side of the head. The place of
formation, motion, and handshape have been modified to produce a
sign that is more fluid than the compound from which it is derived.

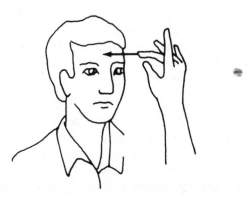

Figure 23. The sign SICK.

Centralization

In looking at centralization of signs over time, Frishberg (1975) has found that signs have moved down from the face, in from the side, and up from the waist. She suggests that this results in the hollow of the throat being a center point of the signing space. She gives several examples: DON'T-CARE, moving down from the forehead to the nose; YOUNG and WILL/FUTURE, moving up from the waist to the shoulder; and FEEL, LOVE, and PLEASE, moving in from the heart to the center of the chest. The only exception to this trend has been that signs made on the face have tended to move outward toward the sides so that the mouth and eyes are more easily seen (presumably an aid to speechreading).

Changing Role of the Head and Face

Over time, signs that previously included head movement as part of their formation have transferred this movement onto the hands or simply have lost the head movement component. The sign PATIENT used to include a lowering of the head as the A hand moved down in front of the lips. Now the head remains still while the hand performs the movement. Frishberg (1975) described the change that occurred in the sign COMPARE. The old sign was made "holding two flat hands facing the signer, separated. The eyes moved from one to the other and then the hands moved together, eyes focused on both at once." The current sign uses the hands only, either rocking alternately, probably a vestige of the former eye movements, or rocking together, a change in movement that can be viewed as an increase in symmetry.

Head tilts and facial expressions play an active role in ASL, more often than not in a larger context than the single sign. Certain signs still retain distinctive facial expression as part of their formation, but these are relatively rare. Head tilt has been observed to indicate relative clauses (Liddell, 1978), whereas facial expression has often been cited as an indicator of negation, question, affirmation, and other functions usually attributed to intonation in spoken languages. These are discussed in greater detail in Chapter 4.

Borrowing from English through Fingerspelling

Initialized Signs   The inclusion of a handshape (DEZ) from the manual alphabet in a sign to make that sign somehow "correspond" to an English word is called initialization. Typically, a sign is initialized in several ways, thus creating several distinctive signs from a single ASL sign. Although some deliberate initializations clearly violate rules of allowable sign formation (Chapter 7), others are linguistically permissible and may even be accepted into the daily language. The acceptance of such signs, and other invented signs, varies from person to person. Some deaf people, who have been told most of their lives that signing is "inferior" or "not grammatical," may feel that these signs are "improving" the sign language, that they make the sign language "more precise." Others recognize the artificiality of these signs and stigmatize people who use them as "obviously hearing signers" (even though some deaf people may use them). Upon meeting a new deaf person, I first have to determine if this person will be offended if I sign with him, and then what kind of signing to use. Some people may view my use of obviously initialized signs as a mark of my being non-native; others may view my lack of them as being professionally inappropriate. Flexibility of signing styles is discussed further in Chapter 6.

Creation of New Signs   Battison (1978) reported that short fingerspelled English words may change into signs through a variety of modifications. Medial letters may be lost, leaving only the first and last letters. The remaining handshapes may assimilate according to the number of fingers involved. At the same time, the handshapes may dissimilate along the open/close dimension (i.e., if the first handshape is open, e.g., 5, then the second will be closed, e.g., S, or vice versa). Movements may be added (remember that fingerspelled letters, except 'j' and 'z', do not move except as a transition into the next letter handshape). These may include 1) linear movement (for example, the *new* sign ALL derived from fingerspelled a+l may move down a list to indicate all the items in a list, or sweep across the horizontal plane (from side to side) to indicate all the people or things) or 2) reduplication (repetition, usually of open/close change in handshape). The location may also change (fingerspelled words are made in a constrained box about shoulder height on the same side of the body as the hand that is doing the spelling) to other areas within the signing space. Finally, the sign may add a second hand. These combined changes remove the word from the realm of fingerspelling into the lexicon of signs. Battison suggests that the target of these processes is to produce a double handshape sign (not necessarily made with both hands) which changes its handshapes during formation. This process is presumably productive and open ended. Spoken languages in need of a vocabulary item may invent new words, compound already existing words, or borrow words from other languages. These processes, which allow borrowing from English (or theoretically any spoken language), provide ASL with the same word innovation options as other languages.

ALTERNATE DESCRIPTIONS

The descriptions of signs presented so far are referred to as the "traditional" descriptions, in that they have not specifically considered possible ways that the descriptions of signs might be consistent with, and described in terms of, spoken languages. Several recent attempts to do this are presented in this section. None of these analyses should be considered final, and the differences among some of them may not be apparent to the casual reader. However, the perspectives that are represented here differ from the traditional, and are likely to recur in future sign grammars or in the next generation of sign systems.

Since Stokoe, Casterline, and Croneberg's (1965) pioneering work, linguists have pondered the parallelism of the descriptions of sign language and oral language. Although at first glance this might seem to represent oral language bias as discussed in Chapter 1, the issue is really more subtle. Until now, linguistic models of language have been shaped entirely by oral languages, although they claimed to be models of "language" and not just models of speech. It therefore becomes a relevant and fair question to ask whether the current linguistic frameworks can be applied to sign languages. The idea is not to mold the description of sign language into an oral language framework, but to see if the *structure* of the oral language framework comfortably fits on sign languages. If, for example, the phonological level of a language, as treated in generative phonology, describes the processes involved when elements of the language occur in sequence, then one might expect to find similar processes (assimilation, metathesis) in both oral and sign languages. Or, if the smallest segmental unit of a language is viewed as a matrix of distinctive features chosen from a universal set of features constrained by marking conventions, then it should not matter whether that segment is spoken or signed. Several attempts to investigate the relationship between sign language and linguistic frameworks are discussed herein.

As with so much linguistic theory, no analysis is ever *the* analysis. Rather, each analysis provides point of departure for the next, and one should expect that any analysis presented here (mine included) will eventually be superseded by another which will provide a more consistent description and will account for more data, presumably without the flaws of the present models.

Of the several alternatives to be discussed, three deal primarily with handshape, and two, Friedman (1976b) and Kegl and Wilbur (1976), deal with the remaining parameters. Thus, handshape is discussed first, in such a way as to reflect the differences in approaches and comparisons to Stokoe's analysis. The other parameters are then discussed in turn.

The reader is reminded that this section is likely to be slow reading
for the nonlinguist and that skimming up to the chapter summary may
be sufficient for most nontechnical purposes.

Handshape

Friedman's (1976b) phoneme inventory for handshape is given in Table
5. It should be noted that Friedman's list includes all of Stokoe's
handshapes plus several others (5̈ (bent5), 3̈ (bent3), V̈ (bentV), Horns Ч,
7, T, M, N, D (separate from G), and G_2 (as in fingerspelling), making
a total of 29. In many cases, she has been able to isolate the environments in which certain variants (allophones) of each phoneme occur.
Factors that affect the variants include whether a sign makes contact
at the thumb tip or on the side of the hand, whether or not the
handshape appears in a loan sign, or whether the sign is involved in
processes of assimilation or reduction. Friedman demonstrates the
phonemiticity of many (but not all) of her handshapes with minimal
pairs.

Friedman (1976b) departed from Stokoe's description of ASL by
providing a different analysis of "phonetic elements of the four articulatory parameters . . . and their distribution in a non-classical phonemic analysis." She indicated that her analysis differs from Stokoe,
Casterline, and Croneberg's (1965) in that: 1) she has presented a
different phonemic distribution, "2) ongoing processes, such as neu-
tralization due to changes in certain handshapes, and potential mergers
and splits are taken into account; 3) loan phones are treated as extra-
systematic elements; 4) predictable elements are accounted for; and
5) pervasive iconic (= non-arbitrary) and scalar (= non-discrete) elements are incorporated into the phonological system" (p. 1). (Point 5
is discussed in more detail in Chapter 5 under "Iconicity.")

Friedman has rejected the possibility of a distinctive feature analysis for American Sign Language: "[W]hile the use of the diacritics
. . . amount to a partial feature analysis, there would be little or no
motivation for taking on the trappings of a *full* feature analysis. . . .
Until it can be demonstrated that generalizations about variations in
handshapes, either historical or synchronic, can best be formulated in
terms of recurring features—thereby giving the feature analysis ex-
planatory value—" (p. 23), such an analysis is not needed. Psychol-
ogists, however, have found distinctive features of considerable utility
in studying oral language memory and perception (cf. Miller and
Nicely, 1955; Wickelgren, 1965). Therefore, in addition to their use in
descriptive linguistics, it should not be too surprising that features
have been demonstrated in psycholinguistic studies of visual perception of ASL.

Table 6. Summary: Phonemic inventory

Phoneme	Variant	Environment
/A/	A	
	Å	contact with thumb tip
		iconic signs
	S	side contact
		loans
		neutral end or initial shape
/O/	O	
	tapered-O	free variation
	bO	end shape (in double-shape signs with closure of L)
/B/	B	free variation
	B̊	free variation
		required in signs with thumb tip contact
	B̂	end shape in double-shape signs with BEND KNUCKLES movement
/C/	C	
/5/	5	
	4	plurality
	5̈	end shape in signs with BEND FINGERS movement
/5̈/	5̈	
/F/	F	
	bO	reduction
/G/	G	
/X/	X₁	
	X₂	contact with middle joint
/L/	L	
	L̈	end shape in signs with BEND FINGERS movement
	L w/bent thumb	iconic signs
		anchored index finger
/H/	H	
	Ḧ	palm-side contact
/V/	V	
	V̈	end shape with BEND FINGERS movement
		iconic signs
/V̈/	V̈	
/3/	3	
	3̈	end shape in signs with BEND FINGERS movement
/3̈/	3̈	
/Y/	Y	
	8	reduction
	ʮ	assimilation
		iconic signs

continued

Table 6—continued

Phoneme	Variant	Environment
/Ⴘ/	Ⴘ	
	Ⴘ	free variation
/ზ/	ზ	
	8	*CLOSE* or *OPEN* movement
/7/	7	
	unspread-7	
/T/	T	
/M/	M	
/N/	N	
/D/	D	
	bD	free variation
/E/	E	
/G₂/	G_2	
/K/	K	
/I/	I	
/W/	W	
/R/	R	

From Friedman, L., *On the Other Hand: New Perspectives on American Sign Language,* © 1977 Academic Press, New York. Reprinted by permission.

In their effort to determine the distinctive features that might be involved in visual perceptions of signs, Lane, Boyes-Braem, and Bellugi (1976) presented handshapes masked by visual "snow," and analyzed the resultant confusion matrices with clustering and scaling techniques. They proposed a set of 11 distinctive features for the ASL handshapes (see Table 7).

Lane, Boyes-Braem, and Bellugi based their features on the notions of the fingers and/or thumb being either "closed" (as in a fist) or "extended" (as in the number 5). Compact hands, then, are closed, with no fingers extended. Broad refers to those hands with three or more fingers extended. In their feature system, a handshape cannot be both compact and broad. The feature ulnar refers to handshapes that have at least the fifth finger extended; full hands have (at least) four fingers extended. The feature concave is used for handshapes with two or more bent fingers (as in C or O). Dual hands have only two fingers extended, index hands have only the index finger extended, and radial hands have the thumb (and possibly some fingers) extended. Touch is used for handshapes in which at least one fingertip is in contact with the thumb (as in F or O). Spread hands have two or more fingers that are spread apart, and finally, if two fingers (but not thumb) are overlapping, the feature cross is used. Correspondences and differences between this and other feature systems are discussed later.

It is important to point out here, however, that these features are perceptually descriptive and their utility in the formation of phonological rules has not yet been tested.

Table 7.   Features for handshapes

Handshape	Compact	Broad	Ulnar	Full	Concave	Dual	Index	Radial	Touch	Spread	Cross
	+				+				⊕		
	+				+				⊖		
	+				−		+		⊕		
	+				−		+		⊖		
	+				−		−		⊕		
	+				−		−		⊖		
	−	+		+				⊕			
	−	+		+				⊖			
	−	+		−				⊕			
	−	+		−				−	⊕		
	−	+		−				−	⊖		
	−	−	+					⊕			
	−	−	+					⊖			
	−	−	−			+				⊕	
	−	−	−			+				−	⊕
	−	−	−			+				−	⊖
	−	−	−			−	+	⊕			
	−	−	−			−	+	⊖			
	−	−	−			−	−	⊕			
	−	−	−			−	−	⊖			

From Lane, Boyes-Braem, and Bellugi (1976) with permission.

Although Tjapkes (1976) proposed features for several aspects other than handshape, she described the handshape features in greatest detail. They are based on articulatory considerations but only cover 16 possible handshapes. The feature adjacent extension is defined such that [+adjacent extension] means "linear, adjacent extension of all fingers," e.g., B, whereas [−adjacent extension] means "adjacent flexion of all fingers," e.g., S. Radial extension is similarly defined such that [+radial extension] means "linear, radial extension of all fingers," e.g., 5, whereas [−radial extension] means "radial flexion of all fingers," e.g., C. [+Index extension] describes "flexion of middle and ring fingers, extension of thumb, index, and little fingers," e.g., 𝌁 , whereas [−index extension] means "flexion of index, middle, and ring fingers, extension of thumb and little fingers," e.g., Y. [+Index intersection] defines R as "flexion of thumb, ring, and little fingers, extension and intersection of index and middle fingers," and [−index intersection] defines H as "flexion of thumb, ring, and little fingers, adjacent extension of index and middle fingers." The handshape for the sign WHO (apparently G, but possibly X) is described by the feature [+middle flexion], "flexion of thumb, middle, ring, and little fingers, extension of index finger," whereas the handshape in LIPREAD (described as V, but possibly V̈) is described as "flexion of thumb, ring, and little fingers, divergent extension of middle and index fingers." The feature right angle extension is defined such that the positive value means "flexion of middle, ring, and little fingers, extension of thumb and index finger," e.g., L, and the negative value means "flexion of thumb and index finger, extension of middle, ring, and little fingers," e.g., F. The handshape A would be described by the positive value of the feature thumb extension, "flexion of index, middle, ring, and little fingers, extension of thumb," whereas its negative value, "flexion of thumb, index, middle, and ring fingers, extension of little finger," describes I. Finally, the feature thumb flexion is defined so that [+thumb flexion] describes W, "flexion of thumb and little finger, extension of index, middle, and ring fingers," and [−thumb flexion] describes 3, "flexion of ring and little fingers, extension of thumb, index, and middle fingers." Although not explicitly stated in Tjapkes, it seems as though the features are determined in such a way that for any handshape, only one of the features will have a positive value, while all other features will be negative. Traditional distinctive feature systems (for spoken languages, but applicable here also) allow for combinations of features with more than one positive value. Thus, Tjapkes's system differs conceptually from the other systems presented here.

Table 8. ASL DEZ (handshape) symbols with tentative feature representation

Distinctive feature	S	E	O	C	B	4	T	A	Á	Ë	B₂	¨5	5	ʊ	G	X	D	G₂	Ö	L	I	Y	Ч	Ψ	7	8	H	N	V	R	3	K	M	W	6	F_s	9	F	M_t	N_t
Closed	+	+	−	−	−	−	+	+	+	+	−	−	−	−	+	+	−	−	+	+	+	+	+	+	−	+	+	+	+	+	+	+	+	+	+	+	−	+	+	+
Thumb	+	−	−	−	−	−	−	+	+	+	+	+	+	−	+	−	−	+	+	+	+	+	+	+	−	−	−	−	−	−	+	−	−	−	−	−	+	+	−	−
Spread	−	−	−	−	−	+	−	−	−	−	−	+	+	+	−	−	−	−	+	+	−	−	−	−	+	+	−	−	−	−	−	−	−	−	−	−	−	−	+	−
Bent	−	−	+	−	+	+	+	−	−	−	−	−	−	+	−	−	−	−	−	−	+	+	+	+	+	+	−	−	−	+	−	+	+	+	−	−	+	−	−	+
Fore	−	−	+	+	+	+	+	−	+	+	+	+	+	+	+	+	+	+	+	+	+	+	+	+	+	+	+	+	+	+	+	+	+	+	+	+	+	+	+	+
Mid	−	−	+	+	+	+	+	−	+	+	+	+	+	+	−	+	−	+	+	+	+	+	+	+	+	+	+	+	+	+	−	+	+	+	+	+	+	+	+	+
Ring	−	−	+	+	+	+	+	−	+	+	+	+	+	+	−	−	−	−	−	−	−	−	−	−	+	+	+	+	+	+	+	−	−	+	+	+	+	+	+	+
Pinky	−	−	−	−	−	+	−	−	−	+	+	+	+	+	+	+	+	−	−	−	−	−	−	−	+	+	+	+	+	+	+	−	+	−	+	+	+	+	−	−
Contact	−	+	−	+	−	−	−	−	−	−	−	−	−	−	−	+	+	−	−	−	−	−	−	−	−	−	−	−	−	−	−	−	−	−	−	−	−	+	−	−
Crossed	−	−	−	−	−	−	+	−	−	−	−	−	−	−	−	−	−	−	−	−	−	−	−	−	−	−	−	−	+	+	−	+	−	−	−	−	−	−	+	+

From Woodward (1973a) with permission.

44

Woodward's (1973a) features are presented in Table 8. They are also based on articulatory characteristics, but cover a larger number of handshapes than does Tjapkes, and are additive in the sense that more than one positive valued feature can occur in a matrix describing a single handshape. Woodward defined 10 features that can describe 40 handshapes. The feature closed, when positively specified, indicates fingers curled into the palm (although some fingers may be extended as the result of other feature specifications), and where possible the thumb is across the fingers, as in the handshape S. In fact, S is defined as [+closed] and negative for all other features. The feature thumb when positively specified moves the thumb from across the fingers to straight up next to the index edge of the hand (A in Figure 1). The feature spread can refer to either the fingers, if extended, or the thumb. The handshape 5 differs from the handshape B in that the former is specified as [+thumb, +spread] but the latter is specified as negative for both features. The feature bent is used for bent fingers that are not in contact with other fingers or the thumb. Each finger extended (and possibly bent) has its own feature. Thus, there is a feature fore, which when positively specified indicates that the forefinger is extended, and three other features, mid, ring, and pinkie, which are similarly defined. Contact between the thumb and any finger is indicated by the feature contact, and the crossing of any digit (fingers or thumb) is indicated by the feature crossed. Because of the great detail and the large number of handshapes specified by this feature system, it was determined to be the most useful (to date) in allowing a generative analysis of handshapes (Wilbur, 1978a; see following "Illustrative Example").

Kegl and Wilbur (1976) attempted to determine a set of distinctive features on the basis of articulation, perception, and theoretical descriptive utility. Both Tjapkes's and Woodward's feature systems were unknown to them at that time, but their system combined aspects from both of them. The feature system is presented in Table 9.

Drawing upon the basic distinction indicated by Lane, Boyes-Braem, and Bellugi, two features, extended and closed, were defined to refer to maximally opposed handshapes. Extended refers to the straight extension of the fingers; closed is its opposite, the fingers being curled into a fist (S). Unlike Lane, Boyes-Braem, and Bellugi's definition, however, a handshape can be both extended and closed, as illustrated by the following set of minimal feature specifications:

[+extended, +closed]	G
[−extended, −closed]	O
[+extended, −closed]	B
[−extended, +closed]	S

Table 9. Features for handshapes

Distinctive feature	G	H	V	L	X	3	Ч	Ҹ	W	O	B	5̈	5	B̈	8	ʁ	F	C	S	A	I	Y
Extended	+	+	+	+	+	+	+	+	+	−	+	+	+	+	+	+	+	+	−	−	−	−
Closed	+	+	+	+	+	+	+	+	+	−	−	−	−	−	−	−	+	+	+	+	+	+
Spread	−	−	+	−	−	+	−	−	+	−	−	+	+	−	+	+	−	−	+	−	−	+
Thumb	−	−	−	+	−	+	−	−	+	−	−	+	+	−	−	+	−	+	+	+	−	+
Pinky	−	−	−	−	−	−	+	+	−	−	−	−	−	−	−	−	−	−	−	−	−	+
Bent	−	−	−	−	+	−	−	−	−	−	−	+	−	+	+	−	+	+	−	−	−	−
2 Adjacent	−	+	+	−	−	+	−	+	−	−	−	−	−	−	−	+	−	−	−	−	−	−
3 Adjacent	−	−	−	−	−	−	−	−	+	−	−	−	−	−	−	−	+	−	−	−	−	−

From Kegl and Wilbur (1976) with permission.

Thus, if no other features are positively specified, [+extended, +closed] implies that only the index finger is extended (G), whereas [+extended, −closed] implies that all the fingers are extended and unspread (B). [−Extended, −closed] is the handshape O, where the fingers are not extended straight out, nor are they curled into the palm, but rather are curled slightly away from the palm and meet the thumb. Finally, when no finger is extended and all are curled into the fist with the thumb across the second joint, we have [−extended, +closed], the handshape S. Thumb is used for extended thumbs (as in Å) and pinkie is used for extended pinkie (as in I or Y). Bent is used when any finger is bent (as in X). The features 2adjacent and 3adjacent (conceptually similar to Tjapkes's adjacent extension) refer to the number of adjacent fingers (not thumb) that are extended (not the total number of extended fingers, however, unless all are adjacent, i.e., none are bent down) and that obey the convention:

> Adjacency Convention: If the handshape is [+extended, +closed], start counting adjacent fingers at the index finger. If the handshape is [+extended, −closed], start counting at the pinkie edge. When the proper number of adjacent fingers has been reached, put the next finger down in contact with the thumb (if the handshape is also marked [+thumb] this contact will not be maintained). These features are not relevant to [−extended] handshapes.

The Kegl and Wilbur model contains a number of implications that should be considered more carefully. One is that there are two basic features, extended and closed, which together produce four classes with the four handshapes G, O, B, and S as the least marked elements. This departs from previous descriptions of unmarked handshapes in that there are only four here, whereas traditionally there are six (G, O, B, S (or A), 5, C; see "Linguistic Constraints," Chapter 2). The two outsiders in this system are C and 5, both of which are of unclear status. In this system, they are both treated as derived from B (although alternatives are possible, for example C could be derived from O with some kind of feature for open). 5 differs from B by one feature value, C from B by two. The implication that C and 5 are therefore more marked than G, O, B, S is difficult to evaluate because no coherent set of markedness conventions (in the sense of Chomsky and Halle, 1968) has been established for ASL, nor has linguistic theory in general resolved the issue of how to evaluate the markedness of individual segments. For example, we could consider [+spread] to be the unmarked value of spread, thus giving us G, O, 5, and S as our least marked set without in any way changing the feature matrix. Or we could have used a feature like contracted to derive B from 5. Thus, although this feature analysis (or any feature analysis) may describe the handshapes (locations, motion, etc.), the question of whether the description is valid is still open. The handshapes that have not yet been described with this system (7 and babyO, for example) may provide the clues to the flaws (whatever they are) in this model. Similarly, handshapes that are describable in several ways, such as C, 5̈, 8, and open8, add pieces of information to the puzzle.

After this somewhat extended caveat, the final disclaimer is almost unnecessary. The handshape O is described with negative values on all features. It is not intended that this should be interpreted as according special status to O in the form of "least marked handshape," but rather as an artifact of the notational system.

Other implications that may be of interest include a closer relationship between G and X than heretofore implied in the descriptions, a separation of F and W (as with Woodward, but not Lane, Boyes-Braem, and Bellugi), and a relationship among S, A, I, and Y (note that Lane, Boyes-Braem, and Bellugi and Friedman have used A as it appears in the fingerspelling alphabet, whereas Woodward specified three separate forms, S, A, and Å. I have chosen S as basic; see "Illustrative Example" below). The validity of these and other implicit implications remains to be determined (possibly through corroborating evidence from child language data, historical change, and traditional means of investigating psychological reality).

Illustrative Example: Phonology of ASL   The discussion in this section has many purposes. One is to argue for considering S to be a basic handshape, from which A may be derived. A second purpose is to illustrate how the environment in which a handshape occurs can affect which handshape will actually occur. A third purpose is to demonstrate how contact, which has been largely ignored to this point, plays a role in the phonology of ASL. A fourth purpose is to show that some handshapes may be derived from others, and that one can make a distinction between derived and basic handshapes. As a result of accomplishing the fourth task, the fifth can be argued, namely, that there are two levels of phonological processing in ASL, the underlying representation (the form of the lexical entry) and the surface representation, and a set of phonological rules which relates one to the other. Having thus established this crucial fact about the phonology of manual languages, one can then conclude that the basic tenets of generative phonology, with some allowances in notation for modality-specific information, can be applied to ASL.

Within the framework of generative phonology, information contained in the surface representations that is predictable by rule from the underlying representations may be omitted from the lexical entry. The recognition of two distinct levels is a fundamental difference

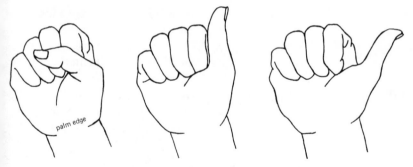

Figure 24.   The handshapes S, A, and Å.

between generative phonology and earlier versions of structural descriptive linguistics. It would be of significant theoretical interest (and great surprise) if ASL as a representative of manual languages did not need a separation of levels and hence did not need a generative analysis (as suggested by Friedman, 1976b, 1977). The purpose then is to consider a limited set of signs that illustrate predictable differences between underlying and surface forms, and to propose an analysis that begins to apply generative phonology to ASL (Wilbur, 1978a).

Three handshapes that are considered initially are S, A, and Å (Figure 24). The S handshape is illustrated by the signs displayed below (written here in Stokoe notation as described in the beginning of this chapter). Note that the notation does not reflect the differences among S, A, and Å. The English meanings are in double quotation marks, e.g., "shoes," and a description of the formation of the sign is cumbersomely given in English in parentheses. The examples are not exhaustive, and were randomly chosen (with ease of description in English as a qualifying criterion).

$A_D^! A_D^{\times \cdot}$	"shoes"	(two S hands in neutral space, contact at index edge of hand, may be repeated)
$A_D^! A_D^{\div a}$	"break"	(two S hands together in neutral space at index edge of hand, twist apart)
$\bar{A}A^\omega$ or $\bar{A}A^{\times \omega \cdot}$	"make, fix"	(two S hands, contact index edge of one to pinkie edge of the other)
$\bar{A}\!\!\diagup\!\!A^{\ominus \times}$	"year"	(two S hands, index edge of one to pinkie edge of other, one hand circles around other and repeats contact)

$\bar{A}A^{\overset{e}{\times}}$	"coffee"	(two S hands, contact index edge of one to pinkie edge of other, top hand makes several small rotations reminiscent of grinding)
$AA^{\wedge\sim}$	"car, drive"	(two S hands in neutral space, index edge up with no contact, move up and down several times)
$AA^{)(\cdot}$	"cold, winter"	(two S hands in neutral space face each other and shake lightly)
$_DA_D^{\times\cdot}$	"work"	(two S hands crossed at the wrist, both palms face down, top hand taps several times on lower hand)
$G_{\wedge\varphi}\,A^{\times}$	"hit"	(one S hand makes contact with an upright G hand, contact on S hand at third joint, on G hand on extended index finger)

The A handshape is illustrated below.

$A^{\mathsf{I}}A^{\perp}$	"together"	(two A hands come together in neutral space with contact at the second joint of the hand, then move together away from body)
$A^{\mathsf{I}}A^{\times}$	"with"	(two A hands come together in neutral space with contact at the second joint of the hands)
$A^{\mathsf{I}}A^{\overset{\square}{\times\div}}$	"without"	(two A hands, contact at second joint, move away from each other and open into a 5 hand)
$[]A_T^{\overset{e}{\times}}$	"sorry"	(one A hand contacts chest at second joint and forms several circles in rubbing motion on chest)
$\}A^{\overset{\mathsf{I}\cdot}{\times}}$	"everyday, daily"	(one A hand contacts side of cheek at second joint and rubs back and forth several times)

Ā$_a$A$_o$$\overset{\varrho}{\times}$	"wash"	(one A hand rubs against other A hand at second joints or against palm of B hand)
[]A$_T$A$_T$$\overset{N}{\times}$	"bath, bathe"	(two A hands rub on chest with second joint contact)
∩A$_T$$^\times$	"stupid, dumb"	(one A hand contacts forehead with second joint)
Ḡ$A_o$$\overset{z}{\times}$	"practice, polish"	(one A hand makes second joint contact with extended index finger of G hand and rubs back and forth)
UA$^{\times\cdot}$	"secret"	(one A hand bars lips with face of thumb, Figure 25)
UA$\overset{\vee}{\times}$	"patience, patient"	(one A hand grazes down chin with face of thumb)

Finally, the Ȧ handshape is illustrated by this sample of signs.

UȦ$^\perp$	"not"	(one Ȧ hand makes thumb tip contact under chin and snaps away from body)
UȦ$^{\times\cdot}_{\perp}$	"nuts"	(one Ȧ hand makes contact with teeth at thumb tip and snaps away from face)
}Ȧ$^{\times T\times}$	"yesterday"	(one Ȧ hand contacts cheek near mouth with thumb tip and moves back towards ear for a second contact)
}A$^\perp_a$	"tomorrow"	(one Ȧ hand contacts cheek with thumb tip and twists sharply forward)
∩Ȧ$^\times$::ȦȦ$^\times$	"remember, memory"	(one Ȧ hand contacts forehead with thumb tip, then comes down to contact other Ȧ hand at thumb tips in neutral space)
UȦ$^\times$::B$_a$Ȧ$_o$$^\times$	"letter, mail"	(one Ȧ hand contacts mouth at thumb tip then contacts palm of B hand with thumb tip)
A$_o$A$^\perp$	"follow"	(one Ȧ hand moves slightly behind the other in neutral space along the same path)

$A^{\prime}A^{\perp}$ *or* $A^{\prime}A^{\perp}_{\times}$	"pass"	(one Ȧ hand starts out behind the other as for "follow" then moves ahead of the other)
$\bar{\dot{A}}\dot{A}^{e\ \sim}_{\vee}$	"mingle, each other"	(one Ȧ hand, thumb facing down, circles around the other, thumb facing up, while it rotates around the first)
$\underline{B}_{D}\dot{A}^{\perp}$	"under, underneath"	(one Ȧ hand is located spatially below the B hand which faces down)
$\checkmark A^{\dagger}$	"refuse, won't"	(one Ȧ hand moves sharply up toward the shoulder)
$\dot{A}^{\perp}$	"self"	(one Ȧ hand may be located in several places in neutral space if associated with another pronoun, e.g., himself, but meaning simply "self" is located in an unindexed place in neutral space)

In order to present a complete and coherent discussion of these data, some review of information is necessary. Thus, one further purpose served by this section is to provide a summary of the descriptions presented so far.

As was seen in Table 1, Stokoe provides a list of possible values for each parameter (handshape, location, and motion) without attempting to interrelate the parameters. He indicates for example that Y handshape has two variants—thumb and little finger extended from fist (referred to here as Y) and index finger and little finger extended, parallel (referred to here as "horns" ꟿ). We do not know what factors are involved in the choice of these two variants (e.g., motion, location, orientation, contact, dominant vs. nondominant hand, stylistic variation, dialect differences, etc.) or why ȣ (open8) is listed as both a variant of Y and as a separate value of the handshape parameter but "horns" is not. Similarly, and more to my point, 'a' and 's' as formed in the manual alphabet (here A and S, and ignoring 't') are given as variants of A with no indication of what their conditioning environments (if any) might be. Ȧ is not included in this list. Instead, it is discussed as part of the "Conventions of Writing American Sign Language" (Stokoe, Casterline, and Croneberg, 1965, pp. xii–xiii), from which one might infer that it occurs in free variation, although it is not clear that this is an intended inference. Within this framework, then, A, Ȧ, and S are treated as allophonic variants of the phoneme A without specification of the conditioning environments.

Friedman's handshape analysis is presented in Table 6. Note that contact and movement have been indicated, as well as loan status and iconicity. Friedman's analysis included all of Stokoe's handshapes and several others, 5̈ (bent5), V̈ (bentV), 3̈ (bent3), 7, T, M, N, D (separate from G), G_2 (G in the manual alphabet), and Ч ("horns," separate from Y), making a total of 29 (compared to Stokoe's 19). The number of handshapes listed is obviously a function of deciding what has phonemic status and what is allophonic (alternatively, what is basic and what is derived). Also, some of the handshapes are not listed in Stokoe's parameter list (probably because he does not consider them phonemic) but are treated in the section on writing conventions. Thus, they are *implicitly* included in his analysis.

Friedman, unlike Stokoe, explicitly allows for a handshape (e.g., bent5̈) to be both allophonic (of 5) and phonemic (as bent5̈). This is the reason that her analysis is a nonclassical phonemic analysis, i.e., it does not adhere to the biuniqueness principle (Chomsky, 1964), which classical phonemic analyses sought to maintain. Stokoe's treatment of open8 as both a variant of Y (indicated in parentheses) and as a separate handshape (it is a separate value of the handshape parameter) is also implicitly a rejection of biuniqueness, but does not appear deliberate as in Friedman's analysis.

Essentially, the biuniqueness principle states that, given any segment (e.g., B̂), one ought to be able to relate it to one and only one phoneme (i.e., B). Clearly, that cannot be done here, since, for example, bent5̈ can be a token of either 5 or bent5̈ (notice numerous others). This problem (in the form of phonemic overlapping) plagued the structural linguists (Chao, 1934; Hockett, 1942, 1948, 1954; Sapir, 1925; Swadesh, 1934; Swadesh and Vogelin, 1939; Twaddell, 1935). Chomsky (1964) argued for the necessity of abandoning the biuniqueness principle as a restriction on phonological solutions. Thus, in not adhering to the biuniqueness principle, Friedman advanced the state of sign language phonology beyond the structural linguistic level. However, the rejection of biuniqueness in spoken language phonology was accompanied by the development of a generative phonological framework which depends crucially on distinctive feature descriptions for segments. Friedman explicitly rejects the necessity or viability of a distinctive feature analysis for ASL, thus also rejecting the possibility of a generative analysis. Indeed, although she has designated some handshapes more basic than others (phonemes as opposed to allophones), she has not gone the next step to predicting or deriving the nonbasic handshapes from the basic ones in anything beyond a list of relevant conditions.

In oral language, we can describe vowels by their height, their position in the mouth, their roundness (or lack thereof), their nasality (if present), etc. The descriptors for consonants refer to place of formation, presence or absence of voicing or nasal resonance, and manner of articulation (e.g., stop vs. fricative). Each of these features refers to a class of segments which have a particular characteristic in common (the class of voiced consonants, the class of velars, the high vowels). The search for distinctive features for signs aims at providing the same level of descriptive adequacy now available for spoken languages. Several distinctive feature systems were discussed here in detail. Each *defines* a different number of features and accounts for a different number of handshapes. Of importance for the data being considered here, two (Kegl and Wilbur, Tjapkes) do not provide a convenient characterization for A, whereas others (Lane, Boyes-Braem, and Bellugi, Tjapkes) similarly fail for Ȧ. Woodward is able to conveniently characterize all three handshapes of interest here: A, S, and Ȧ. The differences among them can be illustrated with his two features, thumb and spread:

	S	A	Ȧ
thumb	−	+	+
spread	−	−	+

Of the three, only Kegl and Wilbur explicitly attempt to organize the handshapes in terms of shared features as suggestions for natural classes (related to the four handshapes given above, G, O, B, and S). However, none of the frameworks for features has yet been carried to the next logical step, which is to attempt to characterize handshape variants as a function of their conditioning environments with the use of features in phonological rules.

When a distinctive feature analysis for ASL handshapes is provided, the issue of the phonemic status of each handshape is avoided, as is the issue of biuniqueness. Unfortunately, I cannot propose a complete solution to the occurrences of these variants, but I can illustrate how such a solution might be pursued. Of crucial concern is the relationship between handshape variant and type of contact (although motion may eventually be relevant). It may be observed that the handshape S occurs if there is no contact at all or if there is contact of the hand at its index edge, at the pinkie edge, at the wrist, or at the third joint of the hand (Figure 25). This is true whether the contact is with the other hand, the chest, or face. The handshape A occurs primarily when there is contact at the second joint of the hand and when there is contact at the thumb face (e.g., "secret"). The handshape Ȧ occurs when there is thumb tip contact or when there is no

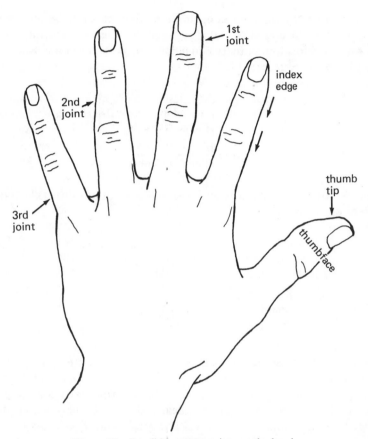

Figure 25. Possible contact points on the hand.

contact at all. The handshape-contact relationship presented so far can be summarized as:

S $\left\{\begin{array}{l}\text{no contact}\\\text{hand edge}\\\text{third joint}\\\text{wrist}\end{array}\right.$

A $\left\{\begin{array}{l}\text{second joint}\\\text{thumb face}\end{array}\right.$

Ȧ $\left\{\begin{array}{l}\text{thumb tip}\\\text{no contact}\end{array}\right.$

Given this distribution, an argument can be made for S as an underlying handshape. Ignoring Ȧ when it occurs in a "no contact" environment for a moment, we can argue that the variants A and Ȧ occur in particular contact environments which are complementary to S. That

S occurs in both the "no contact" environment and the elsewhere environment (third joint, hand edge, wrist, etc.) suggests strongly that it is the basic form, the others being derived. We might then formulate two phonological rules:

$$/\text{S}/ \rightarrow [\text{A}] \; / \; \left[\begin{array}{l} \underline{\hspace{3cm}} \\ \text{second joint contact} \\ \text{thumb face contact} \end{array} \right]$$

$$/\text{S}/ \rightarrow [\dot{\text{A}}] \; / \; \left[\begin{array}{l} \underline{\hspace{3cm}} \\ \text{thumb tip contact} \end{array} \right]$$

Using Woodward's features and a shorthand notation for S, we can write these rules as:

$$\begin{bmatrix} +\text{closed} \\ -\text{thumb} \\ -\text{spread} \end{bmatrix} \rightarrow [+\text{thumb}] \; / \; \left[\begin{array}{l} \underline{\hspace{3cm}} \\ \text{second joint contact} \\ \text{thumb face contact} \end{array} \right]$$

$$\begin{bmatrix} +\text{closed} \\ -\text{thumb} \\ -\text{spread} \end{bmatrix} \rightarrow \begin{bmatrix} +\text{thumb} \\ +\text{spread} \end{bmatrix} \; / \; \left[\begin{array}{l} \underline{\hspace{3cm}} \\ \text{thumb tip contact} \end{array} \right]$$

The minor role that has been allocated to contact is emphasized by the fact that there are not yet features for contact that characterize the types of contact evidenced here. (The description of contact provided by Friedman below does not deal with contact on this level, but rather with describing if a sign has a contact, and if so whether that contact is at the beginning, at the end, continuous throughout the formation of the sign, or repeated as in double contact signs. Points of contact such as those needed in the above rules have not yet been treated in this light.) Both rules are phonetically motivated. In the S handshape, the thumb crosses the second joint area and is thus "in the way" of comfortable second joint contact. It should be pointed out that second joint contact is not physically impossible with the S handshape, but its nonoccurrence in ASL is linguistically constrained. Similarly, those handshapes that require thumb tip contact (which may in turn be conditioned by the type of motion in these signs) would be awkward to produce (but not impossible) with the S handshape. ("Awkwardness," however, is simply a matter of what we are used to.) For some signers who have long thumbs, A and Å are not distinguished in some signs that require thumb tip contact (but apparently always in signs where Å is not derived from S, see below). Thus, their rule might be something like:

$$\begin{bmatrix} +\text{closed} \\ -\text{thumb} \\ -\text{spread} \end{bmatrix} \rightarrow [+\text{thumb}] / \begin{bmatrix} \overline{\text{second joint contact}} \\ \text{thumb face contact} \\ \text{thumb tip contact} \end{bmatrix}$$

Further evidence for the "thumb position-contact" relationship comes from other handshapes in which one can observe a similar change in the thumb. For example, a G handshape (or related X, H, V, and Ÿ) can also be observed to move from an S-position thumb (crossing second joint) to an A position (in this case, straight up against the third or fourth finger edge, as the index finger and possibly the third finger are raised). Thus, G∧ ˈG∧ × "meet," which involves second joint contact, is made with A thumbs rather than S thumbs. It is, however, possible to use S thumbs for "meet" if the contact is changed from second joint contact to the bottom edge of the palm. When these handshapes (G, X, etc.) occur with no contact, or with contact involving the extended finger(s), both S and A thumb positions appear to occur in free variation, with S being favored. Friedman (1976b) reports Ḃ as an Ȧ-thumb position variant of B. Similarly, Battison, Markowicz, and Woodward (1975) discuss Ȧ thumb for L from G, 3 from V in dialect variations. Thus, the rules presented are probably specific instances of a more general process governing thumb behavior, which we are not as yet in a position to specify.

Returning now to Ȧ when it occurs in "no-contact" environments, it must be emphasized again that a full solution is not being presented here, but rather an outline of how such a solution might be approached. So far, it has been suggested that A and Ȧ in thumb tip contact environment are derived from S. The remaining occurrences of Ȧ appear not to be derived from S, but instead are either basic or derived along other dimensions. I will assume that at least some of the occurrences of Ȧ are basic and it will be these basic forms that I contrast with the Ȧ handshapes derived from S.

Certain occurrences of Ȧ in no-contact environments illustrate classifiers as discussed in Kegl and Wilbur (1976) and Kegl (1976a, 1978c). A full appreciation of the function of classifiers in ASL will not be possible until a much later discussion of the syntax of ASL (see p. 103 and Chapter 4). At this time, a very brief description is given to orient the reader. Classifiers (the term attributed to Frishberg, 1975) are a form of pronoun in ASL that seem to be defined primarily by the handshape. They are substituted into a sentence when potential violations of signing space occur (when the "bubble" might otherwise be broken by a straight arm or circular moving signs). They also occur in place of a noun when that noun cannot phonologically blend into the verb (see p. 103). A partial list of classifiers includes:

G—general person

V—ambulatory (by legs)

3—vehicle

Ϥ—airplane

Ȧ—general object, usually taller than wide

B, palm up—flat object, movable

B, palm down—flat object, immovable

B, forearm to fingertip—tall object (or long?)

C—containers, objects with salient insides (bowl, box)

The Ȧ classifier seems to represent objects that can be moved by an independent source. Its occurrence in this capacity is illustrated by "follow," "pass," "mingle, each other," "under, underneath," "self," and others. The occurrence of classifiers in these forms is morphophonologically governed. When these classifiers occur, they may serve as dummy pronominal elements which in certain environments can be replaced by other lexical items.

The sign FOLLOW (made with two Ȧ hands) has been observed with one G hand following one Ȧ hand, and also with two G hands (J. Woodward, personal communication). At present, it appears that only other classifiers can substitute for Ȧ (J. Forman, personal communication).

For example, $B_\upsilon\dot{A}^\perp$ "under, underneath" in citation form is made with one Ȧ hand below a palm-down B hand. To indicate "The person walked under the bridge," the Ȧ handshape in "under" would be replaced with the classifier for "by legs," an upside-down V hand. If the sentence were "The car drove under it," the Ȧ hand in "under" would be replaced with the classifier for "by vehicle," a 3 hand. Similarly, "He found the bowl under the table" would be made with the container classifier C hand in place of the Ȧ hand of "under." These substitutions illustrate a process that is not phonologically conditioned. Thus, not any Ȧ hand may be replaced. Crucially, none of the Ȧ handshapes derived from S may be substituted for. These facts argue for treating Ȧ classifiers as basic.

Other occurrences of Ȧ seem to co-occur with upward movement, as in $[]\dot{A}\dot{A}^{\diamondsuit}$ "live, address"; in alternating up and down movement, as in $\dot{A}\dot{A}^{\wedge\sim}$, "which"; or down only movement, as in $[]\dot{A}_\upsilon\dot{A}_\upsilon^{\times}$ "coat." Thus, some generalization with respect to the vertical axis eventually may be possible here, either in terms of the direction of motion, the motion itself, or the vertical orientation (thumb edge up) of the hands themselves.

Another group of signs with the Ȧ handshape may also possibly be related to the movement. Examples include $\dot{A}^a$ or A° "other, else," and $\dot{A}^{\overset{a}{\vee}}$ "any," which includes a twisting of the wrist. In general, possible relationships such as this between movement and handshape have not been investigated in sign language research. The potential for a systematic rather than a spurious relationship deserves further consideration.

The analysis presented here, however incomplete, diverges from the others in at least one significant aspect, namely, that it recognizes that certain information in the occurrence of handshapes may be predictable and as such need not be entered into the underlying representation of a sign as it is entered into the lexicon (for further reanalysis along similar lines, see Chinchor, 1978b).

This implies that ASL, like other natural languages, can and should be characterized by a generative framework. Given that the phonological component of a grammar deals with the effects of segments in context and then feeds into the phonetic component of the grammar, it should not be surprising that manual languages have phonological characterizations similar to oral languages.

Other processes that require considerable further investigation, but that are suggestive of phonological derivational processes, such as assimilations, are discussed separately (see Chapter 3, "Phonological Modifications") as they deal with signs in context. The consideration of alternate descriptions of the formational characteristics of isolated signs now continues.

Location

Stokoe's values for the location parameter were presented early in this chapter. Within his system, signs that did not contact any part of the body were described as made in neutral space, a location that contrasted with the remaining 11 locations on the body.

Friedman (1976b) continues to follow Stokoe's division of locations into neutral space and body locations. Table 10 presents her list of places where signs are made. She maintains that the major areas are those discussed by Battison, Markowicz, and Woodward (1975) (see p. 27)—head, trunk, arm, and hand. Her list differs from Stokoe's in that she has separated out some places which Stokoe treated as simple variants of others (e.g., side of the forehead as a variant of forehead) and has indicated conditions in which those places might occur (for example, she indicates that side-forehead occurs in two-handed signs).

Kegl and Wilbur (1976) chose to distinguish signs in neutral space from signs on the body by use of the feature contact. This allowed specification of different locations *within* neutral space by having all signs described with reference to the body areas—those that distinctively touch the body are marked [+contact] (this is phonemic—in actual signing, a signer might not make contact, but in citation form the sign touches the body) and those that have traditionally been lumped into neutral space are marked [−contact].

Three features, head, trunk, and hand, were chosen for the major areas; thus the neck can be treated as a special (but not major) area

Table 10.   Place of articulation

Place	Conditions of occurrence
Neutral space	
Head	
Whole face	
Whole face	
Top of head	Iconic signs
Upper face	
Forehead	
Side-forehead	Double articulator signs
Eyes	Iconic signs
Side-eyes	Contact
Nose	
Center	
Under	Iconic signs
Side	Double contact; twist
Lower face	
Chin	
Mouth	Iconic signs
(Under-chin)	
Cheek	
Center	
Side	Thumb tip contact
Ear	Iconic signs
Neck	
Center	
Side	Iconic signs
Trunk	
Chest	
Center	
Stomach	Iconic signs
Waist	Iconic signs
Shoulder	
Arm	
Upper arm	
Elbow	
Dorsal forearm	
Ventral forearm	
Dorsal wrist	
Ventral wrist	
Hand	

From Friedman, L., *On the Other Hand: New Perspectives on American Sign Language,* © 1977 Academic Press, New York. Reprinted by permission.

(Table 11). Each of the major areas may be further divided into the periphery (extreme) and the center (central). The use of the features top and bottom divides each area into three subareas (like high and low in vowel height). Table 12 gives the current version of the location feature matrix. Note that the feature dorsal is only relevant to hand and arm signs, since one cannot make signs on the back of the head or trunk. (In the National Theater of the Deaf performance of "Parade," a deaf Nathan Hale, hands tied behind his back, turns his back to the audience and signs, "I regret that I have but one life to give for my country." The audience's response acknowledged their appreciation of this creative violation of normal signing constraints.)

Another relevant feature which has not been included in this matrix would be something like ipsilateral (or contralateral, or perhaps both will be needed) to indicate that the sign is made on the same or opposite side of the body from the hand that articulates it. It is not clear whether this is a location feature or a manner of articulation feature, much like the features that indicate speed of a sign.

With this set of features the same binary features can be used to define the phonetically relevant points within the major areas, thus eliminating the need to have separate values in each area such as chin, wrist, etc., used by Stokoe, Casterline, and Croneberg (1965) and Friedman.

Orientation

As indicated, orientation appears in Stokoe's system only as part of the specification of the wrist when used as a place of articulation for a two-handed sign. Battison recognized the necessity of treating ORIENTATION as an independent parameter, given that one can have minimal pairs on the basis of orientation alone (THING, palm up, vs. CHILD/REN, palm down). It has since become obvious that orientation for both the palm and the fingers (determined at the metacarpals) must be indicated. Consider the different directions the fingers can point when the hands are held with the palms facing inward to the body—up, down, toward each other, as well as several possibly distinct intervals in between. Thus, the direction in which the fingers face must be indicated in the descriptions of the sign. Anyone who has been frustrated in an attempt to reconstruct a sign from an English description will appreciate this fact.

Table 11.   Features for major places of formation

	Head	Neck	Trunk	Hand	Arm
Head	+	+	−	−	−
Trunk		+	+	−	−
Hand				+	−

Table 12. Feature assignments for location

Locations	Features								
	Head	Trunk	Hand	Extreme	Central	Top	Bottom	Lateral	Dorsal
Forehead	+	−	−	+	−	+	−	±	
Eyes	+	−	−	−	−	+	−	+	
Center nose	+	−	−	−	+	−	−	−	
Side nose	+	−	−	−	+	−	−	+	
Mouth	+	−	−	−	−	+	−	−	
Upper cheeks	+	−	−	−	−	−	+	+	
Cheeks	+	−	−	+	−	−	+	+	
Chin	+	−	−	+	−	−	−	−	
Ears	+	−	−	+	−	−	−	+	
Shoulder	−	+	−	−	−	+	−	+	
Chest	−	+	−	−	−	+	+	±	
Waist	−	+	−	−	−	−	+	+	
Hips	−	+	−	+	−	−	−	+	
Fingertips	−	−	+	+	−	+	−	−	±
Finger base	−	−	+	−	−	+	−	−	±
Center palm	−	−	+	−	+	−	−	−	±
Fleshy part	−	−	+	−	−	−	+	−	±
Wrist	−	−	+	+	−	−	+	−	±
Edge of hand	−	−	+	+	−	−	−	+	−
Upper arm	−	−	−	+	−	+	−	−	±
Lower arm	−	−	−	+	−	−	+	−	±
Elbow	−	−	−	−	+	−	−	−	±

From Kegl and Wilbur (1976).

Friedman takes an interesting approach to the problem of specifying orientation. She defines orientation for each individual handshape (Friedman, 1976b, pp. 68–70) by supplying the appropriate interpretation that should be placed on the orientation when it is
specified. For example, if the orientation of a sign with the handshape
C is given, then the orientation is interpreted as being determined by
the palm, whereas if the handshape is V, then the orientation is determined by the direction of the palm and/or fingertips (see Table 13). It
seems that no handshapes have their orientation defined solely by the
fingertips, because they have either 1) a specification for palm and/or
fingertips or 2) the direction of the palm (as in O and D). Two handshapes, A and M, have orientations that are determined by the side of
the palm or fingers. Friedman's framework does not as yet provide a

Table 13.   Orientation defined

Hand configuration	Orientation in the direction of. . .
A	finger or palm-side
O	fingertips (palm)
B	palm and/or fingertips
$\hat{B}$	palm
C	palm
5	palm and/or fingertips
4	palm and/or fingertips
$\ddot{5}$	palm
F	palm and/or fingertips
G	palm and/or fingertips
X	palm
L	palm and/or fingertips
H	palm and/or fingertips
V	palm and/or fingertips
$\ddot{V}$	palm
3	palm and/or fingertips
$\ddot{3}$	palm
Y	palm
8	palm
8	palm
7	palm
M	finger or palm-side
D	fingertips (palm)
E	palm
G_2	palm and/or fingertips
K	palm and/or fingertips
I	palm and/or fingertips
W	palm and/or fingertips
R	palm and/or fingertips

means for determining the proper interpretation of orientation for those handshapes that can have either palm *or* fingertip definitions. The values that the orientation parameters may have in Friedman's framework are TOWARD, AWAY, UP, DOWN, RIGHT, and LEFT (and combinations thereof). She points out the problem of specifying slight variations that may occur in the way the hands are held (IN may not really be directed *in*, etc.). This problem relates to the issue of whether the features are supposed to characterize all of the (phonetic) details of the sign (in this case, the exact details of how the hands are held) or only those details that are distinct (phonological). There is no simple solution to this dilemma.

Kegl and Wilbur (1976) also took an unusual approach to the problem of orientation by defining features that could be used for both palm and fingers. Six binary features were needed, three for the palm and three for the fingers. Since the palm can face in six primary directions—up and down, toward the body and away, toward the opposite side of the body or toward its own side (right palm facing right, left palm facing left)—three features were used. The first feature, palmup, was defined such that [+palmup] means that the palm is facing up, as in THING, whereas [−palmup] means that the palm is facing down, as in CHILDREN. Another feature, palmin, was defined with [+palmin], meaning that the palm is facing the body, and [−palmin], meaning that the palm is facing away from the body. Finally, palmside was defined such that [+palmside] means that the palm faces the opposite side of the body and [−palmside] means that the palm is facing its side. The reader will note that the only really comfortable way to have [−palmside] is when the fingers face down and the elbows are extended outward to the side or when the fingers face up as if one is pretending to be Sampson pushing the pillars out from under the roof.

To specify finger orientation, three more features were defined, similar to those for the palm—fingerup, fingerin, and fingerside. The metacarpals serve as a more constant reference point, because the fingers may bend in toward the palm, thus obscuring the direction in which they would be pointing if they were extended straight. A line extending from the metacarpals is used to define finger orientation, whether the fingers are extended or bent.

Clearly, certain combinations of the palm and finger features are physically impossible. The fingers and the palm are always at a right angle to each other, thus preventing such combinations as [−palmin, +fingerin] (palm out, fingers in). Other combinations, such as [−palmup, +fingerin], are physically possible but linguistically prohibited in ASL. It should be noted that these features are not specified for each handshape, but rather for each sign, and that for each sign, only one palm feature and one finger feature may be indicated. Furthermore, within this framework, predictions are not made as to which orientations will/can occur with which signs. These and other constraints on allowable feature combinations are written in the same way and in the same part of the grammar as the symmetry constraint mentioned earlier (segment and sequence structure rules, possibly at some later date reinterpreted as morpheme structure rules/conditions).

Motion

The motion of signs provides an enormous challenge to linguists attempting to describe the language, to book publishers attempting to depict the language, and to those brave souls who are attempting to determine an orthography or transcription system for the language. If signs did not move, one could conceivably utilize the same type of description system used for speech, considering each segment as a separate unit with place of articulation and manner of articulation (shape of the articulator(s) and position in the cavity, mouth, or signing space). The temptation to utilize this analogy between oral and manual language has led some researchers (Friedman, 1974; Newkirk, 1975) to investigate motion as a parallel to oral language segment types— stop, fricative, affricate, etc. A stop, for example, would be a sign whose motion came to an abrupt halt; a fricative might be a sign with continuous motion, e.g., wavy fingers; and an affricate would be a sign whose motion included a sharp flick of the finger(s), e.g., CRAM, HATE, ELIMINATE/GET RID OF. Other parallels have also been offered.

A brief glance at Stokoe's movement parameter values reveals a number of redundancies in the system, which he himself has indicated with brackets. These include vertical motion, sideways motion, horizontal motion, rotary motion, and interacting motion. The first three, one will notice, are identical to the three axes utilized in the description of orientation—up and down, side to side, and toward and away from the body. This redundancy has led both Friedman and Kegl and Wilbur to separate the description of the direction of motion from the motion itself. Direction is discussed first, followed by motion.

Direction of Motion   Friedman (1976b) recognizes movement along the three possible axes: the vertical axis, the horizontal-depth axis (movement toward or away from the body), and the horizontal-width axis (side to side). She proposes (1976b, pp. 48–50) a feature direction with 10 values: *up, down, up-and-down, toward, away, to-and-fro, right, left, side-to-side,* and *nondirectional. Up, down,* and *up-and-down* are defined, obviously, on the vertical axis; *toward, away,* and *to-and-fro* are defined on the horizontal-depth axis; and *right, left,* and *side-to-side* are defined on the horizontal-width axis, where *right* and *left* are defined as "movement in the direction of the dominant side (side of the dominant hand) (and away from the non-dominant side) and in the direction of the non-dominant side (and away from the dominant side), respectively" (p. 49). The need to define *right* and *left* like this results from the fact that modifications of the actual hand positions may in turn contribute to modifications in the perceived direction of motion (as opposed to the citation direction of motion).

The system proposed by Kegl and Wilbur (1976) for characterizing direction of motion capitalizes on the fact that their orientation features discussed above uniquely define the position of the hand in space. Given this information, it becomes possible to simplify specification of the direction of motion. Two features are defined, relative to the hands, not to the body—palmo and fingero, the names being shortened forms of *palm o*rientation and *finger o*rientation. These two features indicate the direction of the motion by reference to the orientation features. For example, a sign specified as [+palmo] will move along an axis perpendicular to the palm, regardless of the orientation of the palm (if the palm faces either up or down, movement will be vertical; if the palm faces sideways, the movement will be horizontal-width; if the palm faces toward or away from the body, movement will be horizontal-depth). A sign that is [+fingero] will move along an axis defined by the metacarpals. A sign that is [−palmo, −fingero] will move along the axis defined by the extended thumb (or where it would point if extended, or, viewed alternatively, in the direction defined by the edge of the hand, either pinkie edge or thumb edge). (The combination [+palmo, +fingero] is not possible.) Thus, if the palm faces down and the fingers face away from the body [−palmup, −fingerin], a sign that is [+palmo] will move either up or down (or alternating) as specified by the movement features discussed below. If the sign is [+fingero], it will move either toward or away from the body. If it is [−palmo, −fingero], it will move to the side since this is the direction of the extended thumb. In each case, in order to know which way the hand moves, one must know both the hand and finger orientation and the values of palmo and fingero.

This is clearly not a direct phonetic feature system, in that the interpretation of two features depends crucially on the values of up to six other features (no more than two at a time, however, one palm orientation and one finger orientation). Furthermore, the type of motion—straight, circular, alternating, etc.—is specified by still other features. At this point, it is not clear if this type of phonological feature system is worth pursuing.

Movement (Motion)   One of the redundancy conditions on the movement of signs is the symmetry condition discussed earlier. If both hands are moving, the motion must be symmetrical (identical) or alternating opposites (e.g., one goes up, the other goes down, and vice versa). One can divide the discussion of movement then into movements in which one hand is involved and movements in which two hands are involved.

Friedman (1976b, 1977) discusses five types of movement that involve interaction of the two hands (see display on next page). Alternate is the movement alluded to above, where one hand does the symmetrical opposite of the other hand, usually more than once, whether it is up and down, to and fro, or side to side. Signs such as MEET approach, whereas signs such as BUT separate. Friedman intends these characterizations to refer only to two-handed signs, and not to signs in which one hand stays still while the other comes to it (and makes contact) or leaves it. The feature value cross would be used to describe a sign such as WORK, where one hand crosses the other and taps lightly on the back of the wrist. Link involves linking or grasping of the fingers, as in JOIN, or the hand, as in BELIEVE. Friedman proposes a single feature, interact, with the values alternate, approach, separate, link, cross, and noninteracting. Noninteracting signs are those in which either the two hands move parallel to each other or in which only one hand moves.

Friedman also characterizes the movement of a sign if it makes contact with the body with a feature contact that has six values: continuous contact (contact is maintained throughout the production of the sign as it moves); holding contact (the sign is made in one place of articulation, the movement is probably hand rotation or flexion, and the contact is likely to be an extended finger, usually the thumb); end contact (the sign starts without contact with the body, but ends with contact); beginning contact (sign starts in contact with body and moves away); double contact (sign makes contact at two *different* places, such as KING, which makes contact at the contralateral shoulder and then the ipsilateral waist); and finally noncontact. Friedman (1974) has described the relevance of these feature values to the characterization of stress in ASL. When stressed, contact signs may become noncontact and noncontact signs may become contact (but this is not a symmetrical process—when noncontact signs become contact, it is likely to be end-contact) (see Chapter 3, ''Stress'').

Another aspect of Friedman's framework deals with the movement of the joints of the hand and wrist and of the arm. For the hands and wrist, she indicates six types of movement: bend-fingers, bend-knuckles, bend-wrist, wiggle (obviously for fingers), and open and close action of the hands. Open and close are used for those handshape changes that do not appear to be properly analyzed as a sequence of two separate handshapes. For movement of the entire arm, she suggests three more movement types: straight, twist, and circular. These nine types of movements are the possible values of the feature she calls manner.

Movement in Features

Interact[1]

Alternate	
Approach	
Separate	
Cross	
Link	
Noninteracting	

Contact

Continuous	
Holding	
End	Contact
Beginning	
Double	
Noncontact	

Direction

Upward	
Downward	Vertical
Up-and-down	
Right	
Left	Horizontal-width
Side-to-side	
Toward	
Away	Horizontal-depth
To-and-fro	
Nondirectional	

Manner

Straight	
Twist	Macro
Circular	
Bend-fingers	
Bend-knuckles	
Bend-wrist	Micro
Open	
Close	
Wiggle	

[1] From Friedman, L., *On the Other Hand: New Perspectives on American Sign Language,* © 1977 Academic Press, New York. Reprinted by permission.

Kegl and Wilbur's (1976) discussion of movement is not as extensive as Friedman's, and only a few facets of the two frameworks can be compared. Kegl and Wilbur defined a feature forward, which indicated that the sign moves along the axis defined by palmo and fingero. The interpretation of this feature again depends on the orientation and direction of motion features. The positive value for forward refers to motion in the direction that the palm, fingers (metacarpals), or thumb (as indicated by the direction of motion features) are facing (indicated by the orientation features). Thus, if the palm faces up, [+forward] means straight motion upward (assuming the sign is marked [+palmo]) and [−forward] means that the motion is downward. If the palm faces downward (and the sign is marked [+palmo]), then [+forward] is downward and [−forward] is upward.

Like Friedman, Kegl and Wilbur also defined a feature alternate (actually, Friedman's was a value of the feature interact). If a sign is specified as [+alternate], it moves back and forth along the axis indicated by the direction features. Another feature that was defined by Kegl and Wilbur is circular and is similar in intent to Friedman's circular, although theirs is not restricted to movement in which the arm is involved. Other features that were noted but not fully defined by Kegl and Wilbur were those for repeated contact, or continuous movement along the place of articulation (as in a sign that moves smoothly up the arm, e.g., LONG), or speed of production (e.g., fast vs. slow reduplication; see Chapter 3 under "Reduplication").

SUMMARY

A sign may be viewed as a conglomerate of several features of parameters (exactly how many is not determined), and distinctive feature approaches, although not yet definitive, are apparently appropriate. Signs are subject to physical, perceptual, and linguistic constraints, and may also be highly redundant (e.g., two-handed signs that move identically). Changes in sign formation over time have supported descriptions of allowable signs, in that signs that did not fit these constraints tended to evolve into signs that do. Violations of these constraints may be used for creative humor. In Chapter 7, unintentional violations of these constraints by educators unaware of them are illustrated by invented signs that are clearly inappropriate.

ASL, which exists in a bilingual environment, has a productive mechanism for borrowing from English by creating new signs from fingerspelled words. This contributes to an expanding and changing vocabulary. Yet these new signs obey the existing sign constraints, and are made up of combinations of the same features or parameters as existing signs. This type of information has been used in the past by linguists to argue that a language had productive word-formation and phonological rules. The possibility of analyzing ASL within the framework of generative phonology is important, particularly because generative phonology itself was developed with only spoken language data. Its potential use with ASL not only lends support to generative theory, but suggests insights into those characteristics of language structure that may transcend modality.

The brief introduction to classifiers in this chapter requires some extra emphasis. Classifiers are one-handed signs that behave differently from other one-handed signs. As was demonstrated, classifiers may be part of a two-handed sign, e.g., the Å that occurs in the sign UNDER, and in some cases, may substitute for each other, as when 3, C, or V substitute for Å in UNDER, depending on context. The conditions for this substitution are discussed under "Grammatical Modifications" in Chapter 3, but the fact that it happens is unique. To substitute another handshape for one hand in SHOE, or in ONION, or in DECIDE would create a different sign. When substitution occurs in UNDER, the sign still means "under." What has changed is the information regarding what object or noun is being discussed; in this sense, classifiers are pronouns (more to come in Chapter 3). The descriptions of classifiers given in this chapter are presently undergoing further theoretical and empirical investigation (Wilbur, Bernstein, and Kantor, 1978) and are likely to be modified in the future. In addition, Kegl (1978c) has identified other classifiers which have not been listed here.

CHAPTER 3

SIGNS IN CONTEXT

CONTENTS

This chapter considers those processes that affect the formation of signs in context. The somewhat arbitrary division between the end of this chapter and the beginning of the subsequent chapter is purely for expository purposes, as is the casual separation of this chapter into phonological, morphological, and grammatical modifications. The theoretical issues that relate to such divisions (Wilbur, 1973a,b, 1974a, 1975), although interesting to the linguist, are sidestepped here in the interest of presenting the information in a coherent fashion. A major purpose of this chapter is to emphasize the modifications of sign formation that may occur, so that the reader will be fully acquainted with the insufficiency of a sign description (as presented in Chapter 2) or of a drawing or picture of a sign (as is usually found in sign dictionaries). This is not to say that anything is necessarily wrong with them, but to stress that a language cannot be used appropriately if only the vocabulary is known but none of the rules.

    This chapter is divided into three sections. The first, ''Phonological Modifications,'' focuses on changes in a sign caused by the preceding or following sign (assimilation), the bending of a sign in contact with the other hand or the body, repetition of the sign for various purposes, changes in sign formation under conditions of linguistic stress, and omission or deletion of part of a sign, both historically and in present-day ASL as part of a compounding process. The second part, ''Morphological Modifications,'' covers a variety of processes, such as reduplication, and morphemes, both independent (numerals, auxiliaries) and bound (negative suffix, aspect markers). These modifications may serve two purposes: 1) to derive new signs from others (derivational morphology), as when in English the ''-er'' suffix is added to ''farm'' to create ''farmer,'' and 2) to inflect signs for number, aspect, and tense, as when the English verb ''farm'' is marked with ''-s'' in ''he farms'' or with ''-ed'' in ''he farmed.'' Derived forms may also be inflected, as when the English word ''farmer'' is made plural, ''farmers.'' The third section in this chapter, ''Grammatical Modifications,'' is intended to be a gentle introduction to ASL syntax. Included are verb modification in space to indicate subject and object, more information on classifier pronouns, as well as other types of pronouns, a discussion of the process by which a noun phrase is established in a conversation (which usually must be done before a pronoun can substitute for it), and information on hypothesized internal structures for the noun phrase itself.

PHONOLOGICAL MODIFICATIONS

The processes described below are not yet well documented in the literature as synchronic processes, and may at some later date be shown to be dialectal, stylistic, or even fast signing phenomena. Battison, Markowicz, and Woodward (1975) and Battison (1974) referred to assimilations of movement, location, orientation, and handshape, but did not provide examples or the degree to which they occur. Their regularity in another study was sufficient to warrant hypothesizing their existence as rules (Kegl and Wilbur, 1976).

Assimilations

Assimilation in general is a process whereby two unlike elements become more similar because of their proximity in context. This increase in similarity may result from the first formed element becoming more similar to the second (regressive assimilation), or from the second element becoming more similar to the first (progressive assimilation), or from modifications in both elements (mutual assimilation). In spoken language, these elements are sounds; in manual language, they are signs. In spoken language, the sounds may change their place of articulation or their manner of articulation. Similarly, signs may modify their location, handshape, or other characteristics. In this context, modifications of facial expression are also addressed. To date, no complete description of facial expression has been offered. Grammatical uses are discussed in their appropriate spots, but assimilation of facial expression is a phonological process in the same sense as assimilation of sounds or signs.

Assimilations of Location   Assimilation of location has been observed between two consecutive signs. In each case so far, it has been regressive assimilation, with the second sign conditioning adjustment in the formation of the first sign. For example, in a signed version of "The Three Little Pigs" (Kegl and Chinchor, 1975), while the wolf tries to gain admittance to the house of the three little pigs, he signs LET ME IN repeatedly. In some cases, the formation of LET is modified in that the right hand moves from waist level (where LET is normally signed) to chest height, in anticipation of the formation of the sign ME. In a few cases, both hands of LET were raised to chest height in anticipation of the following sign. In another example, WE REFUSE, regressive assimilation of location caused the sign WE to *metathesize* its two places of articulation (contact first at right chest, then at left chest, *became* contact first at left chest, then at right chest) in anticipation of the formation of REFUSE at the right shoulder. The existence of this kind of internal metathesis has been overlooked previously, and even has been thought impossible.

Assimilations of Handshape   The example WE REFUSE also illustrates assimilation of handshape, again regressive assimilation. The sign WE is usually made with an H hand (or for some people, with a G hand), or in initialized versions with a W, but is made with an A hand as an assimilation to REFUSE, which is made with an A. Other types of handshape modifications which are observed are not strictly phonological; they include blending of an object into its verb (modifying the handshape of the verb GIVE to the shape of its object BOOK, thereby executing GIVE and BOOK simultaneously, written hereafter as BOOK-GIVE), the blending of numbers into nouns (changing the handshape of WEEK, which is actually "one week," to reflect two, three, or four weeks), and the creative combinations of handshapes with certain motions, locations, and orientations to produce name signs. These are discussed in appropriate sections.

Assimilations of Facial Expression   Discussion of facial expression has been extremely limited so far. The roles of facial expression, head tilt, eyeblink, and eye gaze are so important in the syntax of ASL that their functions are described in their relevant places. However, certain facial expressions are distinct to particular signs; for example the distinction between LATE and NOT-YET is that the latter is made with an accompanying slightly extended tongue whereas the former is made the same manually, but without the tongue (Baker, 1976). Thus, at some level, it makes sense to talk about signs that are made with distinctive facial expressions, or lexical facial expression. What has been observed (Kegl and Wilbur, 1976) is the assimilation of signs with neutral facial expression (i.e., lacking lexical facial expression) to signs with lexical facial expression. In at least one example, the assimilation is not regressive, but progressive. The sign BIG may be made with puffed cheeks. The sign TREE has no lexical facial expression of its own. The sequence BIG TREE may be signed in a variety of ways. The simplest (but not necessarily the most acceptable) form would be BIG TREE, with neutral facial expression on both signs. The next possibility would be the unassimilated version, with BIG made with puffed cheeks and TREE made with neutral face (acceptability doubtful). The assimilated version would have puffed cheeks held across the formation of both BIG and TREE. Another possibility is to delete the manual formation of BIG and have a coalesced sign BIG-TREE, in which the hands form TREE but the facial expression is puffed cheeks from the sign BIG. One linguistically impossible version is BIG with neutral face followed by TREE with puffed cheeks. That this is unacceptable argues for treating this process as assimilation (with copying) onto TREE, rather than claiming that puffed cheeks alone is an alternate version of the sign BIG (Baker, 1976). Within the description suggested here, the coalesced form results from assimilation followed by deletion of BIG.

The scope of such facial expression assimilations has yet to be determined (but see initial discussion in Liddell, 1977). We have yet to investigate what happens when a sign with lexical facial expression is placed in a context where the syntactic requirements include a different facial expression (negation, question formation, conditionals, etc.), except those discussed on p. 137.

Bending

There are, of course, signs that are made with already bent handshapes (e.g., X), but of concern here is a process of bending that arises from one hand coming into proximity or contact with the other hand or some part of the body. For example, when the fingertips of the B hand come into contact with the body at the chest or with the other hand, the result is B̈. Similarly, the V hand of LOOK/SEE bends as it comes close to the palm of the other hand in SCRUTINIZE. Even the suggestion of a contact with a surface causes bending, as in WINDOW-SHOPPING, where the closer a person gets to the window to look, the more bent the fingers become, although the fingers may never actually touch the palm (SCRUTINIZE and WINDOWSHOPPING may actually be surface variants of a sign meaning "to look carefully at"). Interestingly, the V hand when used as a classifier "by legs" does not bend in contact with the palm, as in STAND, except morphologically for meanings that imply bent knees (KNEEL, CLIMB) or animal legs. However, if one were to talk about the ceiling falling in, or someone crawling into a tight spot, or some other situation where the space is reduced but the knees are not actually bent from standing position, the V hand would bend in contact with the palm. Other aspects of this process remain to be delineated.

Reduplication

Reduplication is the repetition of an element two or more times. In discussing reduplication in ASL, Fischer (1973a) distinguished two speeds of reduplication, fast and slow, and two suprasegmental features that may co-occur optionally with these, a horizontal sweeping movement and a rhythmic rocking of the body. She noted that fast reduplication cannot co-occur with rocking, and that slow reduplication cannot co-occur with the horizontal sweeping movement. These rules are formalized as:

1. Verb $\longrightarrow$ [+Reduplication]
2. [+Redup] $\longrightarrow$ [±Fast]
3. [−Fast] $\longrightarrow$ [±Rocking]
4. [+Fast] $\longrightarrow$ [±Horizontal Sweeping]

Rule 4, for example, says that a verb sign that is made with fast reduplication may or may not have horizontal sweeping motion, and also (by omission) implies that fast reduplication may not co-occur with a rocking motion. The meanings of these reduplications and sweeping and rocking motions are discussed on p. 81.

Stress

Sentence stress and whatever might parallel syllable stress have not been specifically investigated for ASL. Friedman (1974, 1976b) detailed the modifications that result in sign formation from emphasis or contrastive stress. The major modifications this type of stress entails are change of motion (or duration of motion) and change in contact.

    Overall, a stressed sign tends to be produced larger, tenser, and more rapidly than its corresponding citation form. In measurements made comparing stressed and unstressed signs, Friedman (1976b) reported that the mean duration of a stressed sign was 833 msec, compared to 366 msec for unstressed signs. However, the actual movement part of this duration was only 150 msec for the stressed signs compared to 267 msec for the unstressed signs. The remainder of the duration was composed of "holds," either 1) before and after the movement, 2) before the movement but not after, 3) after the movement but not before, or 4) for some signs, no hold at all. Holds before the movement averaged 367 msec for the stressed signs compared to 150 msec for the unstressed signs, whereas holds after the movement averaged 617 msec for the stressed signs compared to 100 msec for the unstressed signs.

Changes in motion vary according to the type of movement in the citation form. Motion along a straight line, twisting motion, and motion that involves bending of the wrist are modified to become larger, more rapid, and tenser, whereas other nonstraight movements, such as circular, bending of fingers, bending of knuckles, opening, and closing, become tenser and more rapid, but by their nature of formation cannot become larger. Signs that involved repetition in their citation forms tend to lose that repetition. For example, movements such as bending of the fingers, knuckles, or wrist, wiggling of the fingers, twisting, and circular motions are usually made more than once in citation form, but only once in stressed form. Similarly, signs that involve what Friedman calls "interacting" movement (such as approaching, separating, linking, crossing, or alternating of the two hands) usually involve repetition but tend to lose it completely in stressed form. A sign that might be made with alternating up and down movement in citation form, e.g., IF, loses the alternation and instead is made with a single downward thrust of both hands. Signs made with alternating movement toward and away from the signer's body become a single movement away from the body. At the same time, these modified single dimension movements have become straight action movements, and thereby become large and rapid. Signs that involve linking of the hands or fingers as part of the citation form start out with them linked in the stressed form and move away from the signer's body. Signs that move from side to side in unstressed form tend to move toward the nondominant side (usually the left) when stressed.

Wiggling movement, in losing its repetition, becomes a straight motion sign, and thus it also becomes larger and more rapid. In addition, it becomes ballistic (forceful thrusting motion), as do many other straight action signs (whether basically straight or straight by derivation), particularly if their direction of motion is away from the body, up, or down. Upward or outward ballistic straight motion signs may also result in full arm extension (making the sign larger).

The type of contact that an unstressed sign has may also affect how its motion is modified under stress, as well as affecting its stressed contact. Signs that have two points of contact develop an arching motion between the first and second contact under stress. Some signs with one contact, either beginning or end, may also develop this arc. Signs that are produced with continuous contact in unstressed form retain that contact and, instead of being made quicker, are made more deliberately and slower. Friedman reported measurements of mean duration of movement for the stressed signs as 467 msec, compared to 267 msec for the unstressed signs.

Signs that are noncontact in their unstressed forms, usually those that are also straight movement and directional signs, add a final contact point, becoming what Friedman calls "end contact." Similarly, signs that are made with an initial contact in their unstressed forms tend to add a final contact, becoming "double contact." Interestingly, signs that are initially "end contact" tend to become noncontact when stressed, with the exception of those whose final point of contact is on the nondominant hand. This led Friedman to suggest that the loss of contact in these stressed signs serves in the interest of avoiding possible bodily injury to the signer which might result from a large, rapid, possibly ballistic sign making its final contact with the head (DUMB) or chest (MYSELF). Those signs that are made with holding contact in their unstressed forms become noncontact in their stressed forms, while also becoming straight action, large, rapid, and possibly ballistic, thereby making maintenance of contact a physical strain.

Friedman also noted a tendency in the opposite direction of that reported above, namely, that some signs tend to become circular in formation rather than straight. For example, some straight signs with final contact on the nondominant hand tend to become circular in motion when stressed. Other straight motion signs, such as OLD, may become side-to-side in their stressed forms. Finally, a circular motion sign that is repeated in unstressed form loses its repetition, as indicated above, but may also become only a partial circle.

Friedman's analysis of stress illustrates the types of phonological processes that may be found in sign language when one considers the effects of context on the formation of signs. Further investigations may reveal some other factors that have not yet been recognized.

Deletion

Battison (1974) described types of deletion that may occur in ASL and related them to the structural complexity of the signs. He noted four types of deletion: 1) deletion of a contact (also viewed as deletion of a location), 2) deletion of one part of a compound, 3) deletion of movement (e.g., loss of repetition in stressed signs), and 4) deletion of one of the hands in two-handed signs.

It is the latter type that Battison concentrated on. Recall that two-handed signs are restricted in their handshapes and movements by the symmetry condition, allowing three classes of signs: 1) one hand moves, the other stays still, and they both have different handshapes, 2) one hand moves, the other stays still, and they both have the same handshape, and 3) both hands move (and they therefore have the same handshape and same or mirror image movement). Battison reports that these structural groups are correlated with the acceptability of deleting one of the hands. In the first group, deletion of the moving hand is prohibited, probably because the nondominant hand does not provide sufficient information to identify the sign, thereby making the signal unintelligible. Deletion of the nondominant hand in this group of signs is permitted for only a few signs (THAT, WEEK, LATER). In the second group of signs, deletion of the nondominant hand is more readily acceptable, but Battison reports that the signer frequently attempts some type of substitute for the missing hand, perhaps contacting another part of the body or an object, or "ghosting" the movement as though the other hand were there. In the third group of signs, where both hands move, deletion of one hand is more frequent. Frishberg (1975, 1976a) reported that deletion of one hand in two-handed signs made near the face was an obligatory diachronic process. Synchronically, it is optional for two-handed signs made in neutral space, with the exception of signs with alternating movement or with crossing of the arms (HUG, BEAR, SKELETON). Deletion is also not allowed if the contact that the two hands make with the body is not symmetrical, as in the sign RESPONSIBILITY, where the contact (for right-handed signers) is at the right shoulder, and is asymmetrical in the sense that the right hand touches the ipsilateral shoulder (the right one) but the left hand touches the contralateral shoulder (the right one) instead of the symmetrical situation where the left hand contacts the ipsilateral shoulder also. As the degree of redundancy increases in two-handed signs (group 1 is the least redundant, group 3 the most), the freedom for deletion increases.

Bellugi (1975; Klima and Bellugi, 1979) discusses deletion in the context of the process of compounding. Bellugi identifies compounds as having two separate parts which are (or were) clearly identifiable lexical items, the composite of which functions as one sign and the meaning of which may differ from what would be predicted from the sum of its two parts. She notes that compounds in ASL experience temporal compression of the two parts, particularly of the first part, such that the entire compound may take only as much time to make as either of its parts signed in isolation (i.e., the whole compound takes as much time as an average single sign). In measurements made of the compound parts and their corresponding signs in isolation (e.g., BED_SOFT "pillow" compared to BED SOFT "the bed is soft") within appropriate sentence frames, Bellugi found that within the compound, the first part lasted an average of only eight videotape fields (there are 60 fields per second) whereas the second part averaged 21 fields. When the compound parts were signed as single signs in larger phrases (i.e., not used as part of a compound), the signs that functioned as compound first parts averaged 46 fields and the signs that had been compound second parts averaged 55 fields. Thus, when not compounded, these signs behave as separate single signs, but when they are compounded, they are greatly reduced.

The reduction and weakening occurs primarily in the movement of the sign. Signs that are normally made with repeated contact lose their repetition. Full circular motion is reduced to a partial, brief arc. Signs that are made with brushing movement (Friedman's contiguous contact) may reduce to a brief contact and may lose contact altogether (if the brushing is normally repeated, a single brush may remain, or may reduce as single brushing movement does, to brief contact or no contact). Other movements (nodding, twisting, opening, closing, alternating) are weakened and reduced. The common pattern of double contact, which Bellugi refers to as "touch-move away-touch," is reduced to a single contact (especially if both contacts are in the same place) or contiguous contact (by "slurring" the movement and not actually moving away from the point of contact).

Other changes that affect the production of signs in compounds are determined by the number of hands used in the first and second parts of the compound. If the sign is made with one hand for the first part and two for the second, the nondominant hand of the second part may already be in place while the first part is being executed. If the first part has two hands, and the second only one, the nondominant hand may drop or may be held during the second part. If both parts are made with two hands, the compound may actually be made with one (subject to the constraints of deletion discussed by Battison). If both parts are made with one hand, there is a high likelihood of finding handshape assimilation occurring. Since the first part is so greatly reduced and the second part is much longer compared to the first, one might predict that the second handshape would condition regressive assimilation, and, in fact, in many cases this is what happens. The ultimate in compression, of course, is when the two signs merge into one and the diachronic origin is no longer synchronically apparent to the signer.

Frishberg (1978) investigated synchronic remnants of compounds that experienced deletion. When deletion of one part of the sign (whether first or second) left behind a sign with a complex movement (like wiggling, twisting) or a sign that is two-handed, symmetrical, with no contact between hands or body, then no further modification of the sign occurred and no trace of the deleted part has been left. However, in many signs, deletion of one part of the sign resulted in a subsequent modification in the formation of the sign, which Frishberg argued is appropriately described as "compensatory lengthening." In oral languages, it is not uncommon for the deletion of a consonant to be accompanied by the lengthening of a neighboring vowel. In ASL, the deletion of one part of a sign has resulted in a lengthening of movement, either by repetition or by a complication of the movement (addition of wiggling or circular motion). The loss of one part of the compound, and the subsequent repetition of motion, also led to modifications in the location of certain signs. Usually, this reduced two locations (one for first part of sign, one for second) to a repetition at one location. Frishberg observes that if the former compound involved a crossing of the "major area" boundaries (see p. 28 and Table 5), the location of the resultant sign was double contact at the former second location (based on discussion in Frishberg, 1975, the physically lower location is expected also). However, if the former compound involved two contacts within the same major area, the resulting location was midway between the two former locations.

Summary of Phonological Modifications

These sections have illustrated the modifications that may affect the formation of a sign. In context, a sign may change its handshape, motion, location, speed of formation, number of hands involved, and duration. Signs that have no lexical facial expression of their own may assimilate neutral face to the facial expression of a neighboring sign, although the domains of this assimilation (within a noun phrase, across a noun and verb phrase) remain to be determined. Historical changes may leave behind traces of sign parts that have been deleted, and temporal compression of the two signs may allow the formation of a compound sign. In the present discussions, the pressure for signs to modify has been primarily formational and contextual. Several of these processes may also participate in modifications for semantic or grammatical purposes.

MORPHOLOGICAL MODIFICATIONS

Unlike phonological modifications, morphological modifications of signs reflect changes in their meaning or function. These processes include both derivational processes (deriving new words from other words, possibly changing parts of speech) and inflectional processes (adding tense, number, person, aspect, and other information). Morphology shares linguistic borders with phonology, syntax, and semantics, and there is therefore overlap in the types of processes discussed in each of these sections (the reader will notice reduplication as an illustration of this overlap), but the functions served in each of these components is different. Within morphology, the distinction between derivational morphology (see below) and inflectional morphology (see below) is difficult to determine clearly. The separation that has been made here is somewhat traditional, with those processes that are not clearly one or the other delegated to a separate section.

Derivational Morphology

Reduplication serves a variety of functions in this section. In addition, numerous morphologically related families of signs have been identified, for which generalizations remain to be formalized. Also active are the numerals, which can combine with nouns (blending) or in turn can be modified by the nouns they describe.

Reduplication   As indicated, reduplication can serve either a phonological or morphological function (for discussions of the general theoretical differences, see Wilbur, 1973a,b, 1974a, 1975). It can also be either derivational (augmentative, continuitive, durative, deriving nouns from verbs) or inflectional (plural).

Frishberg and Gough (1973a) identified reduplication as a process that affects time nouns. Repetition of the sign WEEK with continuous brushing motion produces WEEKLY, similar reduplication of MONTH produces MONTHLY, and TOMORROW produces EVERYDAY/DAILY. The sign YEAR loses its circular motion (one S hand circles around the other and taps it) so that the brushing repetition of the top hand against the bottom one can produce YEARLY (usually made with the G hand, denoting ONE, as in "once a year"). Slow repetition (with concomitant wide circular path) indicates duration. Done this way, repetition of WEEK indicates "for weeks and weeks." Similarly, MONTH can be reduplicated to mean "for months and months," and DAY "for days and days." Other triplets include ONCE, reduplicated regularly for SOMETIMES, and slowly with circular motion for ONCE-IN-A-WHILE, and AGAIN, reduplicated regularly for OFTEN, and slowly for OVER-AND-OVER.

Kegl and Wilbur (1976) separated this type of reduplication, where the noun can be repeated several times, from reduplication that indicates augmentation (enlargement). For example, "big bowl" is produced by signing BOWL followed by a larger version. Only one repetition is possible for this type of reduplication. These two different reduplication rules have been formalized by Kegl and Wilbur (1976) as:

To form "every week":

X   /WEEK/   Y
     [+Redup]
1   2   3 $\longrightarrow$ 1 2^n 3

To form "big bowl":

X   /BOWL/   Y
          [+Augmented redup]
1   2   3 $\longrightarrow$ 1   2   [2+augmented]   3

Fischer (1973a) discussed reduplication (as formalized earlier in this chapter) in its derivational function as it applies to verbs to indicate aspect. Verbs can be divided into stative ("appear," "seem," "looks like," etc.) and nonstative (active), which can be further divided into durative ("sleep," "talk," "eat," etc.) and nondurative ("kill," "win," "find," etc.). These divisions are semantic in nature and therefore are expected to be appropriately differentiated in every language. Stative verbs must be reduplicated quickly whereas nonstative verbs can be reduplicated slowly or quickly, when reduplication is being used for aspectual marking. Slow reduplication of a nondurative verb is interpreted to mean that the action was iterated ("kept on Xing and Xing and Xing," as in "winning and winning and winning"), whereas slow reduplication of a durative verb indicates that the action was continued ("Xed for a long time," as in "talked for a long time"). In addition, a slowly reduplicated verb can be "rocked," in which case the sign is interpreted as meaning "Too much X." Fast reduplicated forms usually indicate a type of plural. If the reduplication is accompanied by a horizontal sweeping motion, the sign is interpreted as having either a plural subject or a plural object, each of which does X. Fast reduplication without horizontal movement is interpreted as "habitually does X." Thus, the speed of reduplication, the rocking motion or absence of it, and the presence or absence of horizontal sweeping of the hands can be used to indicate various semantic relationships.

Supalla and Newport (1978) discussed the use of repetition in the formation of deverbal nominals (nouns derived from verbs) and associated forms. His discussion includes another aspect of sign formation which has not been characterized extensively, namely, manner of formation (see also Friedman, 1976b). Supalla began by defining two basic types of sign movement—unidirectional and bidirectional. Within the category of unidirectional, he identified three types, *continuous, holding,* and *restrained,* and within the category of bidirectional, he identified only two of these, *continuous* and *restrained.* He illustrated *continuous* with the example of someone swatting frantically after a fly and missing, *holding* as the abrupt end of the motion as the fly is squashed with the fly swatter, and *restrained* as the tense, controlled motion one would use to avoid splattering the fly all over the table (the hand usually bounces back from the contact, reacting to the abrupt stop and the tenseness of the muscles). Supalla observed that in verb-noun pairs, such as SIT and CHAIR, FLY and AIRPLANE, DRIVE and CAR, the noun required at least one repetition of the basic movement, whereas the verb, although possibly reduplicated in the manner discussed by Fischer, did not require it. Repetition is insufficient, however, to derive nouns from verbs. There is also a concomitant change in the manner of formation. Whether the verb is continuous or holding (Supalla indicates that verbs tend not to be restrained), the corresponding noun is restrained. Thus, FLY is unidirectional continuous and AIRPLANE is unidirectional restrained. SIT is unidirectional holding and CHAIR is unidirectional restrained. DRIVE is bidirectional continuous and CAR is bidirectional restrained. As indicated, verbs may be reduplicated for various aspectual meanings. Cyclic reduplication of nouns carries the meaning "X after X after X" (e.g., "car after car after car") and is a reduplication of the already repeated movement (distinguishing it from the repetition of the verb).

Morphologically Related Families   This section describes a group of related families discussed in Frishberg and Gough (1973a). The processes involved in creating these families and their possible synchronic existence remain to be determined. The order of presentation follows that of Frishberg and Gough.

Families Based on Motion Differences   Certain signs are related to each other in that their production is identical except for the direction of motion. The opposite pairs APPEAR (index finger moves up through base hand palm-down fingers) and DISAPPEAR (the index finger moves down from the base hand palm-down fingers), IMPROVE (dominant hand jumps up nondominant arm) and GET-WORSE (dominant hand jumps down nondominant arm), and CHASE (one A hand approaches other in circling motion) and EVADE (one A hand circles away from other) are clearly differentiated by their opposite direction of movement. In many cases, downward direction tends to be associated with negative meanings.

Another group is differentiated by the sharpness or softness of formation (Frishberg, 1972). Soft signs are gentle and repeated; sharp signs are made with extra intensity. MULTIPLY has a soft variant, FIGURE-OUT. YELLOW has both a soft variant, YELLOWISH, and a sharp variant, DEEP-YELLOW (other colors may undergo this process also).

The signs STUDY and CRAM, DIRTY and FILTHY, and AFRAID and TERRIFIED are related by a change from wiggling of the fingers (in the first of each pair) to "spritz" (sharp bursting open of the fingers from a closed fist). Frishberg and Gough provide at least 13 such pairs. They considered it to be a derivational morphological process similar to the others that have been discussed in this section, and I have placed it with the rest for convenience, although Friedman (1974, 1976b) provides an alternate analysis in terms of stress (see "Stress," this chapter) which is also appropriate for these forms.

Handshape Changes During Movement   The signs included in this section are not considered compound signs even though there is a change in the handshape. Friedman (1976b) considers them to have movement specifications of "open" or "close," thus avoiding the need to indicate two separate handshapes. Although one of the handshapes involved may be any handshape, the other one is usually one of the unmarked handshapes, either maximally open (B or 5) or maximally closed (S or A). Frishberg and Gough discuss a group with initial open hand and final closed flatO, all seeming to have a meaning related to taking of information: COPY, XEROX, TAKE-A-PIC-TURE, EAVESDROP, LEARN, etc. The opposite movement, ending with an open hand, relates the signs INFORMATION, ADVISE, IN-FLUENCE, CONTAGIOUS, CONSULTANT, and others.

Similar closing motion can be found in another semantically unrelated (to the above) group, in this case with the closed hand either S or sometimes F: FIND, PICK-UP, CHOOSE, TAKE, TAKE-UP, ACCEPT, CATCH, MEMORIZE, etc.

A separate group, implying negative emotions and other negative connotations, often employs a flicking of the fingers from an 8 handshape to an open 5. This group includes BAWL-OUT, HATE, AWFUL, and with an initial closed hand, NOTHING. It may be possible that these forms fall within the reanalysis of negative incorporation provided by P. Jones, discussed below.

Families Based on Handshape   Many signs that express emotions are produced with the open8 handshape—EXCITE, DEPRESS, FEEL, LIKE, INTEREST(ED/ING), TOUCH—and appear to be related to those negative emotion signs mentioned above.

WH-words tend to be made either with a G hand or a B hand: WHO, WHAT, WHERE, WHEN, and WHAT-FOR are made with G; WHAT, WHERE, and HOW may also be made with B. Frishberg and Gough indicate that they found no semantic or syntactic criteria for differentiating the different forms of WHAT and WHERE, although WHERE with the B hand is probably related to the sign HERE, also made with the B hand. The G hand forms may be related to G hand used for pointing (Hoffmeister, 1977).

The handshape Å occurs in two semantically unrelated families. One is a group of negatives: NOT, DENY, REFUSE, BLAME, ALCOHOLIC, SUFFER, STUPID, and others. The other group involves the use of Å as a classifier (introduced in Chapter 2) in verbs such as FOLLOW, CHASE, EVADE, FALL-BEHIND, FAR, AHEAD, PASS, BEHIND, and also seen in the preposition UNDER. In the "Illustrative Example" (Chapter 2), the possibility of substituting other handshapes in place of Å into these signs was explained. At that time, it was critical for understanding the difference between basic and derived phonological representations in ASL; later, it will be critical for understanding the verb and its behavior within the verb complex. At this point, it is sufficient to indicate that in fact it is the motion of these signs (and the spatial location for UNDER) which *defines* the sign itself, and that the handshape Å seems to be serving as a dummy handshape that can be replaced by a variety of other handshapes (G, V, 3) which indicate information about the subject and object of the verb.

The G handshape serves numerous functions in ASL: as the handshape used to index points in space; as a classifier for people; as the general handshape in many signs, such as WEEK and MONTH, meaning "1 week" and "1 month," and which can be replaced by other numbers; and simply as a handshape in certain signs. Frishberg and Gough indicate a group of signs which share meanings or opposites depending on whether the two G hands are parallel to each other (AGREE, ALIKE/SAME, etc.) or pointing at each other (DISAGREE, OPPOSE, HURT, ARGUE).

Another handshape that serves a similar variety of functions to those of G is V. In some signs, it is related in meaning to vision: SEE,

LOOK-AT, WATCH, READ, and the previously mentioned SCRU-TINIZE and WINDOWSHOP. BentV is found in BLIND, DOUBT-FUL, and ORAL/LIPREAD. The bending of the V in the previous forms is a combination of the V for vision and the bending of V to indicate difficulty: PROBLEM, HARD, NERVY, BLIND (hard to see), STEAL, ANALYZE, DEVIL, DOUBT. Before leaving V in its function as an indicator of vision, it should be mentioned that popular myth suggests that the two fingers of the V hand in such signs as SEE reflect the two eyes. However, it has also been suggested that the V in these signs has come to ASL through the influence of the French signs, which were brought to the United States by Laurent Clerc and Gallaudet. The French sign made with V is said to be an initialized sign (V for VOIR "to see") of an older French sign made with a G hand, which is used in conversation on a videotape of a 60-year-old deaf Frenchman made by Francois Grosjean at Northeastern University. We do not know the fate of the initialized sign in France, but if this story is true, the initialized version seems to have been retained here, except that I have also seen SEE with a G hand used by several informants from Philadelphia.

The other use of V is as the "by legs" classifier (although Frishberg and Gough do not call it this) in such signs as DANCE, STAND, KNEEL, CLIMB, LAY-DOWN, GET-UP, FALL, TOSS-AND-TURN, ROLL-IN-THE-AISLE-WITH-LAUGHTER, RESTLESS, JUMP, etc. Bent V occurs in variations of the verb SIT, as in SIT-IN-A-CIRCLE, SIT-ON-A-BENCH.

Families Based on Location   One of the most frequently indicated families based on location is the group of signs that separates into male and female according to its place of formation on either the forehead or cheek/chin, respectively. Thus, on the forehead there is BOY, MAN, FATHER, GRANDFATHER, BROTHER; on the lower cheek area there is GIRL, WOMAN, MOTHER, GRANDMOTHER, SISTER.

Many negative signs are made under the chin. These include NOT, DENY, NOTHING, NONE, WRONG, UNFAIR.

A family can be created by initializing one sign with several different handshapes. On the back of the hand, one finds NATION (with N handshape), INSTITUTION (with I), and CHURCH (with C), probably based on ROCK and MOUNTAIN. Several signs in the same area include a circular motion before contact with the back of the hand, including NATURAL (with N handshape) and ISLAND (with I).

On the back of the wrist there are the signs USE, WORK, BUSI-NESS, DUTY, APPOINTMENT, HABIT, ESTABLISH.

One obvious group made at the mouth is that related to speech: SHOUT, SCREAM, CURSE, QUIET, SHUT-UP, SECRET, MUTE, WHISPER, THANKS, PRAISE, SAY, TELL, INSULT, ANSWER, TALK, ANNOUNCE, DIALOGUE, PROMISE, TRUE, LIE, and COMMUNICATE.

The nose is often used for derogatory or negative signs: UGLY, STINK, IGNORE, RELUCTANT, BORED, BULLSHIT, DON'T-CARE, FOOL, STRICT, LOUSY, KIDS, FUNNY, and many others.

The use of the palm in many of the signs cited by Frishberg and Gough seems to be related to "book-learning": DRAW, WRITE, READ, PENCIL, PAINT, LETTER, PRINT, PUBLISH, STU-DENT, LEARN, SCHOOL, LETTER, LIST, and others. It is possible to offer another analysis of this, not considering the palm of the nondominant hand to be the location of the sign made by the dominant hand, but instead considering the handshape of the nondominant hand (flat B) to be the important factor, in particular as representing yet another classifier (flat object).

Initialized Sign Families   Aside from those already mentioned, many families have been created through the initialization process. The days of the week, Monday through Saturday, are each represented by a circular motion made in neutral space and a different initialized handshape for the corresponding English name. Thus MONDAY is made with an M, TUESDAY with a T, WEDNESDAY with a W, THURSDAY with an H, and so on. SUNDAY is apparently unrelated to the other days formationally (and seems to be related to the sign PREACH). Signs for royalty include KING with a K, QUEEN with a Q, PRINCE with a P, LORD with an L, and EMPEROR with an E, the only difference between them being the handshape. Similarly, a single sign for group or class or category, originally made with a a C hand, has led to a family with GROUP (G hand), ASSOCIATION (A hand), CLASS (C hand), FAMILY (F hand), ORGANIZATION (O hand), TEAM (T hand), and WORKSHOP (start with W, end with S). It seems that ASL initially had few color terms, probably BLACK, WHITE, something to indicate RED or possibly it meant general color, and maybe some other color term made in neutral space with a shaking hand. Frishberg and Gough speculate that this proto-color term might have been BLUE, because the motion is possibly related to "waves" or "water." At present, this shaking hand serves for the colors BLUE (B hand), YELLOW (Y hand), PURPLE (P hand), GREEN (G hand), but the sign for RED (made at the mouth) has been initialized for PINK (P hand), and apparently unrelated signs exist for ORANGE and GRAY.

Assorted Remaining Families   The remaining are smaller families which indicate various morphemes and processes relating them.

One is the use of the hands for feet: SHOES, SOCKS, WALK (citation form). Another is a group related semantically to indicate change with similar motion: CHANGE, BECOME, VICE-VERSA, INTERPRET/TRANSLATE. Another group indicates disjunction; they differ by handshape, probably through initialization, but have the same alternating up-and-down movement: IF (F hand), OR/WHICH (A hand), MAYBE (B hand), and UNDECIDED (S hand). The concept of connected communication appears to be represented by several signs which utilize the F handshape: SENTENCE, STORY, NAR-RATE, and INTERPRET. The meshing of things together is reflected in signs that interconnect the fingers from both 5 hands: HARMONY, MACHINE, FACTORY, GEARS, INTEGRATE.

This list is by no means exhaustive, either of groups or of the members in them. It should be clear from these examples that it is not unreasonable to talk about the internal structure of signs or of derivational processes that relate them.

Numbers and Numeral Modification   The number signs in ASL and their many variants represent a family in the same sense as those discussed by Frishberg and Gough. A general description of numbers is included in Stokoe, Casterline, and Croneberg (1965), Appendix B. They list the cardinal numbers from 0 to 22 and provide information on producing 23-29, 30-99, 100, 1000, and 1,000,000. They note two alternatives for 13 through 15, and note 16 through 19 are a combination of 10 plus the proper unit. Also included are instructions for higher combinations of numbers; for example, "numbers between one hundred and ten thousand may be signed by presenting the configuration for the hundreds digit, the sign for 'hundred' and the sign for the remaining two digit combination, or by presenting the three digits in order with a slight downward or outward thrust and successive displacement to the side" (p. 295). Finally, they discuss the ordinal numbers and indicate that there are separate forms for "first" through "tenth," but that for higher ordinal numbers, the cardinal number is used followed by the fingerspelled −t+h (a borrowing from English), and that −st, −nd, and −rd are not used. They describe various modifications that may affect numbers, such as changes in orientation to indicate such things as standings in a league or place in a list, and modifications of movement to use in approximations (e.g., shaking the 6 hand to indicate "approximately six").

Chinchor (1978a) and Kannapell (n.d.) have investigated the numeral system in considerable detail. The formation of the numbers from 0 to 1,000,000 is not simply a matter of learning the numbers from 0 to 9 and rules for their combinations. There is considerable variation in their formation, and numerous modifications that may affect them in context.

Chinchor (1978a) notes that, when used to count, the numbers 1 to 5 may be made with the palm facing either toward or away from the signer (depending on the person) whereas the numbers 6 to 9 always face away from the signer. When signing long strings of numbers (phone numbers, social security numbers, etc.), the palm always faces away from the signer. Further orientation changes are discussed after the remaining numbers have been described.

The number 10 is the first number to be made in citation form with a characteristic movement. The A or Å hand is used and is wiggled slightly from side to side. The numbers 11 and 12 are made similarly, in that both are made with the same starting point, a fist facing toward the signer's body, and are produced by the rapid extension of either the index (11) or the index and middle (12) fingers. The numbers 13, 14, and 15 can be made similarly to 11 and 12, with the proper number of fingers extending rapidly from the fist, or they can be made with the proper number of fingers extended (from the fist, palm still facing signer) and waving back and forth. Another formational process exists for all of the numbers from 11 to 19: they can be made as a compound of the sign 10 (without its wiggle) followed by the appropriate digit 1 to 9 (all face palm out). This latter process does not seem to be widely used. For the numbers 16 to 19, their formation as a compound of 10 plus a digit can be made with 10 (A or Å) in its normal upright (thumb up) position or with the fist turned to the side (thumb faces nondominant side, like manual alphabet letter A) so that the hand does not change orientation during the actual formation of the number. Sixteen through 19 may also be made by forming the appropriate single digit, palm out, and twisting it, similar to the way the number 10 is shook. A third possible formation for the numbers 16 to 19 is to form the appropriate digit, palm facing out, and to rub the thumb against the finger that it contacts (i.e., thumb rubs against pinkie for 16, against ring finger for 17, against middle finger for 18, and against index finger for 19).

The number 20 illustrates a general process, namely, that the tens (20, 30, etc.) are made with a digit closing to 0, but at the same time, 20 is an exception to the general rule in that the digit used is not the simple digit 2 (V hand) but an archaic form (believed to be from French Sign Language) of the number 2 (L hand). Thus 20 is made by the sequence L hand changes to babyO (Figure 1). The numbers 21 and

23 to 29 are also made with the L hand followed by the corresponding single digit (e.g., 23 is L followed by 3). The number 21 has a shortened form which is made with a bending thumb, the way we imitate shooting with a gun. However, the number 22 follows a pattern which holds for other double digit numbers, 33, 44, 55, etc. It is made with V instead of L, and consists of V hand followed by V hand moved slightly to the right (33 is 3 hand followed by the 3 hand moved slightly to the right, etc.). The number 25 also may deviate from the generally given citation form, in that it may be formed by making an L handshape and waving the remaining three fingers, or alternately by wiggling an open 8 middle finger.

Fortunately, the numbers 30 to 99 tend to be more regular. Thirty, 40, 50, 60, etc. are made with the single digit closing to a 0 (O hand). Thirty-one through 39 are made with the 3 hand followed by the corresponding single digit, and in the case of the double digit 33, a slight movement to the side is included. The remaining numbers up to 99 pattern accordingly.

One hundred is made with the number 1 (G hand) followed by the C hand (with no assimilation). Two hundred, 300, 400, and 500 may be made similarly as the digit followed by the C hand, but more frequently involve assimilation so that 200 is made with a V hand which bends to V̈ (simulating the shape of C while not actually including all the fingers that C uses), 300 is made with a 3 hand that bends to 3̈, 400 with 4 bending to 4̈, and 500 with 5 bending to 5̈. From 600 to 900, there is no assimilation between the digit and the following C handshape.

The sign for thousand is made by hitting the nondominant B hand with the fingertips of the dominant hand in an M handshape (M is actually B̈ with the thumb tucked underneath the fingers) which has been hypothesized to come from the French *mille,* "thousand." For million, the movement of thousand is repeated once, and for billion the movement is repeated twice (for a total of three contacts with the palm). For numbers other than 1000, 1 million, etc., the single digit is separate from the formation of the thousand or million sign.

Chinchor divides modifications that can affect signs in context into changes in motion, changes in location, and changes in orientation. Each of the changes is either associated with a change in the use of the number itself (e.g., cardinal to ordinal, exact to approximate) or reflects an increased relationship with the noun it modifies.

Changes in Movement   As indicated earlier in Stokoe, Casterline, and Croneberg (1965), the change in production from a sharp, clear formation to a slightly shaking formation reflects a change from precision (exactly 7) to approximation (about 7). This can be used whether a mathematical number is being rounded off or the number of people who showed up for a party is being indicated. For emphasis, the formation of the number is tensed and may move inward toward the signer during its formation. A certain coolness about the number (for whatever contextual reasons) can be indicated by a relaxing of the hand and fingers and a slight flexing of the wrist. A major semantic and functional difference is indicated in the change from cardinal (counting) to ordinal (reflecting order) numerals. The primary change in formation is a pronounced twisting of the numbers 1 to 9, usually from a facing outward position to palm facing the signer. Similarly, numbers can be twisted in this same manner to indicate dollars, although if ambiguity needs to be avoided the sign DOLLAR can always be added. When DOLLAR is used, the twisted numeral is not used; instead the numbers 1–5 are oriented inward and 6–9 are oriented outward. Another modification of movement, shaking, can be used to indicate speed (reputed to represent the movement of the speedometer needle). This shaking is potentially ambiguous with the shaking used to represent approximation.

Changes in the direction of movement can also reflect differences in function. To indicate a stack of $100 bills, the sign 100 can be repeated in a downward moving direction; to indicate $50, the sign 50 would be repeated in the same downward moving direction. In counting down a list of things, the numbers also move downward, usually with a change in orientation from fingertips upright to fingertips sideways.

Changes in Location   Chinchor (1978a) indicates that changes in location for number signs may result from one of two processes; the number sign can change its location through assimilation to a preceding or following sign, usually an associated noun (the result of assimilation is still two separate signs), or the number sign can change its location by actually being blended into another sign (creating one sign with the number for its handshape, but with the movement and location of the other sign). Assimilation of location tends to occur when digits follow the sign CENT, which is made on the forehead. The numbers are not actually made on the forehead, but lower in front or to the side of the face; this is quite different from their usual place in neutral space at about shoulder height. Another example of assimilation is the relocation of the number sign to the location of the sign AGE/YEARS-OLD. Number signs can also relocate to indicate the scores of different teams; "one for them, the other for us" would be formed with their score out in neutral space and with our score near the signer's chest.

If the signer feels no particular affinity for either team, the location of baskets or goalposts can be set up (left and right neutral space) and the scores given accordingly. When talking about the players on a team, the number on their shirts is made in contact with the signer's shirt. Numbers can also be located in different places along the time line (see "Time and Tense," below) when they are blended into signs that are made along this line.

The process of blending creates a single sign with a number for its handshape. An alternate of the AGE/YEARS-OLD and number combination is to actually blend the number into the formation of the sign AGE/YEARS-OLD. Blending also occurs when the number handshape is made at the location of the sign TIME to indicate, for example, 6 o'clock. Numbers can also be blended into time indicators such as HOUR, DAY, WEEK, MINUTE, MONTH, and YEAR. However, such blending is not unrestricted for all numbers. There seems to be a greater degree of freedom for the numbers 1, 2, and 3 to incorporate into other signs, whereas 4 and 5 are generally more restricted (5 even more than 4), being only marginally acceptable to some people and unacceptable to others. The numbers 6 to 9 can blend in only a few instances, and 10 and higher cannot incorporate at all. Zero appears to have blended (and lexicalized) into the sign KNOW to yield a sign made with the zero handshape at the location for KNOW, which means KNOW-NOTHING.

Change in Orientation   Chinchor (1978a) reported the change in orientation that occurs when the numbers 1 to 5 are used in enumerating objects (palm facing out) and when numbers are used to count down in a list (palm in, fingertips facing sideways instead of up). The use of palm out and the fingerspelling box for producing long strings of numbers can also be considered an orientation change (as well as a change in location from neutral space).

One factor that may affect whether a change in orientation for numbers when enumerating objects will actually occur is the location of the object sign itself. If the sign is made in the peripheral areas of the signing space, the number may assimilate its location to that object and may then adopt an orientation identical to or close to that of the noun sign, thus appearing to contradict the generalization that numbers face inward when enumerating objects. Chinchor indicates the phrase 3 CHILDREN as such an example, with the 3 moving to the location of CHILDREN and adopting a downward orientation, rather than an inward one. This seems to be more prevalent for peripheral signs than for central signs.

Discussion of the role of the numbers in the ASL pronominalization must await further exposition of the structure of ASL noun phrases and the processes of pronominalization that can affect them.

Inflectional Morphology

The formation of plurals for nouns and the indication of number on verbs, tense and time markers, and aspect are addressed in this section.

Plurals   Fischer and Gough (1978) described four different types of verb modifications that could be made to indicate plural subject and/or plural object: definite (individual), indefinite, collective, and dual. These processes are reflections of the same process of number agreement in English (e.g., "John walks," "John and Mary walk"), although of course they do not reflect the same rule.

The definite (individual) plural can apply to all verbs. It has a meaning that implies that each of the people or things performing the action does so individually, not collectively (i.e., something like "John left and Mary left and Bill left"). In addition, the people or things involved must be definite (i.e., it cannot be used for "some people left"). In order to understand how both this process and the others below work, it would be convenient to establish three arbitrary points in space in front of the signer's body: point 1, about 6 inches away from the signer's body in front, on the right about even with the right shoulder, at mid-chest height; point 2, somewhere to the left of point 1, same distance away from the body and same height, toward the center of the chest area but not directly in the center (this midline is used for reference to the addressee, second person reference); and point 3, similarly placed on the signer's left, same height and same distance from the body (the distance from the body, the height, and the degree of leftness or rightness are subject to a number of individual signer variables, as well as the total number of references actually being made). For ease of translation, John will be referred to with point 1, Mary with point 2, and Bill with point 3. The definite (individual) plural that corresponds to "John left and (then) Mary left and (then) Bill left" or "They each left separately" is made by facing point 1 and making the verb sign, then facing point 2, repeating the sign, and then facing point 3 and repeating the sign. This process includes repetition of the verb, a horizontal movement which is not a horizontal sweep, and a reorientation of the body and/or head and face which is referred to as "body shift" (Kegl, 1976a).

The indefinite plural has a meaning that implies that "many, but not necessarily all" of the people or things involved performed the verb action. It can be collective, as in "Many of them did it together." The indefinite plural is formed by fast reduplication of the verb sign (without pauses in between) moving around in a horizontal sweep (suppose it starts at point 1 and arcs around to point 3).

The collective plural, which means basically that everyone or everything is involved in the performance of the verb, is made with a single production of the verb sign accompanied by a horizontal sweeping of the hands, body, and/or eyes. Thus the formation of the sign might begin at point 1 and end somewhere near point 3, or the sign could be made closer to a single point, perhaps point 2, while the head and/or eyes turn from point 1 to 3. All verbs that can form a collective plural can also form the indefinite plural, but not vice versa. However, a generalization as to what factors allow or prohibit collective plurals remains to be determined.

Fischer and Gough indicated a couple of alternate pluralization processes that can be used for the collective and indefinite plurals. These include using two hands where in the singular only one hand is used (possibly along with reduplication and horizontal sweep as described above) and incorporating number into the verb sign. If the verb is made with a G hand (same handshape as the number 1), then its formation with the V hand (number 2) is the plural, which Fischer and Gough have termed "dual." The set of verbs that can take this form is limited. If the verb has a V handshape (LOOK), then these forms can be made:

1. "John looks at me." LOOK (hand moved to point 1 to indicate John, hand faces toward signer to indicate "me"). (Formalized notation for indicating this is developed later in the "Grammatical Modifications" and "Syntax" sections.)
2. "John and Bill look at me." LOOK (one hand moves as above at point 1, left hand made as above at point 3). (This is also the dual.)
3. "Everybody looks at me." LOOK (made with both hands as above, not necessarily at points 1 and 3, and with four fingers extended on each hand instead of two (V hand) to indicate "many").

Jones and Mohr (1975) concentrated on the formation of plurals for nouns themselves. They indicated that nearly all nouns can form a plural with the quantifier MANY as an indicator. Many nouns also undergo reduplication and other modifications to form the plural. They formalized several generalizations regarding these modifications, which are paraphrased here:

1. If a noun sign is made with one hand at a location on the face, its plural is generally made by repeating the sign alternately with both hands accompanied by a turning of the head from side to side (which may be a reflection of the horizontal sweep so prevalent in verb pluralization agreement). Exceptions to this are GIRL (which follows the next rule) and FLOWER and APPLE (which require use of a quantifier).

2. If a noun sign is made with an end contact, a beginning contact, a double contact, contiguous contact (contact during the entire formation of the sign, such as the dominant hand brushing up the nondominant arm for LONG), or involves a change in orientation during its formation in the singular, the plural is made by reduplication and usually with a horizontal sweeping arch. Exceptions seem to include OPERATIONS (surgical), which makes the subsequent repetitions slightly lower vertically than the preceding formation, and YEARS, which involves only one repetition, is horizontal to begin with, and does not add the horizontal arch to its formation in the plural.

3. Noun signs that involve some type of wiggling movement or that have a holding contact with some other movement are pluralized by continuing the movement (not reforming the sign) while moving the hands horizontally. Nouns that have bending wrist movement or circular movement are pluralized by continuing their movement but without the horizontal movement.

4. In general, any noun that involves repetition of movement in its singular does not undergo the above modifications of movement for plural, but takes a plural quantifier such as MANY instead (or a number).

   Time and Tense   It has been noted by many sign language researchers that ASL does not provide tense marking on each verb in each sentence as, for example, English does, nor does it require a tense marking on each sentence as do Walbiri and Luiseño. Instead, ASL allows the time of the conversation to be marked at the initiation of that conversation and does not require further marking (although it *may* be) until the time reference is changed (as for example in Malay). Fischer and Gough (1972), Frishberg and Gough (1973b), Friedman (1975a), and Cogen (1977) have all addressed aspects of the time marking system in ASL and modifications that may occur within that system.

Frishberg and Gough (1973b) describe the ASL "time line," a line that passes alongside the body from behind the head to a distance no greater than the full extent of the arm in front of the body, passing just below the ear. The space right in front of the body indicates the present, slightly more forward indicates near future, and greater distances forward reflect very distant future. The near past, of course, cannot be signed behind the body, so the space above the shoulder just about in line with the ear is near past, and distances farther back over the shoulder indicate distant past. Frishberg and Gough also indicate several signs which are used along this time line. For times in the past, there are (at least) four: PAST, BEFORE, LONG-TIME-AGO, and ONCE-UPON-A-TIME. They are differentiated by orientation of the hand (PAST and BEFORE face back over the shoulder and LONG-TIME-AGO and ONCE-UPON-A-TIME face the cheek), length of movement along the time line (BEFORE has a short movement, the others have a longer movement), and number of hands involved (PAST, BEFORE, and LONG-TIME-AGO are made with one hand, ONCE-UPON-A-TIME is made with two). The signs FUTURE, WILL, LATER, and IN-THE-FAR-FUTURE are similarly related, although none of them uses two hands (and many authors treat WILL and FUTURE as a single sign).

The signs TOMORROW and YESTERDAY are made on the cheek and move either forward or backward along the time line, respectively. Movement along the time line can become part of other time signs which are not normally made on the time line. The signs WEEK, MONTH, YEAR are made in neutral space in front of the signer's body, but can move forward or backward in space to indicate "a week from now/next week" or "a year ago/last year." With the incorporation of numbers, phrases such as "3 weeks from now" can be made with the handshape 3 making the movement of WEEK in its normal location across the nondominant palm followed by an added movement out past the palm and forward away from the signer. For the sign MONTH, movement in the past direction along the time line is permissible, but movement forward into the future direction is blocked by apparent structural constraints. Thus, "next month" is produced with a form of the sign NEXT and the sign MONTH.

It has been shown how reduplication of time signs such as MONTH, YEAR, and TOMORROW yields MONTHLY, YEARLY, and DAILY/EVERYDAY, respectively. To obtain "every Monday" or its equivalent with the other days of the week, except Sunday, reduplication cannot be used, because the signs are already made with a repetitive circular motion. Instead, the hand makes a smooth movement downward ("going down the Mondays on a calendar"). For "every Sunday," a combination of DAILY and SUNDAY (made with its forward-backward shake replaced by a smooth downward movement) is used.

If no time is marked at the beginning of a conversation, it is assumed to be the time of the speech act itself, the present. Time can be established by the time adverbials discussed above (YESTERDAY, NEXT THURSDAY, etc.), perfective markers (FINISH, NOT-YET, see p. 99), or the signs FUTURE, PAST, PAST-CONTINUOUS. The sign PAST-CONTINUOUS has been translated into English as "from then until now," "up to now," "ever since," and "have been," and is formed with both G hands pointing slightly palm down toward the body at shoulder height and then turning out until fingertips are pointing upward and hands are about 6 inches from the body. The use of one of the signs FUTURE, PAST, PAST-CONTINUOUS causes a shift in the interpretation of the time line. For example, using the sign PAST causes that part of the time line previously interpreted as present to become past. Thus, within a conversation established in the past, the use of the sign TOMORROW might be interpreted as "the next day" (i.e., the day after the event that was just mentioned) rather than "tomorrow" (i.e., the day after the speech act itself). Thus, the base of time reference can be adjusted to permit time before and after a specified time in the past to be discussed in the present conversation.

Aspect   In the section on morphological modifications that result from reduplication of verbs, several aspectual possibilities were indicated: continuitive, habitual, distributive, durative. P. Jones (1978) has described a different type of aspect, the unaccomplished aspect. Langacker (1972) separated "unaccomplished aspect" from "incomplete aspect" by suggesting that the former is a future action that is incomplete in the present but not in the future, whereas the latter is incomplete in both the present and future. Unaccomplished aspect occurs in Diegueño and Luiseño, both related southwest American Indian languages.

According to P. Jones, there are four ways to form the unaccomplished aspect in ASL, all of which affect the movement of a sign. They are: A—cutting the movement short, B—retracting the movement, C—making a "false start," and D—the movement overextending its target. Unaccomplished aspect A would apply in a sentence translated as "My cat is dying" where the sign DIE, which requires both B hands (one palm down, the other palm up) to reverse their orientations, would never complete the reversal of orientation. Thus, the hands might stop part way in their turning over. In unaccomplished aspect type B a sign would start its movement, stop before completing its movement, and then return to its original position. Type C is illustrated by the sentence "I am trying to do my homework," where the ASL FINISH MY HOMEWORK is made with the sign FINISH moving only slightly and hesitantly (and tensely) rather than its usual swift flicking of the wrists. Finally, type D is illustrated by the verb HIT made with the dominant A hand overshooting its normal ending position on the nondominant G hand (translated as "almost hit/tried to hit"). Jones pointed out that the verb MEET can undergo types A, B, and D, an observation that is relevant to the discussion of grammatically constrained iconicity in "Iconicity and Linguistic Description" (Chapter 5). The role of movement in ASL is still not completely understood, although it is clearly a defining factor in the formation of verbs (and in modulations of adjectives; see Klima and Bellugi, 1979). Jones's analysis of modifications within this parameter (as opposed to repetitions or additions to it) for a morphological function is an important step in separating what is visual representation and what is linguistically controlled.

Other Morphological Modifications

This third section is offered to avoid trying to fit ASL morphology into any preconceived idea of what morphological components should look like (Wilbur, 1973a,b, 1974b, 1975). The line between derivational and inflectional processes becomes more indistinct as one gets farther away from languages in which every morpheme is a clearly identifiable unit (in ASL it clearly is not). We have seen that morphological modifications may affect handshapes, locations, orientations, direction of motion, and movements of even apparently simple signs. This final section on morphology includes a conglomerate of 1) an actual inflectional suffix for negation, 2) two stand-alone signs which may have perfective marker status, separate adverbial status, and/or auxiliary status, and 3) so-called bound morphemes (THINGS-GO-PAST, DRIPPY-LIQUID).

Negative   In Chapter 6 (see "Variation Within ASL"), the history of the negative suffix and the variation that occurs in its use are presented. The traditional description and a more recent modification of that description are provided here.

In ASL, the negative suffix, which is thought to be derived from the French Sign Language NOT, can occur only with certain signs, and when it does, it must always follow the sign. The signs KNOW, LIKE, WANT, HAVE, and GOOD can form a type of contracted negative, called "negative incorporation" by Woodward (1973a,b,c, 1974a), whereas others form their negative with the ASL sign

NOT, usually preceding the verb, or the signs DON'T, STOP, or REFUSE/WON'T. The traditional description given to the contracted forms is a description first of how the sign is made, followed by a description of the negative form, apparently involving "a bound outward twisting movement of the moving hand(s) from the place where the sign is made" (Woodward and DeSantis, 1977b) (Figure 26). P. Jones (1978) has offered two additional generalizations concerning the negative morpheme: 1) the orientation of the negative morpheme is opposite to the orientation of the sign it is negating (KNOW and LIKE have inward orientation and are negated with an outward orientation, whereas WANT and HAVE have an upward orientation and are followed by a downward-oriented negative) and 2) regardless of the handshape of the unnegated sign, the negative morpheme is made with a 5 hand (LIKE changes from 8 to 5 for LIKE-NOT, WANT changes from the handshape CLAW to 5, HAVE changes from B̈ to 5).

FINISH and NOT-YET   Friedman (1975a) referred to FINISH and NOT-YET as perfective markers, FINISH as positive and NOT-YET as negative. She illustrated these with the sentences EAT YOU FIN-

Figure 26.   The sign DON'T-KNOW. The contraction involves an outward twisting of the hand from the place the sign is made.

ISH? "Have you eaten?" and I NOT-YET SEE MOVIE "I haven't seen the movie (yet)."

Fischer and Gough (1972) concentrated primarily on FINISH. They indicated that there are "seven different meanings and at least four grammatical functions" (p. 1). The first use of FINISH is as a main verb that appears to make EQUI noun phrase complements: WHEN YOU FINISH EAT, WE GO SHOPPING "When you finish eating, we will go shopping." Fischer and Gough do not provide an argument that this is in fact EQUI, leaving the above example open to interpretation as a perfective marker in the sense intended by Friedman, "When you have finished eating/ when you have eaten." The important thing is that FINISH comes before the verb EAT.

Fischer and Gough noted several different uses of FINISH as an auxiliary. One may be restricted to adults' signing to children, however, in that the use of FINISH as a past tense marker is observed when signing to a very young child, but as the child matures linguistically, the parents resume use of the normal past tense indicators (see "Time and Tense," this chapter). As an auxiliary, FINISH follows the verb and functions as a marker of completed action, perfective tense.

Two other uses of FINISH do not occur in the verb complex, but seem to be peripheral to the sentence itself. One is the use of FINISH to mean "that's all." It usually comes at the end of the sentence, and is often preceded by an intonation break (pause). It would be used in such instances as "You mean that's all he said?" or "That's all that's going to happen?" The other use of FINISH has the sense of "I've had enough" or "Have you had enough?" It is usually done in the direction of the subject or object of the activity and is often made with only one hand instead of the two used for the other instances discussed above.

Structurally, Fischer and Gough note that FINISH most often occurs at the end of a clause, and tends to occur in the sequence Sentence FINISH Sentence, as in YOU EAT FINISH, WE GO SHOPPING, which can be viewed as YOU EAT (Sentence), FINISH, WE GO SHOPPING (Sentence). As a perfective marker, it almost always comes after the verb, and occasionally appears as a proclitic attachment to the verb (in much the same way the negative morpheme attaches) with such verbs as SEE and READ. As a main verb, FINISH almost always precedes the verb of an embedded sentence. In those instances where it does not, an intonational pause usually occurs. When FINISH is used in the sense of "already," it generally precedes a verb or adjective.

When FINISH occurs as the main verb in a negative sentence, the negative precedes FINISH and cannot come between FINISH and the following verb. When FINISH is used in the sense of "already" or as a perfective marker (which comes after the verb), it cannot appear in the same sentence with a negative, and instead NOT-YET is used. Thus "John has not yet met Mary" must be signed JOHN NOT-YET MEET MARY and not *JOHN NOT FINISH MEET MARY.

Bound Morphemes   It has been suggested that verbs such as FOL-LOW, CHASE, EVADE are critically determined by their motion, allowing various handshapes to substitute for the Å they are made with in citation form. Certain signs are defined primarily by their hand-shapes (numerals especially, and the classifiers, discussed in more detail below); certain locations can take on semantic functions (forehead=male, cheek=female, nose=derogatory, etc.); the direction of motion can be important in the interpretation of the meaning of a sign (e.g., Frishberg and Gough's examples in which up is positive and down is negative); and orientation is not a predetermined feature of a sign's description (as seen by the modifications of orientation that can affect the numerals). Thus, although each sign in ASL can be described in isolation utilizing these parameters, in context, any one (or more) of these parameters can be morphologically modified, creating the need for a nonstatic description of ASL (i.e., it is insufficient to describe the sign in isolation and consider it a complete description of the sign). The following two examples of bound morphemes illustrate the need for recognizing a level of description other than the apparent surface forms. Both of these morphemes, THINGS-GO-PAST (Kegl, 1978c) and DRIPPY-LIQUID, can be analyzed as underlying mor-phemes that have no citation forms of their own, yet can occur in various other signs to form what Frishberg and Gough have called "sign families." Nonetheless, they have been previously overlooked, in much the same way that Jones's (1978) unaccomplished aspect was overlooked, because they have been treated as "visual pictures," a term that does indeed characterize what they are but fails to provide a linguistic description for their use.

Kegl (1978c) identified the defining characteristic of the morpheme THINGS-GO-PAST as its movement in relation to the signer. The morpheme varies its handshape, location, and orientation according to its intended referent. For example, when driving in a car and watching the fence or telephone poles go by, one sees a series of straight upright poles approach the car, pass by the car, and disappear behind the car. Such a description is based not on the perspective of the car driving past the poles (which obviously do not move) but on the perceived movement of the poles as seen by a stationary person sitting in the moving car. The world appears to pass by the person in the car rather than the actual reality of the car and person passing by a stationary world. The signer, in describing this scene, uses two upright G hands and moves them back and forth (alternately or together) along the time line (this is its location; whether the time line itself is actually to be analyzed as part of the sign remains to be determined), reflecting the approaching and passing of poles. Suppose that instead of sitting in a car, the person is now seated in an airplane. The world goes by underneath, and of course does not appear vertical as the telephone poles did, but appears as horizontal, flat land below. In this case, the morpheme THINGS-GO-PAST is realized with two flat B hands, palms down, moving alternately in toward the signer, back out, and in again, at chest height, and the signer may look down at the hands while they are moving. A bowling ball might go down the alley with the same flat B hands, palms down, but perhaps slightly higher, below the chin (treating the head as the ball). These two representations of THINGS-GO-PAST appear to be completely different signs, but can be seen to be related by the similarity of movement that defined THINGS-GO-PAST.

The other bound morpheme illustrated here is defined by both its movement (wiggling downward movement) and its characteristic hand-shape 5̈ (or variant 4̈), thus making it more obvious than THINGS-GO-PAST. It occurs in the signs GRAVY (dripping from the bottom-side of the nondominant B hand), DROOL (formed at the side of the mouth), and in occurrences of BLOOD/BLEED. For BLOOD/BLEED, the back of the hand of the nondominant hand is used as a general location, but usually the sign incorporates the location of the body part that is bleeding (e.g., "bleed from the head" would be made at an appropriate spot on the head, "bleed from the upper arm" would be made at the upper arm). One can "bleed from the nose" or even "have a runny nose" with variations of this same sign.

Summary of Morphological Modifications

In these sections on morphology, numerous examples have been given of relationships between signs. In some cases, processes that appear to be general have been identified. In other cases, the similarities have been identified, but further analysis remains to be completed. In addition, there probably remain many other such relationships that have yet to be identified. Associated changes in semantic content for these modified signs also remain to be studied.

GRAMMATICAL MODIFICATIONS

This section begins to describe the modifications in sign formation that serve specific grammatical functions, and continues discussion of familiar concepts such as noun and verb phrases, without arguing for either and without considering their roles within larger contexts, such as sentences or discourse. Chapter 4 is concerned with sentences and formalizations of various concepts described here.

An Introduction to Verb Behavior and Pronouns

Fischer and Gough (1978) investigated various linguistic properties of verbs as they are reflected in ASL. Included in their study are:

1. Strict subcategorization: whether a verb takes an object, prepositional phrase, verbal complement, and other syntactic categories
2. Selectional restrictions: semantic constraints on the subject, object, type of preposition, complement, etc.
3. Directionality: whether the sign moves between subject and object—agent-beneficiary incorporation (Woodward 1973a,b,c)
4. Incorporation of location: whether the sign is produced closer to the place of formation of its subject, object, or indirect object, if any
5. Reversibility: whether the sign changes the orientation of the hand depending on its subject, object, etc.
6. Incorporation of size or shape: changes in the movement or hand configuration to indicate physical features of the subject, object, etc.
7. Incorporation of manner: whether the sign changes in speed or intensity to indicate the manner in which the action is performed
8. Incorporation of number: fast reduplication with horizontal movement, possibly with the relevant number of fingers extended to indicate how many were involved in the action
9. Habitual: fast reduplication, no horizontal movement
10. Continuous: slow reduplication
11. Reciprocal: whether the verb can (or must) take two arguments (subject and object) that perform action on each other
12. Reflexive: if the sign adjusts to reflect the difference between I-X-MYSELF and SOMEONE-X-ME in terms of the object of the action

The modifications relating to indications of subject and object are the focus of discussion in this section.

In the section on plurals (this chapter) three points (1, 2, and 3) are arbitrarily established in space and are used to demonstrate the difference between certain forms of plurals. In that section, the sentences "John looks at me" and "John and Bill look at me" are illustrated, with John at point 1 and Bill at point 3. These sentences show that the verb LOOK is made at point 1 when John is the subject and at point 3 when Bill is the subject. In both cases, the object of the verb is the signer, and therefore the sign is made with the fingertips pointing toward the signer. Fischer and Gough's notion of "reversibility" has been used previously to refer to the ability of many verbs to modify their location and direction of movement or orientation according to their subjects and objects, but reversibility implies only a two-way change, from A to B or from B to A. Kegl (1976a,b) expanded this notion further to allow for more possibilities. If we make the sign at point 1 and face it toward point 3, we have "John looks at Bill," which is similar in structure to the preceding forms but is not strictly speaking a reverse of either of them. Rather than talk about verbs reversing, one can refer to the ability to modify so as to *agree* with their subjects and (if possible) their objects (Kegl, 1976a, 1977). They may agree in location or by orientation or direction of motion. In the sentence "John looks at me," the verb LOOK agrees with the subject John in that it is made at point 1, and it agrees with the object "me" in that it is oriented toward (but not made at) the signer. One could not sign "John looks at me" by making the sign LOOK at point 1 but pointing away from the signer, or pointing toward point 2 or 3. Thus, the verb LOOK is required to agree with both its subject and its object.

Another verb, GIVE, agrees with its subject in the same way that LOOK does (i.e., it is made at the same point as its subject) but it agrees with its object (actually indirect object) by moving to the point where the object has been referenced. Thus, in "John gave Bill the book" or "John gave the book to Bill," the verb GIVE starts at point 1 and moves to point 3 (what happens to BOOK is discussed later). "John gave me the book" would start at point 1 and move in toward the signer. "I gave you the book" would start at the signer and move out toward the addressee.

With these examples, we can see that Fischer and Gough's three verb characteristics, directionality, incorporation of location, and reversibility, are reflections of the same grammatical process of verb agreement. What seems to be important is whether the verb has an inherent movement, such as GIVE, or a characteristic handshape that can be relocated, reoriented, but still recognized, such as LOOK (but not completely reoriented—orientation of the V hand down is used for verbs like STAND).

There are certain verbs, which have been referred to as body anchor verbs, that are made in contact with the body or at a characteristic location near some part of the body. Some, such as the verb SAY, cannot move their starting point, but can adjust their end orientation or direction of movement. The sentence "I said to Bill . . . " would be made with the sign SAY starting at the signer's mouth and moving outward in the direction of point 3, whereas "I said to John . . . " would move outward toward point 1. However, body anchor verbs such as KNOW, which is made at the side of the forehead with a B hand palm in, or HAVE (possession), which is made with B̈ hands at the chest, do not move as part of their formation (the only movement involved is transition from the preceding sign to this one and from this one to the next one), and therefore cannot move to agree with their objects. Even more important is that by their very nature of formation, body anchor verbs are made at the signer's body, and cannot therefore move around to agree with their subjects. If we want to indicate "John knows . . . ," we must move the whole body over to point 1. In actual signing, moving the whole body may be considered extreme and forced. Instead, a slight shift of the right shoulder forward, or a tilt of the head to the right, or eye gaze to the right would be sufficient to indicate point 1 for the subject. For the present, these variations are considered together under the name of "body shift."

In those examples where the verb can agree with a particular point in space, an appropriate translation into English would also be "The person at point 1 gave the person at point 3 something." In an ASL conversation, the actual nouns, in our case, John, Bill, and Mary, are introduced at the beginning (ours were established in the section on plurals; since then we have only moved into or away from the established points) and subsequent references are made through use of the points in space. These points are serving as *part* of the whole pronoun system in ASL (they are not the actual pronouns as claimed by Lacy, 1974). Kegl (1976a,b, 1977, 1978a) considered the points themselves agreement points or agreement markers. We have seen three different ways in which reference to these points can be made: 1) making the verb start or end at that location, 2) orienting the verb toward that location, and 3) body shifting toward that location. These different methods of referring to the point in space are also part of the pronoun system (Kegl, 1976a).

Kegl, Lentz, and Philip (1976) and Kegl (1976a) have described the body anchor verb cases as situations in which the body itself is acting as a pronoun. Until the pronoun is moved to the appropriate point, we cannot determine to whom the pronoun refers. (In English, this can be seen by the fact that *he* and *she*, as well as the other pronouns, can only be interpreted with respect to the nouns that have been established as their antecedents. In addition, if a conversation contains reference to both Mr. Smith and Mr. Jones, the pronoun *he* can become difficult to use because of its possible ambiguous interpretation. In ASL, this never happens because of the added differentiation of the locations in space.) In the simplest case of the formation of KNOW or SAY, the signer is talking about himself "I know . . . ," "I say," and his body remains in the normal signing position, which is the position for first person reference. The signer's body can shift position for third person references to other points (e.g., 1, 2, 3). Thus use of the signer's body in this way is referred to as "signer's body pronoun" (henceforth SBP). One limitation on SBP is that it cannot be used for the second person reference "you," and in fact there is no need for this because the addressee is (presumably) always present and can be referred to by pointing or head tilt or eye gaze. The fact that the addressee is always there but at the same time occupies the grammatical position for second person reference leads to the designation "real body pronoun" (RBP). However, second person is not the only RBP that can occur. If we continue our conversation, and Bill walks into the room, we can no longer use point 3 for Bill, but must instead refer directly to Bill, who is now serving as an RBP (albeit third person, not second).

The third type of body pronoun that Kegl describes, unlike the other two, cannot be seen. It is in fact a *projected* body pronoun (PBP), which may be placed at a particular "point"—rather, a projected space that is treated as though a body were there. If Bill offers Mary a glass of wine, he does not do so at waist level height where the points of reference are established. Thus, the signer may shift to point 3, face point 2, and offer a glass at mouth height on the PBP at point 2. Similarly, Kegl (1976a) gave an example of a signer talking about helping her aunt put on her earrings. The sign EARRINGS-PUT-ON (which is a verb with its object incorporated, about which more is said later) is made on the PBP at earlobe height. Another example is that of a signer relating a conversation between himself and a child. The child may be established at some point in space, but the signer will always sign down (and look down) to the child, reflecting the difference in size between the SBP and PBP. These modifications in height made in the signer's production of signs indicate that a description based solely on the point in space is insufficient, and that the signer is behaving as though a body were actually there.

What we have seen so far is an interaction among verb behavior, the use of space, and the use of the body as pronoun. Further investigations (Kegl, 1977, 1978a; Kegl and Wilbur, 1976) of verb behavior and space reveal another category of pronouns. First we need another point in space, point 4, which we can arbitrarily put farther out from the body than points 1, 2, and 3, and also arbitrarily establish it on the right side of the signer (it can be directly in line with point 1, but it must be far enough away so that the two are perceptually distinct, perhaps 4 or 5 inches further out). Point 4 is the store. If the sentence to be signed is "I went to the store," the single-hand sign GO with a G hand might be used, and would start at the signer (SBP) and end at the store (point 4 vicinity, it does not have to be right at point 4 on waist height level but can be comfortably above point 4, just so it is clearly at point 4 and not near point 1). In this case, the verb GO can "incorporate" direction; in fact, it must since its very meaning is to start at one place and end at another. The difference between "I went" and "I went to the store" is that we have established a definite end point for the sign GO whereas without point 4 there is no clear end point and therefore no clear, unambiguous interpretation of "I went" without the context in which it is used. Another verb, DRIVE (Figure 27), which is made with up and down alternating movement, loses its up and down movement when it adopts a forward movement. Therefore, "I drove" would be made with the citation form of the verb DRIVE with the hands alternating up and down, whereas "I drove to the store" would be made with the handshape of citation DRIVE, but with smooth or slightly arched movement (depending on degree of stress) starting at the signer (SBP) and moving to point 4 (Figures 28 and 29). Such forward movement is not permitted for other up and down or back and forth verbs such as WALK, nor are any further nonhorizontal modifications on DRIVE permitted. Thus, if we wanted to say "I drove all over town" or "I drove around in circles for hours" or any other variation of DRIVE that is not a straight line, the citation form DRIVE cannot be used. The sentence "I walked for a long time" can be made with reduplication of the citation form of the verb WALK (B hands, palm down, alternating movement) (Figure 30), but "I walked to the store" cannot be made with the citation form of the verb WALK. In the case of "driving around in circles," the recognizability of the verb DRIVE would be destroyed by attempting to make the up and down movement go around in circles, not to mention that such

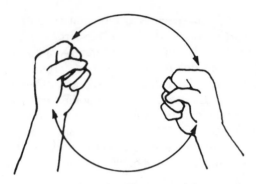

Figure 27.   DRIVE is made with an up and down motion.

simultaneous combinations of up and down movement with directional movement (straight or circular) seem to be prohibited in all but the most restricted of cases. The fact that DRIVE is used for the meaning "drive to the store" is an interesting and presumably exceptional behavior for the verb DRIVE. In the case of WALK, "walk to the store" has the same problem, namely, it cannot move up and down and forward at the same time, and if it loses its up and down motion, it presumably loses its identity. In addition, one *cannot* make the sign WALK with up and down movement and use one's feet to carry one from the initial signing position to point 4 (in other words, one should not have to go anywhere to say something about going places, and feet are definitely outside of the signing space).

Of course, the claim that ASL is a language implies that the above sentences can be conveyed in some linguistically constrained form,

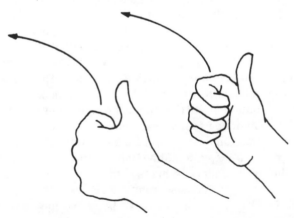

Figure 28.   DRIVE-TO starts at the signer and moves to point 4 in a smooth, arched movement: "I drove to the store."

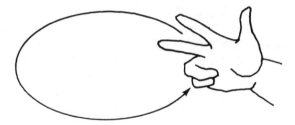

Figure 29.   DRIVE-AROUND is indicated by a circular movement. Notice the different handshape.

and one of the most interesting and exciting aspects of ASL syntax is the manner in which these forms are produced. There are in fact alternate forms, which are another form of pronoun, that are used in place of the above verbs. These are defined primarily by their hand-shape and preferred orientation, and have more freedom of movement than the citation forms WALK and DRIVE (and others). Frishberg (1975) mentioned them briefly and referred to them as "classifiers" because their use reflects classification of their noun referents into categories based on their perceptual and functional properties. A de-scription of oral language classifiers provided by Allan (1977) helps to put these forms in perspective. Allan surveyed 50 unrelated classifier languages (English is not a classifier language) and reported that in these languages, classifiers served to focus on certain qualities or features of their noun referent in very precise ways. For example, a classifier might identify a class of objects that is one-dimensional, two-dimensional, or three-dimensional, flexible or rigid, "of prominent curved exterior," long, or round. Other characteristics of animacy, humanness, mobility, and functions have also been observed in clas-

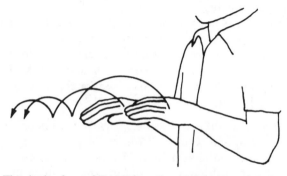

Figure 30.   The citation form of WALK is made with B hands, palms down, alternating movements.

sifier categories. Kegl and Wilbur (1976) provided an introduction to ASL classifiers, Kegl (1976a,b) described their behavior in more detail, and Ellenberger and Steyaert (1978) and Kantor (1977) have reported on their acquisition by deaf children of deaf parents (see pp. 161 and 162).

Kegl (1976a) provided a tentative list of classifiers and their categories for ASL. ASL classifiers can be divided into animate and inanimate objects. The animates are also classified as stationary or moving (or movable); the inanimates are also classified by shape. Kegl's (1976a) list of features and the ASL classifier groups they define is:

1. General person (animate): a G hand, usual orientation is fingertip up
2. Person ambulatory (by-legs): V hand, usual orientation is fingertips down for "stand," "walk," "kneel," but may have other orientations
3. Person by vehicle (by-vehicle): 3 hand, orientation is fingertips sideways (as opposed to the number 3 which has its citation orientation fingertips up), may be used for cars, motorcycles, boats, trains, etc.
4. Plane: ५ handshape, may be used for airplane
5. Stationary object taller than it is wide (also may be used as dummy general object): Å hand, used in place of objects such as bottle, house, lamp
6. Stationary object taller than it is wide which cannot be moved by an independent source or which is intended to be stationary: arm extended upward from elbow to fingertips, B handshape, used for buildings, trees, walls, etc.
7. Flat objects that can be moved: B hand, palm up; can be used for book, paper, mirror, etc.
8. Flat object that is not supposed to be moved: B hand, palm down, can be used for bridge, floor, rooftop, ground, etc.
9. Hollow, curved object with rim: C handshape, palm facing sideways, can be used for glasses, cups, jars, and in "The Three Little Pigs" (Kegl and Chinchor, 1975) is used for chimney, pot of boiling water, and door frame

The exact definition of these classifiers is currently under investigation (Wilbur, Bernstein, and Kantor, 1978).

Returning now to the sentences "I went to the store," "I walked to the store," and "I drove to the store," and recalling that the store is at point 4, we find classifiers in the last two but not in the first. "I went to the store" is made with the verb GO (with a **G** hand that could also be analyzed as the general person classifier) starting at the signer's body and moving to point 4. The sentence "I walked to the store" as indicated previously is not made with the citation verb WALK, but instead is made with the classifier "person ambulatory (by legs)," a **V** hand, fingertips down, which moves with back and forth finger movement from the signer's body to point 4 (Figure 31). (This sign is the only one so far observed that permits alternating movement while adopting directional movement.) "I drove to the store" is made, as indicated earlier, with the modified form of the citation form DRIVE. "I drove around in circles" is made with the vehicle classifier (**3** hand) starting near the signer's body and moving around in a circular path (at least two repetitions) (Figure 29).

Because these classifiers are single handed and have a preferred orientation but no movement or location specifications of their own, they can be used to describe movement along different dimensions, e.g., horizontal direction, as in "walked to" or "drove around," or vertical dimensions, as in "drive up and down the hills," which cannot be made with the citation form of the verb DRIVE, but must be made with the classifier (Kegl and Wilbur, 1976).

One last characteristic in Fischer and Gough's (1973) list of verb characteristics remains to be discussed before this introduction to verb behavior can be concluded, namely, the incorporation of size and shape by means of changes in handshape or motion. We have seen in THINGS-GO-PAST how handshape and location can be affected by what subject is meant, and in the discussion of augmentative reduplication how motion can be modified to indicate size. Focusing primarily

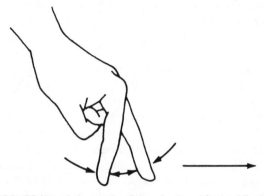

Figure 31.   WALK-TO is made by moving fingers back and forth while the hand moves forward.

on handshape changes here, there is a process by which the object of a verb can be incorporated into the verb formation by means of change in handshape (the general procedure is referred to as object incorporation, the change in handshape itself may be referred to as blending). An ideal verb with which to illustrate this process is GIVE: "John gave Bill an elephant" is made with the verb GIVE starting at point 1 and moving to point 3, preceded or followed by the sign ELEPHANT (word order discussions are reserved until Chapter 4), but "John gave Bill the book" may be signed with handshape modification of the verb GIVE from its citation form with flatO to the handshapes used in the sign BOOK (B hands) in the same orientation as the sign BOOK but without the opening movement of the sign BOOK. This combined sign, written BOOK-GIVE (in the tradition of notation for other object-incorporating languages in which the object is written before the verb) starts at point 1 and moves to point 3, but is not necessarily preceded or followed in this sentence by the actual separate sign BOOK (depending on the context and how the sign is executed, using the separate sign BOOK may actually be unacceptable). Another example might be "Bill gave John the chair." In this case, the sign CHAIR (a dominant H hand contacts the dorsal side of a nondominant H hand) may be made at point 3, then both hands may be moved horizontally to point 1 (using the H handshapes and not forming the flatO handshapes for GIVE). The difference among these three examples is a result of the phonological structure of the object signs involved. ELEPHANT is made in front of the nose and moves horizontally away from the signer in a downward then upward sweeping motion, as does the elephant's trunk, and cannot therefore be moved in a horizontal direction between points 1 and 3 without destroying the sign. It thus does not (and cannot) incorporate with the verb GIVE. The sign BOOK is made in neutral space, starting with two B hands, palms together, which open out in the same manner that a book opens. These handshapes alone, however, are sufficiently recognizable without this movement that the sign can drop the movement and is then phonologically compatible with the movement of the verb GIVE (the location and orientation are also compatible). In the last example, CHAIR-GIVE, the movement of the verb GIVE cannot be produced until after the movement of the sign CHAIR, but the end configuration of CHAIR is then compatible with the verb GIVE and it is moved between points 1 and 3 with the handshapes of CHAIR and the movement of GIVE. Similar to this last example is the combination of HOUSE and MOVE (or GIVE): the sign HOUSE involves the two B hands touching at the fingertips, separating from each other on a downward slant, and then reorienting to fingertips up position for a straight downward movement. In this final position, the two hands can retain the handshapes and orientation for HOUSE and move from point 1 to point 3 (or whatever). It is important to recognize here that the phonological structure of the two signs to be combined must be in some way compatible before the actual blend can be made.

With this background, conditions on classifier usage can now be discussed; this is followed by a discussion of the relation between the body pronouns, the classifiers, and yet another form of pronoun, the hand index. Kegl and Wilbur (1976) indicated a variety of situations that would engender the use of a classifier. The use of classifiers to avoid destroying the formation of a sign by the addition of movement for directional purposes (WALK vs. WALK-TO) has been illustrated. At the same time, signs need not extend beyond the signing space; thus whenever a potential violation of signing space occurs, the signer must either shift to mime or use a classifier form. Also, classifiers allow discussion of activities that are performed with parts of the body outside of the signing space, such as the legs and feet. Another situation in which classifiers may be used is when object incorporation is syntactically feasible but phonologically impossible. If the topic of discussion for the last 15 minutes has been the LAMP that John has given Bill, there is no need for the sign LAMP to be used every time it is referred to. It may be established as a point in space (point 5) and referred to in a variety of ways which are discussed in more detail in the section on noun phrase. However, to indicate "John gave it to Bill last week on Thursday" where the conversation has made it clear what *it* is, the classifier Å can be used on top of the nondominant B hand, palm up, starting at point 1 and moving to point 3 (doing so in the absence of having set up a separate point for the lamp would mean that now both Bill and the lamp are at point 3 and must be further differentiated for future discussion, e.g., using general person G for Bill and general object Å for the lamp, or repeating the complete noun or BILL). One final aspect of classifier usage is what Kegl (1976b) calls "linking indexing." If we had been talking about a chair, and both Bill and the chair were now at point 3, we might wish to link them together, perhaps in the context of Bill standing on the chair to reach something. This could be accomplished by using the dominant hand V handshape with fingertips down resting on the palm-up B hand of the nondominant hand, indicating a person standing on a flat, movable surface, namely, the chair seat. Bill and the chair may be said to have been link-indexed together (more about indexing later in this chapter).

In some cases, classifier usage has been identified as obligatory, whereas in others, its use is optional. All the factors that affect the optional use of classifiers have not yet been determined, but Kegl (1976a) reports that stylistic factors may be involved. She indicates that an "empathy hierarchy" seems to exist, such that the degree of intimacy a signer feels with the person(s) being discussed affects whether a body pronoun, a classifier, or a third pronoun type, hand indexing, will be used. The least intimate seems to be hand indexing, in which the nondominant hand can assume the numeral handshapes for FIRST, SECOND, THIRD, FOURTH, or FIFTH (depending on how many people or objects are being discussed) and the dominant hand is used to indicate which of these are relevant to the sentence. The narrator of one videotaped version of "The Three Little Pigs" (Kegl and Chinchor, 1975) uses the 3 hand for the three pigs, rather than establishing three points in space, and then uses the dominant hand to indicate which pig is being discussed. The dominant hand can assume the G handshape and make contact with any of the fingers on the nondominant hand (i.e., touch the index finger to indicate the second pig) or can assume a V hand for two pigs or a 3 hand for all three. Using the V hand (called the "dual" by Fischer and Gough, 1978; Lacy, 1974), the signer can indicate the first and second pig by moving between thumb and index finger, or the second and third by moving the dominant hand between index and middle finger, or the first and third by moving from thumb to middle finger with an arc that obviously indicates that the second finger is not being included. The 3 hand (called "trial" by Lacy, 1974) here means all of the pigs, but in a situation where all five fingers on the nondominant hand were extended, could be used to indicate that three out of those five did something inclusively and probably collectively. In the case of separate behavior on the part of the three out of the five, the G hand might be used to point to each of the fingers individually, possibly with separate repetitions of the verb (as discussed in the definite, individual verb plural).

Between the classifiers and the body pronouns, Kegl considers the body pronouns to be more intimate. Thus, if there is a choice possible, and if the signer is discussing close friends, the body pronoun (and use of body shift) seems to be chosen over the use of classifiers.

In this section, verbs and pronouns have been introduced and a variety of their behaviors presented. Formalization of this discussion, such as is available, in terms of familiar linguistic notation (i.e., trees and rules) is given in Chapter 4.

An Introduction to the Noun Phrase

In order to use any of the preceding processes to discuss a noun (person or object), the noun must first be introduced into the conversation. Obviously, the actual sign for the noun must be made. If no further reference to that noun will be needed, or if that noun will not participate in any of the verb-noun interactions previously discussed (e.g., the noun only occurs with body anchor verbs which do not agree with their object, or whatever), then no point in space need be established, and the production of the noun sign by itself is sufficient (e.g, "Where's the X?" requires only the production of the noun sign, WHERE, and question marker). For most other purposes, a point in space must be established. These points in space have been used here for descriptions of the verb behavior without explicit statement on how these points were established. The procedure for establishing the point in space is referred to by Kegl (1976a,b, 1977, 1978a) as "indexing," and the point in space to which the noun is related is part of the "index." The remainder of the index, called the "deictic marker," is dependent on how the point in space is established. In general, the deictic marker is a pointing gesture toward the point that is being established. It can take several handshapes: G hand for humans, Ψ for general nonhumans, and A (or Å) for reflexive$_2$-intimate (intimate in the same sense as the previously discussed empathy hierarchy, reflexive in that it has the same handshape as the regular reflexive, reflexive$_1$, and in keeping with the general linguistic literature which refers to such intimate forms as types of reflexives). This pointing gesture may be made before, after, or simultaneously with the noun sign. Kegl (1977) illustrates this description with a tree for ASL noun phrases (NP):

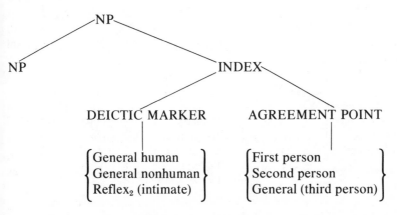

Since the index can precede, follow, or occur simultaneously with the noun, the tree must be considered to be unordered (that is, it can represent all three temporal possibilities). The allowability of unordered trees is critical to Kegl's analysis of ASL syntax.

Before continuing with methods of indexing nouns, the possibility that the NP is in fact a pronoun (PRO) must be considered. To review, a pronoun can be one of the three body pronouns (SBP, RBP, PBP), a classifier G hand (which is simultaneously a classifier and the number 1, meaning "single"), the numbers 2 and 3 (V hand and 3 hand) for dual and trial, plural (usually 5 hand), and may occur independently or as part of the verb (as with classifiers or when the verb starts and ends at particular agreement points) (see also Lacy, 1973, 1974). Pronouns can also be inclusive (e.g., the V hand made between signer and point 1 means "John and I"), exclusive (the V hand made between point 1 and point 2 can mean "John and Mary but not Bill"), and distributive (this is parallel to the individual plural discussed by Fischer and Gough (1978); each reference is made separately, perhaps by pointing with the G hand to each agreement point or possibly as part of the verb when the verb is repeated separately at each agreement point). If the noun phrase is actually a pronoun, the deictic marker may also be possessive (B hand) or regular reflexive$_1$ (Å hand with the same sense as the English reflexive), and can indicate number as well as inclusive, exclusive, or distributive. In addition, there is the possibility of the body remaining in its usual position ("neutral") but not necessarily meaning "first person." These possibilities are illustrated by Kegl (1977) in this tree:

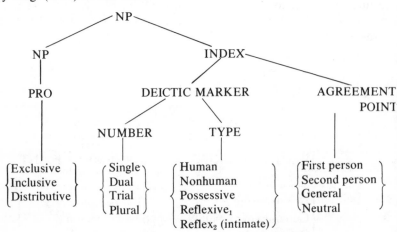

Extensive discussion of indexing also comes from Kegl (1978a). Indexing through pointing deictic markers (regardless of handshape) has already been indicated as a means of establishing the point in space to which a noun (or noun phrase) will be related. Other means of establishing this point in space are also available, some of which may actually precede the formation of the noun sign itself. For example, an index can be established by simply starting a verb at a particular point, without necessarily having the noun already established. That is, the movement of verb between subject and object (if any) may be sufficient in certain circumstances to establish an index. Hand indexing, which was illustrated with the three pigs (Kegl and Chinchor, 1975), establishes each finger as an agreement point for some noun phrase. A reference to the first pig (single) may be made with the G handshape of the dominant hand contacting the thumb of the nondominant hand which is serving as the agreement point. To refer to all three pigs, the 3 hand (trial) is used on the dominant hand and sweeps past the three fingers (also 3 hand) on the nondominant hand. This system is parallel in usage to points in space, but is limited by the number of fingers. Another, even more limited, way of indexing is to use the right hand for one agreement point and the left for the other. This obviously limits one to a discussion with two general references. There are several other methods of indexing which tend not to precede the actual noun, although this is not an absolute rule. One is the use of body shift, which by itself establishes an index, with the signer's body as the pronoun. Another is the use of eye gaze to a particular point. A third is the use of a particular facial expression, posture, or rhythm for a particular referent (Frishberg, 1976b). Finally, there is the linking indexing mentioned previously, which may be accomplished by a combination of the preceding types.

Noun phrases that are not specifically assigned to an agreement point or otherwise indexed, perhaps because no further reference will be needed, are considered to have "null" indexes (Kegl, 1976a). The possibility exists that definite/indefinite distinctions which are reflected in English by the determiners *the* and *a(n)* are distinguished by whether a noun phrase has an index (definite) or not (indefinite).

In a further consideration of the structure of NPs in ASL, Chinchor (1978a) suggested that within a NP, there is a classifier phrase (CP) composed of a quantifier (Q) and a classifier (C). The order within the noun phrase and within the classifier phrase is variable (indicated by dotted lines in the tree) and is represented:

```
                        ╱─NP──────╲
                      ╱              ╲
                    ╱                  ╲
   N ◄─────────────────────────────────► CP╲
                                          ╱    ╲
                                        ╱        ╲
                                      Q ◄──────────► C
```

Chinchor argued that the ability of the quantifier and the classifier to blend (producing a single sign) is evidence of a stronger relationship between them than between the classifier phrase and the noun, which can assimilate (leaving two signs) but not blend. Chinchor identified allowable blendings between the quantifiers ONE, TWO, THREE, and MANY with the person classifier in a variety of contexts. She also suggested that in ASL, measure phrases (MP; inch, mile, etc.) behave parallel to classifier phrases, with the quantifiers ONE through TEN blending with time measures and CENT. The time measures include WEEK, YEAR, MONTH, HOUR, MINUTE, and DAY, with each having a different set of allowable blendings with the numeral quantifiers. For example, Chinchor indicates that WEEK can blend with ONE through FIVE, but MONTH can blend only with ONE through THREE. Also, the allowable blendings change for each time measure when compounded for past and future along the time line. Finally, Chinchor noted that unit phrases (UP) also behave like classifier phrases within the NP. The numeral quantifiers ONE through NINE can blend with the unit HUNDRED to form ONE-HUNDRED, TWO-HUNDRED, etc.

Although the order of occurrence is free within the NP, and within CP, MP, and UP (of course, order cannot be determined when blending has occurred, but we are referring here to order of unblended quantifier and classifier, measure, or unit sign), Chinchor notes the additional support for her analysis that the noun cannot interrupt the CP, MP, or UP. For example, if there is an unblended numeral followed (or preceded) by a classifier, the noun cannot come between the numeral and classifier. This demonstrates the integrity of the classifier, measure, and unit phrases which Chinchor has proposed. Although the word order within these phrases may be free, Chinchor observes that different measures (time, weight, age, height, money, speed, length) appear to have different ordering preferences. For WEEK, YEAR, DAY, MONTH, HOUR, MINUTE, DOLLAR, MILE, TIMES,

POUNDS, and OUNCES, the preference seems to be for the (un-blended) numeral to precede the measure sign. For others, eg., CENT, TIME, AGE, WEIGHT, and HEIGHT, the quantifier generally fol-lows the measure sign. Chinchor's use of the difference between as-similation and blending in determining the structure of these phrases is an interesting one. It suggests the type of linguistic arguments based on ASL itself that can be proposed. It also demonstrates the innovation required on the part of the linguist to avoid oral language bias.

Summary of Grammatical Modifications

Verbs may move around in space to indicate subject and object infor-mation. At the same time, handshape substitutions may occur, with classifiers appropriate for the subject or object. Several processes are available for indexing a noun phrase into the conversation for future reference. Several types of pronouns are available, and numerals may be involved for "dual" and "trial" forms. Within the noun phrase, there seems to be a noun and a possible modifier phrase. Within the modifier phrase, blending may occur, but between the modifier phrase and the noun, only assimilation may occur, not blending.

SUMMARY

The list of processes in which noun and verb signs can participate should have by now made it obvious that learning signs from a dictionary or from a signed English teacher does not equip one to converse with a native user of ASL. The type of information that is contained in this chapter has been too often ignored in sign language classes. The presence of increasingly larger amounts of grammatical information in sign language books (cf. Fant, 1972a,b; Hoemann, 1975a,b; Madsen, 1972; Stokoe, Casterline, and Croneberg, 1965, Appendices A,B,C,) as well as two books to specifically advise sign language teachers of their need to obtain and teach this information (R. Ingram, 1977; Hoemann, 1978) represents both increasing awareness of the need for this information to be passed on to those in contact with deaf people and increasing amounts of such information becoming available from sign language researchers. The extent to which the information pre-sented here can be exploited for language training in nondeaf popula-tions needs to be further researched. The visual representations pos-sible with the numerals, plural, time line, and verb modification in space are all possible training advantages, particularly with retarded individuals. Some discussion is contained in Chapter 9, but it is far easier to raise the possibilities than to demonstrate their effectiveness. Chapter 4 looks at not only the behavior of signs in syntactic environments, but also arguments that have been generated over the appropriate linguistic description for these behaviors.

SYNTAX

CONTENTS

This chapter steps back from the description begun in Chapter 3 (see "Grammatical Modifications") in order to provide historical perspective on linguistic descriptions of ASL, after which recent alternatives are discussed. The chapter includes a major issue of concern, namely, word order behavior in ASL, as well as discussions of individual syntactic structures.

EARLY DESCRIPTIONS

There can be no doubt that the appendix on syntax from Stokoe, Casterline, and Croneberg (1965), which is derived from Stokoe's (1960) first outline of ASL structure, has been the foundation for nearly all of the topics of more recent descriptions. Stokoe, Casterline, and Croneberg provide a functional definition for what they consider an utterance, that portion of linguistically meaningful body activity preceded and followed by nonlinguistic body activity. Defined this way, the signer may be seen to go from repose to signing to repose, and they note a high degree of consistency between the signer's position in repose before and after signing. They also discuss other clues to pauses and junctures (such as those presented in Covington, 1973a,b). Recent research by Baker (1977) on conversational turn-taking and regulators and by Grosjean and Lane (1977) on the relationship of pausing and syntax certainly derive their roots from Stokoe, Casterline, and Croneberg (see Chapter 5 for discussion of both).

    The discussion of "parts of speech" in Stokoe, Casterline, and Croneberg covers such diverse topics as how to determine if a sign is a verb (discussed more recently by Fischer and Gough, 1978), the use of space for indicating grammatical information (the linguistic description of which has been the concern of nearly everyone since), the time line and its function, the use of various signs such as auxiliaries (CAN'T, CAN, FINISH, NOT-YET, which Stokoe, Casterline, and Croneberg call "have not," MAY/MIGHT, LET, SHOULD, MUST, etc. discussed by Fischer, 1972 1978), the use of facial expression in a variety of structures (Baker, 1976; Baker and Padden, 1978a,b), and the combination of directional preposition and verb (ASL ENTER compared to English "go in," where in English the particle "in" can stand as a separate word). They also note a trend for nominal phrases or conversations to proceed from stating the broadest descriptor first followed by those of narrower reference. One example that is frequently cited from them (cf. Hoemann, 1975a) is WASHINGTON MONUMENT ELEVATOR, instead of the English practice of stating the narrowest reference, the elevator, first through the use of prepositions, e.g., "the elevator in the Washington monument."

One interesting aspect of the discussion in Stokoe, Casterline, and Croneberg of the use of space is the suggestion that it is parallel to verb inflection, and that certain structures, such as GIVE (made from the addressee to the signer), which can be translated "you give me . . .," might better be translated in the passive, "I am given . . . ," which they prefer to consider as "reversal of personal reference." Such consideration of how a passive (or other structure) might be rendered in ASL in terms of ASL grammatical mechanisms is a far cry from those who determined that ASL does not have a passive simply by looking for markers comparable to those in English (form of the verb "be" plus past participle of the verb plus "by" phrase for agent). Thus although Stokoe, Casterline, and Croneberg eventually decided that ASL did not have a passive, they did so by considering the structure of the language itself and not by comparison to English. The possibility that their initial thought of using passive translation may be appropriate has resurfaced in Kegl (1976b, 1977, 1978b).

Another early description of ASL syntax comes from McCall (1965). She described a corpus of 700 strings from deaf adults in terms of transformational-generative grammar. In her analysis, she noted the function of ASL auxiliaries, time adverbials, negatives, question markers, facial expression, reflexive and possessive pronouns, reduplication, and the use of space for personal reference. Although it is not possible to be certain, her rules seem to have been written parallel to English phrase structure rules with the transformations which change word order or delete words to correct for differences between English and ASL surface structure. The utility of this framework (with appropriate modifications to strive for ASL deep structures rather than

English deep structure) has not been pursued until recently (Chinchor, 1978a; Kegl, 1976a,b, 1977, 1978a,b,c,d; Kegl and Wilbur, 1976; Liddell, 1977). Although its effectiveness and required modifications are still being investigated, Liddell's (1977) and Kegl's (1977, 1978a,b,c) analyses demonstrate the utility of standard linguistic argumentation and description for ASL sentences (see further details below).

Fant (1972a) provides a short and generally useful introduction to the grammar of ASL except for some details which again are based on comparison with English. He states that "signs are not inflected as words are," whereas we now know from Frishberg and Gough (1973a), Fischer and Gough (1978), and Kegl (1976a,b, 1977, 1978a,b,c) that many modifications of signs may be considered inflective. Fant does, however, note the type of inflection of movement that Supalla and Newport (1978) discuss. He also states that "there is no passive voice," which may be a matter of description rather than reality. For pronouns, Fant recognizes pointing (indexing) used for subject and object, as well as possessive and reflexive, but not the other types, such as use of the body as a pronoun, classifiers, or hand indexing, as do later researchers. Fant also reviews such aspects of sign modification as movement in space, number incorporation, inclusive and exclusive pronominal interpretations, negation, characteristic differences in ASL word order from that of English, the time line, question formation, and use of facial expression.

In addition to the above discussions, which specifically address ASL syntax, there are three other references that should be mentioned. These are books designed primarily to teach ASL as a language, rather than to describe it linguistically, and they address ASL syntax as it relates to the structure to be taught in a particular lesson. Thus, they are not comprehensive, but they are filled with examples and details for the ASL learner. They include Fant (1972b), Madsen (1972), and Hoemann (1975a). (A recent pamphlet by Ingram, 1977, outlines considerations for teachers of sign language, as does Hoemann, 1978).

WORD ORDER IN ASL

Discussions of ASL word order in recent linguistics papers have been widely discrepant, creating what Kegl (1976b, 1977) calls "the word order controversy." The positions taken by Fischer (1975) and Friedman (1976a) with respect to ASL word order diverge partly because of their differing concepts of the treatment of verb behavior (whether verbs are inflected) and their concepts of ASL pronominalization. To set the stage for this discussion, an early study by Tervoort (1968) must be mentioned, if only to demonstrate the difficulty earlier researchers had in applying their concepts of how oral languages behaved to the study of manual language. Following the discussion of Tervoort, Fischer's and Friedman's positions are presented, after which the remaining pieces of the puzzle are fitted together with analyses from Kegl (1976b, 1977) and Liddell (1977).

The Word Order Controversy

This discussion of Tervoort (1968) is based on a more extensive discussion in Chinchor et al. (1976) of his research, the implications that it had for subsequent studies (e.g., Schlesinger, 1970), and the linguistic conclusions that could have been drawn about the nature of linguistic universals (cf. Wasow, 1973) had Tervoort (or Schlesinger) been correct. (Recall the discussion of Schlesinger, 1970, and Bode, 1974, in Chapter 1.)

The framework in which Tervoort was operating led him to look for universals in terms of word order. He took a single sentence YOU ME DOWNTOWN m-o-v-i-e f-u-n? (translated loosely as a request to someone to go downtown to a movie with the signer), wrote down the glosses in all possible permutations, and presented the written forms to 120 student teachers (some of whom were deaf) in a teacher-training program who were familiar with features of communication among deaf children. They were asked to judge each permutation on the basis of the order of the signs and groups into which the signs might fall.

Aside from the considerable difficulties involved with asking nonnative signers to judge strings of signs out of context because of sociolinguistic (Chapter 6) and psycholinguistic (Chapter 5) factors, there is a major problem with transcribing signs in terms of English glosses. Signs move around in space to indicate various grammatical functions that are not depicted by the English word transcription. Presenting the glosses in written form, rather than the signed sentences themselves, invites judgments from an English language perspective. His findings, then, that none of the permutations was considered ungrammatical by the majority of judges, cannot be taken as evidence that word order is free in ASL. Further judgments that groups of the signs YOU and ME and of the signs MOVIE, DOWNTOWN, and FUN were preferable to sequences in which, for example, YOU and ME were separated by another sign, also do not contribute to arguments that ASL has particular syntactic preferences, because these judgments could be made semantically rather than syntactically.

Fischer's (1975) paper basically argues that ASL has become a subject-verb-object (SVO) language like English, possibly through increasing influence from English itself. Fischer constructed sign sequences and presented them to native signers for interpretation. The presented sentences consisted of various permutations of two nouns and a verb: NVN, NNV, VNN. (When either of the two nouns can be interpreted as subject or object, the sentence is referred to as "reversible," e.g., "John kicked Bill," but if only one noun can logically or reasonably be considered the subject or object, the sentence is "nonreversible," e.g., "John kicked the chair.") Fischer reports that the interpretations provided by her informants were:

1. NVN was interpreted as SVO
2. NNV was interpreted as either a) conjoined subject-verb (N and NV), or b) OSV
3. VNN was interpreted as either a) verb-conjoined object (VN and N), or b) VOS

Fischer's conclusion from these interpretations was that ASL is an underlying SVO language. This does not mean that SVO is the only allowable surface word order: "Other orders are allowed under the circumstances that (a) something is topicalized, (b) the subject and object are non-reversible, and/or (c) the signer used space to indicate grammatical mechanisms" (Fischer, 1975, p. 21). Variations from the basic SVO order can be signaled by "intonation breaks" which Fischer characterizes as consisting of pauses, head tilts, raised eyebrows, and/or possibly other nonmanual cues (the details of these nonmanual cues are discussed more fully by Liddell). Thus NVN is interpreted as SVO, contains no breaks, and is considered the underlying order. N,NV may be interpreted as O,SV with the object topicalized and a break between it and the remainder of the sentence (an example of a topicalized object in English would be "as for the rhubarb, John ate it"). The sequence VN,N may be interpreted as VO,S with a topicalized verb phrase, followed by the subject with a break after the verb phrase (symbolized by the comma). (An example of a topicalized verb phrase in English is "As for doing the dishes, John will.") In discussing Fischer's data, Liddell (1977) notes that although these three orders include the subject in all three sentence positions, initial, medial, and final, this does not indicate random word order in ASL. Instead, he adds the observation that "if the subject or object accompanies the verb, the subject precedes the verb and the object follows the verb" (p. 109).

   Friedman (1976a) takes issue with Fischer for basing her analysis on sentences that were presented to signers rather than on discourse excerpts and for not separating verbs into classes (body anchor, movable for subject and object, etc.) (pp. 127–128). Based on her analysis of discourse samples, Friedman claims that "word order is relatively free, with the exception of the tendency for the verb to be last" (p. 142) and that "the vast majority of propositions in ASL discourse appear on the surface as either a verb alone, subject verb (SV) or conjoined subject plus verb (SSV, SSSV). Constructions like SVVV are common and can be analyzed as subject+verb, deleted subject+ verb, etc." (p. 135). Friedman states that in the texts she analyzed, SVO order was present but relatively infrequent. She argues for basic underlying SOV by pointing out the relatively large number of OV constructions, which she argues results from deleted subjects. (Liddell, 1977, critically examines Friedman's claims at length and rejects this analysis.) Friedman's assumption that there are no grammatical inflections for verbs (she does not consider the modifications discussed in Chapter 3, "Grammatical Modifications," to be inflections) leads her to propose several strategies that signers use to identify subjects and objects in the absence of fixed word order (as in English) or case markings and inflections (which allow languages like Latin to have relatively free word order) (Friedman, 1976a, pp. 139–140):

1. With intransitive verbs (e.g., "sleep"), only one noun phrase ("argument") may occur, namely, the subject (e.g., "John slept," but not *"John slept the bed").

2. With transitive verbs that can have two or more semantically nonreversible arguments, there is no problem since their roles are determined by the meaning (e.g., "John pushed the blanket," but *"The blanket pushed John").

3. For transitive verbs that allow the subject and object to be reversed, several possible strategies are presented:
   a. the signing space is used to establish locations of referents and verbs are moved between them
   b. the body and body space are used to distinguish referents
   c. some ambiguous transitive constructions are avoided by choosing one-place verb constructions instead of two-place constructions (i.e., in English, "anger" is a two-place construction as seen in "John angered Mary," but "angry" is a one-place construction as seen in "Mary is angry"; Friedman is suggesting that ASL uses the latter but not the former to avoid ambiguity)
   d. heavy reliance on context

Friedman (1976a, pp. 141–142) summarizes the discourse situation in ASL as:

1. "Nominal signs are articulated and established in space, either by indexic or marker reference or by body position" (as discussed in Chapter 3).

2. After this, "verb signs are then (a) manipulated between or among these previously established locations for nominal referents or (b) articulated on the body which is in the appropriate pre-established position for agent or experience" (as in Chapter 3).

3. The first verb is assumed to have first person subject unless an actual subject is indicated. Subsequent verbs that also appear without overt subjects are still interpreted as first person. Whenever a verb appears without a subject in connected discourse, the subject is "assumed to be the same as the last one given, until a new subject is mentioned."

4. As indicated earlier, word order appears relatively free, with a tendency for the verb to occur last.

5. The appearance or nonappearance of a noun sign after its initial establishment in the discourse seems to be in free variation, with its appearance functioning possibly as an indicator of emphasis, contrast, or clarification.

6. At most, four or five different referent locations may be used within a single discourse. These locations can then be used for later pronominal reference.

Friedman is suggesting that ASL has a series of avoidance strategies for processing and producing signed utterances that are necessary to compensate for constrained syntactic rules. Fundamental to her approach is the claim that the recognition of iconic representation in ASL requires abandonment of standard linguistic notation and concepts (see further discussion in "Iconicity," Chapter 5). Other researchers have retained standard descriptions (Chinchor, 1978a; Kegl, 1976a,b, 1977, 1978a,b,c; Kegl and Wilbur, 1976; Lacy, 1974; Liddell, 1977), requiring whatever iconicity is present in the language to be constrained by linguistic rules for sign structure and syntax.

Another related description within Friedman's framework is that of Edge and Herrmann (1977). Edge and Herrmann do not specifically address the question of word order, because they assume, along with Friedman, that word order is free, that verbs are uninflected, and that the signer uses the various previously mentioned strategies to avoid ambiguity. These assumptions lead them to posit a description of ASL discourse that is composed of loosely defined "lists," of which there

are six types that are hierarchically ordered but for which there are n(
defining characteristics of internal structure. These lists are seen a
composed of a heading mechanism followed by whatever the signe
has to say about the head. The six heading types, in their hierarchica
order, are (with my explanation in parentheses):

1. Body movement (what has been referred to as body shift)
2. Real-word indexing (RBP, including second person reference
   "you")
3. Grammatical indexing (setting up points in space or hand indexing
4. Marking (classifiers)
5. Naming (producing the noun itself)
6. Headless lists, which can occur in the following situations:
   a. context disambiguates subject and object
   b. the subject is first person
   c. "the verb has directional movement or orientation that clearly
      indicates its subject" (Edge and Herrmann, 1977, p. 154)

As far as I can determine, all of the mechanisms they discuss are
describable within Kegl's formalism without further extension. As
previously indicated, Liddell (1977) considers Friedman's arguments
for specific orders and rejects them. Kegl (1976a,b, 1977) considers
the above strategies and Friedman's nonacknowledgment of verb inflection, and rejects her claim of totally free word order in ASL.

Perspective on the Role of the Point in Space in ASL

Before continuing with this discussion of the word order controversy,
some further elaboration of the role of the point in space and its effect
on the linguist's description of ASL is needed. Only Liddell's (1977)
discussion of ASL word order does not depend on an analysis of the
role of the point; his description relies primarily on nonmanual indicators of grammatical function. As for other researchers, the point in
space makes an enormous difference in their perspective on word
order.

In Lacy's (1974) presentation of pronominal reference in ASL, he
considered the point in space to be an "index" in the sense of Mc-
Cawley (1970). McCawley suggested that for semantic representations,
a clause is appropriately separated into a "proposition" and a set of
noun phrases. Each noun phrase is associated with an "index" which
indicates its position (role) in the proposition. An example from
McCawley illustrates the sentence "the man killed the woman":

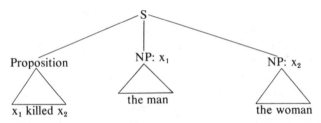

Lacy adopted this semantic representation for syntactic purposes in describing ASL by noting the parallel structure in ASL that associates each noun with a unique index. For Lacy, the pronoun itself is the pointing gesture to the point in space, and the pronoun cannot be interpreted without its "index." He noted that personal pronoun "indexes" are placed in space according to several general rules, some of which have already been mentioned. Neutral body position for the first verb of a discourse utterance is considered to be first person, as Friedman indicates above. The center of the front of the signer is reserved for second person referent ("you"), and third person referents may be placed in space as we did earlier (all three points in a line) or alternating first third person referent on the right of the signer, second third person referent on the left, etc., as indicated in Figure 32.

Lacy (1973) reported that the point in space that locates each pronoun referent is sufficiently well defined in three-dimensional space that once the signer establishes the location, other members of the conversation will direct their pointing so that a line extending from the end of the index finger (G hand) will (more or less) pass through the point location of the intended referent. This information adds to the

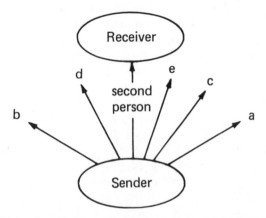

Figure 32. a = first third person reference, b = second third person reference.

claim that these pointing gestures are linguistically conventionalized in a way that pointing as used by nonsigners is not.

Friedman's (1975a, 1976a) concept of the point in space is that it is the actual pronoun. Thus, pointing is simply a means of indicating which pronoun is meant, and starting a verb at a particular point may be viewed as a pronoun followed by a verb. This perspective contributes to her view that there are no inflections on the verb.

Kegl's (1976a,b, 1977) concept of the point in space is what was formalized in Chapter 3, namely, an agreement point which, together with a deictic marker (not only the G hand, but also À, Ψ , and B), may serve as an index for a noun phrase or pronoun, and which at the same time serves to mark the verb in the form of an inflection. Thus a verb made at some point, say point 1, is inflected in the sense that it has been moved to point 1 to agree with its subject. If a pronoun is present, it may be signer's body pronoun (SBP) realized at point 1 to make the verb (e.g., body anchor verbs), or it may be a classifier handshape that will be made as part of the verb, or it may be indicated by a preceding or following index made with a deictic marker, or eye gaze, or rhythm, or handedness, or, finally, it may be left null through a process of topic chaining (Kegl, 1976a). Kegl (1978d) indicates that what all of these different types of pronouns have in common is that they are established as a special characteristic of a particular noun phrase so that the NP can be unambiguously referenced.

ᴵ Independently, O'Malley (1975) presented an analysis of ASL pronominal reference very similar to that of Kegl. O'Malley identified dummy location markers (points in space) which are unambiguously assigned to NPs for future pronominal reference. O'Malley noted that the establishment of these location markers can precede, follow, or co-occur with the NP itself, and that future reference may take several forms. In addition, he separated pronouns into two types, anaphoric and deictic: "a pronoun is anaphoric if and only if it consists of a point to an established reference location for some NP or a point produced with the sign(s) for a NP . . . ; otherwise, the pronoun is deictic and refers to the object toward which the point is directed" (p. 7). (O'Malley's use of "point" here refers to the pointing gesture, not the point in space.) O'Malley also considered the location markers to serve as verb inflection. Finally, O'Malley argued that pronominal reference in ASL always enables unambiguous reference.

Edge and Herrmann (1977) have taken a compromise position: they consider the points in space, body pronouns, and classifiers (not specifically named as such) all to be pronouns. Thus, they are working within the framework established by Friedman that verbs have no inflections (since the point is a pronoun, it is not an inflectional marker).

These different linguistic descriptions of the role of the point in space obviously lead to different conceptions of how verbs behave in ASL, and subsequently how word order is to be viewed.

Resolution of the Word Order Controversy

Kegl (1976b, 1977) identified a number of difficulties with Fischer's and Friedman's approaches. She noted, as did Friedman, the risk involved in presenting sentences to signers for interpretations or judgments (as Fischer did) as opposed to more naturalistic data (as suggested by Friedman), but nonetheless, following Fischer's methodology, she presented similar sentences to signers, using both inflected and uninflected verbs.

When signers were presented with sentences in which the signs were in NVN order but the verb was not inflected, they interpreted the sentences as SVO. However, when asked when such a sentence would be used, they typically responded that an ASL signer would not sign the sentences that way, but that the sentences were understandable. They also suggested that hearing people might sign the sentences that way. One informant rejected all sentences that were presented without inflection on the verb.

When signers were presented with sentences in which the words were in the same order and the verb was inflected, the sentences were accepted as natural and were indicated as being preferred. If the verb was inflected and the words were in a non-SVO order, most signers accepted the sentences, but some indicated that they were stylistically awkward and that SVO order would be preferred.

The signers in Fischer's and Kegl's investigations were able to give consistent interpretations of sentences with uninflected verbs even though they are unacceptable in ASL. Kegl (1976b) attributes this to the bilingual nature of most signers. Although they may not be fluent readers and writers of English (see discussion, Chapter 8), they are nonetheless familiar with English in written and spoken form and in its signed equivalent, signed English (see Chapters 6 and 7). English has very little or no inflection of the verb (for person), no incorporation, no indexing (although there are pronouns and determiners which perform similar functions), and a fairly rigid fixed word order. Therefore, in cases where signers are presented with sentences that lack indexing and verb inflection, they may rely on English-related strategies (namely, word order) to determine grammatical relations. This bilingual phenomenon should be kept in mind (recall Chapter 1).

Kegl's concept of the function of the point in space as part of an inflectional system in ASL also leads to a different interpretation of the data than Friedman's. Friedman seems to have advocated avoidance strategies rather than syntactic structure for ASL (as exemplified by Edge and Herrmann, 1977), and although Friedman was concerned with separating verbs into their classes, she did so according to the *number* of arguments they could have and whether those arguments were semantically reversible. Kegl has separated verbs according to their *inflection,* and subsequently postulated the following solution to the word order controversy:

> The Flexibility Condition: The more inflected the verb is, the freer the word order may be.

Thus, there is an interaction between verb inflection and word order. One may find that if a verb is fully inflected (for subject and object), that all word orders may occur (as Friedman suggested) and that signers may express word order preferences (as Kegl found). In addition, the types of intonation breaks reported by Fischer (and discussed more fully by Liddell, see below) may be reflections of optional rules like topicalization for conversational focus or emphasis, rather than as markers of non-SVO word order.

In ASL, then, the word order is relatively free at the level of major constituents; that is, the ordering of noun phrases with respect to each other and to the verb is free if the verb is inflected. Ordering within the NP may be somewhat free (as it is between NP and INDEX, discussed in Chapter 3, and in Chinchor's arguments concerning the N and classifier, unit, or measure phrases). The NP itself maintains integrity, in that it may not be broken up (similar evidence for a VP in ASL has not yet been offered).

Formalization of the Sentence and Verb Complex

Reference to "major constituents" brings up another facet of ASL that has not been explicitly discussed, namely, the sentence itself, and formalization of the verb behavior. Although Liddell (1977) utilized a formal node for verb phrase (VP), he did so without defending its use. Kegl (1977) indicated that no evidence is presently available for positing a VP constituent for ASL and suggested that until such time as

a VP can be adequately demonstrated, the sentence can be characterized by a tree without a VP, but with a verb complex (VC):

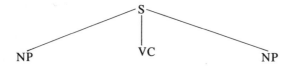

As long as the verb is inflected, constituents sharing the same node in
the tree (i.e., connect to the same upper point) are ordered freely
within that constituent. A full representation of an ASL sentence (from
Kegl, 1977) might look like:

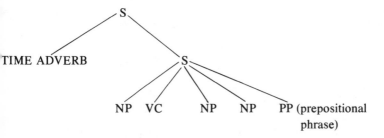

Kegl's (1977) and Chinchor's (1978a) modified formalization of the
structure of a NP (albeit incomplete) have already been presented. By
comparison, the verb structure is sufficiently complex to have been
left until now for formalization. The verb carries much of the grammatical information in the ASL sentence. The unit that has been
referred to as the "verb" may be viewed as a complex composed of
pronominal agreement markers for the subject and object, the verb
itself into which NPs can be incorporated by object incorporation, and
possibly the bound morpheme for negation (see Chapter 3). In addition, directional and locative information (the last two referred to as
"registration markers" by Kegl) are indicated in the verb by various
derivational processes. (Forman and McDonald, 1978, have suggested
that prepositions in ASL may be treated as verbs themselves, while
Kegl, 1978d, has suggested that verbs are in fact underlying prepositions.) Also present in the verb complex is aspectual information, such
as reduplication for the progressive, habitual, durative, etc., and
changes in the movement of the verb for unaccomplished aspect.
Except for the auxiliaries and unbound negative, the verb complex
(VC) is a single unit. Display A shows Kegl's (1977) representation.

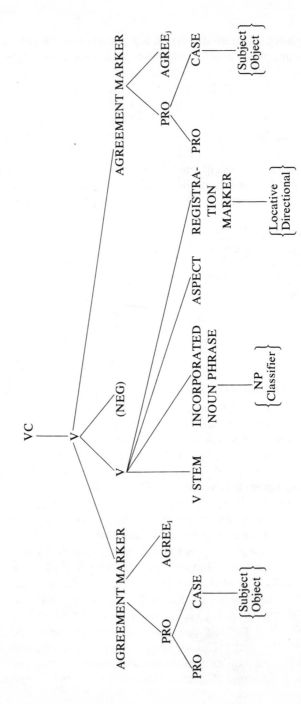

Display A.

Various parts of the above VC have already been illustrated: movement to agreement points, change in orientation of the sign, negative incorporation with the bound negative morpheme, and body shift. The incorporation of a NP was illustrated with the verb GIVE, into which the entire noun BOOK can be incorporated, whereas classifier usage was illustrated by WALK and DRIVE. In addition to the NP and classifiers listed under incorporated noun phrase above, those shape specifiers discussed in Klima and Bellugi (1979) (handshapes that indicate the shape of an object, such as two F hands that separate from each other to "trace" a pipe or rod) should probably be included in this category. Registration markers result from a process that Kegl (1977) treats as the blending of a verb and a preposition. Thus, a combination of the verb DRIVE and the preposition TO can be made if DRIVE loses its up and down alternation, but with a straight linear movement to location 4 ("the store"). With the classifier "by vehicle," we can get DRIVEAROUND (3 hand moves around in circle), DRIVEUNDER (3 hand moves underneath the nondominant hand), DRIVEOVER (3 hand moves over nondominant hand), etc. *without* using the separate preposition in the same sentence (this is the full meaning of incorporation). (Viewed within a relational grammar framework, the effect of this process is to make what in English is the object of the preposition, e.g., "to the store," the direct object of a verb in ASL, e.g., DRIVETO STORE. Although the practical effect of such a change is minimal to the signer (primarily that the preposition is not separately articulated), it is important to the linguist trying to describe the grammar.)

The structure of the verb complex given above is a full expansion of the possible forms. There are various rules that may neutralize agreement markings in some cases depending on the amount of redundancy in the sentence (Liddell indicates that indirect quotes may be just such a case, whereas Kegl indicates topic chaining). In other words, the tree does not necessarily represent the surface form of the sentence. In addition, two further additions must be made to the VC tree, that of auxiliary (AUX) and the unbound (separate sign) negative (NEG). When all three are present, the ordering is AUX NEG VC. Therefore, we have:

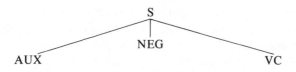

Kegl (1976b, 1977) has argued on the basis of these presented descriptions that in addition to verb agreement, in which the verb's agreement points are identical to the agreement points established for the subject and/or object NPs, one can also identify case marking for *subject*. Kegl (1976b) argued that the use of the signer's body is a grammatical marking for subject, as well as setting up one hand for the subject and the other for the object. In Kegl (1977) this was refined to allow only the body to be the marker of subject. She has also argued that directionality of the verb, moving away from the agreement point, may indicate agentivity. Based on her 1977 analysis, Kegl (1978c) provided a possible argument for a passive in ASL (recall that John is at location 1, Bill is at location 3; Kegl's transcription is simplified for use here):

1. PRO_1-HIT-PRO_3 "He (John) hit him (Bill)" (HIT made with non-dominant G classifier at point 3, body shift to point 1, S hand of HIT starts at point 1, moves to point 3 and contacts extended index finger)
2. PRO_3-HIT-PRO_1 "He (Bill) hit him (John)" (HIT made with G classifier at point 1, body shift to point 3, S hand starts at point 3 and moves to point 1 for contact with G hand)
3. PRO_3-HIT-PRO_1 "He (John) is hit by him (Bill)" (HIT made with G hand at point 1, body shift to point 1, S hand starts at point 3, moves toward signer at point 1 and contacts G hand)

The difference in meaning between examples 2 and 3 is that one is the passive reading of the other. The difference in formation is not where the hands start or end, but where the body is (location 3 in example 2, location 1 in example 3).

Empirical Perspective on the Word Order Controversy

Liddell (1977) provides an empirical analysis that supports Fischer's claim that ASL is underlying SVO; at the same time his discussion hints at the variability that led Kegl to the flexibility condition (apparently Liddell was not familiar with her work).

Liddell begins by demonstrating that, contrary to Friedman's claims, word order is significant in ASL, and that, for example, in a simple yes/no question "Did the woman forget her purse?", the *only* allowable order in ASL is $\overline{\text{WOMAN FORGET PURSE}}^{\text{q}}$, SVO (further explanation of Liddell's notation and the marker "q" is given below). Considering first NVN sequences, Fischer had said that they were interpreted as SVO and that any other order must have intonation breaks in it. Liddell indicates that in fact SVO can have intontation breaks in it also, and that when such an intonation break occurs, the reading is S,VO with the subject topicalized. His measurements indicate that a noun sign that is in initial position but not a topic (i.e., SVO) is roughly 11 fields (0.18 seconds) longer than the average duration of a noun sign in medial position (the shortest position). Signs in final position were approximately 17 fields (0.28 seconds) longer than medial position, whereas noun signs that were topics (i.e., S,VO or O,SV) were held about 22 fields (0.37 seconds) longer than medial position. Thus, his data indicate that part of the "intonation break" Fischer referred to is a result of longer duration of the topicalized sign. Liddell also identifies a particular facial expression and head position, which he calls "t," that marks topics. "t" is a combination of the head tilted backward slightly and the eyebrows raised. It co-occurs with the topicalized sign, then disappears for the remainder of the sentence. Thus, the change of facial expression and head position after the topic combined with the duration of the topicalized sign itself provides the cues that Fischer identified as intonation breaks.

Liddell identifies several other distinctive nonmanual cues that indicate grammatical information in the ASL sentence. One of them is the "q," mentioned above. "q" is defined by a leaning forward of the body, the head forward, and the eyebrows raised. It is used as a marker of yes/no questions, and, as indicated by the line above the entire sentence $\overline{\text{WOMAN FORGET PURSE}}^{q}$, the nonmanual signal is held across all three manual signs (unlike "t," which is held only across the topic). Another nonmanual signal, "n," is a negating signal composed of a side-to-side headshake, and a special facial expression in which a primary feature is the turning down of the corners of the mouth. The sentence $\overline{\text{DOG CHASE CAT}}^{n}$ is translated as "The dog didn't chase the cat" or "It isn't the case that the dog chased the cat" (in other words, the whole proposition is negated). According to Liddell, when the topic marker "t" and the negative marker "n" are both present in the same sentence, the "n" does not co-occur with the "t," giving $\overline{\text{DOG}}$ $\overline{\text{CHASE CAT}}^{n}$ "As for the dog, it didn't chase the cat." A third nonmanual signal that needs to be introduced before continuing with word order is "hn," head nod. Liddell identifies "hn" as a slow, forward head nod (as opposed to others that can occur) which signals assertion and/or existence, and appears to be required in those syntactic structures in which the subject of the main clause (for some reason, not embedded clauses) is separated from its verb. Such cases include topicalized verb phrases VN, N, $\overline{\text{CHASE CAT}}^{t}$, $\overline{\text{DOG}}^{hn}$ "As for chasing the cat, the dog did it," where "hn" is required with DOG. Gapping sentences (as in a list, "I brought cake for dessert, Susie the drinks, Bob the silverware, and John the salad," which has the structure NVN, NN, NN, etc.) require "hn" on the second noun in each gapped construction. Similarly, the English sentence "John is a doctor" is signed in ASL as JOHN DOCTOR with no main verb. Liddell indicates that "hn" is required in JOHN $\overline{\text{DOCTOR}}^{\text{hn}}$ to distinguish it from JOHN DOCTOR "John's doctor." Finally, if a noun phrase and its pronoun (indicated by indexing with a deictic marker, not body shift or verb agreement) both occur in the same sentence (presumably for emphasis), then the pronoun is obligatorily accompanied by "hn." Liddell suggests that "hn" behaves as a parallel to English "be" and "do," especially in its function when the main verb is missing (environment for do-support in English) and for emphasis ("John *did* go to the movies"). He argues for a model of underlying "do" for English and underlying "hn" for ASL.

With these nonmanual signals, Liddell can also argue in favor of Fischer's contention that O,SV and VO, S are derived from underlying SVO by topicalization. He has shown ($\overline{\text{DOG}}^{\text{t}}$ $\overline{\text{CHASE CAT}}^{\text{n}}$) that when a subject is topic, it does not fall within the scope of the "n" signal. He can also demonstrate that when the object occurs initially, it is accompanied by "t" and does not fall under the scope of "n," e.g., $\overline{\text{CAT}}^{\text{t}}$ $\overline{\text{DOG CHASE}}^{\text{n}}$ "As for the cat, the dog didn't chase it" but *$\overline{\text{CAT DOG CHASE}}^{\text{n}}$. This illustrates that certain changes in underlying word order must be accompanied by certain nonmanual signals. Failure to identify those nonmanual signals might lead to the belief that any word order is acceptable (e.g., Friedman). Similar to the above example, when a verb phrase is topicalized, Liddell showed that "t" occurred on the verb phrase and that the subject was required to have "hn," $\overline{\text{CHASE CAT}}^{\text{t}}$ $\overline{\text{DOG}}^{\text{hn}}$. In addition, when the verb phrase is topicalized, it does not fall within the scope of negation, e.g., $\overline{\text{CHASE CAT}}^{\text{t}}$ $\overline{\text{DOG}}^{\text{n}}$ "As for chasing the cat, the dog didn't."

The status of SOV sentences was also disputed by Fischer and Friedman. Although Friedman claimed that word order was free, she also contradicted herself by arguing that surface OV forms came from deleted underlying subjects, presumably SOV. Fischer noted that SOV may occur when the nouns involved are semantically nonreversible, e.g., MAN BOOK READ can only mean "The man reads the book." However, Liddell found that some sentences that were interpretable n just this way nonetheless were considered unacceptable by his nformants, and also that there are certain sentences which he claims nust be SOV to be acceptable. Those that are unacceptable as SOV are just those that contain uninflected verbs, and in fact, one of his examples, MAN MOVIE SEE, was considered unacceptable without nflection, but acceptable when the verb was inflected by using eye gaze to establish an index for MOVIE and then orienting the verb SEE toward that index to agree with MOVIE. Those that must be signed SOV, Liddell claimed, involve iconicity and other mimetic devices. For example, he indicated that the sentence WOMAN PIE PUT-IN-OVEN "The woman put the pie in the oven" is acceptable only if the nondominant hand for PIE (B hand) is the one that is active for the verb PUT-IN-OVEN and that it is unacceptable if the other hand is used. Liddell considered this to be evidence that "the iconicity of the sequence is important for this SOV sequence" (p. 140). Viewed with the formalization given by Kegl, this example can be seen to contain a number of the possible parts of the verb complex. The sign PUT-IN-OVEN already consists of PUT and a locative phrase, "in the oven." Using the nondominant hand of PIE as the hand that does the putting involves the combination of the B hand classifier (object, flat (more or less), movable by outside source) and the verb PUT, thus being an example of object incorporation through the use of a classifier.

These data, then, are consistent with the formalism proposed by Kegl. Liddell's comments on variability, "judgments as to the grammaticality of these sentences would vary depending on where the sentence fell on the continuum (i.e., how well the relationship between the verb and the object is depicted)" (p. 143), is exactly what is predicted by the flexibility condition.

Finally, Liddell observed that when classifiers for location are involved, e.g., "The cat is lying on the fence," the unmarked ASL order seems to be OSV, FENCE CAT LIE-ON-IT. In the articulation of this sentence, the sign FENCE is made, and then what Liddell calls the 4 classifier (4 hand, fingertips facing sideways, used for fence, wall, general erect rectangular objects) is made with the nondominant hand and held while the sign CAT is made, after which the V̈ classifier (bent legs) is made and placed in position with respect to the 4 classifier. The positioning of the two classifiers indicates whether the cat is on the fence, next to the fence, under the fence, etc., and Liddell considers the entire sentence to be composed of locative object-locative subject-locative predicate. He suggests, then, that although SVO is the general underlying order for ASL sentences, the order OSV is unmarked in the case of locatives (unmarked in the sense of there being no intonation breaks and no special nonmanual signals).

MORE NONMANUAL SIGNALS

Numerous functions can be served by parts of the body above the neck. Eye gaze can be used to perform an indexic reference or even to establish the reference (Baker, 1976; Fischer, 1975; Friedman, 1976a). Raising the eyebrows is part of the topic marker "t" involved in yes/no questions (Baker, 1976; Bellugi and Fischer, 1972; Stokoe, Casterline, and Croneberg, 1965), whereas the identification of the negative headshake goes all the way back to Stokoe (1960). Eyeblinks have been shown to be relevant to the proper interpretation of conditional sentences and questions (Baker and Padden, 1978a,b). The use of head tilt backward for topic marker and forward in questions has been discussed above, and is discussed further for relative clauses below. Liddell (1977) identifies use of facial expression and head position in five contexts: 1) as abstract grammatical markers ("t," "q," "n," etc.), 2) as adverbs, 3) as parts of lexical items (tongue position in NOT-YET), 4) as part of pantomime, and 5) to indicate emotional states of the signer.

Liddell (1977) identifies three nonmanual signals which he argues function as adverbs in ASL. They are "mm," made with the lips together and slightly pushed out, with a slight head tilt, "cs," made with the shoulder raised and the head turned to the side of the raised shoulder and a characteristic facial expression, and "th," made with the lips apart and pushed out with tongue protruding (as when making the English sound "th," hence the name).

The adverb "mm" indicates that everything is normal and proper (e.g., engine running ok, people feeling relaxed and comfortable) and co-occurs with the verb. In the following example, [I:continuous] is Liddell's notation for continuous aspect on the verb: MAN

FISH$^{\text{[I:continuous]}}$ $\overset{\text{mm}}{}$ "the man is fishing with relaxation and enjoyment." If the question "Is the man fishing with relaxed enjoyment?" is asked, the "mm" signal falls within the scope of the "q" signal (which covers

the whole sentence) MAN FISH$^{\text{[I:continuous]}}$ $\overset{\overline{\text{q}}}{\underset{\text{mm}}{}}$. With these and other data, Liddell argues that "mm" is actually an adverb and should be represented in a tree as:

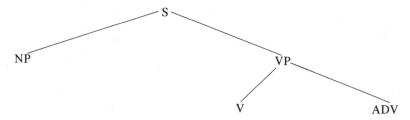

Similar arguments are given for "cs," which seems to have a meaning related to proximity of time or physical distance (e.g., "just yester-day," "brand new," "right behind," etc.) and "th," whose semantic interpretation involves "lack of control, inattention, unintention, and unawareness" (Liddell, 1977, p. 77) (e.g., "clod," "clumsy," "care-less," "make lots of mistakes," etc.). These nonmanual signals do not seem to be in the same group as the puffed cheeks which Baker (1976) described as being completely nonmanual, but which Kegl and Wilbur (1976) reanalyzed as remnants of deleted manual signals that can co-occur. Liddell's nonmanual adverbs do not have manual lexical signs that accompany them, their behavior is subject to linguistic con-straints, and they are not therefore open to the same kind of reanalysis.

Another form of nonmanual signal that Liddell reports is that used to indicate an emotional state of the signer without actual use of the manual sign that could co-occur. For example, the sentence "I was surprised that I liked John" can be signed with the signs PRO.1 LIKE JOHN (I am using Liddell's notation for first person reference PRO.1 here). The facial expression for surprise, signaled by dropped jaw and wide eyes, develops during the signing of this sequence. In that sense, it is unlike the nonmanual adverbs described earlier, which are formed, held for a specified syntactic domain, and then disappear abruptly. A similar nonmanual signal that develops during the signing sequence is "anger," made with dropped jaw, bared teeth, eyebrows down, and tensed lower eyelids. Both of these, he argues, are not part of the surface clausal structure in the same way that the nonmanual adverbs were, in the sense that they cannot be negated or questioned, whereas the nonmanual adverbs could be.

SUBORDINATION AND RELATIVE CLAUSES

Thompson (1977) claimed that ASL does not contain surface structures with subordinate clauses and that those sentences that look like they contain embedded sentences are really sequences of two sentences or coordinate sentences. Liddell indicates a number of problematic aspects of Thompson's argument, including contradictions between his claim and his data, which seem to arise from the way in which he translated the ASL sentences into English. Since Liddell (1977, 1978) reports several types of subordinate clauses and provides a nonmanual marker "r" for the relative clauses, his presentation, rather than the arguments against Thompson, are the major focus here.

Liddell identifies numerous subordinate clauses in ASL. One of them is the WH-complement illustrated by the following sentence (produced in the context of someone having been magically transported to a new location): DON'T-KNOW WHERE GONE "He didn't know where he had gone." There are no reasons to think that this is a direction question and there are no pauses in the string. Liddell indicates that the compound KNOW____THAT may also take sentential complements, as he illustrates with PRO.1 KNOW____THAT GIRL TALL "I already knew that the girl is tall." The compound KNOW____THAT seems to involve the particular meaning of already knowing, such that PRO.1 KNOW____THAT would be translated as "I already know that." However, KNOW____THAT cannot take a simple direct object, as Liddell illustrates with *PRO.1 KNOW____THAT GIRL, which is unacceptable and does not mean "I know that girl."

One of Thompson's arguments is that ASL does not distinguish between direct speech ("John said, 'I . . . '") from indirect speech ("John$_1$ said that he$_1$ . . . "). Liddell observes that just this distinction can be indicated by the presence or absence of body shifting. In the sentence with body shift, the verb SAY is not required, nor in many cases is the PRO.1 for "I." Thus, Liddell supplies the following examples (1977, p. 189, renumbered for use here):

1. JOHN (SAY) ^{shift} PRO.1   "John said, 'I'm tired."
    TIRED
2. JOHN SAY PRO.3 TIRED   "John said he (John) was tired."

In example 1 a direct report of what John said is given, whereas in 2 a report of the essential content of what John said is given using pointing to indicate John. In example 2 there is a subordinate clause, PRO.3 TIRED "he was tired."

Another of Thompson's arguments, with which Liddell appears to be in agreement, is that the verbs HAPPY, ANGRY, SURPRISED, RELIEVED, SORRY, and PROMISE do not take complements. However, neither Thompson nor Liddell indicates what alternative mechanism, if any, is used to report "Mary is sorry that she scared the cat away.'' One possibility is MARY SCARE-AWAY CAT, (PRO.3) SORRY.

Liddell's most extensive discussion and analysis of subordinates is for restrictive relative clauses. He indicates that these clauses can occur in initial, medial, and final position within an ASL sentence. Furthermore, they are accompanied by a nonmanual signal ''r,'' which is composed of raised brows, a backward tilt of the head, and raising of the cheek and upper lip muscles. In English, all relative clauses have what is known as an ''external head,'' that is, the noun about which the relative clause is providing information is outside of the relative clause itself. Consider ''The man who bought the yellow raincoat is John's father's best friend.'' The relative clause ''who bought the yellow raincoat'' provides information about ''the man,'' which is the subject of the predicate ''is John's father's best friend'' and the outside head of the relative clause. Within the relative clause, the relative pronoun ''who'' is considered to have replaced an underlying ''the man'' so that the underlying form of the relative clause would be ''the man bought the yellow raincoat.'' English does not allow ''the man'' to be repeated and substitutes ''who'' as subject of the relative clause in the surface structure.

Other languages do not work like English. They may have what is known as an ''internal head,'' where the noun that is being modified occurs *within* the relative clause itself. Thus, in languages with ''external heads,'' the noun that is the head of the relative clause appears in underlying structure twice, once in the main sentence and once in the embedded sentence, whereas in languages with ''internal heads,'' the noun that is the head appears in underlying structure only once. The characteristics of an internal head relative clause that Liddell summarizes are that 1) it has the structure of a sentence, 2) it serves the same function that a simple noun phrase would in the main sentence, and 3) it is treated and interpreted as though the noun phrase in it that serves as the head is performing the function described in 2. Having established this, Liddell discussed several relative clause types in ASL that appear to have internal heads. For example, the sentence

RECENTLY DOG CHASE CAT COME HOME ''The dog that recently chased the cat came home'' has an internal head DOG which functions as the subject of COME HOME; at the same time RECENTLY DOG CHASE CAT is a sentence itself and is marked with the nonmanual signal ''r'' (which stops at the end of the embedded part). Interestingly, Liddell observes that RECENTLY, which co-occurs with the nonmanual adverb ''cs,'' appears to have both ''cs'' and "r" at the same time. "It seems then that the nonmanual aspects of certain lexical items, expressions associated with individual signs or compounds, and non-manual grammatical markers are independent and additive" (Liddell, 1977, pp. 214–215).

Liddell considers the possibility that RECENTLY DOG CHASE CAT COME HOME is really two sentences concatenated temporally, but reports that when signers were asked to produce the two sentences separately, the nonmanual marker "r" was not used.

Liddell also made some measurements similar to those he used to support Fischer's claim of an intonation break in non-SVO ordered sentences. In this case, he used the sign CAT in a variety of positions in a relative clause. He reports that in medial position, the shortest duration, CAT lasted about 14 fields (0.23 seconds), in final position, 24 fields (0.4 seconds), and in initial position, 20 fields (0.33 seconds). When CAT occurred in initial position in the relative clause, it was always as the object of an OSV sequence. Looking at DOG when it occurred in relative clauses as the subject, he found that, in initial position and functioning as the head of the relative clause, DOG lasted 27 fields (0.43 seconds), but if not functioning as the head it lasted only 17 fields (0.28 seconds). In medial position, if DOG was the head, its duration was 22 fields (0.37 seconds), whereas if it was not the head, it lasted only 14 fields (0.23 seconds). Thus, the function of the head of a relative clause contributes to an increase in sign duration, as does final position (as reported by Grosjean and Lane, 1977) and initial position (as illustrated here).

Also involved in relativization are three forms of the sign THAT, none of which is the actual citation form given in sign textbooks (dominant Y hand contacts nondominant B hand, palm up). Liddell refers to these as THATa, THATb, and THATc. THATa is made with no base hand at all, the dominant hand is in the Y handshape, raised about shoulder height, and drops down from the wrist in a single motion. It is accompanied by "r," and serves to mark the entire relative clause as a subordinate clause, apparently to avoid ambiguity. In some cases, topicalization of the relative clause accomplishes the same purpose and THATa is not used. The topicalization of a relative clause, however, is not clearly marked with "t," since the nonmanual aspects that characterize "t" happen to be a subset of those that characterize "r"; thus to determine that it has been topicalized, order of occurrence (initial position) and possible duration changes may be used as cues.

THATb is also made with no base hand and almost no motion. If any motion is present, it may be a slight shaking of the forearm or a moving of the wrist. Liddell suggests that it is made and held in order to give the addressee an opportunity to let the signer know that he (the addressee) knows the person or thing being described by the relative clause. After the signer receives this signal form from the addressee (possibly by head nod), the signer uses THATc, which is articulated similarly to THATa, except that THATc "begins with a backward motion, while THATa begins with a forward motion. THATc is also made with a more clear cut end to the arm motion. That is, THATc ends with a hold and THATa does not" (Liddell, 1977, p. 235). Using the occurrence of "r" as a means of determining what is within the relative clause and what is not, Liddell finds that THATb is within the clause and THATc is not. THATb then serves the function of "you know which one I mean," although it is not a syntactic question, and THATc reiterates "yes, that's the one I mean." If the relative clause is not in final position, THATc is optional. However, if the relative clause is in final position, it must either be followed by THATc or an affirmative head nod.

Finally, on the behavior of THATa, Liddell notes than when it occurs between a noun phrase and a verb phrase, it functions as a subordinator, but when it precedes a noun, it is functioning as a demonstrative (as in English "that book").

Liddell (1977) has covered a wide range of syntactic structures and markers in ASL. He also provides sophisticated linguistic argumentation for the description of many of these structures, and for topics not discussed here, such as determining the head of a relative clause. The serious student of syntax is advised to refer to the complete work and not to rely on the summary herein.

Before leaving the topic of relative clauses, two other descriptions have been suggested that should be mentioned; although they are not supported to the same degree as Liddell's, they may still be valid choices for ASL signers. One is Hoemann's (1975a) observation that the main sentence appears to be signed higher in the signing space than the relative clause. Clearly, this can only hold for those signs that are made in neutral space; nonetheless, it is a strategy that permits the signer to set off the main clause from the relative clause through the use of space. The second is reported in Fischer (1974). She notes that signers may use handedness for such sentences, establishing one hand for the main clause and the other for the relative clause. Again, this is restricted in that signs that take two hands, or that move around in space for inflection, may be ambiguous as to whether they are in the main clause or the relative clause. Both of these strategies need to be pursued further.

OTHER SYNTACTIC STRUCTURES

The above discussions have covered a wide range of syntactic structures, including negation, questions, topicalization, relative clauses,
WH-complements, locative predicates, gapping, predicate nomina-
tives, adverbs, verb agreement, pronouns, and word order. In contrast, this section is small. There are still some uses of facial movements that remain to be covered, as well as one verb construction that
is of interest.

In their study of ASL conditionals, Baker and Padden (1978)
report that in conditional statements at least four changes could be
observed between the first clause and the second clause: eyeblinks,
release of nasolabial contraction, brow lowering, and initiation of head
nodding. In conditional questions, at least two changes occurred. They
report that in both conditional statements ("If it rains tomorrow, I will
go to the library") and conditional questions ("If it rains tomorrow,
will you go to the library?"), the "if" clause was marked with raising
of the eyebrows. In the statements, but not the questions, the "if"
clause was followed by an eyeblink. In the conditional statements, the
second part would have the brows returned to their normal position,
unless the statement was also negative, and changes in gaze direction
and head orientation would occur as appropriate. In the conditional
questions, the question part continued to have raised eyebrows (part
of the "q" marker), gaze at the addressee, and the head forward or
cocked to one side. Finally, whereas ASL may have a lexical marker
IF (Baker and Padden noted the fingerspelled i+f) in the first part, it
does not have the equivalent of "then" as a sign in the second part.

As Liddell indicated, the yes/no question marker "q" includes
raised brow and wide eyes. Others have observed that for WH-ques-
tions, the eyes are narrowed and the eyebrows are squished. ASL
WH-questions have WH-words to signal them, but these words (WHO,
WHEN, WHERE, WHAT, etc.) may occur in other than initial position (English WH-words are restricted to initial position for questions).
Fant (1972a) and Kegl (1977) observed that "bracing" may occur with
WH-question words, for example, WHO PRO+GIVE+PRO$_{2p}$ BOOK
WHO "Who gave you a/the book?" (literally, "who gave you a/the
book, who?"). Kegl considers this to be part of a more general bracing
process in which a single word, entire phrase, or whole sentence can
appear on both sides of a sentence (initially and finally). Kegl also
suggests that bracing may serve as a test for constituency, in that
whatever may brace a sentence must be a constituent (this is parallel

to Liddell's use of the scope of the nonmanual markers to determine if some element was part of a phrase or not).

Fischer (1974) reports several rules which appear to operate in ASL. She notes that Ross's (1967) coordinate structure constraint is operative for ASL. She also notes that FOR is used to introduce purposive clauses (e.g., "for the purpose of") and that "unless" clauses are introduced by WITHOUT. She notes that auxiliaries in ASL include FINISH (perfective), BETTER (polite imperative), CAN, CAN'T, WILL, MUST, FROM-NOW-ON (future continuous marker), HAVE-BEEN (past continuous marker), NOT-YET (negative of FINISH), HAPPEN, SUCCEED, and possibly SEEM. These auxiliaries have the possibility of occurring at the beginning and/or end of a sentence without a change in meaning from its position in the middle of a sentence. In an embedded sentence, "the auxiliary can occur initially or preverbally, but not at the end" (Fischer, 1974, p. 17). She postulates rules for auxiliary hopping (to move the auxiliary around), NP fronting (for topicalization), sentence topicalization, and VP topicalization. From the formalization of these last few rules, she concludes that Ross's (1967) complex NP constraint is also operative in ASL.

Both Kegl (1977) and O'Malley (1975) postulate deletion rules to handle those cases in which independent pronouns (such as pointing) do not occur in surface forms. Kegl postulates one relevant rule, copy drop. The rule of copy drop is dependent on the semantic notion of specificity, which refers to whether the NP or its copy (pronominal copy) indicates the narrowest set of possible references:

> Copy Drop: Given NP and NP copy, NP deletes if NP is less than or equal to the copy with respect to specificity.

Thus, if the noun BOOK is incorporated into the verb GIVE, it is equal in specificity to the independent (unincorporated) noun BOOK, and consequently the unincorporated BOOK is deleted. However, if noun incorporation is blocked for phonological reasons, and a classifier is used in the verb instead, the NP is more specific (refers to a narrower set of references) than the classifier, and deletion from the NP is blocked. Similarly, if the independent NP is modified (made more specific, e.g., BOOK BLUE), then neither an incorporated noun (BOOK) nor a classifier would be more specific, and deletion would be blocked. Finally, if an independent pronoun is emphatic or demonstrative, or the pronoun in the verb has a null agreement point, deletion is blocked (because the incorporated pronoun is less specific than the unincorporated pronoun).

O'Malley posits several deletion rules that are very similar to Kegl's. He notes that the most deletable pronoun in ASL is first person singular, but only in subject position ("I"), and posits an optional rule of I-deletion. Another optional (and mirror image) rule is pronoun deletion, which deletes independent pronouns when the verb is inflected to convey the same information. He indicates that the function of these two rules is to "simplify sentence structure by removing redundant elements" (O'Malley, 1975, p. 16) and that the information deleted by both rules is uniquely recoverable.

Fischer and Gough (1972) suggest that ASL might have a rule of EQUI-NP deletion (*equi*valent *NP deletion*). O'Malley argues that just such a rule can be postulated. In transformational grammar, a sentence like "I want John to go" is treated as though it comes from two underlying sentences, "I want" and "John go," through a process of complementation, whereby one sentence is modified to fit into the other (inserting the "to" in English). Consequently, a sentence like "I want to go" is treated as coming from two underlying sentences, "I want" and "I go," where the second occurrence of "I" is deleted by EQUI-NP deletion. O'Malley indicates that EQUI-NP deletion in ASL seems to be two rules, one that exactly parallels the English rule (the presence of which may be an ASL borrowing from English) and one that is restricted to avoid EQUI-NP application to sentences with auxiliaries, negatives, and modals. O'Malley's suggestion that signers have two parallel rules for the same structure in ASL is similar to that of Quigley, Smith, and Wilbur (1974), who suggested that deaf students might have parallel rules for English relative clauses (and possibly other structures). Again, the bilingual situation must be kept in mind.

SUMMARY

A variety of syntactic rules exist in ASL, many appreciably different from English. However, none of these rules indicates that ASL is extraordinary with respect to other languages of the world (except of course in how the output structure is constituted after application of morphological and phonological rules). The importance of a linguist's perspective on the function of various aspects, such as the point in space, has been emphasized in terms of how it may affect the linguistic description that is given and the conclusions that are reached. Thus, Forman and McDonald's (1978) and Kegl's (1978d) suggestion that ASL prepositions may be underlying verbs could eventually result in new insights into ASL structure.

Many new questions are raised by the information given here. ASL is an inflected language; how does its structure compare to that of other inflected languages? Can an argument be made for a VP in ASL? If not, how are the structures drawn by Liddell (1977) or the rules and conclusions reported in Fischer (1974) affected? What other facial and head cues are there? Are there other means of marking either grammatical relations or cases? Is ASL an ergative language, as Kegl (1976b) has suggested?

Of particular interest to this author is the further specification of classifiers in ASL. Although questions concerning their particular syntactic environments still remain, the major concern at present is details of the categories that each classifier delineates and the changes in focus that result in a single object being classified by different classifiers in different situations. Wilbur, Bernstein, and Kantor (1978) devised a series of experiments to empirically determine what possible characteristics of a classifier would be relevant to determining which objects it could replace. In a pilot study, subjects were presented with a classifier on videotape in a neutral context (e.g., upright G hand moves up to an upright forearm) as though one had come into the conversation in the middle and missed the establishment of the particular NPs being discussed. The subjects were asked to circle on an answer sheet all of the objects (out of a total of seven) that the classifier could have meant (in this example, the classifier in question was G, which was re-presented alone and statically after the moving neutral context given above). Tentative results from these data suggest that G need not be human, but merely animate; that C is used for objects that are characteristically containers; that the V classifier (person ambulatory) can actually be used for three- and four-legged inanimate objects so long as the sign is not moving; and that the 3 vehicle classifier may be used for a variety of conveyances, which on land must have wheels, but on water need not, and which must be characteristically used for (long-distance?) conveyance (i.e., not for surfboards, roller skates, sleds, or other sports vehicles). This type of information, when finalized, will be helpful in allowing comparison between ASL and other classifier languages (such as those discussed in Allan, 1977), while at the same time placing constraints on what may be allowable iconic or visual representation in ASL.

Recent developments in the linguistic description of ASL have been staggering; much of the information reported in this chapter is less than 2 years old, some of it less than 1. The reader can compare this chapter with the syntax section of Wilbur (1976) and see the enormous difference, yet we have only scratched the surface.

CHAPTER 5

PSYCHOLINGUISTIC ASPECTS OF ASL

CONTENTS

This chapter reviews investigations of the consequences of visual/
manual language. The first and most obvious aspect is the potential
for iconicity, direct visual representation of a sign's meaning. Second,
there is the acquisition of sign language and its relation to spoken and
potential language acquisition universals. Third is the perception and
production of sign language, particularly compared to that of spoken
language. Fourth is the intriguing question of how language in a visual/
manual mode might result in modifications of brain functioning as
evidenced by cerebral lateralization. Fifth is the potential cognitive
modifications in memory processes, an area that is still in need of
further research.

ICONICITY

Perhaps the most controversial and misunderstood aspect of manual
languages is their apparent iconicity. The possibility of relating the
formation of a sign with some real world aspect of its meaning has led
many to the erroneous assumption that sign languages are "pictures"
in the air, and therefore unable to function or qualify as true languages.
Often a sign will be presented to a new learner with an etymology
attached to help "explain" the formational characteristics, e.g., girl—

the strings on a bonnet, boy—the visor on a cap. Such stories, whether true or not, provide memory aids to the learner. Significantly, such explanations are totally lacking in observations of interactions between deaf parents and their sign language-learning children (Moores, 1977).

In discussing iconicity, one can focus on several issues. How transparent are signs to people who are unfamiliar with signs? That is, can one tell what someone is signing without learning signs first? What are the factors involved in iconicity and what are the theoretical consequences of these factors?

Transparency for the Nonsigner

Several procedures have been utilized to attempt to measure the degree of transparency that certain signs may have to the nonsigner (Bellugi and Klima, 1976; Hoemann, 1975b). Bellugi and Klima (1976) presented 90 ASL signs and their English translations to a group of hearing nonsigners and asked them to describe the basis for the connection between the sign's meaning and its formation as they saw it. They found that for over half of the signs, there was general agreement among the subjects as to the possible relationship. Thus, if the meaning is known, a relationship can be determined for some signs. Bellugi and Klima termed this type of sign *translucent*. They next investigated the *transparency* of signs—what Lloyd and Fristoe (1978) have called *guessability*, namely, the likelihood of determining the correct meaning of a sign by a nonsigner. They used the same set of 90 signs with a different group of hearing nonsigners. They found that for 90% of the signs presented, not even one subject was able to determine the correct meaning. The remaining 10% (BED, BUTTON, EAR, EYES, MARBLE, MILK, OPERATION, PIE, and SURPRISE) were identifiable by some but not all subjects. Thus, most of the signs were not transparent to most of the subjects.

A third technique that Bellugi and Klima used was a multiple choice test constructed using the correct meaning and four alternatives chosen from the incorrect guesses of the preceding study, with some likely but incorrect foils added in. Again, the same 90 signs were used with a different group of 10 hearing nonsigners. The correct response rate was no better than chance (18.2% correct compared to 20% chance), indicating that under these more constrained conditions (choices given rather than free choice as above), the ASL signs were *opaque*. For 12 of the 90 signs, a majority of subjects guessed the correct meaning (BED, BUTTON, BODY, BOTH, BLOSSOM, DAY, EAR, EYES, ODOR, OPERATION, SURPRISE, and YEAR). For

36 of the 90 signs, no subject chose the correct meaning. Interestingly, a number of the signs that were never identified are ones that are commonly given stories when they are presented to people learning signs: BOY, CANADA, EARTH, GIRL, GRAVY, HOME, IDEA, SCIENCE, SUMMER, WEEK.

Bellugi and Klima (1976) also discussed the lack of evidence for a role for iconicity in memory, based on Bellugi, Klima, and Siple (1975), Bellugi and Siple (1974), and Klima and Bellugi (1975). Finally, they reviewed several grammatical modifications that signs can undergo, and pointed out that the identifiable iconic parts of certain signs are actually lost in grammatical contexts. The issue of iconicity and grammatical modifications is returned to below.

Possible Types of Iconic Representations

The results that Bellugi and Klima obtained are not surprising. There are many aspects of a real world action or object that might serve as the source for a sign. Although a spatial/visual language naturally takes advantage of its power to depict, each language seems to choose a different aspect to represent, thus providing an arbitrariness that renders the sign opaque to the nonsigner. Furthermore, as Frishberg (1975, 1976a) has shown, signs have historically changed away from iconic depictions and toward more arbitrary representations.

Mandel (1977) discussed several ways in which a sign can conceivably be iconic. He first distinguished *direct* representation, where the gesture is the thing being referred to, as for example the drawing of a house-like outline for the sign HOUSE or the pointing to the nose for NOSE. Nondirect representation, or *metonymy* (Battison, 1971; Schlesinger et al., 1970), refers to the use of *part* of an object or action as a reference for the whole, as for example when the grinding action is used for the sign COFFEE, even if the coffee being discussed is instant or drip (this is similar to the American English use of the word "blackboard" for boards that may be green, blue, or red). Mandel further distinguished *presentation* and *depiction*. *Presentation* refers to the use of a token of an object or activity, either by mime (BASEBALL) (Mandel does not separate sign from mime, but rather includes mime as a type of sign) or by indexing (NOSE). *Depiction*, on the other hand, may be either *substitutive*, as when the articulator is formed into the shape of an object (CUP), or *virtual*, in which the articulator is used to trace a picture in space (HOUSE).

The types of representations that Mandel identifies (and other subcategories included in them) provide a pool from which manual languages can pick and choose. Thus for any vocabulary item that may be iconically based, different sign languages will have different forms, adding to the opacity of the signs themselves. Chinese Sign Language even uses depiction for Chinese characters (forming the character with the fingers or tracing the character in the air) that are themselves former iconic representations of real word objects. One can see the original connection when it is explained, but few would be foolhardy enough to suggest that Chinese characters are iconic and can be read without actual training.

A similar discussion of iconicity is contained in Cohen, Namir, and Schlesinger (1977) (on Israeli Sign Language). Although they do not go into the same detail that Mandel does, they do note differences between free pantomime and iconicity that has been conventionalized into signs, and the fact that different sign languages may pick different characteristics to represent and could therefore have different signs, each of which might still be guessable to the nonsigner. They, like Mandel, include in their discussion of iconicity those signs which move their starting and end points to agree with their subject and object, those which incorporate location or direction, and classifiers (although they do not specifically name each as such).

Iconicity and Linguistic Description

DeMatteo (1977) suggests that iconicity must be incorporated into the grammar of ASL, not simply as part of it, but rather as the base of it. Although unable to specify the details of how such an incorporation might be made, he does suggest that a visual analogue grammar that does not contain discrete units, such as NP, might be possible. He includes as part of his argument for the nondiscreteness of ASL many of the same things that Mandel and Cohen, Namir, and Schlesinger do: verbs that agree with their arguments, signs that include location and direction, object-incorporating verbs (WASH as in WASH-DISHES, WASH-CAR), and classifiers (again, none of these are specifically named as such).

Much of DeMatteo's argument rests on surface similarities between the verb MEET (two G hands, each starting at its appropriate subject index point and both eventually coming together) and other verbs with different movement. For example, in "The boy and girl meet," the two hands start at their previously designated points and move together, usually in the middle of neutral space in front of the signer. In "The boy and the girl passed each other without stopping," the verb would be made without an end contact and of course the hands would pass each other going in opposite directions. In "The

oy avoided meeting the girl" or "The boy avoided the girl," the hand
hat is co-referent with the boy would eventually turn in a different
lirection from the direction that the girl is moving in. DeMatteo pro-
ides other similar examples which he feels argue for a description in
vhich each of these is seen as a modification of the movement of the
verb MEET rather than as separate verbs. Furthermore, it is his
contention that the modifications that do occur are visually based
iconic changes that are potentially infinite, and therefore cannot be
aandled within current theoretical frameworks.

To say that iconicity is part of the structure of ASL is one thing;
o say that it is the basis for the linguistic description of ASL is quite
another. In one example, DeMatteo suggests that the signer's choice
of the verb-locational preposition combination FLY-OVER rather than
the sequence FLY OVER is "the more visually based representation,
choosing descriptive signs or mimic signs in order to create an icon in
the signing space" (1977, p. 121). Such a statement overlooks the
nonoccurrence of the preposition OVER in any kind of surface sequence of verb + preposition (possibly for the reason suggested by
Kegl, 1978d, that verbs are really underlying prepositions) and that the
citation form of OVER (and other prepositions, cf. AROUND,
UNDER) only occur in citation environments ("What is the sign for
X?") and signed English sequences. Suppose, however, that there
existed a grammatical constraint in ASL that allowed OVER to occur
in sequences only in stative, descriptive environments (e.g., "The
lamp that hangs over the desk has a Tiffany shade"). If such a constraint existed, we would be primarily interested in determining 1) its
existence, and 2) its domain of application (other locative prepositions?
what counts as a stative verb in ASL?). To know that the signer
produces a particular form, which to the listener seems to create a
more appropriate visual image of the described event, does not necessarily indicate that he does so free from linguistic constraint. In
order to investigate such constraints, and the phonological and syntactic descriptions given elsewhere in this book, it is necessary to
make a number of working assumptions (Kegl and Wilbur, 1976):

1. ASL may be described in terms of discrete elements.
2. There exist constraints on the combinations and permutations of
   these elements. There exist violations of these constraints, and
   native signers can make metalinguistic judgments of grammaticality utilizing these constraints.
3. Elements in proximity interact with each other. In other words
   there are phonological modifications of signs in sequence.

4. There are derivational and inflectional morphological processes.
5. There is a deep structure, a surface structure, and a mapping from one to the other.
6. There exist linguistic universals such as noun, verb, and the expression of grammatical relations in the base.
7. Any linguistic model claiming to provide a consistent description of language should be an appropriate framework in which to attempt an analysis. This framework should allow one to develop tests, arguments, and predictions. In other words, it provides the metalinguistic mechanisms with which to work.
8. Nonmeaningful variation exists, either stylistically or sociolinguistically conditioned. Knowledge of the grammatical system as a whole will allow us to recognize points at which this nonmeaning changing variation occurs.

When iconicity does appear, it must obey the constraints on allowable signs. When visual analogue occurs (e.g., modifying the sign WALK-AROUND to include a slight hill or disturbance in the path), it is linguistically constrained such that 1) the resultant sign cannot violate the phonological conditions on allowable signs, 2) it cannot destroy the syntactic or morphological content of the sentence, and 3) it cannot be semantically distinct from the original meaning in the sense of a minimal pair (Kegl and Wilbur, 1976). Thus, although De Matteo argues strongly for visual analogue grammar based on the apparent continuity of modifications that the verb MEET can undergo one must contend that because "The boy and the girl passed each other without stopping" is semantically distinct from "The boy and girl meet," which is distinct from "The boy avoided meeting the girl," etc., they represent discrete semantic concepts, and therefore very likely discrete verbs (which may or may not be derivationally related to each other). If, in fact, there is a separate translation into English (or any other language) for each of the different meanings intended, it argues that there is no apparent reason why ASL could not have separate and distinct verbs for each, at least at the semantic level. De Matteo is concerned that this destroys the hope of "placing finite bounds on the number of lexical items" (1977, p. 114), but if one views this as a complex of derivational and inflectional morphological and syntactic processes with regularities and constraints of application then one can describe internal structure without being blinded by surface continuity.

All of this adds up to a single point: describing something as iconic may be true, but it is also linguistically insufficient.

SIGN LANGUAGE ACQUISITION

Studies of the acquisition of ASL (Ashbrook, 1977; Bellugi and Klima, 1972; Boyes-Braem, 1973; Hoffmeister, 1977, 1978; Kantor, 1977; Lacy, 1972a,b; McIntire, 1974, 1977; Wilbur and Jones, 1974) indicate that children learning ASL pass through developmental stages similar to those reported for children learning spoken languages. For example, Ashbrook (1977), Bellugi and Klima (1972), and Hoffmeister (1977) report that the full range of semantic relations found in children learning English (Bloom, 1970) is expressed by children in the early stages of ASL acquisition. Wilbur and Jones (1974) report similar findings for hearing children of deaf parents who are learning both ASL and English.

It seems that a deaf child's first sign may emerge 2 to 3 months earlier than a hearing child's first spoken word (Boyes-Braem, 1973; McIntire, 1974; Wilbur and Jones, 1974). Similarly, in hearing children of deaf parents, the child's first sign may emerge several months before the same child's first spoken words (Wilbur and Jones, 1974). In addition, the child's spoken vocabulary complements his sign vocabulary, with only a small overlap of words that are spoken and signed (Wilbur and Jones, 1974). This indicates that the child is not simply learning spoken words to correspond to signs already known, nor signs to correspond to spoken words already known, at least not in the initial stages (the opportunity for differential usage of signs and speech is probably substantially involved in this difference). (For other studies of hearing children of deaf parents, which are not specifically sign studies but both sign and speech, see Bard and Sachs, 1977; Jones, 1976; Mayberry, 1976b; Sachs and Johnson, 1976; Todd, 1971, 1972; for studies of invented home-signs of deaf children with hearing parents, see Goldin-Meadow, 1975; Goldin-Meadow and Feldman, 1975.)

One further comparison that has been made is that of vocabulary size. McIntire (1974) reports a vocabulary of about 20 signs at age 10 months, the age at which a hearing child is likely to produce his first spoken word. McIntire also reports two-sign utterances at 10 months (two spoken word utterances generally begin at about 18 months) and three-sign utterances at 18 months.

These comparisons of the "first" sign to the "first" spoken word must be considered with caution. There is, of course, considerable difficulty in determining when a child produces his first spoken word, because what may be intelligible to parents who are with the child constantly may not be intelligible to an outside observer. Furthermore, it is not clear whether this difficulty exists to the same degree in both modalities (i.e., is it as hard to determine the first sign as it is to determine the first spoken word?). The above comparisons should be approached with caution for another reason: the number of children studied to date is extremely small. Considerably more documentation is needed for all of these comparisons, but should the differences noted above be confirmed, the earlier emergence of signs is of considerable interest. It is possible that the earlier emergence and growth of signs is attributable to greater control of the hand muscles as compared to the oral muscles.

Phonological Acquisition

The study of the acquisition of phonology in ASL has been limited primarily to the acquisition of handshape. Boyes-Braem (1973) presents a model of handshape complexity that is based on anatomical considerations of the hands and their motor development sequence. Within this model, A is considered the unmarked handshape, and the others are described in terms of the addition of features. Thus, S represents the addition of "opposition of the thumb," 5 is the addition of "extension away from the initial axis of one or more digits," K illustrates the addition of "contact of the knuckle with the thumb," etc. She also provides a number of secondary factors that may be involved: pantomime, anticipation and retention of adjacent handshapes, preference for fingertip contact, nature of the feedback, and nature of the movement of the sign.

McIntire (1974, 1977) modified the Boyes-Braem model, eliminating the distinctions that seem irrelevant to early development (such as the distinction between A and S). She reported four stages of handshape development which are affected by 1) opposition of the thumb, 2) extension of one or more fingers, and 3) contact of a finger with the thumb. In the first stage, only one of the handshapes requires a finger to make contact with the thumb. At this initial stage, the child can produce the following handshapes: 5, S, L, A, G, C, and babyO, in which an O handshape is made with only the thumb and index finger rather than with all the fingers. The second, third, and fourth stages include handshapes that involve touching a finger to the thumb, or more than one of the factors previously mentioned. Stage 2 includes B, F, and adult O. Stage 3 includes I, Y, D, P, 3, V, H, and W, some of which include extension of the weaker fingers (ring finger and pinkie). The fourth stage includes 8, 7, X, R, T, M, N, and E, some of which involve crossing fingers.

Initial analyses of the acquisition of phonology in spoken languages focused on the sequence of acquisition of segments (cf. Jakobson, 1968), similar in many respects to McIntire and Boyes-Braem. Further investigation (Moskowitz, 1970) indicated a crucial interaction between word position and order of acquisition. Thus, Moskowitz found that the word initial position tended to be more stable for consonant pronunciation than either medial or final position. This interaction was also found at the distinctive feature level—when the child learned a distinction, e.g., voiced/voiceless, that distinction may have appeared in initial position, but not in similar segments that occurred in final position (i.e., the child may be able to correctly pronounce *pill* and *bill,* but not *cup* and *cub*). The interaction of context in the acquisition of segments has been pursued even further in more recent studies of oral phonological development within a generative framework (Ingram, 1974, 1976; Menn, 1976; Smith, 1973). The dominance of initial position does not hold up across children; instead, individual strategies seem to characterize different children. In addition to the importance of context, these studies also emphasize the relevance of function. Smith (1973) reported the child's ability to pronounce [v] perfectly in the English word *very,* but at the same time, the child failed to produce it in the remaining words that should properly have it (*very* is referred to by Smith as an "absolute exception" because it is correct and all others are not). Thus, other words that begin with [v] in the adult form were pronounced with [w], [β] or [v] in free variation (not consistently one or the other). Smith emphasized that [v] does not function in the child's system in the same way that it does in the adult's, despite its apparently correct articulation in the one word in which it consistently appears. For spoken segment acquisition, it has become necessary to distinguish between 1) discriminating sounds perceptually, 2) pronouncing sounds correctly, and 3) using sounds appropriately.

These distinctions are undoubtedly relevant to the study of manual language. We might expect to find modification of a handshape depending on the environment in which it occurs (type of motion, orientation, location). For example, a child who can produce the S handshape in a sign like WORK (both hands in S shape, dominant one taps on back of nondominant wrist) might not be able to produce that same handshape in the sign CHANGE because of the difference in motion (twisting wrist) and contact (wrist to wrist). Thus McIntire's stages are relevant primarily to the acquisition of handshapes within single signs, usually simple lexical items (as opposed to the more complex classifiers), although an interaction in complex forms does occur (Kantor, 1977; see below). Within multisign utterances, assimilations, reductions, etc. may occur. The syntactic and semantic components of the child's development must also be investigated for their influence on phonological development. Although Kantor (1977) has done one such investigation, much research remains to be done in this area.

Syntactic Acquisition

Studies of syntactic acquisition, like those of phonological acquisition, are few in number. Lacy (1972a,b) and Ellenberger, Moores, and Hoffmeister (1975) investigated the beginning stages of acquisition of negation by deaf children of deaf parents. Lacy (1972b) reported from his longitudinal investigation that the earliest forms of negation were NO (a sign that seems to be derived from the fingerspelled n-o) and the negative headshake (which is more frequent). The negative head-shake could occur either in linear order with manual signs, or simultaneously with a sign or sign sequence. In a later stage, the use of NO decreased, and the two signs NOT and CAN'T (not a contraction of CAN NOT, but a suppletive form in ASL) were used internally in sentences. As in the acquisition of spoken English, the form for "can't" was acquired before the positive form "can." These developmental stages seem to parallel those reported by Bellugi (1967) in her study of the acquisition of negation by hearing children learning English. Bellugi (1967) reported that children tend to use "can't" and "don't" before they use any other auxiliaries, even "can" and "do." Early negation tends to be outside the sentence, in the form of "no." Later negatives appear inside the sentence, before the verb.

Hoffmeister and Moores (1973) investigated the development of specific reference in deaf children learning ASL. In doing so, they distinguished between formal and informal means of indicating specific reference. The formal mechanisms are the citation forms of the signs THIS (dominant G hand points to palm of nondominant B hand) and THAT (dominant Y hand palm down on the nondominant B hand, palm up). They considered pointing with the G hand to be an informal procedure for indicating reference. This investigation of pointing led to a more extensive study and analysis reported in Hoffmeister (1977), discussed separately below.

Fischer (1973b) reported on the acquisition of verb inflection by two deaf children of deaf parents, Shirley and Cory. Fischer divided the data into arbitrary 6-month stages. For Cory, she analyzed five stages, Stage Zero (age 2), Stage I (age 2 ½), Stage II (age 3), Stage III (age 3 ½), and Stage IV (age 4). For Shirley, there were four stages, from Stage I (same age) on up. Fischer included in her study aspects of verb inflection related to the phonological realization of verb agreement. She divided the verbs into three classes: locational (verbs that can be made at an agreement point other than body anchor verbs), 2) reversing verbs (those that reverse or modify hand orientation toward an agreement point), and 3) directional verbs (those that move between two agreement points). Looking at the phonological realizations, Fischer reported that at Stage Zero, Cory showed no inflections at all, and that verbs that should have been inflected were modified to an uninflected form. At Stage I for both children, Fischer observed only locational verbs, with nonlocational verbs incorrectly modified to be locational (i.e., directional verbs became locational). At Stage II, the children indicated regular overgeneralization of the verb inflection rule (parallel to hearing children first correctly producing *came*, then later incorrectly producing *camed*). Body anchor verbs that were not in any of the above three classes and were correctly produced at Stage I were now incorrectly made into locational verbs. Reversal also appeared at this stage and was overgeneralized. The beginning of directional verbs was also observed at this stage. By Stage III, both girls clearly knew which verbs inflected in which ways, although at Stage IV, Cory was still making occasional overgeneralizations.

Investigations of other complicated syntactic structures have yet to be reported. One would guess that this is primarily attributable to the lack of clear syntactic descriptions of the adult language, but future studies should include object incorporation, choice of pronoun type, and the use of facial expressions and head nods, described in Chapter 4.

Semantic Acquisition

As mentioned previously, semantic relations expressed by children in the early stages of ASL acquisition have been investigated by a number of researchers. Aside from the conclusions that the development of these semantic relations seem to parallel those in spoken language acquisition, one other interesting finding comes from Ashbrook (1977). She originally separated semantic relations expressed through a sequence of signs (as one would do through a sequence of spoken words) from those expressed simultaneously within a complex sign (e.g., agent expressed by verb agreement with that referent point in space, thus one sign starting at that point indicates both agent and action). Her intent was to see if some developmental difference in expression type might exist. In fact, she found no such developmental difference. Thus in the children's language, as in the adult language, both expressions are possible. Comprehensive determination of what governs these choices in the adult language, and their corresponding development in children, still remains to be conducted.

Another type of study on semantics (although it is not specifically called one) is that of Ellenberger and Steyaert (1978). Their primary interest was in the representation of action by one child between the ages of 43 (3;7) and 71 (5;11) months. They reported a developmental trend of: 1) a decrease in the use of pantomime or gestures along with signs that indicate action; 2) a gradual increase in the use of abstract symbols and a decrease in the use of iconic reenactments of events; 3) when telling stories, a shift from the role of actor to that of narrator; 4) the development of the ability to establish referents in space that can be incorporated into the action sign; and 5) an increasing skill in the usage of signs that can incorporate information about participants in the action (including classifiers in the verbs, for example).

Recent Extensive Investigations

This section includes two studies, those of Kantor (1977) and Hoffmeister (1977), which cannot be neatly categorized into the schema used above. Both of them provide unique perspectives on the structure and acquisition of ASL, and consequently require separate and extended discussion. Kantor's study is cross-sectional and investigates classifier development. Hoffmeister's study is longitudinal and traces the development of various systems in ASL that seem to be based on the pointing gesture (discussed as part of the noun phrase in Chapter 3). Hoffmeister's study was conducted as part of a larger investigation at the University of Minnesota (Hoffmeister, 1975; Hoffmeister, Ellenberger, and Moores, 1975; Hoffmeister, Moores, and Best, 1974; Hoffmeister, Moores, and Ellenberger, 1975a,b; Moores and O'Malley, 1976; Morgan, 1975; O'Malley, 1975).

The purpose of Kantor's (1977) study was to obtain data on the developmental stages through which deaf children pass in acquiring the adult form of classifiers. The description of classifiers laid out in Kegl (1976a,b), Kegl and Wilbur (1976), and discussed in Chapter 3, was treated as the adult form to be learned. Within this model of classifiers, classifier signs are linguistically complex, requiring syntactic, semantic, and phonological information for appropriate choice and function. If they are linguistically complex, and if there is any relationship between linguistic complexity and ease/order/age of acquisition, then one might expect that classifiers would take longer than other signs for deaf children to learn, although this relationship is not necessarily so direct (Wilbur, in press a). They may also require different strategies because of the interaction of phonological, syntactic, and semantic components with their proper use.

Kantor conducted a cross-sectional study, using nine children, ages 3 to 11 years. All children were congenitally, profoundly deaf with deaf parents. They were presented with a story specifically designed for elicitation of classifiers, signed by a native user of ASL on videotape, after which they were asked to retell and discuss the story with a deaf houseparent. This interaction was videotaped for later analysis. The children also were given imitation and comprehension tasks to provide a complete picture of their abilities.

The results of this investigation can be more easily discussed in light of a model of classifier usage modified from a more general model of development suggested by M. Bernstein (cited in Kantor, 1977, p. 48). "The use of a classifier in any utterance can be illustrated in the following way":

1) There is a proposition to express.
2) If the environment requires a classifier, substitute one and attach it to the verb.

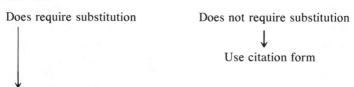

Does require substitution   Does not require substitution

Use citation form

3) What is the appropriate form
   a) semantically (what are the properties of the noun, i.e., is it taller than it is wide, etc.)
   b) phonologically (what are the parameters of the actual sign)
   c) syntactically (where does it move; what are the agreement points?)

The first step in classifier usage, then, is the syntactic recognition that one is needed. Kantor found that even the youngest children in the study were making this recognition, and only one or two real violations of the conditioning environments for classifier usage occurred. If a classifier was not actually used, then either 1) deletion occurred such that no form was used or 2) the citation form of the verb was used without the element that would have conditioned the classifier (e.g., without verb agreement or without the directional preposition, this information simply being omitted). If a classifier did occur, it was likely that other modifications would occur.

The remaining steps that are required for total mastery of the classifier system do not come until much later, in the sense that proper substitution of a classifier in one environment did not ensure that the same classifier would be substituted in another environment, and phonological modifications occurred as a result of the differences in syntactic environments. Similarly, handshapes that were used appropriately in simple signs (such as 3 in the numeral, or V in the sign SEE) were not used correctly in the classifier forms in a consistent manner. These developmental discrepancies within each child parallel the findings in spoken language acquisition discussed above with respect to function and linguistic complexity.

Looking at Kantor's data group by group reveals developmental stages and details of the children's strategies and patterns. The youngest group (3;0 to 3;11) had limited control over classifier usage. They were able to demonstrate comprehension of the classifier forms, as evidenced, for example, by substituting the citation form WALK in an imitation task where the by-legs classifier was presented. In terms of what control the children did have, the by-vehicle classifier seems to be the most advanced, the tall-upright object classifier next, and the by-legs classifier the least developed. The children's errors consisted mostly of deletions (simply not using the form at all) and modifications of handshape, orientation, and, for the by-legs classifier, motion. One common substitution was the use of the 5 hand in place of the 3 hand for the by-vehicle classifier and in place of the V hand in the by-legs classifier. This substitution of 5 for 3 and V is in keeping with McIntire's suggestions that 5 is developmentally easier. (The complexity of V is increased when it occurs in signs like WALK-TO, which involves a combination of linear movement ("to") and finger wiggling movement ("walk"). Very few signs actually involve this combination; most other signs have linear movement or some type of angular movement (twisting, wiggling, flicking, etc.) but not both.) However, the motoric simplicity of 5 is interacting with the other requirements on classifier usage: 5 is not used solely because it is motorically simpler, as evidenced by these same children using 3 and V correctly in nonclassifier forms. This is further illustrated by another example. In an imitation task, Kantor found that a child who could imitate by-vehicle correctly in a sentence with only one classifier nonetheless modified the handshape of that same classifier in a sentence that contained four classifiers and verb agreement. It is also significant that, whatever modifications of handshape, orientation, or motion the children made, the resulting sign did not violate the phonological constraints of ASL.

The middle group (ages 5;8 to 6;0) expanded the semantic domain of their vehicle classifier to allow its use for "trains" (the younger group used it for "car" and "motorcycle"), while still using tall-upright object classifier with a restricted subset of nouns (e.g., "tree" but not "building"). In the by-vehicle classifier, a variant handshape

Table 14. Percent correct and error types in combined comprehension, imitation, and production tasks

	Modifications	Deletions	Substitutions	Correct usage
Youngest	45%	20%	12.5%	22.5%
Middle	6.4%	17%	10.6%	66%
Older	3.3%	9.8%	3.3%	83.6%
Oldest	0	0	0	100%

(B hand with extended thumb) was more frequent (again, this hand-shape is simpler than 3 within the McIntire/Boyes-Braem model). Finally, use of by-legs increased, but still with modifications of orientation and motion.

In the next older group (6;0 to 7;0), the 3 hand by-vehicle classifier was used in a wider variety of contexts and expanded semantically again to include "trucks" and "parked cars." The tall-upright vehicle classifier was used more consistently, and a fourth classifier, the stationary surface (B hand, palm down) was spontaneously used. By-legs classifiers were still being deleted or modified.

The oldest group (10;0 to 11;0) used all classifiers correctly and productively (see Table 14).

From the types of errors that the children made, their relative performance on the three different tasks, and the changes in abilities over age, Kantor made these conclusions:

1. The late acquisition of classifiers confirms Kegl and Wilbur's (1976) and Kegl's (1978c) description of them as a system of great complexity.
2. Classifiers are not acquired as lexical items per se but rather as a complex syntactic process. This is evidenced by several instances of appropriate classifier usage in some environments and inappropriate usage in others.
3. Classifiers begin to emerge around age 3, but are not completely mastered as a set of rules until 8 or 9 years of age.
4. The deaf child's acquisition of segments is not simply a matter of incremental ability to control the weaker digits of the hand. Rather, it is a complex interaction of the various components of the language.
5. There is an influence of syntactic and phonological environments operating on the acquisition of rules in ASL similar to the effect of environment on spoken language rule acquisition as described by Smith (1973) and Menyuk (1977).

6. The notion of function as described by Smith (1973), Ingram (1976), and Menn (1976) is applicable to the acquisition of segments in ASL.
7. The domain of application for a rule widens as the child matures in much the same way it does in hearing children as described by Menyuk (1977).
8. The earliest handshapes used in initial use of classifiers corresponds to the stages of development suggested by Boyes-Braem (1973) and McIntire (1977).
9. The order of feature acquisition corresponds to the hierarchy suggested by Wilbur and Jones (1974) with the addition of orientation. On the basis of developmental stages within the acquisition of simple single signs, Wilbur and Jones (1974) suggested that the order of acquisition of parameters would be location, movement, and handshape. Kantor found that orientation seems to share the final stage with handshape, resulting in location, movement, handshape/orientation.

Thus Kantor's study confirms a number of important issues regarding the adult description of ASL (such as the complexity of classifiers) and questions about the acquisition of signs by children (developmental stages that display an interaction of various components of the grammar).

It has been indicated that the pointing gesture (deictic marker) combined with the agreement point serves to form an index which functions as part of the noun phrase. Hoffmeister's (1977) study identified various functions that this index can serve in the adult language: as the demonstrative pronoun, as a determiner, as part of the possessive system (with the B hand), or as a reflexive (with the À hand), as well as to indicate the individual plural and specific reference. Hoffmeister named the pointing gesture POINT, and this notation is used for this discussion. His observations indicate that the POINT forms the basis for several developmental stages. For example, the early two-sign productions consist of two POINTs: if a child wishes to indicate that a particular toy is his, this possessor-possessed relationship might be a sequence of two POINTs, one to the toy, the other to the child himself. He also found that the first three-sign utterances consisted of three POINTs: "let's you and me go downstairs" POINT (to addressee) POINT (to self) POINT (down). Subsequent developments in the three-sign stage included one sign and two POINTs, two signs and one POINT, and finally three non-POINT signs. Hoffmeister's intention was to show that the POINT was part of the developmental sequence of ASL and that the child learning ASL used pointing gestures in a manner that was linguistically constrained and functional within a system, which a hearing child's pointing gestures would not be. This observation and his documentation of it should have a profound effect on how nonsigners view all the pointing that a signer uses. Often this pointing is interpreted as limiting a signer to talking about only those objects that are present in the room, "concretely-bound language." As we have seen, agreement points can be established in space for reference to nonpresent objects and persons, which represents a greater linguistic abstraction than pointing to visibly present objects. In fact, Hoffmeister found that a developmental sequence was present, such that the "concrete" pointing was acquired earlier than the abstract pointing. The significance for child language studies is easy to demonstrate. In Wilbur and Jones (1974), there occurred sequences of a noun sign followed by or preceded by a pointing gesture, which one might naïvely assume was there because the child lacked the linguistic ability to say what he wanted and chose to point instead, hoping to be understood. Locative POINTs were not separated from object reference POINTs, nor was it considered that such a distinction might exist. It was incorrectly decided that POINTs did not count. In looking back at the data, it is quite clear that for the subjects in Wilbur and Jones (1974), the earliest two-sign utterances were combinations of sign and POINT, and that such sequences occurred at least a month earlier than two non-POINT signs together. The POINT signs of these subjects obeyed the same type of constraints that Hoffmeister observed, but at that time, of course, it was not noticed.

Hoffmeister's study, as indicated previously, was part of a larger study. In all, some 500 hours of videotape were collected on about 10 deaf children of deaf parents for periods ranging up to about 5 years duration. As far as I know, this is the largest collection of data on the acquisition of sign language in the world. For his investigation of the role of pointing, Hoffmeister chose one child, named Alice, and backed up his findings by selectively sampling the data of other children. Alice's productions were divided into arbitrary units of 1000 utterances each, giving the following stages and ages: Stage I (29 months), Stage II (38 months), Stage III (45 months), Stage IV (50 months), and Stage V (52 months). Stages I through IV are remarkably similar in age to those reported by Fischer (1973b): Stage I (30 months), Stage II (36 months), Stage III (42 months), and Stage IV (48 months). Bear in mind that Fischer decided on her stages by 6-month age intervals (not developmental sequences) and Hoffmeister arrived at his by total output of utterances. Neither of these reports is intended to convey the concept of developmental stage by use of the word "stage" in their units of investigation (i.e., they do not mean stage in the same sense that Brown, 1973, uses it to refer to a range of linguistic development from MLU 1.0 to MLU 2.0).

In the expression of semantic relation, Hoffmeister reported that at Stage I, the use of a POINT and a noun for demonstrative+entity ("that book") or POINT and an adjective for demonstrative+attribute ("that (is) red") constituted 56.3% of all semantic relations expressed. By Stage II, this had decreased to 24.3%, by Stage III to 12.8%, and by Stages IV and V, to about 5%.

At Stage I, the POINT was used to indicate agent, patient, locative, object-possessed, and possessor, and was used syntactically as a demonstrative. All these POINTs had to be directed at a real world object or person visibly present in the environment. In the initial stage, these pointing gestures were constrained to the signer, the addressee, and third person objects present in the room. Also in the early part of Stage I, the possessor-possessed relationship was represented by a POINT to the object followed by a POINT to self, using the G hand for pointing. Later in Stage I, the adult B hand began to replace the G hand when referring to the possessor (but with considerable alternation between G and B). The possessed object again had to be present in the room. When using the B hand to indicate the possessor, the child could "back up" this production with an additional G hand POINT, just to be sure the message was correctly received. Also present in Stage I was the possessive construction N+N (as in "Mommy sock"). Plurals at this stage were indicated by repeated POINTs to the same object (i.e., "lamps" might be represented by pointing several times to a lamp), also sometimes accompanied by the sign MANY/MUCH or a numeral.

In Stage II, the POINT could now be made with a Y hand, herein glossed as THAT, even though it was not produced with the nondominant B hand, palm up, which is used in the citation form. Sometimes the POINT with G hand would be used as a backup for THAT. Occasionally, THAT would actually touch the real world object it was referring to, and then the POINT would be aimed at the object (but not contacted). In the possessive construction at this stage, the possessor could now be a third person (not just signer and addressee), and a new development, the use of HAVE, was seen: CAT HAVE LEG "The cat has a leg." For plurals, a continuous POINT to many pictures was used to mean "all"; pointing to two objects, each with a different hand, was used to mean "both of them"; and two fingers on one hand were used also to mean "both of these" (this latter is not necessarily the V hand, but is the precursor of the adult dual pronoun). In Stage II, Hoffmeister also observed that the POINT was used to establish a particular index, after which the verb was inflected to agree. (Stage II was also when Fischer first observed verb inflections.) In contrast to Kantor's findings of late acquisition of the by-legs classifier, Hoffmeister reported a single use at this stage, but did not indicate if its usage was completely correct. Also present was the use of the signer's body as a pronoun (SBP), as when Alice designated herself to be Goldilocks. In general, at this stage, the use of POINT to indicate reference was frequent.

In Stage III, Hoffmeister reported that developments were primarily in areas other than the POINT, with complex and conjoined sentences appearing. The signed English possessive affix 'S appeared in Alice's signing, correctly from the beginning, reflecting the influence of her schooling on her signing. In this stage, the requirement of real world referent started to fade. Alice set up her G hand as a substitute for SUN (definitely the wrong classifier) and then referred to her finger with the other hand. Hoffmeister commented that the G hand, which had performed so many functions for the child already, was now adapted for yet one more purpose.

In Stage IV, full control of all two- and three-unit semantic relations was observed. All possible forms of the possessive were correctly produced. The reflexive (Å hand) was begun, with the POINT again used as a backup. In the development of the use of the reflexive, one could see the entire developmental sequence reflected again. Aside from the initial backup of the POINT, the reflexive was also initially confined to reference within the conversational dyad (signer and addressee), after which outside third persons could be referenced. In addition, third person reference was at first restricted to real word objects, and then extended to objects that were not present. It is exceptional that this developmental sequence for reflexive was manifested in Stage IV, when control of the other pronominal and possessive POINTs had already been established for reference outside the dyad and to nonpresent objects. (For further details on this aspect, see Hoffmeister, 1978.) In Stage IV, the adult dual pronoun made with the V hand appeared. Finally, although Alice began to use reference to nonpresent objects in Stage III, the remaining control was established here in two ways. In one form, a real word object that was present in the room was used to substitute for another object that was not present. Thus, Alice pointed to a lamp near her while referring in her conversation to another lamp in her room which she had broken. In the other form, arbitrary points in space were established, and the verb was moved between them, with some usage of classifiers if needed, and with the backup of the familiar POINT just in case.

By Stage V, Alice had mastered adult use of the POINT, possessive, plural, reflexive, and verb agreement in terms of establishing arbitrary points in space.

Summary of Acquisition Studies

Although the acquisition studies are severely constrained in generality because of the small number of children studied so far, they nonetheless display similar developmental trends to those seen in acquisition studies of spoken language (which are also based on too few children). Semantic relations seem to develop in parallel fashion in spoken and sign language. Syntactic structures in ASL require several developmental stages before the child learns the correct adult form, as shown for verb inflection by Fischer, and for noun indexing, possessives, plurals, etc. by Hoffmeister. Overgeneralization of rules (e.g., "camed" and "wented" used by children learning English) is documented, demonstrating that the child learning sign language adopts similar acquisition strategies to the child learning to speak. Of interest also is the "fall back" seen in both Kantor's and Hoffmeister's studies. In Kantor's study, the child "fell back" on motorically simpler handshapes when faced with the necessity of making semantic and syntactic decisions in the use of the classifiers. In Hoffmeister's study, the child fell back on the G handshape as she developed from references within the conversational dyad to reference outside of the conversational dyad, and from real world referents to established nonpresent referents.

Unanswered questions remain. How does a child learning to sign acquire the scope of the meaning of a sign? The same question has only begun to be answered for hearing children because of the difficulty in determining what a child thinks something means, as well as the interaction with necessary cognitive development for full interpretation of a word's denotations and connotations. Another question then is what (if any) effect does the visual/spatial modality have on the cognitive development of the child? R. Kantor and M. Bernstein at Boston University are investigating aspects of these questions. Kantor is looking at the interactions of deaf mothers and deaf children as communicative competence develops, and Bernstein (1978) is looking at the role of visual representation in locative predicates (e.g., ON) as it interacts with cognitive and linguistic development (of the concept of, for example, "on-ness"). In addition, the child's acquisition of appropriate facial expression remains to be investigated.

PRODUCTION AND PERCEPTION OF SIGNS

Many of the early linguistic and psycholinguistic studies of ASL were aimed at demonstrating that ASL was in fact a language in its own right. In the process of trying to make this point, psycholinguists were led into some of the less often studied aspects of language use. Thus, included in this section are aspects of pausing, rhythm, breathing, blinking, and the control of conversation. The information derived from these investigations supports the positions presented in Chapter 4 that there is structure to the ASL sentence, that this structure may include hierarchies that parallel internal constituent structure as described for spoken languages, and that this structure affects aspects of the perception and production process. Without the benefit of a comprehensive grammatical description for ASL, psycholinguists have begun by observing measurable variables and then deriving syntactic information from their measurements. Word order was, of course, a prime target for investigation.

Using a memory paradigm, Hoemann and Florian (1976) found that random sequencing of signs produced less meaningful strings, as might be expected based on the Chapter 4 discussion. Not only was meaningfulness reduced by random ordering, but apparently recall was also affected. This is in keeping with the findings of Miller and Isard (1963), who reported that, for English, random organization of words or correct organization but significant reduction in meaningfulness resulted in significantly poorer recall. Tweney and Heiman (1977), also using a memory paradigm, presented nonsense signs or a fingerspelled consonant-vowel-consonant (CVC) sequence embedded in either a grammatical sentence or a random string of signs. The number of nonsense signs and overall number of signs recalled were significantly greater in the grammatical strings than in the random strings. Such studies serve to demonstrate the role of grammatical structure in the processing of ASL and the similarity of sign language processing to spoken language processing.

Other studies, discussed below, investigated particular consequences of ASL structure on processing.

Comparisons of Signing and Speaking

In a series of studies that investigated performance variables such as pausing, rate of signing, and breathing, Grosjean (1977, 1978; Grosjean and Lane, 1977) reported similarities and differences between the two language modes. Parallel to the studies of pausing and syntax in spoken languages (Grosjean and Deschamps, 1975), Grosjean and Lane (1977) found that the longest pauses in a signed story appeared at what might be considered the boundary between two sentences, that shorter pauses appeared between constituents that can be analyzed as parts of a conjoined sentence, and that the shortest pauses appeared between internal constituents of the sentence. Pauses that would not normally show up in conversational signing because of their brevity were elicited by asking signers to sign at half their normal rate and at a quarter of their normal rate. Grosjean and Collins (1978) reported that for English, pauses with durations of greater than 445 msec occurred at sentence boundaries; pauses between 245 and 445 msec occurred between conjoined sentences, between noun phrases and verb phrases, and between a complement and the following noun phrase; and pauses of less than 245 msec occurred within phrasal constituents. Grosjean and Lane's (1977) findings for ASL were that pauses between sentences had a mean of 229 msec, pauses between conjoined sentences had a mean of 134 msec, pauses between NP and VP had a mean of 106 msec, pauses within the NP had a mean of 6 msec, and pauses within the VP had a mean of 11 msec. These results are interpreted as clearly showing that sign sentences are organized hierarchically and that the signs are not strung together without internal constituents (i.e., not as a Markov chain). This supports analyses such as Kegl's, Liddell's, and Fischer's, reviewed in Chapter 4, although it cannot be used to decide between conflicting claims about how the constituents are internally structured. Not specifically addressed in this study was an observation made by Grosjean (in press) that speakers when reading out loud tend to try and cut a sentence into two equals parts, possibly for rhythmic purposes, and that signers appeared to be doing some of the same (both signers and speakers are, of course, constrained by the syntax of the sentence they are producing). This type of intonation and its interaction with that discussed by Fischer (1975) and Liddell (1977) remains to be specifically addressed.

The technique of asking signers to slow their rate of signing created some interesting questions. Grosjean (1977) investigated in detail the effects of rate change, again comparing signers to speakers. If a speaker doubles his actual reading rate, he feels himself to have increased by six times, whereas a listener perceives an increase of three times (Lane and Grosjean, 1973). Thus, produced rates and perceived rates differ in spoken language. Similarly, if a signer increases his signing rate by two, he perceives an increase by six, whereas an observer (signer or nonsigner) perceives an increase by three (Grosjean, 1977). However, unlike Lane and Grosjean (1977), Grosjean (1977) found that when readers double their rate of reading, listeners perceive an increase by four. Regardless of which listener rate is used, the overall effect seems to be that judgments of self-production of speech or signing rates are equivalent for speakers and signers, but that judgments of perceived speech rates tend to be overestimated more than perceived rates of signing. Grosjean suggested that the similarity in judgments on the part of the producers (speaker or signer) may be attributable to similar muscle feedback (despite the different articulation in the two modalities), whereas the differences in the perceivers may be attributable to the different perception systems in use, visual vs. auditory.

Grosjean (1978) looked at the differences in how signers and speakers were able to accomplish these changes in rate. Speakers tend to change the amount of time they pause, whereas signers tend to adjust the time they spend articulating. Grosjean showed that the time spent articulating a sign is modified directly by changes in movement as opposed to any other parameter (e.g., addition of extra location, modification of handshape, etc.). If a signer does modify his pause time, it generally affects both the number of pauses and the length of the pause. On the other hand, speakers primarily alter the number of pauses but not the pause durations, which have a minimum duration of the time needed for a breath. Interestingly, although speakers, because of the very nature of the speech process, must breathe between words, primarily at syntactic breaks, signers maintain normal breathing rhythm while signing, although breathing rate may be affected by the physical effort required to sign at, for instance, three times the normal rate. Grosjean also found that signs tend to be longer in sentence final position than within sentences, and that the first occurrence of a sign within a single conversation is longer than the second or subsequent occurrences of that same sign (controlling for syntactic position).

One further aspect of speaking and signing rate is the comparison done by Bellugi and Fischer (1972) of the time needed to relate a story in both modalities. The same story produced in both modalities contained the same number of propositions, covered the same semantic ground, and took about the same amount of time to produce. However, the modality made a difference: 50% more spoken words than signs were needed (as a result of the differences in ASL and English syntax) but were nonetheless produced in the same amount of time, since spoken words take considerably less time to produce than signs. One implication of this study is that, at some level of processing, there is an optimum time or rate for transmission of information regardless of modality. The finding that signed English (see Chapters 6 and 7) sentences for this same story increased the story time (but not the number of propositions) by almost 50% can possibly be interpreted as a negative indication for signed English use (see "Memory," Chapter 8).

Pause duration may serve as a marker for sentence boundaries. Conversations, of course, must have beginnings and ends also. Eye contact, among other variables, plays a significant role in the marking of conversational turns. A conversation cannot begin without direct eye contact between the signer and the receiver. During the conversation, the addressee must continue to watch the signer, but the signer need not maintain eye contact with the addressee. As in oral conversation, the sender is free to look away, for purposes of organizing thought or to maintain the floor, but must check back with the addressee every so often to be certain that the addressee is following the conversation. A signer can ignore an interruption by not establishing eye contact with the person attempting to interrupt (Baker, 1976, 1977).

Covington (1973a,b) and Baker (1977) have reported on junctures that mark turns within the conversation. For example, Baker (1977) reported on several hand positions that are part of the regulators of turn-taking. When a signer is listening and not intending to take a turn, the hands remain at full extension. When a signer is preparing to sign, perhaps to interrupt or simply waiting for a turn but wanting the present signer to acknowledge that he is waiting, the hands assume half-rest position, generally at waist level and with increased body tension (possibly a slight lean forward). Hands higher than this are in quarter-rest position, a strong indication to the current signer to yield the floor. Of course, a signer can simply begin to sign and hope that the other signer will yield the floor (doing this too forcefully or too often is as rude as it is in speech). The floor is yielded by returning hands to full-rest position or maybe half-rest as an indication of wanting the floor back as soon as possible.

Baker and Padden (1978) investigated the blinking behavior of deaf signers engaged in conversation. As Grosjean and Lane (1977) indicated, speakers do not breathe in the middle of a spoken word but signers may breathe anywhere they please. Baker and Padden reported that speakers may blink anywhere they please whereas signers do not blink in the middle of a sign. Signers appear to blink at phrase boundaries, such as between subject and predicate, or setting off a direct object, or after a time indicator (e.g., YESTERDAY, TOMORROW, etc.). In conditional sentences, signers tend to blink between the first and second clauses if the conditional is a statement but not if it is a question (see "More Nonmanual Signs," Chapter 4). Finally, the addressee does not take his cue of when to blink from the signer (as evidenced by signer blinks not followed by addressee blinks, as well as addressee blinks that immediately precede signer blinks) but nonetheless blinks at grammatical boundaries, indicating that the addressee is anticipating when these boundaries will occur. Baker and Padden suggested that this may be an aid to the linguistic processing of incoming information.

CEREBRAL LATERALIZATION

Research from neuropathology and neuropsychology studies has documented an apparent separation or specialization of the cerebral hemispheres for linguistic or nonlinguistic processing. These reports include the disruption of language and other functions (orienting oneself in space, etc.) from brain damage as well as controlled experimentation on dichotic and visual half-field tasks with normal hearing adults. From these studies, one can infer that in the majority of right-handed hearing adults, the left hemisphere seems to be specialized for language processing and other types of temporal sequencing and analytic tasks, whereas the right hemisphere seems to be more involved in holistic visual-spatial tasks (this statement is greatly simplified, but suffices for purposes at present).

Because of this apparent hemispheric dichotomy, the relationship between cerebral dominance and sign language has recently commanded greater attention. The central issue of concern is how the brain would treat a language that is visual/spatial in modality. The left hemisphere might be supposed to specialize for ASL because it is a language, or the right hemisphere might be supposed to specialize for ASL because it is visual/spatial. It might also be supposed that determining the answer to this question should be an easy matter. Recent literature (reviewed in both Poizner and Lane, 1977, and Neville and Bellugi 1978) and a caveat from Obler (in press) reveal why this is not so.

Empirical Investigations

As background for the methodology of the McKeever et al. (1976) study, consider how a standard dichotic listening test is conducted with hearing adults. Two messages are presented simultaneously through earphones to the left and right ears of the listener. The listener is required to report what he heard. The accuracy of report for each ear, as well as the order of report, the latency or response time of report, and in some cases the evoked electrical potential in each hemisphere, may be of relevance in determining the lateralization or dominance of the listener. In most cases, material presented to the right ear (left hemisphere) is reported better (faster, more accurately, with higher evoked potential and quicker peaking of the electric signal) than that presented to the left ear (right hemisphere) when the material is linguistic in nature; this is possibly reversed for nonlinguistic material. To translate this task for deaf people and for ASL is complicated by two major factors: 1) the eyes are not connected to the brain in the same way that the ears are (each ear "connects" primarily to the opposite hemisphere, and each eye is "connected" equally to both hemispheres, thus requiring a division of each eye's field of sight into hemifields, one connected to the ipsilateral hemisphere, the other connected to the contralateral hemisphere), and 2) ASL moves in space as well as in time, thereby rendering traditional tachistoscopic presentation either difficult or unsuitable. To avoid this latter diffi- culty, McKeever et al. (and several of the next studies also) used only line drawings of ASL signs, line drawings of manual alphabet hand- shapes, and English letters and words. Material was presented appro- priately to the visual hemifields. Hearing subjects showed significant left hemispheric advantage to two of the three tasks involving English words or letters, but the deaf subjects showed left hemispheric advan- tage in only one of the tasks involving English stimuli. On the other two English tasks, they showed no hemispheric difference; however both the nonhearing and the hearing subjects showed right hemispheric advantages for the manual alphabet handshapes and the ASL signs. Poizner and Lane (1977) indicate that this study contains several meth- odological problems, among which are the failure to present nonlin- guistic materials to determine what, if any, lateralization exists (needed to compare with linguistic results), the fact that the hearing and deaf subjects used different response modes, making their results not di- rectly comparable, and most importantly, the data analysis which pooled the high recognition scores for the manual alphabet tasks with the comparably lower scores for the ASL tasks, thus skewing the analysis toward the manual alphabet stimuli.

In their initial study, Manning et al. (1977) presented English words and line drawings, but also included random geometrical shapes (presumably right hemispheric) to deaf subjects and the words and geometric shapes to the hearing subjects. As expected, the hearing subjects displayed a significant left hemispheric advantage for the English words; the deaf subjects showed only a trend in that direction. For the remaining conditions (signs and geometric shapes for the deaf, shapes for the hearing) no hemispheric differences were recorded.

A second study by Manning et al. presented photographs of signs, signs and their corresponding English translation together, and English words alone to deaf subjects and English words alone to the hearing subjects. Unlike Manning et al.'s initial study, in this one the response modes for both groups of subjects was the same, with the subjects required to indicate the appropriate picture on a response board. Again, as expected, the hearing subjects showed a significant left hemispheric advantage for the English words, whereas the deaf subjects showed a trend toward left advantage for the words alone and a trend toward right advantage for the signs alone. The combined sign and English word stimuli revealed little or no hemispheric differences.

Among the methodological problems in the Manning et al. study discussed by Poizner and Lane (1977) are the lack of clear indication of subjects' knowledge and fluency of ASL, a definite concern of cerebral dominance studies with any language (Obler, in press), and the fact that some signs used were not bilaterally symmetric (two-handed signs that have the same handshape and the same or mirror image movement are bilaterally symmetrical around the axis from head to foot down the center of the front of the body, whereas all one-handed signs, and two-handed signs where only one hand moves, are not bilaterally symmetric). This latter factor creates difficulty with respect to visual acuity in terms of the stimuli distance from the fixation point (cf. Siple, 1973).

Phippard's (1977) study included two groups of deaf subjects, one group of orally trained deaf subjects, the other group trained in both oral and manual communication. English letters, variously oriented lines, and faces were presented to the hearing controls; English letters and lines were presented to the orally trained deaf; English letters, lines, manual alphabet handshapes, and faces were presented to the deaf subjects with combined manual and oral communication. The hearing subjects performed as expected, with left hemispheric advantage for the English letters and right hemispheric advantage for the lines and faces. The orally trained deaf adults showed right hemispheric advantages for both the English letters and the lines, whereas the subjects with familiarity in manual communication showed no visual field preferences for the four stimuli types. Poizner and Lane (1977) suggested that interpretation problems for lateralization of ASL were confounded again by lack of indication of knowledge of ASL as a native language, and also by the presentation of manual alphabet handshapes but no signs.

Lubert's (1975) study is similar in nature to the preceding studies, in that materials were presented tachistoscopically with English letters, photographs of ASL signs that did not require movement to be identified, photographs of manual alphabet handshapes, and a dot enumeration task. Unlike the previous studies, the hearing subjects did not show the expected left hemispheric advantage for the English letters, thereby complicating the interpretation of all the other results. Both deaf and hearing subjects showed right hemispheric advantage to the photographs of ASL signs, and no preferences for the dots or the manual handshapes.

Neville and Bellugi (1978) presented to deaf subjects line drawings of a person making signs, 22 of which were bilaterally symmetrical and 20 of which were not (these latter were made on the face, using the right hand for presentation in the right visual field and the left hand for the left visual field). In addition, a dot localization task was used for deaf and hearing subjects (a dot was presented in one of 20 possible positions in a rectangle, and subjects were required to indicate on a response grid where the dot had been). Subjects were tested in both unilateral and bilateral presentation conditions, although hearing subjects found bilateral presentation of the dot localization condition too difficult for it to be continued.

No difference was found in the deaf subjects' performance on the symmetrical and asymmetrical signs, and they were therefore collapsed, yielding a left hemispheric advantage for the unilateral presentation but no differences for the bilateral presentations. Similarly, the deaf subjects showed left hemispheric advantage for the dot localization task when presented unilaterally, but no differences when presented bilaterally. As expected, the hearing subjects showed right hemispheric advantages for the dot localization task.

Neville and Bellugi's discussion of these results adds an interesting dimension to the original alternatives presented in the introduction to this section. First, the fact that there is hemispheric preference for unilateral presentation but not bilateral presentation seems to be partially explicable by a strategy adopted by the deaf subjects to handle the task requirements, namely, to focus their attention (but not their eye gaze) on one visual field for several items, then switch to the other field for the next few items, and then switch back, giving a net effect of no preference. Second, the left hemispheric advantage for signs is an indication of cerebral lateralization for language developing independently from language modality. However, they interpret the left hemispheric advantage for the dot localization task as evidence that because the language modality is visual/spatial, and because the left hemisphere is handling the language, it is also handling the visual/ spatial components which would be right hemispherically lateralized in the person who learns a spoken language. They suggest that this is analogous to the findings that hearing people show left hemispheric advantage for judgments of temporally sequenced nonlinguistic material, presumably because temporal processing is a major function of the left hemisphere (participating, for example, in processing fine distinctions in speech perception).

Poizner and Lane (1977) tachistoscopically presented adult deaf native signers and hearing nonsigners with photographs of the ASL numbers SIX, SEVEN, EIGHT, and NINE (none of which requires movement); photographs of nonoccurring handshapes; Arabic numbers 6, 7, 8, and 9 in print; and four randomly shaped geometric forms. For the hearing subjects, a left hemispheric preference was found for the Arabic digits and a right hemispheric advantage for the ASL signed numbers and the non-ASL handshapes. The deaf subjects showed a right hemispheric advantage for the ASL signed numbers and the non-ASL handshapes. Neither group showed hemispheric advantage for the randomly shaped geometric forms.

Poizner and Lane argued that the right hemispheric advantage arose from processing the "complex spatial properties of the static signs." They suggested that their results are incompatible with theories that assign language to the left hemisphere and visual/spatial processing to the right. They also suggested, but did not discuss, the possibility that ASL may be bilaterally processed. They suggested that their results indicate that language processing of ASL "engages" the left hemisphere, and that the visual/spatial processing of ASL "engages" the right hemisphere, and that the visual/spatial processing in the right hemisphere predominates.

In reviewing the literature, Poizner and Lane (1977) put forth as their major criticism the fact that all previous studies were performed with statically presented signs and that one cannot really know how processing of moving language is done until a more real world experimental condition is constructed. Poizner, Battison, and Lane (1978) presented three types of stimuli—English words, static signs, and signs portrayed with movement—to deaf native signers. Hearing controls viewed only the English words. For the moving presentation, three frames displayed the beginning, middle, and end points of the sign for a total exposure of time of 167 msec; for the static signs, the total exposure time was also 167 msec and consisted of three identical frames of the same sign. As expected, the hearing subjects showed a left hemispheric advantage to the English words. The deaf subjects also showed a left hemispheric advantage to the English words, but a right hemispheric advantage to the static signs. Most importantly, the deaf subjects showed no hemispheric advantage for the moving signs. Poizner, Battison, and Lane interpreted this as possible evidence that ASL requires more bilateral participation than spoken English. However, this interpretation may require further modification in light of the spoken language results reported by Obler (in press).

A Caveat on Interpretation

Obler's (in press) investigation is not a study of cerebral dominance in sign language users, nor is it concerned with deaf subjects at all. Instead it is concerned with the development of cerebral dominance in bilingual hearing adults, with the factors that can affect how this dominance is established, and is thus directly relevant to the interpretation of the results of the preceding experiments. Obler indicates that a review of the experimental and aphasiological literature reveals a generally greater right hemispheric participation (or less pronounced left lateralization) in bilinguals than in monolinguals. She also indicates that the development of dominance may be influenced by such factors as "language-specific effects" (e.g., direction of reading scan, such as right-to-left for Hebrew vs. left-to-right for English), cognitive strategies used in teaching the second language (so-called deductive teaching where traditional drilling is used vs. inductive teaching where conversational approaches are used). All of these may be relevant to the deaf signer even if native, since no deaf adults in the United States have escaped some exposure to the second language teaching of English. They are therefore to some degree (some obviously more than others) bilinguals, and thus the possibility of a greater right hemispheric contribution to the processing of ASL regardless of its visual/spatial properties cannot be dismissed out of hand. This does not mean that ASL will be "in" the right hemisphere or that the left hemisphere is not involved, only that any bilingual situation seems to be confounded by a greater general right hemispheric participation.

MEMORY FOR ASL

Studies of memory with hearing adults have indicated that adults tend to make mistakes in recall based on the phonological properties of the words they hear, particularly if the possibility of utilizing semantic information has been eliminated by the task design. Such studies have determined that several features that constitute a sound segment are crucial to memory coding and recall, even when the material to be remembered is presented visually (e.g., printed word lists) (Conrad, 1962; Wickelgren, 1965). Bellugi and Siple (1974) conducted a similar study to investigate memory for signs in deaf adults. They found that the deaf subjects' performance was similar to that of the hearing in that they made mistakes based on the formational characteristics of the signs themselves. For example, given the word "tea," a hearing person might mistakenly recall it as *key* because of the similar phonological properties. However, a deaf person might mistakenly recall the sign TEA as the sign VOTE, which differs from TEA only in motion. Bellugi and Siple (1974) and Bellugi, Klima, and Siple (1975) reported that mistakes were made according to handshape, place of formation, and motion (orientation and other features like contact were not investigated). Whether there exists a hierarchy of these features is an intriguing question. From the Bellugi memory studies and the acquisition studies mentioned earlier (Kantor, 1977; Wilbur and Jones, 1974) it might be inferred that location would be best remembered, motion next, and handshape and orientation least remembered. However, Freidman (1977), in a short-term memory study, reported exactly the reverse, although the study is confounded by the use of nonsense signs and non-native signers who were not congenitally deaf. Thus further research remains to be done in this area.

Other studies with deaf subjects (Conrad, 1970, 1971, 1972, 1973; Conrad and Rush, 1965; Locke, 1970; Locke and Locke, 1971) have investigated the roles of English phonemics, visual graphemes, and dactylic (fingerspelling) coding in memory processing but have not specifically attended to the possible role of sign features. These studies were primarily concerned with how the deaf person as a bilingual would handle memory processing for English. This question still remains unanswered and is of primary concern for the development of appropriate educational technology, as well as for the theoretical implications for memory (and possibly cerebral) organization. Wilbur (1974a) suggested that, as hearing people seem to convert visually presented written material into its corresponding phonological representation for coding and storage, perhaps deaf people who know ASL utilize it for the coding and recall of written English, converting the English to a sign representation much as a compound bilingual might do. (This hypothesis would still presume the absence of the possibility of using a semantic representation strategy, as one would normally do in more real world situations, e.g., a conversation.) Some support for this hypothesis comes from a study done by Odom, Blanton, and

McIntyre (1970). They compared recall accuracy of deaf signers and hearing nonsigners on two lists of English words—those for which there exists an appropriate ASL equivalent and those for which there is no exact convenient simple sign, thus necessitating fingerspelling. The results were as hypothesized: the deaf subjects performed significantly better on the list of signable words; the hearing subjects, of course, showed no difference between the two lists. Also interesting was the fact that the performance of the deaf subjects on the list of signable words was significantly superior to the performance of the hearing subjects on both lists.

Further research is obviously needed here also. One aspect that must constantly be kept in mind is the interaction of the bilingual nature of many deaf people with the task requirements. Harlan Lane (personal communication) has emphasized the need to avoid creating a "set" for English processing, perhaps by requiring English output, or by giving instructions in English, or by inviting English processing by presenting obviously rhyming English words. Great care must be taken to avoid contaminating memory study results, particularly when potential cross-lingual processing is the desired target of investigation.

SUMMARY

This chapter has presented the empirical results of several recent studies on iconicity, sign language acquisition, perception and production of signs compared to speech, cerebral lateralization for ASL, and memory processing. From the iconicity studies, it has been argued that signs are not transparent to the nonsigner, with a few exceptions. Thus, transparency and iconicity are not strictly the same thing, because although the sign may not be guessable, it may still bear some relationship to its meaning or referent. Several possible relationships between signs and their referents were suggested by Mandel. A recent empirical study by Pearl (1978) has investigated memory for signs as a function of different types of iconic relationships (metonymy vs. metaphor). Other questions have yet to be addressed: 1) What effect, if any, does the (type of) iconicity of a sign have on its learnability? Although Brown (1977) and others have addressed this question in hearing children and adults, the development of young deaf children learning signs as a native language (and the parallel cognitive development) have not yet been studied. M. Bernstein (1978) has proposed a study which will investigate deaf native signing children's acquisition of the concepts of "in," "on," and "under" as it may be affected by the visual representation of "in-ness" in the sign IN, "on-ness" in the sign ON, and "under-ness" in the sign UNDER, whereas the spoken English words do not convey this extra information. Must a child cognitively handle the concepts of "in," "on," and "under" before the iconicity of IN, ON, and UNDER becomes apparent, or does the visual representation in IN, ON, and UNDER contribute to the child's acquisition of the linguistic concepts? 2) If the iconicity of signs is shown to be an aid to learning and memory retention in, for example, hearing adults, can the learnability of noniconic signs be increased by "creating" an explanation or story as to why they are produced the way they are? Can retarded and autistic populations be assisted in learning and retention by inducing awareness of the iconicity of signs (discussed further in Chapter 9)? 3) How do the concepts of transparent, translucent, and opaque relate to the synchronic analyzability of a sign (on knowing the meaning, one can see why it means what it does) as opposed to the need for historical information to reconstruct the sign's former iconicity (e.g., the sign for HOME when made with two flatO hands at the cheek is not synchronically analyzable, but is reconstructable when the etymology that it comes from EAT and SLEEP is supplied)?

Finally, in the section on iconicity, it was argued that whatever visual representation there is in a sign language is constrained to obey the sign structure conditions, the syntactic regulations, and the pragmatic conventions. Similarly, in spoken languages, the rooster crow, cat meow, dog bark, etc., are described differently in different languages so that they fit the constraints of each language.

From the acquisition studies, it can be concluded that there are developmental sequences in the acquisition of ASL, that the time scales for ASL acquisition and spoken language acquisition are similar with the possibility that ASL acquisition may initially be accelerated, and that ASL acquisition, like spoken language acquisition, is affected by motor complexity, syntactic complexity, and semantic complexity, as illustrated by the Kantor study on classifiers. For further research, one can identify several distinct populations of interest: deaf children of deaf parents (studies desperately needed below age 2), deaf children of signing hearing parents below school age (Hoffmeister and Dworski, 1978; Hoffmeister and Goodhart, 1978), hearing children of deaf parents (an initial joint effort is in progress with Lee Williams from University of Denver, Peyton Todd from University of Tennessee, Jacqueline Sachs from University of Connecticut, Ann Strominger from Children's Hospital in Boston, Madeline Maxwell from Pennsylvania State University, and this author), and occasionally for comparative purposes (Hoffmeister and Dworski, 1978), hearing children of hearing parents (nonsigning).

In the perception and production comparisons of signing and speaking, the effect of modality is most clearly seen. Breathing is a critical factor in speaking, but not in signing, whereas blinking is critical to signing but apparently not to speaking.

The most recent lateralization studies indicate that the movement of signs may be crucial to how they are perceived and processed, and that previously reported right hemispheric advantages with statically presented signs disappear when the signs are presented with their movement.

Memory processes related to ASL are the least well studied, and have been primarily confined to isolated word lists. Short- and long-term memory for both ASL and English need to be studied, keeping in mind at all times the bilingual nature of the majority of deaf people.

Finally, shadowing techniques, such as those suggested by Mayberry (1977) for facial expression and McIntire and Yamada (1976) for syntax, need to be further explored for their potential ASL research.

CHAPTER 6

SOCIOLINGUISTIC ASPECTS OF ASL USAGE

CONTENTS

In Chapter 1, ASL and its nearest relatives were discussed. This chapter examines Woodward's (1978) argument that ASL was not "invented" or "started" in France, but that it developed naturally over time, and that it absorbed French signs when they were introduced in 1817, much the way English absorbed many French words after the Norman conquest in 1066. As a natural language, ASL has considerable variation; it is affected by factors such as geography, age and education of the signer, and formality of the situation in which the conversation is taking place. Interaction between deaf and hearing people is greatly affected by the hearing person's general unfamiliarity with ASL and the degree of familiarity with English possessed by the deaf person. In such situations, the use of pidgin (neither group's daily language) has developed (Pidgin Sign English). A signer's fluency in ASL may make him eligible for membership in the deaf community, bound together by linguistic factors rather than just deafness (some members may be hard of hearing or even hearing). This situation contributes significantly to the difficulty of obtaining unbiased information on the structure of ASL and its role in the lives of deaf people. No matter what level of fluency a hearing signer attains, it should never be assumed that conversations with native deaf ASL users are actually being conducted in ASL rather than in Pidgin Sign English.

IN THE BEGINNING

One frequently asked question about ASL is "Where did it come from and when did it start?" One approach to answering the question is to point out the parallel difficulty of answering the question "Where did spoken language come from?" Many theories of the origin of spoken language still compete—the Tower of Babel, a gift from outer space, from the cries of emotions, even that the first languages may have been manual languages which became spoken as man needed his hands for other tasks. Whatever the origins, one thing is clear—where there are humans, there is language.

Nonetheless, one can read in the literature on education of the deaf or on sign language that Thomas Hopkins Gallaudet went to France to study the method of signs and brought back Laurent Clerc, a deaf teacher. The two established the American Asylum for the Education and Instruction of the Deaf and Dumb in 1817 (now the American School for the Deaf in Hartford, Connecticut), which used modified French Sign Language. It is to that point that many people trace the origin of ASL. Woodward (1978) takes issue with this version of ASL history, citing a number of factors that make it highly improbable that these two men were responsible for the establishment of an entire language. The fact that Gallaudet was hearing and Clerc a foreigner (who also strongly encouraged assimilation into the hearing world) makes them both unlikely role models.

If ASL was indeed a direct descendant from the French Sign Language (FSL), introduced in America in 1817, one would expect modern ASL and modern FSL to have a very large number of signs or cognates in common. Glottochronological techniques (Gudschinsky, 1964) can be used to calculate how long ago two languages split by the number of cognates that exist. One standard procedure is to compare two languages on the Swadesh 200-word list. When Woodward (1978) compared the ASL signs for these words with those listed in Oleron (1974), a dictionary of modern FSL, only 61% were cognates. This percentage would date the split between ASL and FSL at between 504 A.D. and 1172 A.D. (with a 90% confidence level). A second analysis was made, comparing the same French signs to those of an 80-year-old man who had attended the Kendall School, Washington, D.C., and who had conversed with Clerc as a child (thus, second generation ASL by the standard history). Again, 61% of the pairs were cognates.

Next, Woodward compared all 872 available FSL signs with their counterparts in ASL, both with younger signers and with the 80-year-old man. These analyses yielded about 57% cognates, which would date the split of FSL and ASL at between 584 A.D. and 835 A.D. Although not all researchers agree on the validity of using these techniques, the resulting figures are so far off the 1817 date that one must suspect either the statistics or the purported history. Woodward, using Russian Sign Language and ASL for data, provides evidence that manual languages change at about the same rate as (or even slightly slower than) spoken languages. Thus if the figures are in error, it is in the direction of underestimating how long ago the two languages would have had to split. Woodward argues instead that the data strongly support a creolization of the FSL signs and whatever signs (i.e., older ASL) were here before Gallaudet and Clerc started their teaching. Furthermore, most of the changes in these forms seem to have occurred in the early to mid-1800s (there is about 90% agreement between modern ASL and records from 1913 to 1918).

VARIATION WITHIN ASL

Woodward (1972, 1973a,b,c, 1974b,c, 1975, 1976a) and Woodward and Erting (1975) investigated several dialects of ASL, primarily Black and White Southern signing, and found 1) that these dialects support the historical changes reported by Frishberg (1975, 1976a), 2) that these dialects indicate that certain of these processes are still in progress, and 3) that other changes not reported by Frishberg seemed to occur. For example, Frishberg reported that signs tended to move up from the waist as part of the centralization trend, but Woodward and Erting found that signs like YOUNG were still made on the waist for some signers. Similarly, Frishberg reported the tendency toward symmetry which often resulted in a one-handed sign becoming two-handed. Woodward and Erting found that in some Black Louisiana signers, DIE/DEAD/KILL was still made with only one hand.

Woodward continued his investigation into the relationship between French Sign Language and American Sign Language as it is reflected in the historical changes that have occurred and in the sociolinguistic variation that exists. Frishberg reported that two-handed signs made on or in front of the face tended to become one-handed. Thus the two-handed versions are older. Woodward and DeSantis (1977a) found that users of modern FSL tended to use more two-handed versions than users of ASL, and that White Americans over the age of 47 tended to use older forms more than Whites under the age of 47. These demographic variables illustrate the widespread systematic variation that can occur.

Woodward (1976b) extensively discussed handshape changes that have occurred. He illustrated four basic types of changes: thumb extension (rule of thumb, Battison, Markowicz, and Woodward, 1975), simplification, metathesis, and maximal differentiation. Variation in location, motion (Woodward, 1976b), and use of face (Woodward, Erting, and Oliver, 1976) have recently been documented.

Battison, Markowicz, and Woodward (1975) reported on the tendency in some dialects for the thumb to be extended in the formation of G and H handshapes. They suggested that this change might be attributable to naturalness of articulation. Several FSL signs have undergone this change to produce modern ASL signs: PLAY, made in FSL with I handshape, now made with Y (I plus extended thumb) in ASL; ACCIDENT, made in FSL with S handshape, made in ASL with A handshape (S plus extended thumb).

Simplification of handshape occurs when the nondominant hand is no longer required to make a sign, and the base hand is usually assimilated to the dominant hand: in FSL, WHEN is made with a B hand and a G hand, in ASL it is made with two G hands; FSL BAD (ASL WORSE) is made with one S hand and one V hand, but it is made in ASL with two V hands.

Metathesis of handshape refers to switching of handshapes from one hand to the other. FSL START is made with a nondominant G and a dominant V; ASL START is made with a nondominant V and a dominant G. Similarly, FSL SHOW is made with nondominant G and dominant B, but ASL SHOW is made with nondominant B and dominant G.

Woodward defined maximal differentiation of handshape (also applicable to movement) as a reversal of perceptible features. Handshape can contrast in relative openness or closeness of the hands. A and S are maximally closed, B and 5 are maximally open. C is medially open—all the fingers are open but are also bent. Some FSL signs with maximally closed A handshape are related to ASL signs with B or C. Some FSL signs with closed S changed to ASL open 5. Woodward diagrammed the historical relation between maximally open, medially open, and maximally closed as:

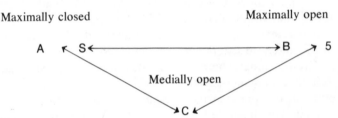

Maximally closed   Maximally open

A   S ⟷ B   5

Medially open

C

He suggested that C may be an intermediate stage in the process of maximal differentiation.

ASL VARIETIES (GRAMMATICAL DIFFERENCES)

Dialect information that has been gathered indicates that there are many forms of ASL. Stokoe (1970b) pointed out that there is a diglossic situation in the deaf community, such that each signer may have available to him several forms of ASL for different communicative contexts. One may view the varieties as a continuum, with ASL at one end and signed English at the other. Informal conversations would tend toward the ASL end, whereas formal speeches, school settings, and the presence of a hearing person would require more English-like signing. Viewed within a two-dimensional model suggested by Stokoe, informal and formal ASL are at one end, and informal and formal signed English at the other. Woodward refers to an intermediate variety of Pidgin Sign English, when the syntactic order is basically English, but inflections and other structures have been modified.

Just as the handshapes of signs vary from dialect to dialect, so Woodward found that the application of syntactic and morphological rules varied. Three rules, agent-beneficiary incorporation, negative incorporation, and verb reduplication, are discussed in detail here.

Woodward (1973a) investigated the possibility of reduplicating the following nine verbs: MEET, MEMORIZE, SEE, WANT, STUDY, READ, KNOW, RUN, and DRIVE. He found that they are implicationally ordered, such that a signer who can reduplicate MEET can reduplicate all of the others, but not necessarily vice versa. The possibilities are given in Table 15. A signer in lect 6 (characteristics of lects are given in detail below), for example, can use and accept reduplication of READ, KNOW, RUN, and DRIVE, but not the others. Lects 6–10, in which less than half of the forms can be reduplicated, are considered most English-like (English does not have productive reduplication, especially not of verbs), whereas lects 1–5, which allow a wider range of reduplication, are considered more ASL-like.

Woodward (1974a) found a similar implicational hierarchy in his investigation of a negative incorporation. Several verbs may add a negative affix, which is an outward twisting movement of the hands. Before discussing the implicational hierarchy that Woodward found and its eventual implication for sign language research, some relevant history of the process of negative incorporation is offered.

Woodward and DeSantis (1977b) discussed this history in detail. According to them, negative incorporation is a purely phonological process in French Sign Language, where the verb is traditionally

Table 15. Verb reduplication implication

Lects	"Meet"	"Memorize"	"See"	"Want"	"Study"	"Read"	"Know"	"Run"	"Drive"
1	+	+	+	+	+	+	+	+	+
2	−	+	+	+	+	+	+	+	+
3	−	−	+	+	+	+	+	+	+
4	−	−	−	+	+	+	+	+	+
5	−	−	−	−	+	+	+	+	+
6	−	−	−	−	−	+	+	+	+
7	−	−	−	−	−	−	+	+	+
8	−	−	−	−	−	−	−	+	+
9	−	−	−	−	−	−	−	−	+
10	−	−	−	−	−	−	−	−	−

From Woodward (1973a, p. 196).

followed by NOT. The FSL NOT is made with a **G** hand, facing outward, pointing upward, and shaking repeatedly from side to side. In general then the hand must twist to an outward orientation for NOT after forming the verb. Assimilation of handshape then affected FSL verbs KNOW, WANT, LIKE, and HAVE, so that they were restructured into single units in ASL (bear in mind that ASL NOT is formationally unrelated to FSL NOT, and that ASL NOT cannot be the source of negative incorporation). These lexical units (DON'T-KNOW, DON'T-WANT, DON'T-LIKE, DON'T-HAVE) were the basis for a generalization of a grammatical process of negative formation which extended to ASL GOOD to form ASL BAD (GOOD-NOT). Although the actual scope of this process is extremely limited, its salience as a generalization (in the sense of Wilbur and Menn, 1975) is demonstrated by overgeneralizations made by hearing people (*DON'T-THINK) and children learning ASL (*DON'T-LOVE).

Given this background, it is interesting that Woodward (1974a) found all possible lects indicated in Table 16. Here lects 1–3 were considered most ASL-like and 4–6 most English-like.

Woodward and DeSantis (1977b) investigated negative incorporation in four areas of France to compare it with Woodward's (1974a) findings. FSL does not have negative incorporation for GOOD, thus there were four verbs that were studied (HAVE, LIKE, WANT, KNOW) and five possible lects that could occur. They found all five lects to exist (Table 17 with total number of people per lect = 60).

Woodward and DeSantis hypothesized that assimilation of the suffix to the verb began with KNOW, proceeded later to WANT, then to LIKE, and then to HAVE in FSL, and finally to GOOD in ASL. This hypothesis is consistent with most signers allowing and accepting negative incorporation for KNOW, fewer accepting it for WANT, fewer still accepting it for LIKE, fewer still for HAVE, and only ASL signers accepting it for GOOD. Thus historical process may well be reflected in synchronic dialect variation (cf. Bickerton, 1975, for spoken language parallels).

Woodward (1973a,b,c,) also found an implicational hierarchy for agent-beneficiary incorporation. In addition, Woodward found that these three rules were themselves implicationally ordered (Table 18). There were lects that had none of the three rules and were thus most English-like, and the implicational hierarchy indicated that a lect with agent-beneficiary incorporation also necessarily had negative incorporation and verb reduplication, a lect with negative incorporation also necessarily had verb reduplication (but not agent-beneficiary incorporation), and a lect with verb reduplication did not necessarily

Table 16. Negative incorporation implication

Lects	HAVE	LIKE	WANT	KNOW	GOOD	Northeastern	Northwestern
1	+	+	+	+	+	17	12
2	−	+	+	+	+	23	14
3	−	−	+	+	+	50	7
4	−	−	−	+	+	10	1
5	−	−	−	−	+	8	2
6	−	−	−	−	−	0	0
Total						108	36

From Woodward and DeSantis (1977b).

Table 17.   Negative incorporation for French signers

Lect	HAVE	LIKE	WANT	KNOW	N
1	+	+	+	+	21
2	−	+	+	+	26
3	−	−	+	+	4
4	−	−	−	+	6
5	−	−	−	−	3
Total					60

From Woodward and DeSantis (1977b).

have either of the other two rules. Again, a lect with all three rules can be considered more ASL-like than a lect with two, which in turn is more ASL-like than a lect with only one, which again is more ASL-like than a lect with none of the three rules. Lects 1 and 2 are closest to ASL and lects 3 and 4 are closest to English.

Aside from geographical factors, Woodward and his associates found that variation in lects is significantly correlated with four variables: 1) whether or not the signer is deaf, 2) whether or not the signer has deaf parents, 3) whether or not the signer learned signs before the age of 6, and 4) whether or not the signer has had some college experience (for deaf signers only). Using the lects from Table 18, these factors are illustrated in Table 19. "One is more likely to find a deaf person, a person with deaf parents, and a person who learned signing before age six in lects that approach ASL; one is more likely to find a hearing person, a person with hearing parents, and a person who learned signing after six in lects that do not approach ASL closely" (Woodward, 1973c, p. 7). Further analysis of these data by L. Anderson revealed that for deaf people with deaf parents, college tends to inhibit use of ASL, whereas for deaf people with hearing parents, college tends to encourage ASL usage (compared to signed English).

Table 18.   Implicational hierarchy for agent-beneficiary incorporation

Lects	Agent beneficiary incorporation lects 1–5	Negative incorporation lects 1–3	Verb reduplication lects 1–5	N
1	+	+	+	84
2	−	+	+	27
3	−	−	+	12
4	−	−	−	18

Table 19.   Factors responsible for variation in lects

Variable	Lects 1,2	Lects 3,4
A. Deaf	97	11
Hearing	14	19
B. Deaf parents	34	2
Hearing parents	77	28
C. ASL 0–6 years	60	5
ASL after 6 years	51	25
D. College	42	2
No college	55	9

PIDGIN SIGN ENGLISH

The widespread dialect variation discussed in the preceding section is coupled with situationally conditioned stylistic variation for individual speakers to create a diglossic continuum. As indicated earlier, informal situations tend to favor use of ASL, and more formal situations require more English-like signing. "Pidgin Sign English" is the term suggested by Woodward (1972, 1973a), Woodward and Markowicz (1975), Stokoe (1970b), and Friedman (1975a) to cover the intermediate varieties along the continuum between ASL and English.

Roughly put, a pidgin is characterized by 1) a mixture of structures from two or more languages, 2) structures that do not belong to either or any of the languages from which they are derived, 3) reduction in structure compared to other languages, 4) not being the native language of any of the people who use it, 5) restricted social situations, such as between employer and employee, but not personally expressive situations, such as between family members, and 6) accompanying negative attitudes toward the pidgin (Woodward, 1973d). Creoles are often described as pidgins that have become someone's native language, although a previous pidgin state is not absolutely necessary for creolization to occur (Hymes, 1971).

Woodward (1973d) indicates the following as linguistic characteristics of PSE (he also emphasizes that considerable further research is necessary for a fuller description):

Articles   PSE has variable use of articles; ASL has no articles as we traditionally think of them; English has *a/n* and *the*. PSE has a sign for *a* and fingerspells *the*.

Plurality   ASL may use reduplication for noun plurals, whereas English adds *-s* to most nouns. PSE uses some noun reduplication and does not generally have an equivalent for -*s*. If the plurality is to be emphasized, the plural noun may be fingerspelled.

Copula   Like Russian, ASL has no copula for present tense sentences such as "John *is* a teacher" (except the required head nod, Liddell, 1977). However, Russian does have copula forms for other tenses, e.g., past tense, but it is not clear if ASL forms can be considered copulas in these other tenses. English has many copula forms (*be, is, am, are, was, were,* plus compounded forms *will be, would be, could be,* etc.). PSE as used by older persons tends to use the ASL sign TRUE/REALLY, whereas newer signs which have been created for educational purposes (primarily initialized forms of TRUE, FUTURE, and PAST) have worked their way back into PSE usage for some signers.

Progressive aspect   The progressive aspect is represented in English by a combination of *be* + verb + *ing* ("is going," "was running"). In ASL, it is represented by verb reduplication as discussed by Fischer (1973a). PSE uses verb reduplication in some environments, but also uses copula + verb (without -*ing*), illustrating the reduced structure characteristic of pidgins.

Perfective aspect   In English, the perfective aspect is indicated by *have* + verb + *en* ("have broken," irregular, "have gone"). ASL uses the sign FINISH. Woodward indicates that an allomorph of "finish," "finish$_2$," is used in PSE, followed by the verb (without + *en* for perfective aspect).

Incorporations   In general, PSE tends to use fewer incorporations than ASL. Woodward and Markowicz (1975) indicate that PSE encompasses lects 4–6 for negative incorporation (Table 15), lects 6–10 for agent-beneficiary incorporation (what we have called verb inflection), and only the numbers 1 and 2 for number incorporation (blending) in pronouns.

In addition to the above, Woodward and Markowicz (1975) also note that PSE tends to be signed in a more restricted, more centralized signing space than that observed for ASL. Facial expression is also more restricted.

The characteristics described for PSE tend to be similar in nature to those of other pidgins:

> These characteristics point up some close similarities between PSE and other pidgins. In most pidgins, articles are deleted; the copula is usually uninflected; inflections such as English plural are lost and most derivations are lost, just as they are in PSE. Perfective aspect in pidgins is often expressed through *finish* or a similar verb like *done* (Woodward, 1973b).

LANGUAGE AND THE DEAF COMMUNITY

The inability to hear is treated by most people, particularly the educational community, as a handicapping condition. The concept of the deaf community as a linguistic minority (Charrow and Wilbur, 1975) bound together by a common language provides a perspective that is foreign to most people. "Members of the deaf community include the profoundly deaf, the hard of hearing, the prelingually and the postlingually deaf, those who have intelligible speech as well as those who don't" (Markowicz and Woodward, 1978), and occasional hearing people with deaf parents may be included. Membership in this minority group seems to be based on two important criteria: "1) attendance in a residential school for the deaf, and 2) communicative competence in ASL (Stokoe et al., 1965)" (Markowicz and Woodward, 1978). According to Meadow (1977), about half of the 90% of deaf children who have hearing parents attend residential schools, where they are enculturated into the deaf community by older children and those who have deaf parents. Although the situation is gradually improving, most deaf children have little or no contact with deaf adults. The use of ASL-like signing (as opposed to the signed English end of the continuum) serves to solidify people within the deaf community while excluding outsiders. Pidgin Sign English serves as a buffer between the hearing and deaf communities (Markowicz and Woodward, 1978).

An Empirical Investigation

Kantor (1978) pursued Markowicz and Woodward's report of the linguistic criteria for membership in the deaf community by investigating the identifiability of signers as native or non-native, hearing or deaf. She conducted a study aimed at determining the ability of signers (native deaf, non-native deaf, native hearing, non-native hearing) to identify other signers (presented on videotape) as native deaf, non-native deaf, native hearing, or non-native hearing, and to determine what factors influenced these decisions. The non-native signers were all second-language (L2) signers (deaf or hearing) who had learned to sign after puberty; native signers had all learned ASL from birth. She reported her results both in terms of the accuracy of the judges and the identifiability of the signers being judged.

Identifiability of the Signers   As suggested by the data above, the native deaf signers and the L2 hearing signers were the most easily identified groups overall (50% and 60%, respectively). In contrast, overall judgments on native hearing signers and L2 deaf signers were extremely inaccurate (10% and 8%, respectively). Instead, the L2

Table 20.   Percentages of judgments influenced by characteristics

Characteristic	Native deaf	L2 Deaf	Native hearing	L2 Hearing
Hands	100%	65%	33%	81%
Rhythm	100%	54%	23%	49%
Kinds of signs	92%	50%	9%	57%
Face	100%	58%	21%	77%
Body	95%	31%	13%	53%
Location of signs	81%	19%	7%	38%
Finger size	9%	0	0	7%

signers were easily identified as deaf (73%) but rarely as L2 (15%) whereas the L2 hearing signers were easily recognized as L2 (79%) almost as often as hearing (66%).

Characteristics that Influenced Decisions   Raters were given several characteristics to check off or describe if they felt it was relevant to their decision regarding the signers to be judged, and were also asked to provide additional characteristics or comments which might be helpful to the experimenter. Table 20 presents the percentages of judgments that were influenced by the various characteristics according to the group being judged.

The hands, face, body, and kinds of signs were the primary telltale characteristics. For the native deaf signers, comments included: "facial expression dominates," "affirmative nodding of head while telling a story," "incomplete mouthing of words," use of mime, use of particular signs ("deaf signs," "expressive signs"), and rhythm of signing, including speed, fluency, and use of space. For the L2 deaf, comments included: "exaggerated mouth movements indicates early oral training," "hesitant speech with the signing," "the speed is halting," and "deaf facial expressions." For the native hearing, comments included: "good use of body emphasis," "fluent use of signs, but pattern of words seems hearing," and "signs are very fluid." Finally, for the L2 hearing, comments included: "way hands shaped while signing too stiff and formal," "body too stiff," "too much false facial expression," "face kind of blah," "facial expression not deafy," "used all easy basic signs," "used same sign too often," "used signs that hearing people use," "sign for 'just right' was the giveaway," "excessive fingerspelling," "fingerspelling too quick," and "slow fingerspelling."

Accuracy of the Raters   The native signers (both deaf and hearing) were most accurate in determining the proper category for the signers being judged. With a 25% chance of making a completely correct judgment (50% probability of getting deaf or hearing correct, 50% chance for getting native or L2 correct, but only 25% chance for getting both characteristics correct for any particular signer), the native deaf and native hearing groups scored 40% and 41% correct, respectively, whereas the L2 deaf and L2 hearing performed less accurately (21% and 34%, respectively). Interestingly, both hearing groups were better able to accurately identify a signer as deaf or hearing, and both deaf groups were more accurate in determining whether signers were native or L2.

Native deaf signers were most accurate at identifying native deaf signers (70%) and L2 hearing signers (68% correct), supporting Markowicz and Woodward's contention that the linguistic abilities helped bind the community together. Similarly, native hearing signers were highly accurate in identifying native deaf (67%) and L2 hearing (73%) signers. The L2 deaf and hearing judges performed considerably below the native groups, suggesting that they were less attuned to the salient characteristics.

SUMMARY

As indicated by Kantor's (1978) results, Markowicz and Woodward's observations are empirically substantiated. Canonical members of the deaf community (presumably the native deaf signers) can easily identify other native deaf signers and nonmember L2 hearing signers, while they experienced difficulty (and probably uncertainty) about the borderline cases of native hearing signers and L2 deaf signers. "Native hearing and L2 deaf were almost never detected with any real accuracy. Native hearing signers were most often mistaken for native deaf and occasionally as L2 deaf but only in one or two cases as L2 hearing. This implies that the factor of hearing is not significant to the signing qualities of native signers. A native signer is a native signer; their 'accent' is equivalent" (Kantor, 1978, p. 10). One qualification on this conclusion seems necessary. Woodward (1976c, 1977a) reports that native hearing signers with deaf parents are unlikely to know the signs for sexual behavior that are used in the deaf community. He suggests that since these signs represent areas of social intimacy, they are reserved for the core members of the deaf community, creating a topic distinction between hearing and deaf native signers.

The implications of this chapter for linguistic research on ASL and for the educational community are profound. As suggested several times in other chapters, the influence of English can never be discounted when studying ASL; here the effect of hearing, particularly of the researcher, is added to the list of cautions. Educators, in addition, must remember that deaf children will eventually be faced with the choice of joining the deaf community after they leave school, and that their decision to do so will be greatly facilitated by knowledge of ASL (not instead of, but in addition to, English). The sign systems currently in vogue in educational programs for the deaf do not resemble ASL or English as much as their creators and proponents think they do (this is discussed in greater detail in Chapter 7). One can also question the effect on deaf children learning the different sign systems when they attempt to enter the deaf community and have 1) different lexical items and 2) little or no knowledge of ASL syntax. Anyone who has labored to learn ASL signs in sign language class or from a book, put them into English word order, and then discovered that they could not follow a native signer in conversation will appreciate the fact that ASL syntax is sufficiently different from English to warrant separate study. As more of the linguistic information passes into sign language teaching books, it will become more difficult for teachers and others in contact with deaf children to use the difficulty of obtaining real ASL as their excuse to know only signed English. Meanwhile, the existence of the deaf community places deaf people in a category apart from those with other sensory, cognitive, or physical disabilities. Although retarded or physically disabled individuals may eventually leave a sheltered environment, marry, and raise families, they are not bound together in the same way by a separate, communal language. In fact, Charrow and Wilbur (1975) and others have argued extensively for treating deaf children as a linguistic minority rather than as a handicapped population. Such a perspective raises the importance of bilingual approaches to educating deaf children, and suggests that teachers of deaf children might benefit from academic programs in bilingual education and teaching English as a second language.

PART II

EDUCATIONAL
CONSIDERATIONS

CHAPTER 7

SIGN SYSTEMS

CONTENTS

The linguistic structure of ASL is sufficiently different from English that true simultaneous communication in ASL and spoken English is very difficult to accomplish. Nonetheless, English is the predominant language in American education and society. For this reason, manual systems have been created in order to permit concurrent signing and speaking using English syntax. That these systems are considerably different from ASL is clear; that they are also significantly different from English (which they are intended to represent faithfully) has recently begun to attract the attention of linguists (Allen, 1975; Charrow, 1975b; Wilbur, 1976).

Wilbur (1976) used the term *systems* to designate those manual methods that have been developed for educational purposes but are not currently used as the home language by large groups of deaf people. A manual system is formally different from both ASL and English, and for many reasons cannot be considered *language* in the same sense that ASL and English are.

It should be clear that the systems do not simply take "the signs of ASL and put them in English word order." They also drastically alter the morphological and phonological processes that users of ASL are accustomed to producing and perceiving (e.g., reduplication, blending, assimilations). The systems were designed to parallel English based on the assumption that signing English would be more effective in teaching written English syntax than signing ASL.

Deaf children's problems with English syntax are discussed in greater detail in Chapter 8 (see "Learning English Syntax"). Given what we now know about deaf children's English difficulties, we cannot rule out the possibility that the same problems that manifest them-selves in written English will not also occur in their acquisition of signed English, regardless of which system is used.

HISTORY OF SIGN SYSTEMS

The first constructed signing system undoubtedly was that of the Abbé de l'Epée, who modified the signs used by the deaf community in France to create a signed French. Markowicz (1976) discussed the Abbé's considerations and procedures. The "methodical" signs were of two types—lexical and grammatical. The grammatical ones were created to more exactly parallel French syntax, whereas the lexical ones, if not original signs, were created to label things that did not already have signs or to make distinctions between French words that might share the same sign. Many of de L'Epée's signs were demon-strated first with a series of pantomimes to convey the meaning to the deaf students, after which the abbreviated sign was presented. Much emphasis was placed on written French syntax, so initially the students were asked questions by means of methodical signs and provided their responses in writing. These "methodical" signs were brought by Lau-rent Clerc and Thomas Gallaudet to the United States, where they were adapted to teach English.

The first English-based system was developed by Sir Richard Paget (1951) in England. He called his system "A New Sign Lan-guage." After his death, Lady Grace Paget and Dr. Pierre Gorman continued his work, revising the system and calling it "A Systematic Sign Language" (Paget and Gorman, 1968). This name was abandoned in 1971 (Paget, 1971) in recognition of the fact that it is not a language (as distinguished in Wilbur, 1976), and the system is now known as the "Paget-Gorman Sign System" (PGSS) (Craig, 1976). Paget was the first to delineate several basic modifications for making signing more closely approximate spoken English. Included were such criteria as: 1) each sign should represent an English word or part of an English word; 2) signs should be ordered in the same order as spoken words are; 3) signs should be inflected to reflect the inflections in spoken words; 4) signs should be adapted to form a small, basic vocabulary for initial use (Bornstein, 1973).

The first system in the United States was developed by David Anthony, who was interested in producing a simplified system to use with deaf retardates. Anthony's (1966, 1971) original system developed into Seeing Essential English (SEE 1), from which Linguistics of Vis-ual English (Wampler, 1971, 1972) and Signing Exact English (SEE 2)

(Gustason, Pfetzing, and Zawolkow, 1972, 1973, 1974) subsequently were derived. Manual English was developed at the Washington State School for the Deaf (1972), utilizing many of the principles and basic assumptions of the other systems, with differences which are noted below. Another system whose use has become quite widespread is Signed English. In discussing this, a distinction must be made (unfortunately not made in Wilbur, 1976) between Signed English as a developed system (Bornstein et al., 1973, 1975) and signed English as a loosely defined means of utilizing ASL signs in English syntactic order without invented grammatical endings or separate grammatical signs and which allows use of ASL syntactic devices such as reduplication and spatialization (as discussed in Part I). signed English also refers to the signing that is used by hearing people who have learned signs but have not received instruction in ASL syntax and thus put the signs together in English order and fingerspell whatever signs they do not know. Thus, signed English may be the most widely used of all the systems but it is the least well defined.

The final system included in this discussion is also not strictly a system, but rather a synthesis of several other systems. The *Perkins Sign Language Dictionary* (Robbins et al., 1975) was originally developed to meet the needs of those working with visually impaired deaf students. The dictionary includes entries from 11 sign text sources, chosen according to criteria which are discussed below. The issue of syntax is discussed at length in the Introduction to the dictionary, where it is suggested that several levels of grammatical markers might be advantageously recognized and that their use is governed by the level of functioning of each child rather than by absolute principles based on English syntax. In light of this, comparisons of the systems are not relevant to the *Perkins Sign Language Dictionary*, and these are reserved for separate discussion.

COMPARISON OF THE SYSTEMS TO ENGLISH

In looking at the relationship between the several available systems as a group and English, three major questions can be addressed: 1) What are the basic guidelines upon which each system has been established? 2) How do these guidelines compare to the structure of English or to the structure of ASL? 3) When do these guidelines break down (when are they inconsistent, counterintuitive) and how serious is this problem?

The creators of each system believe that their system faithfully reflects the structure of English in a visual mode. Because English is a spoken language, many arbitrary decisions have to be made about how to represent spoken English in signs. It may be said of all the systems as a group that they follow English word order. However, they diverge with respect to the structure of signs and the creation of new signs (see Table 21) and the amount of fingerspelling permitted. Several of the systems have made different decisions regarding the formation and use of signs.

The formation of past tense verbs provides an illustration of these arbitrary decisions. In English, verbs can be divided into those which form their past tense by a regular rule and those which are in some way irregular. The regular past tense rule is to add the suffix "ed" to the verb ("talk"-"talked"). The irregular verbs can be subdivided into several groups. There are those for which the past tense is the same as the present, e.g., "hit"-"hit"; those which display internal vowel changes, e.g., "meet"-"met"; those which have vowel changes in both the past tense and the past participle, e.g., "ring"-"rang"-"rung"; others which use "-ought" or "-aught," e.g., "fight"-"fought," "catch"-"caught"; and a few for which the past tense does not resemble the present tense at all, e.g., "go"-"went." The differences are all reflections of processes that occurred earlier in the history of the English language.

There are many ways in which a sign system can code the past tenses of English verbs. One possibility is to represent English past tenses by signing all the verbs in the same way. For example, one could sign the present tense followed by the ASL PAST sign ("talked" = TALK + PAST, "came" = COME + PAST), or one could sign the present tense followed by another past tense marker such as fingerspelled 'd' ("talked" = TALK + d, came = COME + d). Another approach is to divide the verbs into regular and irregular, and use one past tense marking for the regular verbs and another for the irregular verbs: 1) sign the present tense plus the ASL PAST for the regular verbs and another marker, perhaps fingerspelled 'd' for the irregular verbs ("talked" = TALK + PAST, "came" = COME + d), 2) the opposite of 1 ("talked" = TALK + d, "came" = COME + PAST), 3) sign the present tense plus PAST marker for the regular verbs and use new signs for the irregular verbs ("talked" = TALK + PAST, "came" = CAME), 4) sign the present tense plus PAST for the regular verbs and fingerspell the irregular verbs ("talked" = TALK + PAST, "came" = c + a + m + e). Others might be the same as 3 or 4, but using 'd' for the regular verbs. Other possibilities include subdividing the irregular verbs into smaller groups, along the same lines that they are divided in English. All of these approaches

Table 21. Characteristics of manual systems

System	Author(s)	ASL signs?	Fingerspelling?	Basic morphological principle(s)
Paget-Gorman Sign System (PGSS)	Paget (1951) Paget and Gorman (1968, 1971)	No	Only for proper names	One meaning-one sign
Seeing Essential English (SEE 1)	Anthony (1966, 1971)	For the most part	Some	Two out of three: sound, meaning, and spelling
Signing Exact English (SEE 2)	Gustason, Pfetzing, and Zawolkow (1972)	Same as SEE 1	Same as SEE 1	Same as SEE 1
Linguistics of Visual English	Wampler (1971, 1972)	Same as SEE 1	Same as SEE 1	Same as SEE 1
Manual English	Washington State School for the Deaf (1972)	Yes	More than SEE 1	Variable—one meaning-one sign Some same as SEE 1
Signed English	Bornstein et al. (1973, 1975)	Yes	Yes Variable amounts	To string together ASL signs with 14 markers and fingerspelling
signed English Siglish Ameslish	Riekehof (1963) Fant (1964, 1972b) Watson (1964) Bragg (1973) O'Rourke (1973)	Yes	Yes	Pidginization of ASL signs and English markers and word order

From Fristoe and Lloyd (1978) (modified from Wilbur, 1976, p. 453).

can be used in various combinations with initialized signs to create even more possibilities.

The logical possibilities have not been exhausted, but it should be clear from the above examples that the manner of treating past tenses is more or less an arbitrary decision made by the creator of the system. There is nothing about the structure of English that would force any particular combination of the above possibilities. Since English irregular verbs are subdivided into groups, perhaps a manual system that also subdivided them would be preferable to one that did not. However, the number of ways in which the verbs can be subdivided, and the way they are treated once they have been subdivided, is largely a matter of preference. Consider how the past tenses are actually treated.

As indicated earlier, time is indicated in ASL by the use of the time line. The time is generally established by the use of a time adverbial (YESTERDAY, TOMORROW, LAST WEEK), after which if no time indication is given, it is assumed to be at that time. "Time . . . seems to be in sign language a sentence or utterance rather than a verb matter. Unlike an English finite verb, which must indicate tense, a sign verb will remain uninflected for time. Instead, the sentence or utterance as a whole will have whatever time reference the situation or a general or specific time sign has indicated until a change is signalled" (Stokoe, Casterline, and Croneberg, 1965, p. 282).

In the Paget-Gorman Systematic Sign (PGSS), verbs are divided into two groups, those made with one hand and those made with two hands. The one-handed signs form their past tense by simultaneously signing the present tense form of the sign with one hand and the past tense sign PAST with the other. The two-handed signs form their past tense by sequentially signing first the present tense form of the verb and then the PAST sign (PGSS does not use ASL signs).

In general, the past tense in Signing Exact English (SEE 2) is formed by signing the present tense form of the verb followed by the ASL sign PAST. The past participle is formed by signing the verb plus FINISH. Auxiliary verbs ("can"-"could") do not use PAST, they use FINISH.

In Manual English, all verbs form their past tense by using the sign PAST after the verb. However, verbs are divided into regular and irregular for purposes of forming the past participle. For regular verbs, the past participle is the same as the past tense (VERB + PAST). For irregular past participles, the sequence VERB + PAST + FINISH is used.

In Bornstein et al.'s (1973, 1975) version of Signed English, two past tense markers are used, one for regular verbs and one for irregular verbs.

It should now be clear that each system has its own "systematic principle." Each principle is arbitrary in terms of the structure of English. However, as far as the child is concerned, each system has its own set of signs to correspond to different concepts. Since the child does not yet know English, it makes little difference linguistically whether he learns TEAR (with an E hand) as the sign for "tore," or TEAR + PAST, or TEAR + d, or t + o + r + e. The creators of the sign systems hope, however, that the basic principles of their system will somehow become real and meaningful to the child, that the child will learn that all verbs signed one way have something in common. However, there are no data as yet to indicate whether a child realizes that what those signs have in common is that their English equivalents correspond to the regular rule of English past tense formation. Children are most likely to look only for generalizations about the system that they are learning, in order to organize their memory more efficiently and to make their task of comprehension and production easier. It remains to be experimentally demonstrated that these generalizations carry over into their use of English. (See Caccamise, 1976, for another detailed comparison of sign systems.)

GENERAL COMMENTS ON THE SYSTEMS

Before giving a description of each of the systems, several major differences should be pointed out. In the area of sign usage and sign formation, the systems have different principles which serve as guidelines for determining what signs should be used (particularly for the many words not listed in the system's dictionary or manual of usage). For example, the PGSS system utilizes a combination of basic sign + modifier sign to form most of its words. The basic sign is a category, like PERSON or ANIMAL. The modifier sign specifies the nature of the particular intended referent. One hand forms the sign PERSON and the other forms the sign TOOTH ("dentist"), TEACH ("teacher"), FIRE ("fireman"), or STETHOSCOPE ("doctor"). For every meaning there is a separate sign. (Interestingly, Craig, 1976, p. 52, reports that "in practice it has been found that with the possible exception of the "ANIMAL" signs, children are not aware of the derivation of the signs any more than hearing children are aware of the derivation of words until they have acquired considerable linguistic sophistication," thus supporting skepticism concerning the supposed benefits of the sign systems.)

On the other hand, Signing Exact English (henceforth SEE 2) has as a basic principle that if two of the following three criteria are identical for two English words, the same sign is used for both of them: a) pronunciation, b) spelling, and c) meaning. For example, "wind" (breeze) and "wind" (what you do to a clock or watch) are spelled the same but are pronounced differently and have different meanings; therefore they have separate signs. On the other hand, "sock," which can mean both "stocking" and "to hit," is nonetheless spelled and pronounced the same for both of its two meanings and is thus represented by one sign for both widely divergent meanings.

Manual English, like PGSS, generally has one sign for each meaning. The English word "call" is represented with four separate ASL signs in Manual English: NAME, SUMMONS, PHONE, and SHOUT. (SEE 2 would use one sign based on pronunciation and spelling). Bornstein (1973, p. 462) does not believe that an "altered form of the sign word will facilitate the learning of the English word form" and hence Signed English uses ASL signs for all types of English words. These rules are summarized in Table 21.

The systems also differ in their expressed attitude toward the use of fingerspelling. In PGSS, fingerspelling is used only for proper names. In SEE 2, fingerspelling is generally avoided. Manual English, on the other hand, is not opposed to the use of fingerspelling and would permit it, for example, as an alternate form of the past tense formation. In Signed English, whenever an English word cannot be represented by one sign word and one sign marker, fingerspelling is recommended. The amount of fingerspelling in signed English varies, the actual amount depending greatly on the person's fluency in English and whom the person is signing with. The use of large amounts of fingerspelling by users of signed English allows the system to be very flexible and to borrow words from English by simply spelling them. One further advantage is that an adult learning to sign can simply fingerspell any word for which he does not know the sign.

PAGET-GORMAN SYSTEMATIC SIGN (PGSS)

PGSS was developed in England with the intention that the system be discarded by the child when he no longer needed it for communication (i.e., when the child had mastered English). Craig (1976, p. 53) lists the following aims for PGSS:

1. To provide correct patterns of English to enable the deaf child to learn language at an age which is more commensurate with the natural optimum age of language learning in normally hearing children.
2. To increase the deaf child's comprehension by giving clearer patterns of correct language than those which are available to him by speechreading alone.
3. To enable the deaf child to build up an understanding of correct language in conjunction with speech and speechreading. It should provide a sound foundation for the future use of speech and speechreading to be used by themselves where possible or for correct fingerspelling to be used where this form of communication is considered to be most appropriate for the individual child.
4. To encourage in the deaf child a desire to communicate verbally.
5. To accelerate his learning of all school subjects by providing clear, unambiguous patterns of correct language.
6. To encourage the deaf child to express English which would be considered acceptable for his age and environment.
7. To increase the probability of the deaf child's reaching a reading level which would enable him to read with facility, and so benefit him educationally and socially.
8. To offer a method of remedial teaching for those deaf children or young adults whose language has not been adequately developed by other methods of teaching.

Since PGSS was developed in England it does not use signs from ASL. The system is based on pantomimic signs which include 21 standard hand positions and 39 basic signs used in different combinations. Each basic sign serves to group together signs with a common concept. Basic signs exist for FOOD, INSECT, PERSON, ANIMAL, etc. The standard hand configurations serve to differentiate specific lexical items in each group, although a basic sign is not necessary for every sign. As indicated earlier, this internal sign structure seems to be opaque to the children. Craig (1976, p. 52) points out that "although the Basic Signs are not functioning in the way that the authors originally intended they are by no means a useless feature of the system. The instructions for making the signs can be written down clearly and unambiguously, and the Basic Signs form a convenient shorthand in reading those instructions. In addition they are of considerable value to hearing adults learning to use the system since they form the basis of a fairly logical pattern to which the system largely conforms. Because of this relatively logical pattern to the system most of the signs can be learned with comparative ease, though not without some effort.''

Aside from the meaningful signs described above, there are also functional signs in PGSS. The following affixes are listed in Craig (1976):

1. Plural of nouns (regular or irregular).
2. Possessive.
3. Comparative and superlative of adjectives (-ER, -EST). (Those that would be said with "more" or "most" in English are signed with MORE or MOST.)
4. Present progressive (-ING).
5. Past tense of verbs (regular or irregular).
6. Past participle.
7. Third person singular -S in present tense verbs.
8. Adverb (-LY).
9. Adjective (-Y).

The PGSS pronoun system follows the pattern of English pronouns. There are separate signs for first, second, and third person singular pronouns: I, YOU, and IT. The other pronouns are variations of the main sign. For example, the pronoun "he" is signed by combining the pronoun IT in one hand with the sign MALE in the other. Reflexive pronouns are formed by signing the possessive form (formed on the nominative) and then the pronoun SELF. Thus "myself" is MY + SELF. (Implication: the reflexive "himself" is signed as HIS + SELF, a common mistake made by young hearing children, second language learners, and deaf children). Plurals in PGSS are formed by signing the functional sign PLURAL after the noun: NOUN + PLURAL (for both regular and irregular nouns). Possessives are formed by signing the noun and then the functional sign POSSESSIVE (NOUN + POSSESSIVE). Plural possessives have the form NOUN + PLURAL + POSSESSIVE.

All verbs are treated alike in PGSS except the verb "to be." "Be" has six distinct signs: BE, AM, IS, ARE, WAS, and WERE. The other verbs are all used unmarked in the present tense, except third person singular. That is, there are no endings or modifications to indicate first or second person singular or plural, third person plural, or regular vs. irregular verb. The future tense is formed by using a separate sign TIME-FORWARD before each verb (analogous to English "will" + verb). As mentioned earlier, the past tense involves a division of verbs into one-handed and two-handed signs (rather than the English regular vs. irregular), with one-handed signs simultaneously signing the verb and TIME-BACKWARD and two-handed signs sequentially signing the verb and then TIME-BACKWARD. The present participle is formed by a functional sign -ING which follows the verb. The sign PAST PARTICIPLE (PAST PART) is used to form participles from the past tense, i.e., VERB + TIME-BACKWARD + PAST PART, where TIME-BACKWARD follows the rule for past tense formation.

The formation of compound and complex signs is the area in which most of the systems run into trouble. They end up being either internally inconsistent, cumbersome, or counterintuitive. The PGSS system has attempted to avoid the complexities inherent in paralleling English word formation by establishing its own morphological rules, although a few still parallel English. The -ING functional sign can be used to derive nouns from verbs, and the -LY suffix is used to derive some adjectives and adverbs. For the most part, however, the signs are formed on productive combinations of the 39 basic signs and the 21 standard hand configurations. Examples of human signs ("dentist," "fireman," "doctor") were given earlier. Others include "elephant" = ANIMAL + LONG-NOSE, "leopard" = ANIMAL + SPOTS, "lion" = ANIMAL + ROAR. Compound signs are made by combining two or more basic signs: "bedroom" = BED + SLEEP, "scent" = GOOD + SMELL, "contract" = PAPER + LAW, "breakfast" = MORNING + FOOD.

The signs of PGSS are pantomimic in some sense, but could not be taken as universal. For example, the sign for "frog" is ANIMAL + JUMP, which could be taken to refer to a kangaroo in Australia. Furthermore, PGSS violates a cultural taboo on extended middle fingers by using this hand configuration in some of its signs (this hand configuration is allowable in Chinese Sign Language).

SIGNING EXACT ENGLISH (SEE 2)

Signing Exact English (SEE 2) is an outgrowth of David Anthony's original work on Seeing Essential English (SEE 1). Bornstein (1973) reports an overlap between SEE 2 and SEE 1 of 75% (general vocabulary only) to 80% (affixes, pronouns, and Be-verbs included). Signing Exact English was developed by Gustason, Pfetzing, and Zawolkow (1972). The manual and a supplement are currently available from the National Association of the Deaf. The SEE 2 manual includes 2100 words and 70 affixes, with 7 contractions. Words are divided into basic words, complex words, and compound words. The system uses the two-out-of-three principle described above, namely, that the same sign is used for two English words if those two words are alike in two of the three features—pronunciation, spelling, and meaning. One of the ASL signs may be chosen to represent the two words, or a new sign may be invented. The ASL sign would be used if it is "clear, unambiguous, and has only one English translation" (Gustason, Pfetzing, and Zawolkow, 1974). The exception to the basic two-out-of-three principle is that inflected basic forms cannot be used as new basic words. For example, the past tense of "see," "saw," cannot be used as the sign for the verb "to saw."

SEE 2 retains some of the ASL pronoun signs—ME, YOU, and YOUR. Initialized signs have been invented for the other pronouns, using, for example, the E hand for "he," the M hand for "him," and the S hand for "his." Possessive pronouns are formed by adding -S to the possessive adjectives; for example, "yours" is signed as YOUR + S. The exception to this is "mine," which is MY + EN. The reflexives are the same as in PGSS (only using some ASL signs) with the possessive adjective (MY, YOUR, HIS, etc.) followed by SELF for the singular and SELF + S for the plural. Regular plural nouns are formed by signing S after the noun. Irregular nouns are divided— nouns in which the final consonant is a voiceless fricative in the singular and a voiced fricative in the plural ("leaf"-"leaves") are treated as ASL plurals and pluralized by reduplication. Possessives are formed using the contraction 'S (an S hand that moves in the shape of an apostrophe), added directly to singular nouns and after the plural marker S in plural nouns (the plural marker is also an S hand, but it does not move).

Regular and irregular verbs are treated similarly in SEE 2. In the present tense, the third person singular is inflected with -S (same S as the plural marker). The ASL sign PAST is used after the verb to indicate past tense. The future is formed with the ASL sign FUTURE which has been initialized to stand for "will." For the present participle, the suffix -ING is used, and for the past participle the ASL sign FINISH is used after the verb. Auxiliary verbs are differentiated, however. The past tense is formed using the past participle sign FINISH, so "could" = CAN + FINISH. Also, the verb "to be" has several signs associated with it. Some are derived from the ASL sign TRULY, which is initialized with A for "am," R for "are," I for "is," B for "be." To indicate past tense, the ASL sign PAST has been initialized with S for "was," R for "were." Some of these signs for "be" have been accepted into ASL and are now being used by deaf adults in formal situations in many parts of the country.

In every language, words are created by combining one or more morphemes. For example, the word "farmers" is composed of the morphemes "farm" + "er" + "s," where "farm" is a verb stem, "er" is an agentive suffix (one who does), and "s" is a plural marker. The PGSS system does not attempt to parallel English morphology, but the SEE 2 system does. It uses morphemes that are productive and have constant semantic value (thus the meaning of a word composed of morphemes A + B + C should be predictable from the meaning of the individual morphemes themselves. An example of an English word that does not have the meaning of its composite morphemes is "carpet," which has a meaning unrelated to either "car" or "pet"). As with SEE 1, the two-out-of-three principle holds for choice of signs. Since the affix "-ship" (as in "relationship") has the same spelling and pronunciation as the noun "ship," one sign is used for both, even though the meanings are radically different. Complex words are formed by adding an affix if there is one in English, regardless of meaning. For example, the pair "red"-"redden" follows an English rule for deriving verbs from adjectives ("light"-"lighten," "white"-"whiten") and an -EN suffix is used in SEE 2 for these forms. However, the same -EN suffix is used in SEE 2 for words that in English mean something entirely different as a result of an "-en" ending, such as "chick"-"chicken," "mitt"-"mitten," "my"-"mine." (In addition, the -EN sign is actually the past participle FINISH sign, so "chicken" is really signed as CHICK + FINISH. The "chick"-"chicken" pair is particularly disturbing, since it seems that the sign should instead indicate that "chick" is a "little chicken.") Whether or not these system deviances have any effect on children's acquisition of English remains to be seen.

Despite the fact that SEE 2 holds to the two-out-of-three principle even in some very strange situations (as in "-ship," "ship"), it nonetheless includes a number of words that are not formed along this principle at all. Some forms are actually broken down into archaic morpheme divisions ("height" = HIGH + T), or syllable divisions ("sorrow" = SORRY + W, "jewelry" = JEWEL + R + Y, "nursery" = NURSE + ER + Y, "any" = AN + Y). This is not done systematically, however, since, for example, "although," "also," "already" are signed as two signs, e.g., AL + THOUGH, whereas "almost," which could easily be divided like the others, is nonetheless one sign.

With respect to compound signs, SEE 2 uses two signs if the word retains the meaning of the two words that compose it ("babysit," "shepherd") and uses a single sign (ASL or invented) for words that have nonpredictable meanings ("carpet" has its own sign because it has nothing to do with either "cars" or "pets"). Words like "yesterday" and "today" are treated as two signs each, ignoring available ASL signs for both of them. "Hot dog" is also treated as two signs even though the relationship between its meaning and that of "a hot dog" is fairly obscure. Again, it should be pointed out that these are purely arbitrary decisions and that most of the systems have this kind of problem with English morphology, so SEE 2 alone cannot be faulted.

MANUAL ENGLISH

Manual English was developed by the Total Communication Program at the Washington State School for the Deaf in order to provide a system that would parallel English sufficiently well that it could be used in conjunction with normal speech. The system is taught to adults who are in contact with the child so that English structure can be reinforced through signs at all times. Again, it must be noted that English syntax can be presented this way, but that English morphology causes difficulty. Manual English uses more fingerspelling than does SEE 2. A signer also has several options, such as forming a verb tense as VERB + TENSE or of partially spelling the word, e.g., VERB + e + d.

Manual English uses many of the ASL signs. If an English word has more than one meaning, and each of those meanings has a separate ASL sign, then ASL signs are retained. A large number of initialized signs are used. The pronouns in Manual English are the same as those in SEE, except that "mine" = MY + E whereas SEE 2 uses MY + EN. The contractions, plurals, and possessives are the same as in SEE 2. Manual English handles the verb "to be" in the same manner as SEE 2 but differs in its treatment of main verbs, notably in its handling of the past participle. The ASL sign FINISH is used as a suffix marker for the past participle, but, unlike SEE 2, Manual English divides the verbs into regular and irregular. Those irregular verbs that have a distinct word for present, past, and past participle forms, as "speak-spoke-spoken," use the past participle form VERB + PAST + FINISH. (One should bear in mind that distinctions such as this are opaque to all but the most knowledgeable students, for whom this division, as most of the others, is purely an arbitrary one requiring special memorization. That is, the student must learn the list of signs that take FINISH in their past participles as exceptions to the otherwise regular rule of having simply VERB + PAST.) Other irregular verbs, such as "hit-hit-hit" and "come-came-come," are not discussed in the manual. The auxiliary verbs in Manual English are derived from English, ASL, and SEE 2. The auxiliary verb "have to" has its own sign from ASL. Initialized versions of this sign are used for NEED, MUST, and OUGHT TO. "Would," "should," and "could" are treated as the past tenses of "will," "shall," and "can," respectively—WOULD = WILL + d, SHOULD = SHALL + d, COULD = CAN + d. Thus, in Manual English, "I would have been given . . ." would be signed I WILL + d HAVE BE + PAST PART GIVE + PAST + FINISH.

In compound and complex sign formation, Manual English has borrowed some signs from SEE 2, eliminated others, and altered others. Some nonproductive affixes like -NEATH, and YESTER- have been eliminated because of their limited use ("beneath," "underneath," "yesterday," "yesteryear"). Unlike SEE 2, which uses the same -ER suffix for most occurrences of English "-er," Manual English has three -ER signs, one for the agentive "-er" (one who does) using the ASL sign PERSON, one for the comparative "-er" ("bigger," "smaller"), and one for everything else ("prayer," "eraser," "dryer"). Note that in this last category, an eraser is that which erases, and a dryer is that which dries, but a prayer is not that which prays, nor one who prays (one who prays would be agentive and would use PERSON), so that the third group is an arbitrary collection of leftovers.

The principles for complex word formation vary. The basic rule is supposed to be that if no ASL sign exists for a complex word, then an affix may be used to form a sign. However, there are cases where this principle is overlooked, as seen by the use of NEAR + PERSON for "neighbor." The same principle is supposed to hold for compound words, so that "oversight," "grandmother," "gentleman," and "workshop" use the ASL signs, whereas two signs are put together when needed, for example, "houseparent" = HOUSE + PARENT.

SIGNED ENGLISH

Bornstein and his colleagues (Bornstein, in press; Bornstein and Hamilton, 1972; Bornstein et al., 1973, 1975) constructed Signed English for use with preschool and elementary school children. The intention is to provide "a semantic approximation to the usual language environment of the hearing child" (Bornstein, 1973, p. 330). The 2500-word vocabulary is chosen for use with the young child and includes sign words and sign markers. Of these 2500 signs, 1700 are from ASL and the rest are either invented or borrowed from other systems. The 12 sign markers function for basic English structures. The plural is marked by fingerspelling '-s' after the sign for regular nouns, and by reduplication for irregular nouns (again, an arbitrary choice of divisions). The 'S sign for possessive, which has been somewhat accepted into ASL, is used in Signed English. Unlike the other systems, contractions are treated as separate words and have their own signs. Thus, there is a separate sign for "don't," which is not an alteration of "do not." The evidence from early language acquisition in hearing children supports the view that children learn contractions as separate entities ("don't" and "can't" appear in utterances in an earlier developmental stage than "can" and "do" or the other modals, which suggests that they are learned as whole units, rather than as contractions of their component words). Four sign markers are used with the verbs, one for the past tense of regular verbs, one for the past tense of irregular verbs, one for the third person singular present, and one for the past participle. The possible combinations of signs and markers are limited, so anything not covered by these principles is fingerspelled. In all probability, the system is sufficient for the young child and many retarded individuals.

PERKINS SIGN LANGUAGE DICTIONARY

The *Perkins Sign Language Dictionary* represents a synthesis from 11 other sources compiled by the Department for Deaf-Blind Children of the Perkins School for the Blind in Massachusetts. The sources that are included are Babbini (1974), Bornstein et al. (1973), Fant (1972b), Gustason, Pfetzing, and Zawolkow (1972, 1973, 1974), Huffman et al. (1975), Kannapell, Hamilton, and Bornstein (1969), Madsen (1972), O'Rourke (1973), Riekehof (1963), Sanders (1968), and Watson (1973). Thus, this dictionary includes signs from several systems (SEE 1, SEE 2, Signed English) as well as ASL signs or commonly used variations of them. The population for which this dictionary was originally constructed and the objectives that the authors set for their language instruction are discussed in greater detail in Chapter 9. This discussion here is confined to the structure of the system as it might concern those who are teaching normal deaf children. The authors do not see their primary goal as teaching English to the children, thus the dictionary is aimed first at "communication, expressiveness, language for learning, language for thinking, communication skills to enhance a sense of personal worth and relationship to others" (Robbins et al., 1975 p. 17). They see the "acquisition of English as an important secondary goal" for those students who are likely to go on to learn to read, at which time they suggest an attempt at "a reasonably good match between English and the sign system used *but* while maintaining 'meaning', not phonetic or written word, as the basic unit to be respected" (p. 17). Thus, the dictionary is not a system in the same sense as SEE 2, for example, in that it does not provide a series of guidelines based on English spelling, meaning, and pronunciation for choosing signs, but instead has laid out a totally different set of criteria for sign choice.

To begin with, the Perkins group recognizes the need for more than one "system" for a varied population and that the best approach for an individual child may change as the child matures. They are primarily interested in representation of deep structure meaning, rather than English surface structure. They are concerned with systems that are "expressive, focusing on intended meaning and feeling, *not* on stringing together of surface structure words" (p. 18). The systems should be easy for parents and teachers to learn, "relating to English but not to the point of becoming over self-conscious and burdened with affixes and rules" (p. 18). After learning the system, students should also be able to communicate with ASL users and signed English users. For more complex markers, rather than develop a separate set of special signs for English affixes and function words, the use of fingerspelling is preferred.

The vocabulary itself is chosen from several sources. The Lexington *Vocabulary Norms for Deaf Children* aided in choosing word categories. Within each category, vocabulary sets were established. Once the vocabulary was determined, signs were chosen to represent them. The 11 above-named sources were consulted, as were deaf adults, and if necessary a new sign was invented. If more than one sign was available for a given word or concept, the following criteria were used for making a decision (Robbins et al., 1975, p. 19):

(1) The preferred sign was that seeming to be most descriptive of *meaning* (deep structure) rather than of English surface or phonological structure.
(2) An attempt was made to choose signs which had a high consensus of usage among 11 sources.
(3) If there was no consensus, signs advocated by Riekehof and ABC [O'Rourke] were given first priority; those from Bornstein and Watson were given second priority; the other sources were then considered.
(4) Occasionally, a sign was chosen because it was motorically easiest, after the first three criteria above had been met.

The use of these types of criteria, rather than the two-out-of-three principle, or the rigid one sign-one meaning approach, provides a reasonable perspective on using signs to teach children. Of particular importance is the fact that the users of such a system are not misled into thinking that they are providing a perfect parallel for English, and are thus not disturbed when deaf children do not produce the type of sentences that the other systems imply that they should.

A major advantage to the use of the *Perkins Sign Language Dictionary* as a system for teaching deaf children is its flexibility in the area of syntax. Although ASL syntax is not used, neither is strict English syntax. Instead, the dictionary recognizes levels of competence which might require different forms of syntactic expression. Three levels are described (Manual English, Basic Signed English, and Perkins Signed English) which move toward increasing use of fingerspelling, more emphasis on English written structure, and a closer approximation of English syntax.

The first level, Manual English, consists of the Perkins Sign Vocabulary, English word order, and facial and body expressiveness with mime when needed. This is the starting level, and the child may be presented with the second level only when he begins to spontaneously use three or more signs together.

The second level, Basic Signed English, includes the Perkins Sign Vocabulary, English word order, facial and body expressiveness, four sign markers (PAST, PLURAL, POSSESSIVE, and PERSON), and increased fingerspelling for more complicated English structures. A child may be presented with the third level of complexity only after he:

a) is reading stories *not* relating to his own personal experiences and of more than two or three paragraphs, and b) *spontaneously* and *consistently* expressing the following structures in his everyday language:
(1)   Use of PAST MARKER
(2)   Use of POSSESSIVE MARKER
(3)   Use of PLURAL MARKER
(4)   Use of PERSON MARKER
(5)   Use of range of TIME INDICATOR WORDS
(6)   Formulates questions using WHO, WHAT, WHEN, and WHERE (Robbins et al., 1975, p. 20).

The third level of complexity, Perkins Signed English, includes the Perkins Sign Vocabulary, English word order, facial and body expressiveness, the sign markers COMPARATIVE and SUPERLATIVE, and expansion of fingerspelling. During reading or grammar lessons, four other markers may also be used—adverb marker -LY, adjective marker -Y, contraction marker -N'T, and gerund marker

-ING. Robbins et al. (1975, p. 22) offer some guidelines for the use of markers and the different levels:

(1) Importance is placed on evaluating the child's *own* expressive everyday performance in language as a cue to how enthusiastic one should be about the use of English markers.

(2) If the essentials of language (an agent, an action, a time indication, and so on) are not expressed in the simplest forms, by the student, then to push for or expect further differentiation of structure is unrealistic; conversely, if the elements of language structure *are* expressed readily one can assume a reasonable language learning capacity and explore for the possibility of added differentiated structures related to English.

signed ENGLISH

signed English is an outgrowth of the ASL-English pidginization process (Fant, 1964; O'Rourke, 1973; Watson, 1964; see also Chapter 6). It includes a great deal of variation. signed English uses ASL signs strung together in English word order by the use of fingerspelling and some conjunction words. The degree of English word order may vary, however, depending on the amount of fingerspelling used. Thus, the signer may use T+h+e TWO MAN w+e+r+e s+e+a+r+c+h-+i+n+g QUIET for "The two men were searching quietly" in a formal situation and in a less formal situation use TWO MAN SEARCH SEARCH QUIET SEARCH SEARCH, using ASL reduplication to indicate the present progressive. This variability closely approximates the situation in spoken languages, where each person has several styles corresponding to the formality of the situation and whom they are communicating with. Consider for example the difference between everyday speech and formal letter writing, or telephone calls to a friend, or to the boss, or to a client, or to a stranger. What varies is not just the content, but also the linguistic structure, the carefulness of articulation, and the choice of vocabulary items. In signed English this is reflected in the amount of fingerspelling used and the number of rules chosen from English or ASL (see discussion in Chapter 6 on Pidgin Sign English). It provides for greater fluency, since if one does not know a sign, communication can continue uninterrupted by fingerspelling the word. In addition, the need for arbitrary sign formation rules is obviated, since words for which no sign exists can be fingerspelled. This situation tests some new or invented signs from other systems. Some catch on (particularly some initialized signs) and are retained (as, for example, the different signs for the verb "to be") and others are rejected and drop from usage. Dialects develop (a natural situation for any language) and historical changes take place. Furthermore, the teacher can legitimately insist on grammatical signed English in the classroom and still condone the manual communication which goes on outside the classroom as a reflection of these different linguistic styles (nobody really speaks the way English teachers would like them to, but many people expect deaf children to use classroom language outside the classroom, a highly artificial situation). The teacher does not have to learn a new syntax (ASL) nor do the students have to learn many artificial or altered signs. Furthermore, differences in sign usage, such as might occur between users of SEE 2 and users of Manual English, do not occur here.

FINGERSPELLING AND CUED SPEECH

Fingerspelling and cued speech have been separated from the other systems because their relationship with English and speech is different. They are treated individually below.

Fingerspelling

Fingerspelling (dactylology) consists primarily of 26 distinct handshapes which correspond directly to the 26 letters of the alphabet (see Figure 2), although two letters, 'j' and 'z,' require movement as well. A sign for "and" is also included in the standard fingerspelling repertoire. Since the hand configurations correspond to the letters of the alphabet, fingerspelling is a manual representation of written language, and may be used for any language that uses the Roman alphabet (for examples of fingerspelling of non-Roman alphabets, see Moores, 1974). Fingerspelling then has no separate syntax, morphology, phonology, or semantics, but is instead entirely dependent on the linguistic structure of the language it is representing (in this case, English). In this sense, it is similar to Morse Code, which translates each letter of the alphabet into dots and dashes. The consistent pairing of fingerspelling and speech is known as the Rochester Method in the United States (Scouten, 1967) and Neo-oralism in the Soviet Union (Moores, 1974, 1977).

Fingerspelling presents several obvious advantages and disadvantages. In its favor, anyone who can spell can learn the 26 handshapes quickly. Thus, teachers, parents, and clinicians are provided with a quick and easy way to make themselves understood to many deaf people. On the other hand, even though the average adult can learn to fingerspell in short order, learning to perceive and read fingerspelling is another matter. A skilled fingerspeller learns to form words as units, rather than as simple sequences of letters. Thus, the center letters of a word may be assimilated to the surrounding letters, blurring the formation of the letters and creating a perception problem. The skilled fingerspelling reader learns to rely heavily on the first and last letters of a word to help identify that word since there is often a tiny break between the last letter of one word and the first letter of the next word, making the first and last letters more distinct. In rapid fingerspelling reading, one has to make successive guesses as to what is being perceived, in which case a thorough knowledge of the grammar of English (which determines what possible words can follow the words already deciphered) is absolutely essential. In this respect, reading fingerspelling parallels speechreading. The problem of fingerspelling reading can be mitigated if the fingerspeller slows the rate of spelling considerably. This enables the reader to follow the fingers, but destroys the normal rate of conversation, and interrupts the normal flow of speech and intonation.

The reading of fingerspelling is not the only problem associated with it, the other problems being related to the use of fingerspelling with very young children (below age 5). The movements of the fingers are not large, and are usually rapid. Fingerspelling requires a considerably greater degree of manual motor coordination than does signing. Although a child may put two or three signs together into an utterance at about 18 months, fingerspelling does not emerge until much later. Wilbur and Jones (1974) observed nearly none at age 3½ years. In fact, the only spelling seen was the child's own name, which was not done correctly since a double consonant in the name was improperly formed by the child. In addition to the motor problem, very young children have difficulty learning to fingerspell, because the ability to spell is a prerequisite of fingerspelling. Hearing children do not usually learn to spell until they have had considerable experience with reading and spelling practice. Spelling is one of the core subjects of the standard elementary school curriculum. Therefore, one cannot expect a very young child (an illiterate child at that, regardless of whether the child is deaf, retarded, or normal) to acquire fingerspelling without a great deal of effort (drill, patience, practice) and formal training. Language is not learned by means of formal training by hearing children, and consequently the learning of fingerspelling should not be viewed as a normal language learning situation.

This is not to say that children *cannot* learn to fingerspell. Fingerspelling has been shown to be an effective aid in educational settings. Moores (1974, 1977) reviewed several Russian studies that reported success with fingerspelling combined with speech. Moores, Weiss, and Goodwin (1977) followed seven preschool programs for several years. They found that in one program, children taught with the Rochester Method seemed to lag at the early ages, but that by the time the children were about 8 years, their academic performance was significantly superior to children in the oral-only program. The total communication programs fell between the oral and the Rochester methods. In a study specifically designed to assess the effectiveness of fingerspelling as an educational tool, Quigley (1969) compared two preschool programs, one using the Rochester Method (simultaneous fingerspelling and speech) and the other using a traditional oral approach. He followed the two programs for 4 years. At the end, he found that the Rochester Method students were superior in one of two measures of speechreading, five of seven measures of reading, and in three of five measures of written language. The oral group was superior in only one measure of written language. Quigley also compared three residential schools using the Rochester Method with three comparable schools using simultaneous signs, fingerspelling, and speech (probably signed English). No differences in speech or speechreading were found between the two groups. Quigley concluded that "1) The use of fingerspelling in combination with speech as practiced in the Rochester Method can lead to improved achievement in deaf students particularly on those variables where meaningful language is involved. 2) When good oral techniques are used in conjunction with fingerspelling there need be no detrimental effects on the acquisition of oral skills. 3) Fingerspelling is likely to produce greater benefits when used with younger rather than older children. It was used successfully in the experimental study with children as young as three and a half years of age. 4) Fingerspelling is a useful tool for instructing deaf children, but it is not a panacea" (p. 87).

Children of deaf parents who sign and fingerspell have considerable opportunity to observe their parents and to learn from them. In this situation, 1) signing is the primary language that is learned according to developmental stages and without formal instruction and 2) the fingerspelling that is acquired emerges much later and only as an auxiliary. The adult problem of perceiving and comprehending rapid fingerspelling is magnified with the very young child, both in terms of small hand movements and speed. A further caution on the use of fingerspelling is that it is difficult to see in the back of a large audience. Thus a signer can enlarge his signs to accommodate a larger audience by increasing the space utilized in the motion. However, it is not possible to enlarge one's fingers, and even though the spelling can be made more distinct by carefully forming each letter, the gain is not great, and the cost is speed. (This is particularly a problem in interpreting.)

Finally, fingerspelling is slow when compared to signing or speech. To get a feel for what it must be like, have someone read you the last paragraph letter by letter.

Cued Speech

Cornett (1967, 1969) described Cued Speech as a system designed "to enable the deaf child to learn language through exposure to a visible phonetic analog of speech supplied by the lip movements and supplementing hand cues." As Moores (1969) pointed out, the components ("cues") have no meaning independent of their association with those lip movements. (One cue may represent three consonants. The lip movements are required to make a decision.) Thus, the system is most appropriately viewed as an auxiliary to speech and not as a separate communication channel for language. In addition to the system of Cued Speech developed by Cornett, which is described below, several other similar systems were developed in Europe. In the mid-nineteenth century, a French monk, Friar Bernard of Saint Gabriel, developed a system that cued only consonants. Several years later, another Frenchman, Monsieur Fourcade, developed a similar system. Another system was developed by Dr. Georg Forchhammer of the Boarding School for Deaf and Hard-of-Hearing Children at Frederica. Forchhammer's doctoral dissertation reported that the system had a beneficial effect on communication. His system employs hand movements to demonstrate the movement of the mouth organs that cannot be observed during normal speech (glottis, palate, etc.) (Børrild, 1972).

In Cornett's system, there are 36 cues for the 44 phonemes of English. The cues can be divided into vowel cues and consonant cues. Vowel cues are represented by hand positions, and consonant cues are represented by hand configurations. It is therefore possible to represent consonant-vowel pairs by superimposing the consonant hand configuration on the vowel hand position. Diphthongs are represented by a sequence of the first vowel position followed by the second vowel position. The handshapes borrow from those of ASL. The 5-hand configuration of signing is identical to the cue for /m/, /f/, and /t/. The F hand of the fingerspelling alphabet is the cue for /h/, /s/, and /r/. The B hand cues /n/, /b/, and /ʍ/('wh'). The L hand cues /l/, /ʃ/ ('sh'), and /w/. The G hand (upright) cues /d/, /p/, and /ʒ/. Vowel positions are to the right side of the face near the ear, lower on the face by the cheek, below the chin and slightly to the right, and on the right side of the lips. In other words, the cues are made near the face so that they may be easily seen in the perceptual field while the eyes are on the lips, but so that they never come in front of the lips where they would obscure the lip movement.

Like fingerspelling, Cued Speech has its advantages and disadvantages. To its credit, it can be useful for conveying fine phonetic distinctions of either standard or dialectal pronunciation to the already knowledgeable speaker. Success with Cued Speech, in the form of increased accuracy in speechreading, greater vocabulary, greater relaxation among the children, shortening of delay time between learning something receptively and producing expressively, increased communication among the children, and increased intelligibility of the children, has been reported (Rupert, 1969).

Moores (1969) has critically reviewed Cued Speech and I will simply add to his comments as I review his arguments. Objections to the use of Cued Speech can be divided into those that deal with the general assumptions and rationale of the system and those that deal specifically with the system's phonetic base.

1. *Assumptions*   In fact, the first objection is not to an explicit assumption, but to the lack of an explicit distinction, namely, the failure of Cornett to distinguish between language and speech. As indicated above, such distinction is crucial to understanding the nature of language and how language is acquired. Not having made this distinction leads to another assumption, quite commonly held, that language is learned by imitation. It is Cornett's belief that the child will copy the adult cues and thus make himself better understood by the cues even though his speech may not be accurate. This will reduce frustration between adult and child and create a better atmosphere for learning. The problem is that the considerable body of research that exists on the acquisition of language indicates that the role of imitation is nowhere near as central to language acquisition as was previously thought. In investigating imitation, Bloom (1971) was able to sort children into those who do imitate and those who do not. Clearly, those who do not imitate stand as evidence to the contrary of a theory of acquisition by imitation.

2. *Phonetic problems*   Moores pointed out that Cued Speech is intrinsically tied to the sound system and has little or no transfer potential to reading. It is the nature of English orthography that phonemic distinctions are indicated, but predictable phonetic ones are not. For example, in English /d/ and /t/ are pronounced as flaps when they come between two vowels. No one actually says [rayter] for "writer"

and [ryder] for "rider." This flapping process is a general process which holds true for all the words of English for all the speakers. The written forms of the words do not indicate this process, yet it is a phonetic distinction. Likewise, certain unstressed vowels are reduced to a more central, less distinct vowel. This is also not indicated by the orthography. In addition, dialectal pronunciation is of course not indicated by the orthography. One does not write "Cuber" for the New Englanders' "Cuba," although certainly such a major mark of New England pronunciation would have to be cued, otherwise the child would end up missing a major feature of the dialect. The reason for the discrepancy between the written forms and the types of phonetic processes just indicated is that certain phonetic distinctions do not make a difference, even though they are perfectly regular. For example, every voiceless consonant is aspirated at the beginning of an English word. If it were left out, however, its absence might not even be noticed. Cornett's system does not differentiate between those phonetic processes that are dialectal (the fine distinctions mentioned earlier) and those that are redundant, regular, not indicated in the writing systems, and consequently not crucial. It is a far more serious error for the vowel in "bat" to be mispronounced, since it could come out as "beat," "bit," "bait," "boat," "bought," "but," "bet," "bite," "beaut," etc. The system does not set guidelines for the adult as to which phonetic distinctions are important and which are not. In fact, one could suggest that rather than maintain a phonetic base, a phonemic base would be preferable, but then the benefit of indicating fine dialectal distinctions would be lost. This leads to the next point, namely, the competence of the average adult with respect to phonetics. Berko and Brown (1966) remarked, "The untrained adult cannot even approximate an accurate phonetic record." From firsthand experience I can report that learning phonetic transcription is tedious and boring, and is a skill that must be worked at to be developed and maintained. Thus we have the situation of an untrained adult trying to indicate phonetic distinctions which may or may not be important in a manner which may or may not be accurate to a child who may or may not imitate the cues, who may or may not produce them spontaneously on his own, but who is highly unlikely to understand what they indicate, and cannot utilize that information in learning to read. Børrild (1972) reported that a cued speech system has been in use in most Danish schools for nearly 70 years, and that "it is pretty obvious that most pupils having been trained in the mouth-hand system to accompany speech are rather helpless when they have to face pure lipreading. And in spite of the past 70 years, a very small minority only of the population will be acquainted with the mouth-hand system, and a far smaller minority will really master it" (p. 237). Again it should be emphasized that the entire system is geared toward speech and not toward language. Its utility lies in speech therapy, not in initial language learning. Børrild concurred: "It is an indisputable fact that the mouth-hand system is an excellent medium in the articulation training, and that in many cases it is indispensable for adult persons with acquired deafness without any hearing residue but with a normal language . . . " (p. 237).

SUMMARY

The variety of approaches to the goal of representing English in a visual mode demonstrates the arbitrary nature of the choices that are made. Long-term evaluations of the relative effectiveness of the different systems must be conducted, since it seems highly unlikely that they could all be equally effective (unless of course this situation parallels approaches to teaching reading, where there seems to be at least one population for which each method is effective). The need for such comparisons should not be confused with the many comparisons of oral mode vs. manual mode vs. combined mode vs. fingerspelling vs. cued speech which have been conducted to demonstrate that the use of one or more manual modes is superior to the use of oral input only (cf. Beckmeyer, 1976, and Moores, 1974; for initial reading instruction, Wilbur and Flood, 1977, failed to find such an effect but attributed it to inappropriate choice of stimuli). Comparisons of methodology are addressed in more detail in Chapter 8. For purposes of interpreting the problems raised in this chapter with respect to questionable choices and assumptions involving various sign systems, the general trend indicated by most of the methodology studies is that signs, in any form, seem to be more preferable educationally than no signs at all. It remains to be determined if signs in an artificial, English-based system are preferable to ASL or even PSE.

CHAPTER 8

THE USE OF SIGN LANGUAGE IN THE EDUCATION OF DEAF CHILDREN

CONTENTS

All of the preceding information presented in this book would be, to many people, only an interesting academic exercise if it were not for the considerable educational, sociological, and psychological implications that result from the use of ASL and the several sign systems. Included in this chapter is the research available on the feasibility and effectiveness of using manual communication with deaf children. In Chapter 9, similar research is reviewed on the use of sign language with nondeaf populations.

The reader is advised that the information presented here includes any relevant information currently known to me. This means that information, both pro and con, concerning the use of manual communication with deaf children is included. Attempting to extract a simple position on my part is not advised. There is not enough current, objective research and evaluation to reach a truly informed decision, in addition to which it must be recognized that no decision, method, or program is right for every child (see also Moores, in press). There are some guidelines for choosing and some warnings to heed, but the renewed interest in sign language-based programs for deaf children has not been met with a renewed interest in assessing its effectiveness. Too often a decision is made, followed by an ever-increasing feeling of the need to defend it. This does not lead to objectivity, which is so badly needed.

Specific topics included here are the acquisition of language (particularly English syntax, but general acquisition as well), the development of speech skills, socioemotional development, and various aspects of memory. The acquisition of language and the subsequent acquisition of English (if it is not the first language) is of primary importance in the overall education and development of deaf students in the United States. All subsequent academic endeavors depend on language competency, including arithmetic beyond simple nonverbal problems. The acquisition of speech is important insofar as the need exists for deaf people to function in a hearing world. Speechreading skills can provide deaf people with an enhanced ability to enjoy and profit from uncaptioned television, movies, lectures, and social interactions with nondeaf people. Schein and Delk (1974) report that the professional standing and overall earnings are higher for deaf people with good speech than for those whose speech is not good. Social integration in the deaf community (which is really only possible with the knowledge of ASL) is extremely important, possibly as important as a well-adjusted family situation. A deaf person who cannot speak well is almost always uncomfortable in a hearing society, and a deaf person who cannot sign is not an integrated member of the deaf community either. Finally, the development and organization of certain psychological processes, such as memory coding, memory retrieval, and memory rehearsal, may be affected by the modality of the language learned during the child's early years.

ACQUISITION OF LANGUAGE

Learning English Syntax

The general difficulty that deaf children have learning English has been very well documented (Bonvillian, Charrow, and Nelson, 1973; Myklebust, 1964, 1967; Power, 1971; Quigley et al., 1976; Schmitt, 1968; Wilbur, 1977). With respect to reading, Furth (1966a) reported that less than 12% of deaf students between the ages of 15.5 and 16.5 years can read at a fourth-grade reading level or above (as measured on the Metropolitan Reading Achievement Test). This result was confirmed by the Office of Demographic Studies at Gallaudet College (1972).

Traditional studies of the specific problems have focused on the errors, categorizing the number of omissions, substitutions, redundancies, and word order errors (Myklebust, 1964). These categories tend to obscure the causes for the errors and do not provide much guidance to those who are involved in the difficult remediation task. Research on language deficits often reflects current linguistic frameworks, and the area of deaf students' difficulties with English syntax is no exception. The earlier studies reflected classical or structural linguistic approaches which stressed either parts of speech or word order within a sentence (Wilbur and Quigley, 1975). Two more recent frameworks have added considerably to our knowledge of deaf students' problems—transformational grammar, which focuses on relationships that exist with and across sentence types, and pragmatics, which stresses the importance of communicative context for proper use of language structure.

Within the framework of transformational grammar, investigators of deaf students' difficulties with English syntax look for patterns within the errors. Using a stratified random sample of 480 deaf students between the ages of 10 and 18 years (which included students from day and residential programs, oral and manual schools, from each of the nine major geographical areas of the United States), a massive study was conducted of deaf students' difficulty with several groupings of syntactic structures. (For a complete description of the population, methods, and findings, see Quigley et al., 1976; for a general outline of the project, see Wilbur and Quigley, 1975; for a complete text on the topic, see Russell, Power, and Quigley, 1976).

The study indicated that, even by age 18, deaf students do not have the linguistic competence of 10-year-old hearing children in many syntactic structures of English. In some cases, comprehension processing strategies were found beyond the age when a hearing child would have abandoned them (Power, 1971), and non-English rules for producing syntactic structures were found. It was speculated that these rules coexist with the standard English rules for some children (also see Charrow, 1974, 1975a). The possible origin of these rules is discussed below.

Specific Syntactic Structures of English

Passive   In an initial study which tested deaf students' ability to match sentences to their appropriate pictures, Schmitt (1968) found that even by 17 years of age many deaf students had not mastered comprehension of the passive voice. Power (1971) investigated this further, using a performance task to test comprehension. He found steady improvement with age, but by age 18, almost 40% of the students still did not understand the passive. Of primary interest is the strategy the students seemed to be using. If the sentence given was "The truck was hit by the car," the students would interpret this according to a surface subject-verb-object order (referred to here as reading surface order, RSO), e.g., "the truck hit the car." The strength of this RSO strategy is affected by the type of sentence. For example, if the sentence is nonreversible (the subject and object cannot be interchanged), such as "The books were destroyed by the children," comprehension was better than when the sentences were reversible, as in the truck/car sentence above. One significant implication of this information is related to the fact that passive sentences occur as early as the first grade readers for children (hearing or deaf) (Quigley et al., 1976), yet clearly they are not being read properly, even at the oldest ages. It should also be mentioned that only slightly over 40% of the oldest students were able to *produce* a correct passive sentence.

Relative Clauses   The RSO strategy is not restricted to passives, but is also found in the processing of relative clauses. (Actually, the application of the RSO strategy may be useful in comprehension of several English structures, but it happens to work in only some of the structures discussed here.) Quigley, Smith, and Wilbur (1974) reported extensively on the study of relative clauses in English. Deaf students again performed considerably worse when compared with 8- to 10-year-old hearing children. The RSO strategy was found in the students' miscomprehension of embedded relative clauses. Given a sentence like "The boy who hit the girl went home," and a multiple choice, yes-no task, the students responded "yes" to "The girl went home." This indicates again the use of a surface reading, connecting a verb "go" to the closest possible noun phrase for a subject, in this case "the girl." In terms of correct comprehension of the whole sentence, relative clauses, which do not interrupt the main sentence (final relatives), are easier than embedded relative clauses, which separate the main sentence noun phrase from its corresponding verb.

Another interesting process that seems to be operative in deaf students' difficulty with relative clauses is the maintenance in the relative clause of the noun phrase being relativized. Thus, in a sentence such as "The dog which the dog bit the cat ran away," the relative clause should be "which bit the cat," where "which" is replacing the second occurrence of "the dog." Instead, "the dog" has been retained in the relative clause so that both the relative pronoun "which" and the noun phrase "the dog" are present. It is unclear if this is the result of a deliberate copying rule (which it was originally termed) or a failure to delete the noun phrase after inserting the relative pronoun. Nonetheless, metalinguistic judgments made by deaf students on the acceptability of sentences such as these reveal that over 30% of the oldest students in the study consider these sentences to be acceptable.

Questions The copying phenomenon found in relative clauses is also found in Wh-questions (who, what, when, where, why, which, how), confirming that it is intimately connected to the function and usage of Wh-words. An example of a Wh-question with copying is a sentence like "Who did the dog bite the cat?" A task identical to that conducted for relative clauses was conducted for Wh-questions; interestingly, the results from the two studies are so close that the graphs are nearly identical.

The study of questions in general (Quigley, Wilbur, and Montanelli, 1974) indicated that, in terms of comprehension of questions, yes-no questions ("Is the earth flat?") were easier than Wh-questions, which in turn were easier than tag questions ("John didn't come to school today, *did he*?). Metalinguistic judgments of acceptability were also easier for yes-no questions than for Wh-questions. Stages of development were found for the deaf students which paralleled those reported in the literature for young hearing children (Brown and Hanlon, 1970; Ervin-Tripp, 1970; Klima and Bellugi-Klima, 1966). The difference, of course, is the age difference.

Pronouns The investigation of pronouns (Wilbur, Montanelli, and Quigley, 1976) focused on two aspects of English pronouns—which ones to use and when to use them. The investigation of which ones to use was presented to the students in the form of two sentences, the second one containing a blank where a pronoun should go. The first sentence, then, provided the antecedent to the second sentence. The student was required to choose the correct pronoun from three or four choices given beneath the item sentences. Essentially, then, the students were told, "A pronoun goes in this slot—which one is it?" In this situation, even the youngest students (age 10 years) did quite well. The mean percent correct across all age levels was 72% for subject pronouns (I, we, you, he, she, it, they), 74% for object pronouns (me, us, you, him, her, it, them), 63% for possessive adjectives (my, our, your, his, her, its, their), 50% for possessive pronouns (mine, ours, yours, his, hers, its, theirs), and 55% for reflexives (myself, ourselves, yourself, yourselves, himself, herself, itself, themselves).

In addition to the syntactic tests, written language samples were collected from each student in the study, using a sequence of four pictures that "told a story." These written samples were analyzed for correct pronoun usage. Two analyses were done. The first examined pronoun usage when the antecedent of the pronoun was in the same sentence as the pronoun itself. In this case, the students did well, with scores ranging from 75% at age 10 to a high of 93% correct at age 17. The other analysis examined pronoun usage when the referent did not occur in the same sentence as the pronoun, but rather appeared in an earlier sentence. The difference in performance was striking—correct usage ranged from only 40% at age 10 to 80% at age 18. These data indicate that deaf students' problems with pronouns are related to when to use them, not which ones to use.

Conjunctions The rules for conjoining sentences in English seem to cause less difficulty to deaf students than relative clauses, passives, and various verb constructions. Wilbur, Quigley, and Montanelli (1975) found developmental trends similar to those reported by Menyuk (1963, 1964). The easiest type of conjunction for deaf students is the conjoined sentence, especially when the sentences do not share common elements. In this case, the child need only put an "and" between two separate sentences to produce a conjoined sentence. In the most general of cases (there is no syntactic relationship between the two sentences being conjoined), deaf students correctly produced conjoined sentences ranging from less than half (46%) at age 10 to 76% at age 18.

A more difficult conjoined structure is the conjoined noun phrase, with subject noun phrases being easier than object noun phrases. Thus, from two sentences, "Ann went to school" and "John went to school," one sentence, "Ann and John went to school," can be produced with the subject conjoined noun phrase "Ann and John." With this type of structure, deaf students did less well than with conjoined sentences, producing 34% correct at age 10 but increasing to 81% at age 18. Object conjoined noun phrases ("The boy spilled the milk and the cookie box") were even harder, with only 7% correct at age 10 but increasing dramatically to 77% at age 18. In both the subject noun phrase and object noun phrase situations, the largest "error" response was to produce a fully conjoined sentence without reduction to conjoined noun phrases (e.g., "Ann went to school and John went to school," "The boy spilled the milk and the boy [or he] spilled the cookie box."). Because conjoined sentences are an earlier stage of development than conjoined noun phrases, the source of this error is easily understood.

Conjoined verb phrases are the most difficult type of major conjoined phrase. From two full sentences, "John washed the car" and "John waxed the car," a conjoined verb phrase, "John washed the car and waxed it," is the expected form. At age 10, deaf students produced only 3% correct conjoined verb phrases, improving to only 62% by age 18. The fully conjoined sentence "John washed the car and he waxed it" was the most common "error" response. From these data, we can see the same overall pattern (from easiest to hardest) reported by Menyuk (1963, 1964): conjoined sentences (easiest), conjoined sub-ject noun phrases, conjoined object noun phrases, conjoined verb phrases (hardest). This pattern, if it were the only one we had, might suggest a mere delay in deaf students' development. Other data, how-ever, suggested that something more than a mere delay was occurring. Certain structures, initially considered deviant, were found, but those so-called deviant structures now seem to be the result of normal devel-opment strategies and can be explained in a reasonably simple way.

As indicated above, conjoined sentences were the easiest form for deaf students to handle because they are mastered at an early developmental stage. However, the restriction "in the general case" was placed on this discussion because of problems that arise with two more specific cases. If the two sentences were related in such a way that they shared similar subjects or objects, a number of unusual omissions occurred. For example, two sentences, "John washed the car" and "Mary waxed the car," might be rewritten as "John washed the car and Mary waxed," where the object of the second sentence has been deleted. This has been referred to as object-object deletion; the second object was deleted because it is identical to the first object. Likewise, "The boy hit the girl" and "The girl hit him back" might be rewritten as "The boy hit the girl and hit him back," where the second subject has been deleted because it is identical to the first object (object-subject deletion). (For further details, see Wilbur, 1977; Wilbur, Quigley, and Montanelli, 1975.) These structures were origi-nally reported by Taylor (1969). Wilbur, Quigley, and Montanelli (1975) reported reduced performance on sentence rewrite items when deaf students were presented with object-object deletion environments (25% correct at age 10 to 68% at age 18) or object-subject deletion items (44% at age 10 to 45% at age 18) when compared to the general case sentences (again, 46% at age 10 to 76% at age 18). In the written language samples, both object-object deletion and object-subject dele-tion occurred in free production. Interestingly, object-object deletion declined with age (from a small 6% at age 10 down to 1% at age 18), whereas object-subject deletion increased from 12% at age 10 to 32% at age 18. The free production data are consistent with the test results, in that object-object deletion seems to disappear with age in both cases, but object-subject deletion does not.

The first step in providing an explanation for these two rules is to notice that they are not simply random deletions, but that they occur in the second sentence of two conjoined sentences, and that in fact this is one of the environments in which English pronominalizes. Thus one begins by hypothesizing that deaf children are aware of the need for reducing redundancy, which is what pronominalizing does, but instead of pronominalizing, they simply delete. Indeed, this initial hypothesis still seems valid, but requires further discussion. Why does object-subject deletion increase in use but object-object deletion decrease? This question is especially important, given that the above hypothesis attempts to explain both rules as a single process, when they clearly do not behave as a single process. One important implication of the decline of object-object deletion is that it provides evidence that deaf students are still revising and refining their hypotheses about the structure of English even at the oldest ages tested in this study. Furthermore, it is possible to explain the nature of these revisions and refinements within a framework based solely on the structure of English. There are environments in English in which it *is* possible to delete the subject of the second sentence in a conjoined structure. The result of this process is a conjoined verb phrase, such as "The elephant crushed the roots and ate them," which comes from "The elephant crushed the roots" and "The elephant ate them (the roots)." The general rule for English is that the subject of the second sentence may be deleted if it is identical to the *subject* of the first sentence. The deaf students who use object-subject deletion are deleting the second subject when it is identical to the first *object*. Together with object-object deletion, their generalization is probably to "delete a noun phrase in the second sentence if it occurs in the first sentence." This generalization gives correct forms (conjoined verb phrases) as well as incorrect forms. As the deaf students get older, they seem to come to realize that objects are not deleted in English. However, their increasing mastery and use of conjoined verb phrases reinforces the deletion of subjects. Thus, as they mature, a new generalization is formulated—"Delete the subject in the second sentence if it occurs in the first sentence." This generalization produces correct conjoined verb phrases and incorrect object-subject deletion, accounting for the failure of object-subject deletion to disappear. Because there is no similar parallel for objects, the loss of object-object deletion is predictable. This situation suggests that deaf students' problems with English syntax reflect their attempts at coping with increasing, but still limited, data.

Determiners   An analysis of determiner usage in the written language sample (Wilbur, 1977) revealed a pattern opposite to that discussed for the pronouns. Determiners were correctly placed before the noun 61% of the time at age 10, increasing to 76% of the time at age 18. However, of the correctly placed determiners, 25% (mean across all ages) were incorrect in terms of their usage, either being definite ("the") when they should be indefinite, or, indefinite ("a") when they should be definite. Thus, although deaf students seem to know when to use determiners (unlike pronouns), they do not seem to know which ones to use (also unlike pronouns).

Possible Explanations   The above data, together with data on negation (Quigley et al., 1976), verbal auxiliaries (Quigley, Montanelli, and Wilbur, 1976), and verbal complements (Quigley, Wilbur, and Montanelli, 1976), indicate the considerable difficulty deaf students have with English. It has been suggested that deaf children's difficulty in acquiring English is not limited to linguistic processing but extends to their general cognitive ability to form generalizations. Furth (1966b) has demonstrated that the general cognitive ability of deaf people is not greatly different from hearing people in nonlinguistic tasks. Given this information, it has been suggested that deaf people do not develop the ability to apply their nonlinguistic cognitive skills to linguistic tasks. This suggestion ignores the fact that the acquisition of ASL is a linguistic task that many deaf children accomplish easily. However, it is still suggested by some that the difficulty is specific to English but not specific to syntax.

Wilbur (1974b) investigated nonsyntactic generalizations made by deaf students. The task required recognition of English constraints on the structure of allowable words. For example, *blick* could be a word of English, although it actually is not. However, *bnick* could not be a word of English because of the structure of the initial consonant cluster *bn* (compare with Russian which allows initial clusters *zd* and *gd*). One need not know what these words might mean in order to decide which is acceptable to English and which is not. Furthermore, these constraints, unlike spelling rules and "proper" grammatical rules, are not specifically taught to either deaf or hearing children in school. Therefore, any knowledge that deaf children have of these constraints must have been extracted entirely on their own, thus giving an indication of their processing ability relative to English. First-, third-, fifth-, and seventh-grade deaf and third/fourth- and seventh-grade hearing children were tested on their ability to reject incorrectly formed words such as *bnick*. Although the deaf students' scores were quantitatively below those of the hearing children until the seventh grade, the scores were not qualitatively different. That is, violations of English word structure constraints that were easy for the hearing children to spot were also easy for the deaf students, and those that were hard for the hearing children were also hard for the deaf children. It was concluded that deaf students' difficulty in learning the proper rules for the more complex syntactic patterns is not attributable to a disturbance of general linguistic or cognitive processing (see Furth, 1966b), but rather to difficulty in learning the specific rules for English. This is strengthened by the fact that by seventh grade, the deaf and the hearing students performed equally well. It is also supported by the acquisition data in Chapter 5 ("Sign Language Acquisition") which showed that the deaf child learning ASL is a hypothesis-generating and refining creature, similar to the hearing child.

Wilbur (1977) provided an explanation of this difficulty by considering the larger pragmatic environment in which these structures must be used and comparing it with the manner in which they are taught. The study of language within a pragmatic framework includes contextual environments larger than a sentence, such as a paragraph (in writing) or a conversation (in speaking). The context interacts with the syntax in such a way as to allow certain syntactic structures and prohibit others. Consider the two syntactically and semantically related sentences "The car hit the truck" and "The truck was hit by the car." The difference in meaning or function between these two sentences is not at all obvious without the benefit of context. Although they are alternate realizations of the same deep structure, their use in context reflects a difference in function. For example, the passive may be appropriate and the active inappropriate in a given context, or vice versa. An appropriate response to "What hit the truck?" may be either "The car hit the truck" or "The truck was hit by the car." However, if the question is "What did the car hit?" it would be inappropriate to respond with "The truck was hit by the car." The pragmatic domain, then, is concerned with messages intended, sent, and received, in terms of shared knowledge between sender and receiver, expectations of both based on world knowledge, conversational content, and linguistic structure, and the effects of these on choice of syntactic structure.

A primary pragmatic consideration is the separation of old and new information. If information has already been presented, repeated reference to it may become redundant, and thus deletion rules or pronominal rules may apply. One may wish to refer to a specific piece of information already introduced, in which case a definite determiner ("the") would be used. Old information may be put in a relative clause ("The boy whom I told you about"). Within a pragmatic perspective, then, several of the syntactic structures that deaf students have difficulty with seem to form a group in that they are involved in separating old from new information. Three of the structures—pronominalization, conjunctions, and determiners—illustrate the problem. As indicated above, deaf students were able to handle the choice of pronouns when presented with pronoun environments, but experienced difficulty in deciding when to use pronouns. In particular, pronoun usage was easier within a sentence than across two sentences. Wilbur (1977) interpreted this as evidence that deaf students perform better with single sentences than sentences in sequence. The problem with sentences in sequence is that the first one introduces new information ("This is my friend John") which immediately after presentation is considered *old* information. Thus the second sentence, if it refers back to the first, must use a pronoun ("He goes to school with me"). This situation is further complicated in the case of pronouns by the lack of a fixed rule for pronoun usage in English. A pronoun should be used to avoid redundancy when information is referred to several times in succession, but at the same time ambiguity of reference must be avoided. The same general tendency of reducing redundancy is apparent in the deletions that produce conjoined structures, and deaf students' confusion is similarly reflected in their overgeneralization of the deletion process. In fact, the deletions that occur may be alternately viewed as further difficulty with the use or nonuse of pronouns in their function of referring to old information.

Deaf students' difficulty with determiners is also an old vs. new problem. The use of "the" when introducing *new* material is severely constrained ("This is the woman I mentioned to you," where "the woman" must be further modified by a relative clause). In general, "the" is reserved for reference to old information.

As indicated above, deaf students' problem with determiners is not the placement of determiners before nouns, but rather the distinction of definite/indefinite. Determiner usage constraints, and the other pragmatic constraints, must be applied to each individual conversational situation, making the acquisition of such constraints a complicated task.

To what extent is deaf students' difficulty with English attributable to interference from knowledge of ASL? The answer can take a variety of forms: 1) Researchers in the area of second-language acquisition have investigated bilingual interference in a variety of ways. One such study (Richards, 1974) reports that only about 20% of the second-language errors may be attributed to interference from the first language. (I am unconvinced by either the statistic or the method.) 2) The sample used for the studies on English syntactic structures discussed above included students from total communication and oral schools, yet the error patterns pervaded all schools and all grade levels. 3) This is not surprising after the extensive discussion above of the generalizations deaf students are making based on the English data available to them. These generalizations are specific to English. So far, there has been no need to resort to ASL for explanations (although the possibility is not ruled out). 4) Given the extensive description of the structure of American Sign Language in this book, it cannot be argued that deaf students' problems with English are a result of any deficiencies in ASL structure.

Wilbur (1977) argues that part of the problem, particularly that part which is pragmatically controlled, may be attributable to the heavy emphasis placed on the proper structure of the single sentence in the language training programs for deaf children. Older approaches (Fitzgerald, 1929; Wing, 1887) were primarily concerned with the order of words within a sentence. More recent programs, especially those based on transformational grammar, emphasize the function of words in a sentence (grammatical relations such as subject and object) and relationships between sentences (active-passive, declarative-question-imperative, positive-negative). Even so, the emphasis may still be on the structure of the sentence alone, rather than on the use of the sentence within its larger environment. Obviously, both types of study, pragmatic and syntactic, are needed, indeed are crucial, for the development of deaf individuals with high degrees of competence and flexibility in English use.

Despite the lack of evidence suggesting interference, one may still question the relationship between knowledge of manual communication and the development of English syntax.

A specific study of this relationship has been completed by Brasel and Quigley (1977). They defined four groups on the basis of the educational approach of the parents with respect to the child. The parents of the first group used Manual English (ME), the parents of the second group used ASL (referred to as the Average Manual (AM) group), the parents of the third group began intensive oral (IO) training with the child at an early age, and the parents of the fourth group used oral communication but did not use any kind of special early training (referred to as the Average Oral (AO) group). Brasel and Quigley reported that none of the parents in the ME group used any of the "morphemic types of sign language such as Seeing Essential English, Signing Exact English, or Linguistically Oriented Visual English"; Manual English therefore would be equivalent to what has been called signed English here. The groups themselves each contained 18 deaf students, with a mean age for each group of 14.8 years. It should be pointed out that Brasel and Quigley's (1977) groups were confounded in the same way that many other such studies are, namely, that the parents of the deaf students in the manual groups were deaf and the parents of the deaf students in the oral group were hearing. This entails sociological and emotional interaction in addition to the language variable being studied. An extremely detailed description of the sample group, parents, and siblings, including samples of the parents' written English, is given in Brasel and Quigley.

The groups were compared on the same tests of English syntax, the Test of Syntactic Ability (TSA), that were used in the previously mentioned studies (Quigley et al., 1976) and on four subtests of the Stanford Achievement Test (Language, Paragraph Meaning, Word Meaning, and Spelling). The results of the Brasel and Quigley study showed "that the two Manual groups were significantly superior to the two Oral groups on every test measure employed." Although the ME group outscored the AM group on all six major syntactic structure groupings in the TSA, only one of those differences was significant (relative clauses). Furthermore, "no differences were found between the IO and the AO group on any of the TSA subtests although the IO group generally did better than the AO group, and the AM group did better than the two Oral groups." On the Stanford Achievement Test subtests, the Manual English group "was found significantly superior to the other three groups on all four subtests, with the ME group being from one to nearly four grades ahead with its nearest competitor being the AM group" (p. 120). Brasel and Quigley (1977) concluded that "the greatest advantage appears to come when the parents are competent in Standard English and use Manual English with and around the child, as witness the marked superiority of the ME group over both Oral groups on nearly [sic] every test measure employed and that some advantage is found where early Manual communication exists regardless of degree of deviation from Standard English syntax."

The reader is advised to use caution when reading and interpreting the Brasel and Quigley study. The Manual English parents are continually referred to as "language-competent" or "grammatically correct." "Language-competent" should be read as "English-competent"; "language-competent" means that someone knows a language, not necessarily English, so that someone who knows ASL is certainly language-competent, but not necessarily English-competent; thus, the TSA is a test of English, not "language." "Gramatically correct" should be read as "grammatically correct with respect to English"; French and Spanish are certainly grammatically correct with respect to themselves, but not with respect to English. These findings also must be considered with caution for other reasons, such as differences in age of detection between the oral and manual groups, the late age of fitting of amplification for the so-called early intensive oral group, and the fact that many of the parents in the Manual English group were teachers.

Bonvillian, Charrow, and Nelson (1973), Bonvillian, Nelson, and Charrow (1976), and Moores (1974, 1977) also reviewed several studies that have been conducted on differences between groups of deaf students trained orally and manually. These studies cover a wide range of areas (social adjustment and mathematics, for example) not directly related to the topic of English syntax. These studies are reviewed in other sections below.

Early Language Learning

There is yet another aspect of the implications of manual communication for language acquisition that bears discussion. It has been well documented that the brain develops rapidly until puberty, at which time establishment of synaptic patterns ceases (Lenneberg, 1967). At the same time, it has been observed that language acquisition before puberty happens more or less naturally, with children being able to acquire any language(s) to which they are exposed, whereas language acquisition after puberty becomes more of a process of conscious learning (as opposed to more or less spontaneous acquisition). It has been hypothesized that the high correlation between these two events, brain development and language acquisition, is in fact a causal relationship, such that the acquisition of a first language after puberty should be virtually impossible (referred to as the Critical Age hypothesis in Lenneberg, 1967). Furthermore, it has been observed that the most rapid rate of brain development and organization occurs before 5 or 6 years, which is also the time of the most rapid development of language in normal children. As the child grows toward puberty, the establishment of neural synaptic networks and language development slows down. There is, then, a time in the life of a child from birth to about 6 years that is undoubtedly the most critical with respect to the proper acquisition of language.

Consider this with respect to some data from the Brasel and Quigley study. For the ME and AM groups, the children were confirmed deaf at 7 months of age or younger. For the IO and AO groups, the children were confirmed deaf at about 1 year, 2 months. With the exception of the IO group, the children did not begin formal schooling until they were at least 4 years old. The IO group began formal training at around 2 years (recall that the subjects were selected *because* of the so-called early intensive training which they received). In the 4 years from birth until they began schooling, the deaf children in the ME and AM groups had an opportunity to observe the use of language in the visual mode, a mode that functions normally for them. Through this mode they were able to perceive language and use their normal linguistic processes (whatever those might be) to acquire language from their environment, utilizing the same types of early acquisition strategies as young hearing children, and passing through similar developmental stages (one-word stage, two-word stage, the several different semantic relationship stages, etc.).

The deaf child in the AO group received minimal language input (English or otherwise) until he started school at age 4, at which point nearly two-thirds of those crucial years were gone. He had missed the developmental stages that a child normally passes through in language acquisition and had to compensate for them with formal training. The deaf child in the IO group was given a partial opportunity at age 2 to begin the developmental sequence, but this was done in such a way that the child was formally presented with input, based on what the adults thought the child should be learning, in a mode that requires considerably greater effort from the child because of his auditory deficit. Furthermore, the mode and the formal presentation distract from other aspects of language acquisition, primarily syntax and pragmatics. The deaf child has considerable difficulty in mastering English syntax. This can be explained partially by the specific methodology used to teach it, namely, concentrating on the single sentence. Just as overemphasizing the sentence can lead to incorrect assumptions about how such sentences should be constructed and to functional deficits in how such structures should be used in contexts, overemphasizing articulation leads to overlooking both syntax and pragmatics. Recent research on hearing infants (Donahue, 1977a,b; Donahue and Watson, 1976; Watson, 1977) indicates that the child participates actively in conversations with adults (primarily the mother) through a variety of means before the child can talk intelligibly. These include responding to a mother's questioning intonation with a statement intonation (spread across a babbled sequence), mother's imitation of the child followed by the child's imitation of the mother (indicating some knowledge on the child's part of turn-taking cues), and in later developments, the child's use of back-channel communication to the mother (head nods, "uh-huh," "mm," "yea"). These early conversations provide the child with important social and linguistic information. A child learns strategies for dealing with situations in which he has not been understood properly (e.g., repeating himself louder, phrasing himself differently). Other information, such as phrase structure, may come from conversational clues, such as adult pausing and intonation. All of these provide the very young hearing child with help in decoding the language he hears. The language acquisition process is similar in deaf children of deaf parents who learn ASL as a first language. The deaf child's problem arises in the acquisition of English. Heavy emphasis on one particular aspect to the (partial) exclusion of all others is detrimental to the child by depriving him of clues to the decoding of English and the appropriate use of it.

SPEECH SKILLS

If the deaf individual is to function in a hearing world, speech is clearly a useful language tool. It is a common belief that the use of manual communication necessarily hinders the development of speech. Moores (1971) summarized several studies that directly compared early oral preschool children with children who had no preschool. None of the studies cited reported any difference in oral skills (speech and speechreading) between the two groups. One of the studies (Vernon and Koh, 1970) compared deaf children of hearing parents with early intensive oral training to deaf children of deaf parents with no pre-school (i.e., ASL users). Again, no differences in oral skills were found between the two groups, but the students with deaf parents were found to be superior in reading and general achievement.

Several studies have compared deaf children of deaf parents to deaf children of hearing parents. Four of these studies included results that are relevant here (Meadow, 1966; Quigley and Frisina, 1961; Stevenson, 1964; Stuckless and Birch, 1966; for a description of these, see Bonvillian, Charrow, and Nelson, 1973; Moores, 1971, 1974). The four studies reported that the deaf children of deaf parents were superior on some or all of the English skills and general measures of ability. Three of these studies reported no difference between the two groups on measures of speech production, but the fourth reported that the deaf children of hearing parents were better. One of the studies also reported that the deaf children of deaf parents were better on measures of speechreading ability, whereas the other three reported no difference between the two groups.

Direct studies of the effects of manual communication on speech are rare. Quigley (1969) reported no difference in speech or speech-reading for students using the Rochester Method (simultaneous fin-gerspelling) when compared with those using simultaneous signing and speech. A study of children using Swedish Sign (Ahlström, 1972) reported that "speech was not adversely affected by knowledge of signs" (Power, 1974). One study seemed to be contradictory. A group of nine children in a German school for the deaf was being taught using the Rochester Method. When these children were transferred to an oral-only approach, the "quantity and quality of speech improved. Lipreading ability increased partially" (Power, 1974). Studies such as this last one are difficult to evaluate because it is not possible to determine the effects of increased age and the change in social group pressure or in numbers of opportunities to use speech.

What is striking about the studies summarized in Power (1974) and Moores (1971, 1974) is the lack of any direct evidence that the use of manual communication is in fact detrimental to the development of speech skills. If such an interference relationship existed, one would expect to see it reported in study after study. Its absence is thus noteworthy.

Researchers investigating the use of manual communication with other populations with normal hearing (retarded, autistic, language delayed) have reported beneficial effects of manual communication on speech skills, although this may possibly be for other reasons (discussed in Chapter 9).

The development of speech skills is offered as the primary concern of those people who do not choose to use manual communication with deaf children. Children's competence with speech and speechreading has come to represent (whether appropriately or not) a measure of the effectiveness of educational programs, particularly those using manual communication. The use of total communication (meaning here signing and speaking English) is a sensitive issue. Many people have equated the use of total communication (TC) with the use of signs themselves. Thus, a negative comment against TC is often wrongly interpreted as a negative comment against the use of any manual communication. At the risk of being misinterpreted, I wish to sound a note of caution on the use of TC, particularly with respect to the assumptions one makes before adopting it and the expectations one has when using it.

One assumption that underlies the use of TC is that by simultaneously signing and speaking with the child, the child is receiving speech input and speechreading practice, which will lead to the child's own speech production. Put another way, the responsibility for intensive speech instruction may have been abdicated because one assumes that the child is being presented with sufficient speechreading practice as a consequence of the continuous use of TC. The expectation then is that the child's speech skills will not decline, and may even grow, with the use of TC (other skills, such as language, other academic subjects, and social interactions, are also expected to improve). When such an expectation is not met, TC as a whole will be faulted and may well be abandoned. The caution being raised here challenges these assumptions and expectations. First, the child's attention must be split between the two visual systems, manual (sign and/or fingerspelling) reading and speechreading. One should not expect this to be as effective for speech skills as intensive speech training. Unfortunately, TC is not being used properly in many cases, with people not speaking while they are signing, and the child is deprived of *any* speech exposure, whether incidental or intensive. In order for TC not to go down the drain (and all manual communication with it), one must recognize its limitations. If speech is the skill being taught, there is no substitute for intensive speech training. If English, history, math, or science are being taught, TC should be used if necessary, or ASL only if possible and appropriate; one should not pretend to be fulfilling responsibilities in the area of speech skills. Moores (in press) indicates that there are two schools of thought: 1) the bilingual school, with the child learning to sign first, and using sign to learn everything else (English, speech, etc.) later, and 2) the school that says we all know English so let's use it with these children. He points out that the second school predominates. The first position, suggested here for further consideration, is often viewed as a radical perspective, but may turn out to be more viable in the long run. It certainly should not be condemned until all the evidence has been evaluated.

SOCIALIZATION, ACHIEVEMENT, AND EMOTIONAL DEVELOPMENT

The relationship of the use of manual communication to the well-being of the deaf person interacts with the relationship of a deaf person to his parents. Several of the earlier cited studies that compared deaf students of deaf parents to deaf students of hearing parents to determine the relationship of manual communication to the acquisition of English or of speech skills are relevant here (see Table 22). These studies overwhelmingly reported better overall achievement for the deaf students of deaf parents, even though there were differences on some measures, and, in some cases, no differences at all. It is probable that much of this achievement depends directly on better parent-child relations, which in turn are a function of better communication channels.

Moores (1974) summarized several studies comparing deaf students of deaf parents to deaf students of hearing parents. Relevant portions are discussed here, but the reader is advised that these are only summaries. Stevenson (1964) compared 134 deaf students of hearing parents, and reported higher educational achievement for the deaf students of deaf parents in 90% of the comparisons, with 38% of the

students with deaf parents going on
of the students with hearing parent.
ported superior reading, speechread
deaf students of deaf parents, with n
psychosocial development.

Meadow (1966) reported higher se
ment in deaf children of deaf parents
1.25 years in arithmetic, 2.1 years in 1
for these students. In addition, teacher
in favor of the deaf students of deaf pare
independence, sociability, appropriate s   , appropriate responses to situations, fingerspelli_g ability, written language,
signing ability, absence of communicative frustration, and willingness
to communicate with strangers. No difference was noted in speech or
speechreading.

Vernon and Koh (1970) likewise found that deaf students of deaf
parents were superior in reading, vocabulary, and written language,
with an overall achievement of 1.44 years higher than the students of
hearing parents (and no manual communication). No differences were
found in speech, speechreading, or psychosocial adjustment. Quigley
and Frisina (1961) found higher vocabulary levels for the deaf students
of deaf parents, no differences in speechreading or educational
achievement, and better speech for the deaf students of hearing parents. Vernon and Koh (1970) compared the academic achievement of
deaf students of deaf parents with early manual communication to deaf
students of hearing parents with early intensive oral training (John
Tracy Clinic program). They found that the students of deaf parents
were one full grade ahead in all areas and had superior reading skills.
No differences were found in speech or speechreading.

Comparisons of deaf students of deaf parents with deaf students
of hearing parents revealed that 60% of the deaf students of deaf
parents did not have preschool education, whereas only 18% of the
deaf students of hearing parents had not attended preschool. The
hearing parents had a significantly higher socioeconomic status than
the deaf parents, and nearly 90% of the hearing parents had some
contact with the John Tracy Clinic program.

These studies do not tell the whole story, however. The existence
of a deaf community (Chapter 6) that is bound together by a common
language has a profound effect on the perspective from which one
views the relationship between socioemotional development and use
of manual communication. The deaf person, unlike other language-
disrupted persons, has the deaf community to enjoy while growing up

Table 22. Studies of deaf children of deaf parents receiving manual communication

Investigator	Comparison	Programs	Results
Stevenson (1964)	134 deaf students of deaf parents to 134 deaf students of hearing parents	California School for Deaf, Berkeley	Those with deaf parents were educationally superior in 90% of pair matchings. 38% of students with deaf parents went to college, 9% of those with hearing parents.
Stuckless and Birch (1966)	38 deaf students of deaf parents matched to 38 deaf students of hearing parents	American School for Deaf, Pennsylvania School for Deaf, West. Pa. School for Deaf, Martin School for Deaf, Indiana School for Deaf	Children with deaf parents superior in reading, speechreading and written language. No differences in speech or psychosocial development.
Meadow (1966)	59 deaf students of deaf parents matched to 59 deaf students of hearing parents	California School for Deaf, Berkeley	Children with deaf parents ahead 1.25 years in arithmetic, 2.1 years in reading, 1.28 years in achievement. Superior in written language, fingerspelling, signs, willingness to communicate with strangers. More mature, responsible, sociable. No differences in speech or speechreading.

| Quigley and Frisina (1961) | 16 deaf students with deaf parents out of a population of 120 deaf students | Kansas School for Deaf, Michigan School for Deaf, Pennsylvania School for Deaf, Texas School for Deaf, Rochester School for Deaf, California School for Deaf, Riverside | Children with deaf parents superior in fingerspelling and vocabulary. No differences in speechreading and achievement. Children with hearing parents superior in speech. |
| Vernon and Koh (1970) | 32 deaf students with deaf parents matched with 32 recessively deaf students with hearing parents | California School for Deaf, Riverside | Children with deaf parents—an average of 1.44 years superior on academic achievement and superior in reading vocabulary and written language. No differences in speech and speechreading. |

From Moores (1971).

and as an adult. Social functions, religious groups, educational seminars, and political lobbying are all part of the activities within the deaf community. Markowicz and Woodward (1978) report that "ASL serves as the primary linguistic criterion for identification of self and others as members of the deaf subculture, and for the promotion of solidarity within the group." The deaf community may include the profoundly deaf and the hard of hearing, both prelingually and postlingually deaf individuals, those with good speech and those without, and occasional hearing people (usually with deaf parents). At the same time, there are hearing-impaired people who are not members of the deaf community and who have little or no contact with its members. Two criteria that seem to determine membership in the deaf community are 1) attendance at a residential school for the deaf (where deaf children of hearing parents are socialized into the community by older children and peers who have deaf parents) and 2) competence in ASL (Stokoe, Casterline, and Croneberg, 1965).

Charrow and Wilbur (1975) discussed the parallels between the minority deaf culture and other minority groups in the United States. Of particular sociolinguistic interest are the different social conventions and politeness rules for signers than for speakers/listeners. For example, Baker (1977) has described turn-taking signals in ASL conversations (see Chapter 5, "Comparisons of Signing and Speaking") that are different from those in English, and has identified different conventions for eye contact, distance between signer and addressee, and other such cultural differences.

Information is scarce concerning the relationship between manual communication and vocational success, although it is known that good speech skills are highly correlated with employment opportunities and financial rewards (Boatner, Stuckless, and Moores, 1964). Information of psychosocial aspects of manual communication usage continues to be gathered (Bolton, 1976; see especially Bornstein, Woodward, and Tully, 1976; Meadow, 1976). One study (Rainer, Altshuler, and Kallmann, 1963) reported on the marital patterns of deaf women, indicating that 95% of marriages of women born deaf and 91% of marriages of women adventitiously deafened at an early age are to deaf men. They also reported that the better the communication skills (oral or manual), the higher the probability of marriage. However, ironically, once married, the better the communication skills, the higher the incidence of marital discord. Such information, although interesting, does not directly pertain to the use of manual communication itself as much as to the need for improved communication skills. Related articles can also be found in O'Rourke (1972; see Vernon, Meadow, or Schlesinger).

MEMORY

Two questions related to memory and sign language may be profitably asked: 1) What is the effect of knowledge of sign language on the organizations of memory, particularly with respect to English? 2) What is the effect of early acquisition of sign language on the development of memory itself?

Organization of Memory and English

The reader should recall at this point the earlier research on memory (Chapter 5, "Memory for ASL"), where Bellugi and Siple's (1974) investigation of the parameters of ASL is discussed. Their study dealt specifically with the organization of memory for ASL. It was briefly pointed out that when deprived of an opportunity to use semantic information in the recall of words, hearing people tend to make mistakes based on the phonological properties of the words they hear or see; phonological properties of signs produce similar errors in deaf persons. In order to better consider the research that has been done on memory processes of deaf individuals, the research on hearing people is now briefly reviewed.

The recall of lists of unrelated words is heavily influenced by the sounds that constitute those words. Conrad (1962) demonstrated that hearing people have greater difficulty recalling lists of unrelated words that sound alike. Wickelgren (1965) investigated the contributions to memory of the major phonetic distinctive features of which sounds are composed (place of articulation: bilabial, dental, velar, etc.; and manner of articulation: voiced/voiceless, nasal/oral, aspirated/unaspirated, etc.). The use of phonological information for memory coding was shown to be effective regardless of whether the lists were presented in an auditory or visual manner. However, research has also demonstrated that, if at all possible, people will attempt to organize the words to be recalled according to some semantic or syntactic relationship. If a person can relate five words in a list by a sentence, or by remembering that they were all four-legged animals, this information will aid in recall. The use of semantic information provides a greater benefit to memory than syntactic information. In fact, Sachs (1967) found that the actual syntax of a sentence is discarded very shortly after the sentence is seen or heard, probably because once the meaning of a sentence has been extracted, the syntax is no longer useful information. Thus, for hearing people, one can expect that memory for unrelated word lists will be coded on a phonological basis unless semantic clustering can be accomplished, and that memory for sentences will be coded on a semantic basis and not on the form (syntax) of the sentence (Bransford, Barclay, and Franks, 1972; Bransford and Franks, 1971; Crowder, 1972; Franks and Bransford, 1972; LaBerge, 1972; Norman, 1972; Paris and Carter, 1973). Although there are considerable problems with their method, assumptions, and conclusions, Moulton and Beasley's (1975) results do indicate that deaf subjects (like hearing subjects) will take advantage of the semantics of stimulus items when possible, but that they resort to signed-based coding when the meaning cannot be of assistance.

To determine the role of phonological features in deaf people's memory, Conrad and Rush (1965) investigated recall of lists of consonants presented visually (presuming that the same strategies are at work with lists of letters as with lists of unrelated words). Some of the nine consonants used were phonetically similar (B, P, T, C), others were visually similar (A, H, T, I). The recorded error patterns did not support either a phonological or a visual encoding strategy. Locke (1970) investigated the same consonants to determine whether the fingerspelling alphabet was responsible for the errors (and would thus be a coding strategy for deaf persons) but found little support for this hypothesis.

Conrad (1970, 1971, 1972, 1973) determined that it was possible for prelingually, profoundly deaf people to use an auditory encoding strategy. In a school in which the method of instruction was predominantly oral, he compared two groups of deaf students: those for whom the phonological properties of the consonant letters provided at least some support to coding and recall (this group was subsequently rated "above average" in speech quality by independent judges) and those for whom the auditory features seemed to be largely irrelevant (this group was subsequently rated as "average" in speech quality). Conrad inferred that the above average group articulated while reading (not necessarily overtly) whereas the average group did not. He then compared the two groups on recall of visually presented material in two conditions, one in which they silently read the presented material, and the other in which they read out loud the presented material. Recall was not greatly improved by vocalization for the "articulating" group but was significantly hampered for the "nonarticulating" group. The inference is that the articulating group had acquired some form of a phonological code so that actually articulating the material while reading did not either help or hinder them. However, the nonarticulating group had acquired a nonphonological coding system, and reading out loud actually interfered with their normal coding process.

A further study by Locke and Locke (1971) determined that the type of linguistic coding strategy correlated to some extent with the deaf person's articulatory skills. Unintelligible deaf subjects made more errors in recall of visually similar letter pairs than did the intelligible deaf subjects and hearing controls. Furthermore, unintelligible deaf subjects made more dactylically similar confusions (based on the fingerspelling alphabet) than did the other two groups.

The implications of the above studies are: 1) coding strategies are learned, not innate; 2) deaf people have a choice of coding language either by phonological, visual, or manual means; 3) oral training methods do not guarantee phonological coding strategies; 4) deaf people who do not have phonological coding strategies and do not use sign do not give clear evidence of reliance on only one of the other possible strategies.

There is at this point one further clarification that needs to be made with respect to the notion of strategies in memory. One strategy is to use a *code,* and the lack of clear strategies as to what code to use has been discussed herein. This does not imply that deaf people's use of other memory strategies is also necessarily impaired.

In their investigation of memory strategies in deaf adolescents, Belmont, Karchmer, and Pilkonis (1976) reported that when these youngsters are not specifically instructed in memory strategy techniques, they perform considerably poorer than hearing adults, but when given instructions to use fingerspelling as a memory strategy, their performance improves to 100% of the hearing adult performance. They concluded that "deaf people's deficiency reflects in large measure a failure to develop spontaneous use of cognitive processes" for memory efficiency. Karchmer and Belmont (1976) recognized that the Belmont, Karchmer, and Pilkonis (1976) study did not separate possible cognitive deficiencies from deaf individuals' known difficulties with English. They constructed an experiment that tested verbal (English words) and nonverbal (pictures) memory. They found that "deaf subjects' performance was inferior to the hearing subjects' for word lists but not for pictures lists" and that, given instruction in memory strategies (in this case a 4-3 rehearsal strategy), both groups of subjects improved drastically, bringing the deaf students' performance above the level of the hearing students' performance before instruction (but still below hearing subjects instructed in memory strategies). In the 4-3 rehearsal paradigm, the subject rehearses the first four items several times, then whips through the last three. To recall information memorized with this strategy, one recalls the last three first, then searches through the rehearsed four for recall. The three "fast-finish" items test primary memory, and Karchmer and Belmont reported that deaf subjects' primary memory is completely normal. The four rehearsed items test secondary memory, and it was here that differences between the hearing and deaf subjects were noted. Although deaf subjects' accuracy on the picture lists was equal to that of the hearing subjects, they were nonetheless slower to respond. The implications and causes of this difference in speed of processing have yet to be determined.

Other studies of memory have been related to larger educational method evaluations. Kates (1972) compared three groups of deaf children and two groups of hearing children on several language tasks, some of which related directly to memory for English. His groups were: Oral, Rochester Method, Combined (oral and signs), Hearing-Age (hearing subjects matched with the deaf subjects for age, about 14 years old), and Hearing-Achievement (hearing subjects matched with the deaf subjects for general achievement level, approximately 10 years old). On a task that investigated short-term recall memory of unconnected words, Kates found a difference between the Combined group and the Hearing-Age group, and found that the other two deaf groups were not different from the two hearing groups, nor were the hearing groups significantly different from each other. At the same time, short-term recognition memory for the same words was tested (recognition being easier than recall), and no differences were found among the five groups. Kates looked only at the number of words correctly recalled or recognized and did not attempt to determine whether or not a difference existed in the types of mistakes made by the Oral, Rochester, and Combined groups.

Another study in Kates (1972) investigated noun-pair recall with the same subjects; two nouns were presented in a sentence, and all the nouns were in capital letters. Subjects were then given the first noun and were asked for the second. At the same time, subjects were asked to recall the sentence even though they had not been instructed to pay attention to the sentence (incidental recall). Kates found no differences among the five groups, presumably because the nouns and sentences were processed semantically. The last related study by Kates dealt with sentence memory, that is, memory for the exact syntax of a sentence. In this study, he found that the Oral group did better than the other two deaf groups and also better than the two hearing groups. He did not find differences between the two remaining deaf groups and the two hearing groups. Kates's studies do not show consistent trends: the results may be attributable to specific instruction in the different schools.

Several questions can be raised here which unfortunately cannot be answered. One major question pertains to the normal, daily treatment of English input in memory processing in persons who are native or near-native deaf signers. Is English translated into ASL and then coded in memory? Is it simply processed in English to get the meaning, the syntax discarded as suggested by Sachs (1967), and constructed from storage in whatever response mode is required? If semantics is unavailable to help in memory processing, is the English processed using auditory phonological processing, while the ASL is separately treated using sign-based phonology? Is there one memory processing system or two? One relevant study is that of Odom, Blanton, and McIntyre (1970), which indicates that English words that have direct equivalents in ASL are recalled significantly better than words that do not. What happens with whole sentences is not yet known. The answers to these questions are of particular importance to the use of total communication in educational settings where the child may be asked to process separate systems (the signs, the lips, and whatever auditory information is available) simultaneously. If the child is attempting to process the signs using sign phonology and the speech using speech phonology (or its equivalent, whatever that is for speech reading), he is obviously trying to do two disparate tasks at once, raising serious questions concerning the requirements on the child of the use of total communication. Although parallel processing of incoming information has been suggested as a necessary part of input analysis (Neisser, 1967), it is not clear how such a model would be reconciled with multiple modality linguistic input of the type we have discussed here. If in fact such parallel processing exists, it remains to be determined whether the information input from the speechreading is competing with the information input from the manual reading for processing by the parallel processors, or whether separate parallel processors would be assigned to handle each type of input (all still simultaneously). In any case, the processing demands that TC places on the perceptual and cognitive systems is a critical concern for the psychological development of children being exposed to it.

Development of Memory

Related to the preceding discussion is the obvious question: How does learning ASL as a native language affect the eventual organization and strength of the memory process? Put another way, will someone who learns ASL as a first language as an infant have a more effective memory, and thus greater learning potential, than someone who learns ASL when he enters school at age 5? than someone who learns ASL in high school? than someone who learns ASL as an adult? than someone who never learns ASL?

The Kates (1972) study suggested that, in terms of overall amount of information to be remembered at any one time, oral deaf students are not impaired any more than hearing counterparts. Neither are those who use the Rochester or Combined methods. None of the deaf students in Kates's study had deaf parents, so that the comparison is between deaf students who have learned a strategy since entering school and hearing children who have acquired their strategy over normal developmental stages. (For a discussion of normal memory development, see Brown, 1975).

Because the deaf students are not grossly deficient in their memory processing, and yet are significantly behind in their acquisition of English, the focus should be shifted from "how much" memory to "what kind" of memory. If, as the Conrad and Locke studies indicate, many deaf people are using a variety of strategies, will early ASL usage provide a more efficient strategy, which can facilitate later learning of English? Again, the Odom, Blanton, and McIntyre (1970) study is suggestive. The deaf subjects' recall of English words with ASL equivalents is significantly better than the hearing subjects' recall of both lists of English words (those with ASL equivalents and those without). Unfortunately, the central questions being raised here—how does early learning of ASL or other manual coding systems affect memory?—has not been specifically studied.

Perception

In their comparison of signing and speech, Bellugi and Fischer (1972) found that nearly 50% fewer signs than spoken words were used to relate the same number of propositions in the same amount of time. Stokes and Menyuk (1975) and others have suggested that both ASL and English (and other natural languages) are adapted to the human central processing mechanism such that there is an optimal range of time in which linguistic processing occurs. This would include perception, attention, short-term memory, and comprehension and production processing. Because signs take longer to produce (larger muscles move more slowly), a signed language would have to be adjusted so that the semantic and syntactic content could be conveyed in fewer signs in order to keep the length of an utterance within the optimal range. Thus, the function of incorporation and blending rules would be to pack more information into a single sign, and fewer signs would be needed. Stokes and Menyuk suggested that abnormally slowed input greatly taxes storage and retrieval processes. It may be that, when difficulty is encountered in the use of sign systems in the classroom, the unusual length of a signed utterance that contains a separate sign for each English word or morpheme may be to blame. It may be that the utterance exceeds the short-term memory span and that the slow rate of input does not permit sufficient syntactic processing to aid memory coding as the input is received. As yet there are no data to support these speculations, but should they turn out to be correct, the effect would be to make the acquisition of a signed system (as opposed to ASL) a more difficult task for the young child than previously expected.

MEMORY AND READING

Aside from the direct implication that the Odom, Blanton, and Mc-Intyre (1970) study has for memory, it also has another important implication for the teaching of reading. Research on hearing children indicates that children who learn letter-sound association, and then use these associations in reading (by sounding out the word), experience superior reading achievement (Chall, 1967). Consequently, reading materials intended for hearing children rely heavily on the acoustic properties of the words to serve as recognition cues to the beginning reader. Such materials would seem to be inappropriate for use with deaf children, even aside from syntactic difficulties (Quigley et al., 1976). Instead, the study suggested that memory for English words can be strongly affected by associations with signs. Perhaps reading materials written to reflect correspondences between English and ASL would avoid the frustration involved in initial reading attempts. At present, several primary level readers are available that contain a story in English and in Signed English (Bornstein et al., 1973, 1975) where the Signed English is drawn in, usually parallel to the printed English. This type of reader presents the child with a choice of codes and does not have the possible drawback of TC, which requires real-time processing of both signals (signs and speechreading). Although presentation of static pictures is not the same as presentation of actual signs, it will be interesting to observe the results with these readers (assuming their use is maintained) over the next few years.

SUMMARY

The studies reviewed in this chapter suggest that deaf children's problems learning English are not primarily the result of their knowledge of sign language, and similarly that their acquisition of speech is not hindered by their knowledge of sign language. It is also clear that early use of sign language has a beneficial effect on performance in English (as demonstrated by Brasel and Quigley, 1977) and may substantially contribute to the better overall performance of deaf children of deaf parents when compared to deaf children of hearing parents. Although the data do not argue convincingly in favor of signed English forms as opposed to ASL, they do argue that signs in any form are preferable to no signs at all. This conclusion is qualified by the cautions that have been raised, particularly that children should be treated individually, that it should not be assumed that one system is best for all, and that attempts to teach deaf children to speak should not be lessened by the assumption that the children will "pick up" what they need from the TC input.

CHAPTER 9

USE OF MANUAL COMMUNICATION WITH OTHER POPULATIONS

CONTENTS

In recent years, there has been an increasing number of successful reports of the use of manual communication with hearing children with various types of communicative disorders (Fristoe, 1975; Lloyd, 1976; Schiefelbusch, in press). A general trend has emerged from these reports (although obviously not for every case): the introduction of signs has resulted in the establishment of at least minimal communication over and above whatever the child was previously capable of, often followed by an increase in vocalizations even in predominantly mute children, which often improve to intelligible verbalizations in the very same children with whom previous speech therapy had not been successful, and which is often followed by a decline in the child's use of signs (possibly also followed by a decrease in the need for the experimenter to use signs except when introducing new words), which finally may be followed by incidental learning of new words from the surrounding environment (words that are not specifically taught). Clearly, the end of this sequence is an arduous achievement and is not to be expected as an inevitable outcome of the use of manual communication. As Moores (in press) indicates, "it is unrealistic to believe that children with severe cognitive, physical, or emotional handicaps would benefit from exposure to the Rochester Method, with its demands on perceptual and motor integration, with the complete, sophisticated American Sign Language, or with one of its variants [sign systems]." Nonetheless, the reports of success are heartening, although the reasons for success are not at all obvious. Considerations for the use of manual communication and determining reasonable expectations are discussed at the end of this chapter. First, the various reports of manual communication intervention with autistic, retarded, language-delayed, and other populations are presented. The reader is referred to Schiefelbusch (in press) and Kiernan (1977) for discussions of manual communication intervention along with other forms of non-speech language strategies (Blissymbols, rebus, Premack symbols, etc.) with these same populations.

AUTISTIC CHILDREN

Early reports (Rutter, 1968; Webster et al., 1973) of autistic children's responsiveness to the use of gestures (not signs) suggested that manual communication might be a successful approach. Miller and Miller (1973) used ASL signs along with body awareness training with 19 autistic children, using signs limited to particular goals or activities, and reported the development of speech in two of the children. Creedon (1973, 1975) has reported on the success of a TC program with autistic children, indicating improvement in socialization and decrease in self-stimulatory behavior (often noted by other reports, e.g., Bonvillian and Nelson, 1978). Creedon (1976) reported that about two-thirds of the children receiving manual communication intervention initiated some form of speech, including fluent speech for a small number of children. Fulwiler and Fouts (1976) worked with a single autistic boy and reported development of speech accompanying the signs. Schaeffer et al. (1977) and Schaeffer (in press) reported progress along the general trend with three autistic boys ages 4½, 5, and 5½ years. The children were presented with what Schaeffer calls "signed speech," which is the simultaneous presentation of signs and speech. The children progressed from using signs only spontaneously to using signs and speech simultaneously in about 4 to 5 months. After 5 months, all three children had begun to use speech spontaneously without signs, at which point signing was faded for those structures the child could produce in speech. Schaeffer (in press) suggested several methodological advantages that contributed to the children's success in attaining spontaneous speech: 1) the children's constant exposure to signs and speech may have provided important clues to the relationship between signs and speech; 2) when the children were still using signs only in the sessions, the instructor spoke the word while the child signed to encourage the child to imitate it; 3) as soon as the children had developed necessary sound production skills, specific speech instruction was aimed at teaching them to pronounce the words they could already sign; 4) the children were taught to imitate after the instructor rather than to shadow the instructor's voice, forcing them to rely more heavily on their own memory for sounds; 5) when the children began to spontaneously combine speech and signs, they were thereafter required to do so; and 6) the children were taught to coordinate their sign movements and their speech syllables precisely. The necessity and efficiency of each technique for general instruction remain to be determined.

Comparisons of the effectiveness of signs, speech, and combinations of the two with autistic children (parallel to that reported by Moores, 1974, for deaf children) are rare. Webster, Konstantareas, and Oxman (1976) compared the abilities of four autistic children to follow commands, name actions or objects, and imitate as a function of the presentation mode of the instructions. They reported that for all four children, signs were at least as effective as speech, and there was no significant difference between signs only and combined signs and speech. Baron and Isensee (1977) compared comprehension of instructions presented in signs only with instructions presented in speech only and found a definite advantage to the signs (83.5%) compared to the speech (56.2%) over a variety of linguistic variables and contexts (pictures vs. real objects) for a single 12½-year-old girl. Further investigations are obviously needed.

MENTAL RETARDATION

Numerous reports of the use of manual communication with retarded individuals were discussed in Lloyd (1976). These included Bricker (1972), Levitt (1972), Owens and Harper (1971), Shaffer and Goehl (1974), Stohr and Van Hook (1973), Sutherland and Becket (1969), Wilson (1974), and Wolf and McAlone (in press). More recently, Stremel-Campbell, Cantrell, and Halle (1977) indicated the eventual production of speech as a result of manual communication training with six of nine trainable mentally retarded children. The above reports represent only a small portion of the number of programs that are currently using manual communication with retarded individuals. In a nationwide survey of speech, hearing, and language services for the retarded, Fristoe (1975) reported that over 10% of those responding were using manual communication or other nonvocal communication systems (including Blissymbols, rebuses, and communication boards; see Lloyd, 1976, and Schiefelbusch, in press, for discussion of these systems). The results of the survey, and a follow-up (Fristoe and Lloyd, 1977b) indicated a widespread proliferation of the use of manual communication but, at the same time, a minimal awareness on the part of the program of what other teachers, clinicians, and researchers were doing. In many cases, respondents indicated a lack of understanding regarding the difference between using the signs from ASL (usually in English word order) from using ASL itself (the Appendix contains a resource list from Fristoe and Lloyd, 1977a, for those involved in programs using manual communication with retarded individuals).

One of the major concerns of those initiating manual communication programs with retarded individuals is where to start. Because of the concern over what signs to teach, Fristoe and Lloyd (1978) suggested a first sign lexicon based on their analysis of the signs that are currently being used with retarded individuals (including some of the signs in the *Perkins Sign Language Dictionary*) and principles for selection from a variety of sources. Of primary concern are the first sign(s) to be taught; these are generally thought to be functional and give the child some control over his environment, such as EAT, DRINK, and TOILET, or something important to the child like COOKIE or TICKLE. Furthermore, Fouts (1973) indicated that teaching Washoe the chimpanzee signs that involved contact was easier than teaching signs that were made in neutral space and involved no contact. Anecdotal information (Fristoe, personal communication) indicates that this may also be true for retarded children as well. Fristoe and Lloyd (1977b) raised other questions concerning which signs to teach and how to teach them. They questioned whether one-handed or two-handed signs would be easier for the child to master, and whether the reinforcer for correct performance should be the sign's referent or some other reinforcer totally unrelated to the sign's meaning. Concerning the grouping of signs for instructional presentation, Fristoe and Lloyd (1977b) indicated that categories that are conceptually or functionally coherent seemed to be preferable to alphabetic organization, which is used in most sign language manuals (alphabetic based on the equivalent English gloss). Stremel-Campbell, Cantrell, and Halle (1977) indicated that errors increased when two signs from the same category were included in a single learning set, and they suggested that the groupings of signs for presentation should be checked for similarities of handshape, motion, and place of formation.

Another concern about the teaching of signs is the possibility that iconicity contained within the sign may contribute to the sign's learnability. R. Brown (1977) presented evidence indicating that hearing children with normal intelligence were better able to remember iconic signs paired with their proper meaning than signs paired with meanings that did not reflect the characteristics visible in the sign. Stremel-Campbell, Cantrell, and Halle (1977) and Konstantareas, Oxman, and Webster (in press) have indicated that iconicity may be a relevant variable in teaching retarded children. Rogers (1976) did not find such an effect experimentally with four retarded adults. A major concern here is, of course, how iconicity is determined. Lloyd and Fristoe (1978) analyzed the guessability or transparency of those signs that are included in vocabularies for retarded children. They indicated that the percentage of signs in these functional vocabularies that are guessable by naïve adults is higher than that reported by Bellugi and Klima (1976) or Hoemann (1975b) for the language as a whole. Signs may be iconic, however, without being transparent. That is, a sign that is not guessable may still bear some relationship to its referent which might become more obvious when pointed out. In addition, guessability for adults does not necessarily ensure transparency for children, especially retarded children. For further discussion of iconicity, see Baron, Isensee, and Davis (1977) and Wilbur (in press b).

MULTIPLY HANDICAPPED POPULATIONS

The current work using signs with autistic, retarded, and other severely languaged-impaired populations is probably derived from the earlier work using signs with the "deaf retarded" (cf. Anthony, 1966, 1971; Butler, Griffing, and Huffman, 1969; James, 1963, 1967; Johnson, 1963; Sutherland and Becket, 1969). Manual communication intervention has been reported by Hall and Conn (1972), Hall and Talkington (1970), and Hoffmeister and Farmer (1972). Hoffmeister and Farmer reported an increase in receptive and expressive knowledge of signs through a special tutorial program for mentally retarded deaf adults, but no improvement through the same program for two other mentally retarded deaf adults, who also were considered autistic or brain damaged. In addition, subjects with vocabularies greater than 200 signs were observed using two- and three-sign productions in their spontaneous communication.

The *Perkins Sign Language Dictionary,* discussed in more detail in Chapter 7, was constructed at the Perkins School for the Blind to meet the communication needs of a population with the following characteristics (Robbins et al., 1975, p. 16):

1) multihandicapped ($^2/_3$ below 70 IQ.).
2) high incidence of expressive conceptual language problems; . . .
3) high incidence of expressive motor difficulties;
4) acquisition of information (growth of concepts) is difficult . . . due to learning problems *and* the social and often physical isolating effects of dual sensory impairments.
5) the population includes a high percentage of deaf, partially seeing students whose learning needs and later social responsibilities are more

similar to the non-professional, non highly-educated deaf than to any other group.

6) the population includes a high percentage of very visual children for whom visual imagery is most persuasive for thinking.

The program at Perkins, for which the dictionary was developed, does not aim at teaching English as the primary goal. Instead, the establishment of effective communication with whatever structural means is of paramount importance.

DECIDING TO USE MANUAL COMMUNICATION

Because "other populations" includes a variety of possible problems, certain subdivisions must be made along other than traditional labels:

1. There are individuals who, at some point during their lives, indicate that they are capable of both sophisticated comprehension and production but who do not choose to communicate.
2. There are individuals who have excellent comprehension and are capable of good production but who suffer from performance disfluencies (consistently improper word choice, disrupted switching of stylistic level).
3. There are individuals who have excellent comprehension but who have difficulties in production attributable to speech problems.
4. There are individuals who demonstrate comprehension on tasks not requiring verbal output but who cannot speak.
5. There are individuals who demonstrate generalized learning difficulties, of which disturbed language is one manifestation; in such individuals there may be little or no evidence of comprehension or production.

These five general groups are not intended to be all-inclusive, or necessarily mutually exclusive, and they do not take into account etiology. They do, however, represent basic variables to be considered in the remediation process. For example, the first group does not have a language disorder in the *linguistic* sense of language. In most cases of this type, some emotional disturbance is indicated, and unless the emotional problem is directly related to using speech (as in a child who refuses to talk for fear of using up his breath), it is not clear that switching to manual communication will provide any benefit.

In the second group, the disorder can be considered paralinguistic. That is, it relates to factors concerned with socially defined usage of language (conventional meanings of words, proper style for addressing friends as opposed to strangers). This type of problem has been reported with autistic adolescents (Simmons and Baltaxe, 1975). It is not clear what benefit would be gained by using manual communication with this population. The probability of similar problems with ASL cannot be ruled out (that is, signs may be acquired, but paralinguistic difficulties may be manifest in the use of those signs).

In those instances where there is an indication of aphasia (the patient finds it difficult to find the right word or substitutes semantically similar or phonologically similar words for intended words), some benefit may be gained by switching to ASL. Battison and Markowicz (1974), Battison and Padden (1974), and Markowicz (1973) reported that evidence from brain lesions indicate that signs, fingerspelling, and speech are differentially located in the brain and are differentially impaired by lesions. It is possible, then, for speech to be lost while signs remain intact. Battison and Markowicz (1974, p. 16) suggested that "some hearing aphasics may have an intact system capable of producing propositional gestures. That is, the language disruption of some hearing aphasics may be limited to their speech, and they may be capable of learning to sign, all problems of training aside."

Individuals with speech problems may have either nerve problems (dysarthria) or motor coordination problems (oral apraxia). In the case of dysarthria, manual communication would seem to be indicated. In the case of oral apraxia, manual communication might be a beneficial alternative, unless of course the apraxia is actually more generalized to include manual apraxia also.

Individuals who exhibit no expressive language may demonstrate a wide range of comprehension, from nearly none (a few highly frequent utterances that require simple motor responses, such as "stand there" or "put on your jacket") to quite sophisticated (as, for example, reported in Lenneberg, 1967).

In the four groups discussed above where some indication of comprehension was present and there was no indication of generalized learning difficulties, the focus of remediation is on providing a means for expressing language. With the retarded, particularly the severely or profoundly retarded, the establishment of receptive language becomes as important as, if not more important than, teaching means of expression.

In order to acquire a minimal receptive knowledge of a language, an individual theoretically must be capable of symbolic representation, in that he must be able to use something (not necessarily a word) to stand for (refer to, represent) something else (an object or concept). The child who can take a rattle and pretend in overt play that it is a spoon (or some similar type of representation) has indicated the ability to substitute a symbol (the rattle) for the object (the spoon). Within Piaget's (1951, 1952, 1964) theory of cognitive development, the child begins to develop such symbolic representation at Stage 6 of the sensorimotor period (roughly 18 to 24 months of age in normal children). Inherent in Piaget's theory is the notion of "readiness" to acquire language (which does not mean that intervention should be postponed until the child is "ready"; see Chapman and Miller, in press).

M. Woodward (1959) found that many profoundly retarded children and adolescents functioned at a level below Stage 6. In an explicit test of the relationship between Stage 6 functioning and the presence of meaningful language in the severely/profoundly retarded, Kahn (1975) compared a group of eight children who were able to use at least 10 words to ask for various objects with another group of eight children who used no words at all. On four Piagetian tasks of Stage 6 functioning, Kahn found that seven of the eight children who used words functioned at the Stage 6 level on all four tasks, whereas none of the eight children who did not use words functioned at Stage 6 on all four tasks. The two best children of the nonlanguage group were able to reach Stage 6 functioning on only two of the tasks. Kahn's findings were statistically significant: the language group functioned at Stage 6, the nonlanguage group did not. Kahn concluded that attainment of Stage 6 cognitive abilities are prerequisite to language development, therefore cognitive assessment should precede language training. Those children who are functioning at or above Stage 6 might reasonably be expected to profit from training, whereas those below Stage 6 might benefit from activities aimed at raising their cognitive functioning. Other researchers in the field have suggested that, cognitive level aside, language should be made available to children as early as possible to provide a communication system that will eventually result in further language and cognitive development. Yoder (1978) has argued that such communication should take place in an environment in which the child might be motivated to communicate, and that the communication method should be appropriate to the needs and abilities of the child.

WHY DOES IT WORK?

Many factors are involved in the acquisition of signs by these populations (as compared to their failure to acquire speech) and in the subsequent acquisition of speech (for those who do). The early emergence of signs in children who are learning ASL as a native language (see Chapter 5, "Sign Language Acquisition") suggests that signs are motorically simpler (although motor development alone is insufficient to account for the developmental stages observed in the acquisition of ASL). Another possible advantage in using signs is their visibility. The learner is able to see the shape and movement of the modeler's hands and, crucially, of his own hands. Signs are 100% visible, compared to speech, which may range from 10% to 40% visible via speechreading (Jeffers, 1967; H. Schlesinger, 1972). The two sets of hands can be held together to determine similarity, and the learner's hands can be corrected more easily than the learner's mouth. Signs can also be useful if an auditory perceptual disorder is suspected. That is, it might be possible to take advantage of the visual perceptual system if the auditory perceptual system seems to be impaired (not hearing impairment, but auditory attention focusing or short-term auditory memory) (Graham and Graham, 1971). This is particularly true because some signs can be held relatively stationary for a period of time, and can be produced more slowly without too much distortion. Robbins (1976) discussed these and related reasons for the appeal and effectiveness of sign-based intervention.

Fristoe and Lloyd (1977b), in addressing the question "Why does manual communication intervention lead to increased spontaneous vocalizations and even intelligible speech?", included some of the above factors and several others. In all, they listed 16 factors that may be relevant to the effectiveness of the use of signs. The first two are relevant to all nonspeech communication (including the graphic and pictorial-type symbols): 1) removal of pressure for speech and 2) problems of auditory short-term memory and auditory processing circumvented. The next four highlight what nonspeech approaches force the trainer to do: 1) limit vocabulary, particularly to functional forms, 2) simplify the language structure used, 3) reduce excess verbiage (noise), and 4) adjust the presentation rate to ensure comprehension. The next four are training advantages of nonspeech approaches: 1) easier to determine student's attention, 2) enhance figure-ground differential, 3) facilitate physical manipulation (molding) if needed, and 4) facilitate observations of shaping to assess progress. The final six relate to stimulus and processing factors that are inherent in nonspeech approaches: 1) stimulus consistency is optimized, 2) both paired associate learning and match-to-sample learning are facilitated, 3) intramodal symbol meaning associations are simplified, 4) multimodal representation is possible, 5) duration of stimuli is adjustable, and 6) visual representation (iconicity, spatial modifications) is possible.

Undoubtedly there are others at work, because these seem to be insufficient to explain why nonspeech approaches can lead to speech. (For discussion of the success of other nonspeech approaches, see Schiefelbusch, in press; for bibliography on the topic, see Fristoe, Lloyd, and Wilbur, 1977.)

One major problem faced by many programs is what sign system to use. The above populations represent groups that do not have their own communities as do the deaf. They do not have their own community organizations, social structure, and native language. In the absence of a communal language, there are no sociolinguistic grounds for choosing one signing system over another. One consideration would be that, given the structure of signs discussed in Chapter 2, and the role of signs in memory, perception, and in reducing independent movement by the two hands, those forms of manual communication that use ASL signs would be preferable to those that do not. Many of the signs created by the manual systems violate the sign structure constraints, which are presumably perceptually based (Siple, 1973). Another problem that must be faced is that of choosing a limited system which conceivably could be mastered completely by the child, and then possibly having to switch to a different system in order to meet the increasing communication needs of the child, compared to choosing an infinitely expandable system, such as ASL or Signed English. This last point is obviously only a problem if we are fortunate enough to have made significant progress with the child, but nonetheless should be considered beforehand, thus not limiting the child's eventual development by preconceived ideas as to his potential communication skills. Robbins (1976) argued that the goal of choosing such an intervention system should be "*not* to select *a* sign system, *not* to determine which system is the 'best', *nor* which system represents English the least imperfectly," but rather "for a preferred method for a particular child at a particular stage (Moores, McIntyre, and Weiss, 1973)." In addition, she indicated her personal preference for "language goals relating to functional use and development of meaning and of concepts which would enable the student to relate more completely to the world of objects, events and persons as he learns, than goals focusing on production of correctly formed English kernel sentences with perfect morphological components." Robbins also argued that the cognitive behavior of the child must be carefully considered before teaching particular signs. The child will demonstrate concepts such as possession, negation, and plurality, after which one can initiate teaching of such signs as MINE, NO, or MANY. As the child's cognitive level develops, different choices of signs and communicative structures will be indicated. Of primary concern is the need to monitor carefully both the input to the student and the subsequent implications of the output from the student.

SUMMARY

The use of visual communication systems as augmentative or alternative to speech training is clearly in its infancy, but if the outcomes that have been reported so far can be generalized to nondeaf populations at large, we can expect to see more and more nonspeech language intervention programs in the future. The studies suggest that when these visual systems are used, undesirable behaviors are reduced, communication (especially spontaneous communication) is facilitated, and many children begin to vocalize spontaneously. Aside from the implications this research has for nondeaf populations, one cannot help but wonder what effect it will have on those involved in educating deaf children. As more and more people outside the field of deafness become aware of the potential utility of nonspeech systems, sign language will be considered less of an oddity and will be more accepted in general. Similarly, as more nondeaf children profit from these systems and begin to vocalize, educators of the deaf may become less reluctant to use sign language with their students.

Further research on the use of sign language with nondeaf populations needs to focus on the potential utility of such aspects of ASL as use of space for grammatical information, facial expression for grammatical or adverbial information, and reduplication for its various purposes. Each of these devices allows a single sign to carry more information than a single word in English would; thus, these devices may allow a child to convey or receive more information at the single sign stage than would be available in a sequence of signs. For example, instead of signing NO MORE, one can sign MORE with a negative facial expression and headshake. Whether this will facilitate learning and retention remains to be determined.

APPENDIX

MANUAL COMMUNICATION FOR THE RETARDED AND OTHERS WITH SEVERE COMMUNICATION IMPAIRMENT: A RESOURCE LIST

Macalyne Fristoe and Lyle L. Lloyd

Recently an increasing number of clinicians have become interested in the use of signs for communication by retarded, autistic, and aphasic individuals who are not able to communicate effectively by the usual spoken means. Manual communication serves two purposes: it can be a temporary means of communication, used until such time as vocal communication is established and then faded out, or it can be the principal means of communication for an individual who is unable to produce spoken communication.

A number of manual systems are being used for this purpose. The best known is a natural language, American Sign Language (ASL or Ameslan), the language that ranks fourth in use in the United States after English, Spanish, and Italian and is used primarily for communication involving persons who are deaf.[1] In addition, several pedagogical sign systems have been developed. These include Manual English, Signed English, Seeing Essential English, Signing Exact English, Linguistics of Visual English, and Systematic Sign Language, which lie at different points on a syntactic continuum between ASL and English. In addition to these systems there are others that have been designed for use with a single individual or in a single setting. Most are based on the use of a vocabulary of signs from ASL; usually

---

Reprinted from *Mental Retardation*, October 1977, pp. 18–21, by permission.

[1] T. J. O'Rourke, Timothy F. Medina, Angela K. Thames, and Deborah A. Sullivan. National Association of the Deaf Communicative Skills Program. *Programs for the Handicapped,* April 15, 1975, pp. 27–30.

Authors: **MACALYNE FRISTOE, Ph.D.,** Director, Speech Clinic and Associate Professor, Department of Audiology and Speech Sciences, Purdue University, West Lafayette, Indiana 47907; **LYLE L. LLOYD, Ph.D.,** Chairman and Professor, Special Education Section, Purdue University, South Campus Courts, Bldg. E., West Lafayette, Indiana 47907.

they involve the use of ASL signs with English syntax, often presented in a simultaneous (spoken and signed) manner. Some systems use esoteric signs and gestures.

In a national survey of speech, hearing, and language services for the retarded, over 10% of the persons responding indicated that they were using some form of nonverbal communication system (Fristoe, 1975), which suggested that a significant trend toward the use of such programs is developing. Unfortunately, some of these programs were started without benefit of access to the experiences gained and materials developed in other programs, resulting in inefficiency and duplication of effort. Many persons responding to the national survey indicated a desire to know more about manual communication methods, programs, and materials that can be used with the retarded.

In an attempt to provide an opportunity for interested persons to study what is available in this area, the following resource list has been developed. Although most of the materials listed were developed for use with the severely hearing impaired (deaf), they provide a valuable resource to use in teaching manual communication to the staff working with persons with any type of severe communication impairment. Many of these manuals present limited vocabularies of functional words that are particularly useful in programs for the retarded. While most of the references pertain to teaching ASL or pedagogical sign systems, three of the listings (Fristoe, 1975; Lloyd, 1976; Mayberry, 1976) include more general reference material about the use of nonspeech communication systems. To further facilitate exchange of information in this area, the compilers of this list invite readers to send them recommendations for additional listings that would be useful in manual communication for the retarded, autistic, aphasic, and/or multihandicapped.

RESOURCE LIST[2]

Abelson, Bambii Rae. Alpha-Hands Flash Cards. Kenworthy Educational Service, Inc., Buffalo, New York 14205, 1969.
* Abrams, Paula. Simultaneous Language Program for Non-Verbal Preschool Children. Dysfunctioning Child Center, Michael Reese Medical Center, 2915 S. Ellis Avenue, Chicago, Illinois 60616, 1975.

---

[2] This is an expansion of the resource list distributed at the presentation of "The use of manual communication with the retarded," at 54th Annual Convention of the Council for Exceptional Children in Chicago, Illinois, April 9, 1976.

* Items developed especially for use with mentally retarded, autistic, or multihandicapped (e.g., deaf-blind, deaf-retarded).

* Andreas, Judy, David Bell, Janice Bentley, Ginger Buck, and Dolly Klee. Let Your Fingers Do the Talking: A Teaching Manual for Use with Non-Verbal Retardates. Department of Communication Disorders and Education and Training, Craig Developmental Center, Sonyea, New York 14556, 1975. Subsequently distributed by ERIC Document Reproduction Service, P.O. Box 190, Arlington, VA 22210 (Document No. ED 121034).

Anthony, David. Seeing Essential English. Anaheim Union High School District, Anaheim, California 92800, 1971. Subsequently published as The Seeing Essential English Manual. The University Bookstore, University of Northern Colorado, Greely, Colorado 80639, 1974.

Babbini, Barbara E. An Introductory Course in Manual Communication: Fingerspelling and Language of Signs. San Fernando Valley State College, Northridge, California 91300, 1965.

Babbini, Barbara E. Manual Communication: Fingerspelling and the Language of Signs: A Course Study Outline. (Two volumes, one for instructors, one for students). University of Illinois Press, Urbana, Illinois 61801, 1971.

Bornstein, Harry, (Ed.), Lillian B. Hamilton, Karen Luczak Saulnier, and Howard L. Roy. Signed English Dictionary for Pre-School and Elementary Levels. Gallaudet College Press, 7th and Florida Avenue, N.E., Washington, D.C., 1975.

Bornstein, Harry, Lillian B. Hamilton, and Barbara M. Kannapell, Signs for Instructional Purposes. Gallaudet College Press, 7th and Florida Avenue, N.E., Washington, D.C. 20002, 1967.

Bornstein, Harry, et al. Gallaudet Signed English Series. (Many titles are available from Gallaudet College Press, 7th and Florida Avenue, N.E., Washington, D.C. 20002.)

Caccamise, Frank, and Carolyn Norris. Code Book: Sign Language for Messages to and from Deaf People. Alinda Press, P. O. Box 553, Eureka, California 95501, 1975.

Caccamise, Frank, and Carolyn Norris. Food in Signs. Alinda Press, P. O. Box 553, Eureka, California 95501, 1974. (There are three other primers in coloring book form in this series on Animals, Home, and Community.)

Catalog of Captioned Films for the Deaf: Theatrical Films and Educational Films for Adults. Captioned Films for the Deaf Distribution Center of the Conference of Executives of American Schools for the Deaf, Inc., 5034 Wisconsin Avenue, N.W., Washington, D.C. 20016. (Includes films giving manual communication training and practice.)

Charlip, Remy, Mary Beth [Miller], and George Ancona. Handtalk: An ABC of Fingerspelling and Sign Language. Parents' Magazine Press, 52 Vanderbilt Avenue, New York, New York 10017, 1974.

* Creedon, Margaret Procyk, (Ed.). Appropriate Behavior Through Communication: A New Program in Simultaneous Language for Non-Verbal Children, 2nd Ed. Dysfunctioning Child Center, Michael Reese Medical Center, 2915 S. Ellis Avenue, Chicago, Illinois 60616, 1975. (See chapters by Candy Haight and Candy H. Smith.)

Davis, Anne. The Language of Signs: A Handbook for Manual Communication with the Deaf. Executive Council of the Episcopal Church, New York, New York 10000, 1966.

* Elwyn Institute. Signs for Everyday: Books 1 and 2. Elwyn Institute, Elwyn, Pennsylvania 19063, c. 1975.

Falberg, Roger M. The Language of Silence. Wichita Social Services for the Deaf, Wichita, Kansas 67200, 1963.

Fant, Louis, Jr. Ameslan: An Introduction to American Sign Language. Joyce Motion Picture Co., 8320 Reseda Boulevard, Northridge, California 91321, 1972. (Also distributed by National Association for the Deaf, 814 Thayer Avenue, Silver Spring, Maryland 20910.)

Fant, Louis, Jr. Say It with Hands. American Annals of the Deaf, 5034 Wisconsin Avenue, N.W., Washington, D.C. 20016, 1964.

* Foster, Elizabeth. Programmed Language Workbooks for Multiply Handicapped Deaf Children. Indiana School for the Deaf, 1200 E. 42nd Street, Indianapolis, Indiana 46205, 1972.

* Foster, Elizabeth. Programmed Vocabulary Workbook for Multiply Handicapped Deaf Children. Indiana School for the Deaf, 1200 E. 42nd Street, Indianapolis, Indiana 46205, 1971.

* Foster, Elizabeth, Joyce Levy, and Sammy Cullison. Learning Activities for Multiply Handicapped Deaf Children. Indiana School for the Deaf, 1200 E. 42nd Street, Indianapolis, Indiana 46205, 1972. (Two booklets identified as Parts 1 and 2.)

* Fristoe, Macalyne. Language Intervention Systems for the Retarded. State of Alabama Department of Education. (Order from Language Intervention Systems for the Retarded, L. B. Wallace Developmental Center, P.O. Box 2224, Decatur, Alabama 35602), 1976. (This resource lists training programs using manual communication and systems developed to teach manual communication to the retarded.)

Gustason, Gerilee, Donna Pfetzing, and Esther Zawolkow. Signing Exact English. Modern Signs Press, Rossmoor, California. (Order from National Association of the Deaf, 814 Thayer Avenue, Silver Spring, Maryland 20910), 1972.

* Hinkle, Carroll. We Have Hands: A Teaching Manual for Those Concerned With Our Deaf. Green Valley Developmental Center, Greeneville, Tennessee 37743, c. 1974.

Hoemann, Harry W., (Ed.). Improved Techniques of Communications: A Training Manual for Use with Severely Handicapped Deaf Clients. Bowling Green State University, Bowling Green, Ohio 43402, 1970.

Hoemann, Harry W. The American Sign Language: Lexical and Grammatical Notes with Translation Exercises. National Association of the Deaf, 814 Thayer Avenue, Silver Spring, Maryland 20910, 1976.

Hoemann, Harry W., and Shirley A. Hoemann. Sign Language Flash Cards. National Association of the Deaf, 814 Thayer Avenue, Silver Spring, Maryland 29010, 1976. (This material, in perforated book form, replaces the 1973 Sign Language Flash Cards.)

Hoemann, Shirley A. Children's Sign Language Playing Cards. National Association of the Deaf, 814 Thayer Avenue, Silver Spring, Maryland 20910, 1973.

* Huffman, Jeanne, Bobbi Hoffman, David Granssee, Ann Fox, Juanita James, and Joseph Schmitz. Talk With Me: Communication With the Multi-Handicapped Deaf. Joyce Motion Picture Co., 8320 Reseda Boulevard, Northridge, California 91321, 1974. (This is the same as Sign Language for Everyone by the same authors and publisher, except for the addition of a chapter, "Suggested Activities," pp. 219–269.)

Kosche, Martin. Hymns for Signing and Singing. 116 Walnut Street, Delavan, Wisconsin 53115, (undated).
* Lake, Sandra J. The Hand-Book. Communication Skill Builders, Tucson, Arizona 85733, 1976.
Landes, Robert M. Approaches: A Digest of Methods of Learning the Language of Signs. Virginia Baptist General Board, P.O. Box 8568, Richmond, Virginia 23226, 1969.
* Larson, Thalia. Communication for the Non-Verbal Child. Marfex Associates, Inc., Box 519, 90 Cherry Street, Jamestown, Pennsylvania 15907, 1975.
Lawrence, Edgar D. Sign Language Made Simple. Gospel Publishing House, 1445 Boonville Avenue, Springfield, Missouri 65802, 1975.
* Lloyd, Lyle L., (Ed.). Communication Assessment and Intervention Strategies. University Park Press, Baltimore, Maryland 21202, 1976. (See chapters by Ronnie Bring Wilbur; George A. Kopchick, Jr. and Lyle L. Lloyd; and Charlotte Clark and Richard W. Woodcock. In addition, chapters by Joseph K. Carrier, Jr., and by Gregg C. Vanderheiden and Deberah Harris-Vanderheiden present other nonvocal communication systems.)
Long, J. Schuyler. The Sign Language: A Manual of Signs, 2nd Ed. Gallaudet College Press, 7th and Florida Ave., N.E., Washington, D.C. 20002, 1962.
Madsen, Willard J. Conversational Sign Language: An Intermediate Manual. Gallaudet College Press, 7th and Florida Avenue, N.E., Washington, D.C. 20002, 1967.
* Mayberry, Rachel. If a chimp can learn sign language, surely my nonverbal client can too. Asha, 1976, 18, 223–228. (This article reviews briefly a number of sign systems and then discusses teaching manual communication to persons without significant hearing loss.)
O'Rourke, Terrence J. A Basic Course in Manual Communication. National Association of the Deaf, 814 Thayer Avenue, Silver Spring, Maryland 20910, 1973. (This resource provides an extensive "Manual Communication Bibliography" on pages 121–146, which includes an annotated list of many materials for use in teaching signs.)
* Owens, Michael, and Beryl Harper. Sign Language: A Teaching Manual for Cottage Parents of Non-Verbal Retardates. Pinecrest State School, P.O. Drawer 191, Pineville, Louisiana 71360, c. 1971.
Paget, Sir Richard. The New Sign Language. The Welcome Foundation, London, England, 1951.
Paget, Lady Grace, and Pierre Gorman. A Systematic Sign Language. Royal National Institute for the Deaf, 105 Gower Street, London WC-1E6AH, England, 1968. (Sir Richard Paget died in 1955, but Lady Grace Paget continued his work with Dr. Gorman.)
Riekehof, Lottie L. Talk to the Deaf: A Manual of Approximately 1000 Signs used by the Deaf of North America. Gospel Publishing House, 1445 Boonville Avenue, Springfield, Missouri 65802, 1963.
* Robbins, Nan, Janice Cagan, Carol Johnson, Helen Kelleher, Jocelyn Record, and Jan Vernacchia. Perkins Sign Language Dictionary: A Sign Dictionary for Use with Multi-Handicapped Deaf Children in School. Perkins School for the Blind, Watertown, Massachusetts 02172, 1975.
Royster, Mary Anne. Games and Activities for Sign Language Classes. National Association of the Deaf, 814 Thayer Avenue, Silver Spring, Maryland 20910, c. 1974.

Sanders, Josef I., (Ed.). The ABC's of Sign Language. Manca Press, Inc., Tulsa, Oklahoma 74100, 1968.

* Skelly, Madge, Lorraine Schinsky, Randall W. Smith, and Rita Solovitz Fust. American Indian Sign (Amerind) as a facilitator of verbalization for the oral verbal apraxic. Journal of Speech and Hearing Disorders, 1974, 39, 445–456. ("Amerind" is a gesture communication system based on American Indian Hand Talk.)

* Snell, Martha. Sign Language and Total Communication. In Kent, Louise R., Language Acquisition Program for the Severely Retarded. Research Press, 2612 North Mattis Avenue, Champaign, Illinois 61820, 1974. (Chapter 16, pp. 147–184.)

Springer, C. J. Talking with the Deaf. Redemptorist Fathers, 5354 Plank Road, Baton Rouge, Louisiana 70805, 1961.

* Stohr, Pamela G., and Karen E. Van Hook. Have Hands—Will Sign. Ranier School, P.O. Box 600, Buckley, Washington 98321, 1973.

* Talkington, Larry W., and Sylvia M. Hall, A Manual Communication System for Deaf Retarded. Austin State School, P. O. Box 1269, Austin, Texas 78767, c. 1970.

* Topper, Sue T. Gesture Language for the Severely and Profoundly Mentally Retarded. Denton State School, P. O. Box 368, Denton, Texas 76202, c. 1974.

* Vail, Jacqueline L., and Diana L. Spas. A Manual Communication Program for Non-Verbal Retardates. NWSEARCH—Title I, 145 Fisk Avenue, DeKalb, Illinois 60115, c. 1974.

Wampler, Dennis. Linguistics of Visual English. Early Childhood Education Dept., Aurally Handicapped Program, Santa Rosa City Schools, Santa Rosa, California 95404, 1971. (Materials are not currently available.)

Washburn, Arthur O. A SEE Thesaurus: Groupings of Seeing Essential English Signs. Kendall Hurst Publishing, 2460 Kerper Blvd., Dubuque, Iowa 52201, 1973.

Washington State School for the Deaf. An Introduction to Manual English. The Washington State School for the Deaf, Vancouver, Washington 98661, c. 1972.

Watson, David O. Talk With Your Hands. Menasha, Wisconsin: George Banta Co. (Order from author, Route 1, Winneconne, Wisconsin 54986, or American Annals of the Deaf, 5034 Wisconsin Avenue, N.W., Washington, D.C. 20016), 1964.

* Wilson, Paula Starks, Linda Goodman, and Robin K. Wood. Manual Language for the Child Without Language: A Behavioral Approach for Teaching the Exceptional Child. Developmental Team, 79 Elm Street, Hartford, Connecticut 06115, 1975.

* Wilson, Paula Starks, Robin K. Wood, Linda Goodman, and Terry Roberts. Manual Language Dictionary—Functional Vocabulary for the Retarded, Booklets One, Two, and Three. Developmental Team, 79 Elm Street, Hartford, Connecticut 06115, c. 1974. (Order from Earl Robinson, Jr., Occupational Training Center, Mansfield Training School, Box 51, Mansfield Depot, Connecticut 06251.)

REFERENCES

Ahlström, K. 1972. On evaluation of the effects of schooling. In Proceedings of the International Congress on Education of the Deaf. Sveriges Lärarförbund, Stockholm.

Allan, K. 1977. Classifiers. Language 53:285-311.

Allen, N. 1975. What is said and what is signed: The relationship between English and four modes of signing English. Unpublished master's thesis. University of Southern California, Los Angeles.

Anthony, D. 1966. Seeing Essential English. Unpublished manuscript. University of Michigan, Ypsilanti.

Anthony, D. 1971. Seeing Essential English, Vols. 1 and 2. Educational Services Division, Anaheim Union School District, Anaheim, Cal.

Ashbrook, E. 1977. Development of semantic relations in the acquisition of American Sign Language. Unpublished manuscript. Salk Institute for Biological Studies, La Jolla, Cal.

Babbini, B. 1974. Manual Communication. University of Illinois Press, Urbana.

Baker, C. 1976. What's not on the other hand in American Sign Language. In S. Mufwene, C. Walker, and S. Steever, (eds.), Papers from the Twelfth Regional Meeting, Chicago Linguistic Society. The University of Chicago Press, Chicago.

Baker, C. 1977. Regulators and turn-taking in American Sign Language discourse. In L. Friedman (ed.), On the Other Hand: New Perspectives on American Sign Language. Academic Press, New York.

Baker, C., and C. Padden. 1978. Focusing on the nonmanual components of American Sign Language. In P. Siple (ed.), Understanding Language through Sign Language Research. Academic Press, New York.

Bard, B., and J. Sachs. 1977. Language acquisition patterns in two normal children of deaf parents. Presented at the Second Annual Boston University Conference on Language Development, Sept. 30–Oct. 1.

Baron, N., and L. Isensee. 1977. Effectiveness of manual versus spoken language with an autistic child. Unpublished manuscript. Brown University, Providence, R.I.

Baron, N., L. Isensee, and A. Davis. 1977. Iconicity and learnability: Teaching sign language to autistic children. Presented at the Second Annual Boston University Conference on Language Development, Sept. 30–Oct. 1.

Battison, R. 1971. Some observations of sign languages, semantics, and aphasia. Unpublished manuscript. University of California, San Diego.

Battison, R. 1973. Phonology in American Sign Language: 3-D and digitvision. Presented at the California Linguistic Association Conference, Stanford, Cal.

Battison, R. 1974. Phonological deletion in American Sign Language. Sign Lang. Stud. 5:1–19.

Battison, R. 1978. Lexical borrowing in American Sign Language. Linstock Press, Silver Spring, Md.

Battison, R., and H. Markowicz. 1974. Sign aphasia and neurolinguistic theory. Unpublished manuscript. Gallaudet College, Washington, D.C.

Battison, R., H. Markowicz, and J. Woodward. 1975. A good rule of thumb: Variable phonology in American Sign Language. In R. Shuy and R. Fasold (eds.), New Ways of Analyzing Variation in English II. Georgetown University Press, Washington, D.C.

Battison, R., and C. Padden. 1974. Sign language aphasia: A case study. Presented at the 49th Annual Meeting, Linguistic Society of America, New York.

Beckmeyer, T. 1976. Receptive abilities of hearing impaired students in a total communication setting. Am. Ann. Deaf 121:569–572.

Bellugi, U. 1967. The acquisition of negation. Unpublished doctoral dissertation. Harvard University, Cambridge, Mass.

Bellugi, U. 1972. Studies in sign language. In T. O'Rourke (ed.), Psycholinguistics and Total Communication: The State of the Art. National Association of the Deaf, Silver Spring, Md.

Bellugi, U. 1975. The process of compounding in American Sign Language. Unpublished manuscript. Salk Institute for Biological Studies, La Jolla, Cal.

Bellugi, U., and S. Fischer. 1972. A comparison of sign language and spoken language: Rate and grammatical mechanisms. Cognition 1:173–200.

Bellugi, U., and E. Klima. 1972. The roots of language in the sign talk of the deaf. Psychol. Today June:61–64, 76.

Bellugi, U., and E. Klima. 1976. Two faces of sign: Iconic and abstract. In S. Harnad, H. Steklis, and J. Lancester (eds.), Origins and Evolution of Language and Speech. New York Academy of Sciences, New York.

Bellugi, U., E. Klima, and P. Siple. 1975. Remembering in signs. Cognition 3:93–125.

Bellugi, U., and P. Siple. 1974. Remembering with and without words. In F. Bresson (ed.), Current Problems in Psycholinguistics. Centre National de la Recherche Scientifique, Paris.

Belmont, J., M. Karchmer, and P. Pilkonis. 1976. Instructed rehearsal strategies' influence on deaf memory processing. J. Speech Hear. Res. 19:36–47.

Berko, J., and R. Brown. 1966. Psycholinguistic research methods. In P. Mussen (ed.), Handbook of Research Methods in Child Development. John Wiley & Sons, New York.

Bernstein, M. 1978. Acquisition of locative expressions by deaf children learning American Sign Language. Funded by the Bureau of Education for the Handicapped, Research and Demonstration program.

Bickerton, D. 1975. Dynamics of a Creole Continuum. Cambridge University Press, London.

Bloom, L. 1970. Language Development: Form and Function in Emerging Grammar. MIT Press, Cambridge, Mass.

Bloom, L. 1973a. If, when, and why children imitate. Presented at the Institute for Research on Exceptional Children, University of Illinois, Urbana-Champaign.

Bloom, L. 1973b. One Word at a Time. Mouton, The Hague.

Bloomfield, L. 1933. Language. Holt, Rinehart & Winston, New York.

Boatner, E., E. Stuckless, and D. Moores. 1964. Occupational status of the young adult deaf of New England and the need and demand for a regional technical-vocational training center. Final report, Research Grant RD-1295-S-64, Vocational Rehabilitation Administration, DHEW.

Bode, L. 1974. Communication of agent, object, and indirect object in spoken and signed languages. Percept. Motor Skills 39:1151–1158.

Bolton, B. 1976. Psychology of Deafness for Rehabilitation Counselors. University Park Press, Baltimore.

Bonvillian, J., V. Charrow, and K. Nelson. 1973. Psycholinguistic and educational implications of deafness. Hum. Dev. 16:321–345.

Bonvillian, J., and K. Nelson. 1978. Development of sign language in autistic children and other-language handicapped individuals. In P. Siple (ed.), Understanding Language through Sign Language Research. Academic Press, New York.

Bonvillian, J., K. Nelson, and V. Charrow. 1976. Language and language-related skills in deaf and hearing children. Sign Lang. Stud. 12:211–250.

Bornstein, H. 1973. A description of some current sign systems designed to represent English. Am. Ann. Deaf 118:454–463.

Bornstein, H. 1978. Systems of sign. In L. Bradford and W. Hardy (eds.), Hearing and Hearing Impairment. Grune & Stratton, New York. In press.

Bornstein, H., and L. Hamilton. 1972. Some recent national dictionaries of sign language. Sign Lang. Stud. 1:42–63.

Bornstein, H., L. Hamilton, B. Kannapell, H. Roy, and K. Saulnier. 1973. Basic Pre-School Signed English Dictionary. Gallaudet College, Washington, D.C.

Bornstein, H., L. Hamilton, B. Kannapell, H. Roy, and K. Saulnier. 1975. The Signed English Dictionary for Pre-School and Elementary Levels. Gallaudet College, Washington, D.C.

Bornstein, H., J. Woodward, and N. Tully. 1976. Language and Communication. In B. Bolton (ed.), Psychology of Deafness for Rehabilitation Counselors. University Park Press, Baltimore.

Børrild, K. 1972. Cued speech and the mouth-hand system. In G. Fant (ed.), International Symposium on Speech Communication Ability and Profound Deafness. Alexander Graham Bell Association for the Deaf, Washington, D.C.

Boyes, P. 1973. Developmental phonology for ASL. Working paper, Salk Institute for Biological Studies, La Jolla, Cal.

Boyes-Braem, P. 1973. A study of the acquisition of the DEZ in American Sign Language. Working paper, Salk Institute for Biological Studies, La Jolla, Cal.

Bragg, B. 1973. Ameslish: Our national heritage. Am. Ann. Deaf 118:672–674.

Bransford, J., J. Barclay, and J. Franks. 1972. Sentence memory: A constructive versus interpretive approach. Cog. Psychol. 3:193–209.

Bransford, J., and J. Franks. 1971. The abstraction of linguistic ideas. Cog. Psychol. 2:331–350.

Brasel, K., and S. Quigley. 1977. The influence of certain language and communication environments in early childhood on the development of language in deaf individuals. J. Speech Hear. Res. 20:95–107.

Bricker, D. 1972. Imitative sign training as a facilitator of word-object association with low-functioning children. Am. J. Ment. Def. 76:509–516.

Brown, A. 1975. The development of memory: Knowing, knowing about knowing, knowing how to know. In H. Reese (ed.), Advances in Child Development and Behavior. Academic Press, New York.

Brown, R. 1973. A First Language: The Early Stages. Harvard University Press, Cambridge, Mass.

Brown, R. 1977. Why are sign languages easier to learn than spoken languages? Presented at the National Symposium on Sign Language Teaching and Research, Chicago.

Brown, R., and C. Hanlon. 1970. Derivational complexity and order of acquisition. In J. Hayes (ed.), Cognition and the Development of Language. John Wiley & Sons, New York.

Butler, G., B. Griffing, and J. Huffman. 1969. Training program for the retarded blind and the retarded deaf children. Grant No. 2 R20 MR02075-04, Sonoma State Hospital, Eldridge, Cal.

Caccamise, F. 1976. Comparative systems of manual communication. National Workshop in Total Communication, Montana State University, Bozeman.

Chall, J. 1967. Learning How to Read: The Great Debate. McGraw-Hill Book Co., New York.

Chao, Y. R. 1934. The non-uniqueness of phonemic solutions of phonetic systems. Bull. Inst. Hist. Philol., Academia Sinica 4:363–397.

Chapman, R., and J. Miller. Language analysis and alternate communication systems. In R. Schiefelbusch (ed.), Nonspeech Language and Communication: Analysis and Intervention. University Park Press, Baltimore. In press.

Charrow, V. 1974. Deaf English—An investigation of the written English competence of deaf adolescents. Report 236, Institute for Mathematical Studies in the Social Sciences, Stanford, Cal.

Charrow, V. 1975a. A psycholinguistic analysis of "Deaf English." Sign Lang. Stud. 7:139–150.

Charrow, V. 1975b. A linguist's view of manual English. Presented at the World Conference on the Deaf, Washington, D.C.

Charrow, V., and J. Fletcher. 1973. English as the second language of deaf students. Report 208, Institute for Mathematical Studies in the Social Sciences, Stanford, Cal.

Charrow, V., and R. Wilbur. 1975. The deaf child as a linguistic minority. Theory Pract. 14:353–359.

Chinchor, N. 1977. Problems in the study of aphasia. Unpublished manuscript. Brown University, Providence, R.I.

Chinchor, N. 1978a. The structure of the NP in ASL: Argument from research on numerals. Unpublished manuscript. Brown University, Providence, R.I.

Chinchor, N. 1978b. The syllable in ASL. Presented at the MIT Sign Language Symposium, Cambridge, Mass.

Chinchor, N., J. Forman, F. Grosjean, M. Hajjar, J. Kegl, E. Lentz, M. Philip, and R. Wilbur. 1976. Sign language research and linguistic universals. University of Massachusetts at Amherst Working Papers 2:70–94.

Chomsky, N. 1964. Current issues in linguistics. In J. Fodor and J. Katz (eds.), The Structure of Language: Readings in the Philosophy of Language. Prentice-Hall, Englewood Cliffs, N.J.

Chomsky, N., and M. Halle. 1968. The Sound Pattern of English. Harper & Row. Publishers, New York.

Cogen, C. 1977. On three aspects of time expression in American Sign Language. In L. Friedman (ed.), On the Other Hand. Academic Press, New York.

Cohen, E., L. Namir, and I. M. Schlesinger. 1977. A New Dictionary of Sign Language. Mouton, The Hague.

Conlin, D. 1972. The effects of word imagery and signability in the paired-associate learning of the deaf. Master's thesis. University of Western Ontario, London, Ontario.

Conrad, R. 1962. An association between memory errors and errors due to acoustic masking of speech. Nature 193:1314–1315.

Conrad, R. 1970. Short-term memory processes in the deaf. Br. J. Psychol. 61:179–195.

Conrad, R. 1971. The effect of vocalizing on comprehension in the profoundly deaf. Br. J. Psychol. 62:147–150.

Conrad, R. 1972. Speech and reading. In J. Kavanagh and I. Mattingly (eds.), Language by Ear and by Eye: The Relationships between Speech and Reading. MIT Press, Cambridge, Mass.

Conrad, R. 1973. Some correlates of speech coding in the short-term memory of the deaf. J. Speech Hear. Res. 16:375–384.

Conrad, R. 1975. Matters arising. In Royal National Institute for the Deaf (ed.), Methods of Communication Currently Used in the Education of Deaf Children. The Garden City Press, Letchworth, England.

Conrad, R., and M. Rush. 1965. On the nature of short-term memory encoding by the deaf. J. Speech Hear. Disord. 30:336–343.

Cornett, R. 1967. Cued speech. Am. Ann. Deaf 112:3–13.

Cornett, R. 1969. In answer to Dr. Moores. Am. Ann. Deaf 114:27–33.

Covington, V. 1973a. Juncture in American Sign Language. Sign Lang. Stud. 2:29–38.

Covington, V. 1973b. Features of stress in American Sign Language. Sign Lang. Stud. 2:39–58.

Craig, E. 1976. A supplement to the spoken word—the Paget-Gorman Sign System. In Royal National Institute for the Deaf (ed.), Methods of Communication Currently Used in the Education of Deaf Children. The Garden City Press, Letchworth, England.

Creedon, M. 1973. Language development in nonverbal autistic children using a simultaneous communication system. Presented at the Society for Research on Child Development Conference, Philadelphia.

Creedon, M. 1975. (ed.), Appropriate Behavior through Communication: A New Program in Simultaneous Language. Michael Reese Medical Center, Chicago.

Creedon, M. 1976. The David School: A simultanous communication model. Presented to the National Society for Autistic Children Conference, Oak Brook, Ill.

Cromer, R. 1974. Receptive language in the mentally retarded. In R. Schiefelbusch and L. Lloyd (eds.), Language Perspectives—Acquisition, Intervention, and Retardation. University Park Press, Baltimore.

Crowder, R. 1972. Visual and auditory memory. In J. Kavanagh and I. Mattingly (eds.), Language by Ear and by Eye: The Relationship between Speech and Reading. MIT Press, Cambridge, Mass.

DeMatteo, A. 1977. Visual imagery and visual analogues in American Sign

Language. In L. Friedman (ed.), On The Other Hand. Academic Press, New York.

Donahue, M. 1977a. Conversational gimmicks: The acquisition of small talk. Presented at the Second Annual Boston University Conference on Language Development.

Donahue, M. 1977b. Conversational styles of mother-toddler dyads. Presented at the American Speech and Hearing Association conference, Chicago.

Donahue, M., and L. Watson. 1976. How to get some action! Presented at the First Annual Boston University Conference on Language Development.

Edge, V., and L. Herrmann. 1977. Verbs and the determination of subject in American Sign Language. In L. Friedman (ed.), On the Other Hand. Academic Press, New York.

Ellenberger, R., D. Moores, and R. Hoffmeister. 1975. Early stages in the acquisition of negation by a deaf child of deaf parents. Research report #94. Research, Development, and Demonstration Center in Education of the Handicapped, University of Minnesota.

Ellenberger R., and M. Steyaert. 1978. A child's representation of action in American Sign Language. In P. Siple (ed.), Understanding Language through Sign Language Research. Academic Press, New York,

English, S., and C. Prutting. 1975. Teaching ASL to a normally hearing infant with tracheostenosis. Clin. Pediatr. December:1141–1145.

Ervin-Tripp, S. 1970. Discourse agreement: How children answer questions. In J. Hayes (ed.), Cognition and the Development of Language. John Wiley & Sons, New York.

Fant, L. 1964. Say It with Hands. Gallaudet College, Washington, D.C.

Fant, L. 1972a. The American Sign Language. California News 83(5).

Fant, L. 1972b. Ameslan. National Association of the Deaf, Silver Spring, Md.

Fischer, S. 1973a. Two processes of reduplication in American Sign Language. Found. Lang. 9:469–480.

Fischer, S. 1973b. The deaf child's acquisition of verb inflections in ASL. Presented to the Linguistic Society of America Annual Meeting, San Diego.

Fischer, S. 1974. Sign language and linguistic universals. In Proceedings of the Franco-German Conference on French Transformational Grammar. Athaenium, Berlin.

Fischer, S. 1975. Influences on word order change in ASL. In C. Li (ed.), Word Order and Word Order Change. University of Texas Press, Austin.

Fischer, S. 1978. Sign languages and creoles. In P. Siple (ed.), Understanding Language through Sign Language Research. Academic Press, New York.

Fischer, S., and B. Gough. 1972. Some unfinished thoughts on FINISH. Working paper, Salk Institute for Biological Studies, La Jolla, Cal.

Fischer, S., and B. Gough. 1978. Verbs in American Sign Language. Sign Lang. Stud. 18:17–48.

Fitzgerald, E. 1929. Straight Language for the Deaf. The McClure Co., Stauton, Va.

Forman, J., and B. McDonald. 1978. Investigation into the structure of the NP and VP. Presented at the MIT Sign Language Symposium, Cambridge, Mass.

Fouts, R. 1973. Acquisition and testing of gestural signs in four young chimpanzees. Science 180:978–980.

Franks, J., and J. Bransford. 1972. The acquisition of abstract ideas. J. Verb. Learn. Verb. Behav. 11:311–315.

Freidman, E. 1977. The parameters of signs in the short-term memory of the deaf: An initial investigation. Unpublished manuscript. Boston University.

Friedman, L. 1974. On the physical manifestation of stress in the American Sign Language. Unpublished manuscript. University of California, Berkeley.

Friedman, L. 1975a. Space, time, and person reference in American Sign Language. Language 51:940–961.

Friedman, L. 1975b. Phonological processes in the American Sign Language. In C. Cogen, H. Thompson, G. Thurgood, K. Whistler, and J. Wright (eds.), Proceedings of the First Annual Meeting of the Berkeley Linguistic Society. Berkeley Linguistic Society, Berkeley, Cal.

Friedman, L. 1976a. The manifestation of subject, object, and topic in American Sign Language. In C. Li (ed.), Subject and Topic. Academic Press, New York.

Friedman, L. 1976b. Phonology of a soundless language: Phonological structure of American Sign Language. Unpublished doctoral dissertation. University of California, Berkeley.

Friedman, L. (ed.). 1977. On the Other Hand: New Perspectives on American Sign Language. Academic Press, New York.

Frishberg, N. 1972. Sharp and soft: Two aspects of movement in American Sign Language. Working paper, Salk Institute for Biological Studies, La Jolla, Cal.

Frishberg, N. 1975. Arbitrariness and iconicity: Historical change in American Sign Language. Language 51:676–710.

Frishberg, N. 1976a. Some aspects of the historical development of signs in American Sign Language. Unpublished doctoral dissertation. University of California, San Diego.

Frishberg, N. 1976b. Rhythm in American Sign Language. Presented at the Summer Linguistic Institute, Oswego, New York.

Frishberg, N. 1978. The case of the missing length. In R. Wilbur (ed.), Sign Language Research. A special issue of Communication and Cognition.

Frishberg, N. Research on Adamarobe (Ghana) sign language. Hampshire College, Amherst. In preparation.

Frishberg, N., and B. Gough. 1973a. Morphology in American Sign Language. Working paper, Salk Institute for Biological Studies, La Jolla, Cal.

Frishberg, N., and B. Gough. 1973b. Time on our hands. Presented at the Third Annual California Linguistics Conference, Stanford.

Fristoe, M. 1975. Language Intervention Systems for the Retarded. L. B. Wallace Development Center, Decatur, Ala.

Fristoe, M., and L. Lloyd. 1977a. Manual communicaton for the retarded and others with severe communication impairment: A resource list. Ment. Retard. 15:18–21.

Fristoe, M., and L. Lloyd. 1977b. The use of manual communication with the retarded. Presented at the Gatlinburg Conference on Research in Mental Retardation.

Fristoe, M., and L. Lloyd. 1978. A first sign lexicon for non-speaking severely/ profoundly impaired individuals, based on cognitive and psycholinguistic considerations. Presented at the Gatlinburg Conference on Research in Mental Retardation.

Fristoe, M., and L. Lloyd. Nonspeech Communication. In N. Ellis (ed.), Handbook of Mental Deficiency: Psychological Theory and Research. 2nd Ed. Lawrence Erlbaum Assoc., Hillsdale, N.J. In press.

Fristoe, M., L. Lloyd, and R. Wilbur. 1977. Non-speech communication: Systems and symbols. Short course, American Speech and Hearing Association Conference, Chicago.

Fulwiler, R., and R. Fouts. 1976. Acquisition of sign language by a noncommunicating autistic child. J. Autism Child. Schizo. 6:43-51.

Furth, H. 1966a. A comparison of reading test norms of deaf and hearing children. Am. Ann. Deaf 111:461-462.

Furth, H. 1966b. Thinking without Language. Collier-Macmillian, London.

Goldin-Meadow, S. 1975. The representation of semantic relations in a manual language created by deaf children of hearing parents: A language you can't dismiss out of hand. Unpublished doctoral dissertation. University of Pennsylvania, Philadelphia.

Goldin-Meadow, S., and H. Feldman. 1975. The creation of a communication system: A study of deaf children of hearing parents. Presented at the Society for Research in Child Development Meeting, Denver.

Graham, J., and L. Graham. 1971. Language behavior of the mentally retarded: Syntactic characteristics. Am. J. Ment. Def. 75:623-629.

Greenberg, J. 1966. Some universals of language with particular reference to the order of meaningful elements. In J. Greenberg (ed.), Universals of Language. MIT Press, Cambridge, Mass.

Grosjean, F. 1977. The perception of rate in spoken and sign languages. Percept. Psychophys. 22:408-413.

Grosjean, F. 1978. Crosslinguistic research in the perception and production of English and American Sign Language. Paper presented at the National Symposium on Sign Language Research and Teaching, Coronado, Cal.

Grosjean, F. A study of timing in a manual and a spoken language: American Sign Language and English. J. Psycholing. Res. In press.

Grosjean, F., and M. Collins. Breathing, pausing, and reading. Phonetica. In press.

Grosjean, F., and A. Deschamps. 1975. Analyse contrastive des variables temporelles de l'anglais et de français: Vitesse de parole et variables composantes, phénomènes d'hésitation. Phonetica 31:144-184.

Grosjean, F., and H. Lane. 1977. Pauses and syntax in American Sign Language. Cognition 5:101-117.

Gudschinsky, S. 1964. The ABC's of lexicostatistics (glottochronology). In D. Hymes (ed.), Language in Culture and Society. Harper & Row Publishers, New York.

Gustason, G., D. Pfetzing, and E. Zawolkow. 1972. Signing Exact English. Modern Signs Press, Rossmoor, Cal.

Gustason, G., D. Pfetzing, and E. Zawolkow. 1973. SEE Supplement II. Modern Signs Press, Rossmoor, Cal.

Gustason, G., D. Pfetzing, and E. Zawolkow. 1974. The rationale of SEE. Deaf Am. Sept.

Hall, S., and T. Conn. 1972. Current trends in services for the deaf retarded in schools for the deaf and residential facilities for the mentally retarded. Report of the Proceedings of the 45th Meeting of the Convention of American Instructors of the Deaf, Little Rock, Ark., 1971. U.S. Government Printing Office, Washington, D.C.

Hall, S., and L. Talkington. 1970. Evaluation of a manual approach to programming for deaf retarded. Am. J. Ment. Def. 75:378–380.

Herx, M., and F. Hunt. 1976. A framework for speech development within a total communication system. Am. Ann. Deaf 121:537–540.

Hewes, G. 1973. Primate communication and the gestural origin of language. Curr. Anthropol. 14:5–24.

Hockett, C. 1942. A system of descriptive phonology. Language 18:3–21.

Hockett, C. 1948. Implications of Bloomfield's Algonquian studies. Language 24:117–131.

Hockett, C. 1954. Two models of grammatical description. Word 10:210–231.

Hockett, C. 1958. A Course in Modern Linguistics. Macmillan Publishing Co., New York.

Hoemann, H. 1975a. The American Sign Language: Lexical and Grammatical Notes with Translation Exercises. National Association of the Deaf, Silver Spring, Md.

Hoemann, H. 1975b. The transparency of meaning of sign language gestures. Sign Lang. Stud. 7:151–161.

Hoemann, H. 1978. Communicating with Deaf People. University Park Press, Baltimore.

Hoemann, H., and V. Florian. 1976. Order constraints in American Sign Language. Sign Lang. Stud. 11:121–132.

Hoffmeister, R. 1975. The development of location in a deaf child of deaf parents. Unpublished manuscript, Research, Development, and Demonstration Center in Education of the Handicapped, University of Minnesota, Minneapolis.

Hoffmeister, R. 1977. The acquisition of American Sign Language by deaf children of deaf parents: The development of the demonstrative pronouns, locatives, and personal pronouns. Unpublished doctoral dissertation. University of Minnesota, Minneapolis.

Hoffmeister, R. 1978. An analysis of possessive constructions in the ASL of a young deaf child of deaf parents. In R. Wilbur (ed.), Sign Language Research. A special issue of Communication and Cognition.

Hoffmeister, R., and S. Dworski. 1978. Is the message the same in hearing and deaf children? Presented at the MIT Sign Language Symposium, Cambridge, Mass.

Hoffmeister, R., R. Ellenberger, and D. Moores. 1975. Sign language development in deaf children of deaf parents. Presented at the 53rd Annual Convention of the Council for Exceptional Children, Los Angeles.

Hoffmeister, R., and A. Farmer. 1972. The development of manual sign language in mentally retarded individuals. J. Rehab. Deaf 6:19–26.

Hoffmeister, R., and W. Goodhart. 1978. The semantic and syntactic analysis of the sign language behavior of a deaf child of hearing parents. Presented at the MIT Sign Language Symposium, Cambridge, Mass.

Hoffmeister, R., and D. Moores. 1973. The acquisition of specific reference in a deaf child of deaf parents. Report #53, Research, Development, and Demonstration Center in Education of the Handicapped, University of Minnesota, Minneapolis.

Hoffmeister, R., D. Moores, and B. Best. 1974. The acquisition of sign language in deaf children of deaf parents. Research report #65, Research, Development, and Demonstration Center in the Education of the Handicapped, University of Minnesota, Minneapolis.

Hoffmeister, R., D. Moores, and R. Ellenberger. 1975a. The parameters of sign language defined: Translation and definition rules. Research report #83, Research, Development, and Demonstration Center in Education of the Handicapped, University of Minnesota, Minneapolis.

Hoffmeister, R., D. Moores, and R. Ellenberger. 1975b. Some procedural guidelines for analyzing American Sign Language. Sign Lang. Stud. 7:121–137.

Huffman, J., B. Hoffman, D. Granssee, A. Fox, J. James, and J. Schmitz. 1974. Talk with Me: Communication with the Multi-Handicapped Deaf. Joyce Motion Picture Co., Northridge, Cal.

Hymes, D. 1971. Pidginization and creolization of languages. Cambridge University Press, New York.

Ingram, D. 1974. Phonological rules in young children. J. Child Lang. 1:49–64.

Ingram, D. 1976. Phonological Disability in Children. Elsevier-North Holland Publishing Co., New York.

Ingram, R. 1977. Principles and Procedures of Teaching Sign Language. British Deaf Association, Carlile.

Jakobson, R. 1968. Child Language, Aphasia, and Phonological Universals. Mouton, The Hague.

James, W. 1963. Mentally retarded deaf children in a California hospital. Report of the Proceedings of the Forty-first meeting of the Convention of the American Instructors of the Deaf, pp. 573–577.

James, W. 1967. A hospital improvement program for mentally retarded children at Sonoma State Hospital. Report of the Proceedings of the Convention of American Instructors of the Deaf, pp. 272–276.

Jeffers, J. 1967. Process of speechreading viewed with respect to a theoretical construct. In Proceedings of the International Conference on Oral Education of the Deaf. Alexander Graham Bell Association for the Deaf, Washington, D.C.

Johnson, R. K. 1963. The institutionalized mentally retarded deaf. Report of the Proceedings of the Forty-first meeting of the Convention of American Instructors of the Deaf, pp. 568–573.

Johnson, R. 1978. A comparison of the phonological structures of two northwest sawmill sign languages. In R. Wilbur (ed.), Sign Language Research. A special issue of Communication and Cognition.

Jones, M. 1976. A longitudinal investigation into the acquisition of question formation in English and American Sign Language by three hearing children with deaf parents. Unpublished doctoral dissertation. University of Illinois, Urbana-Champaign.

Jones, N., and K. Mohr. 1975. A working paper on plurals in ASL. Unpublished manuscript. University of California, Berkeley.

Jones, P. 1978. On the interface of sign phonology and morphology. In R. Wilbur (ed.), Sign Language Research. A special issue of Communication and Cognition.

Jordan, E., and R. Battison. 1976. A referential communication experiment with foreign sign languages. Sign. Lang. Stud. 10:69–80.

Jordan, E., G. Gustason, and R. Rosen. 1976. Current communication trends at programs for the deaf. Am. Ann. Deaf 121:527–532.

Kahn, J. 1975. Relationship of Piaget's sensorimotor period to language acquisition of profoundly retarded children. Am. J. Ment. Def. 79:640–643.

Kannapell, B. The presentation of the numbers in American Sign Language. Unpublished manuscript. Gallaudet College, Washington, D.C. No date.

Kannapell, B., L. Hamilton, and H. Bornstein. 1969. Signs for Instructional Purposes. Gallaudet College Press, Washington, D.C.

Kantor, R. 1977. The acquisition of classifiers in American Sign Language. Unpublished master's thesis. Boston University.

Kantor, R. 1978. Identifying native and second-language signers. In R. Wilbur (ed.), Sign Language Research. A special issue of Communication and Cognition.

Karchmer, M., and J. Belmont. 1976. On assessing and improving deaf performance in the cognitive laboratory. Presented at the American Speech and Hearing Association Convention, Houston.

Kates, S. 1972. Language development in deaf and hearing adolescents. Final Report: RD-2555-S (14-P-55004). Social and Rehabilitation Service, Department of Health, Education and Welfare, Washington, D.C.

Kegl, J. 1976a. Pronominalization in American Sign Language. Unpublished manuscript. MIT, Cambridge, Mass.

Kegl, J. 1976b. Relational grammar and American Sign Language. Unpublished manuscript. MIT, Cambridge, Mass.

Kegl, J. 1977. ASL syntax: Research in progress and proposed research. Unpublished manuscript. MIT, Cambridge, Mass.

Kegl, J. 1978a. Indexing and pronominalization in ASL. Unpublished manuscript. MIT, Cambridge, Mass.

Kegl, J. 1978b. ASL classifiers. Unpublished manuscript. MIT, Cambridge, Mass.

Kegl, J. 1978c. A possible argument for passive in ASL. Unpublished manuscript. MIT Press, Cambridge, Mass.

Kegl, J. 1978d. ASL agreement. Presented at the MIT Sign Language Symposium, Cambridge, Mass.

Kegl, J., and N. Chinchor. 1975. A frame analysis of American Sign Language. In T. Diller (ed.), Proceedings of the 13th Annual Meeting, Association for Computational Linguistics. Am. J. Comput. Ling. Microfiche 35, Sperry-Univac, St. Paul, Minn.

Kegl, J., E. Lentz, and M. Philip. 1976. ASL pronouns and conditions on their use. Presented at the Linguistic Society of America Summer Meeting, Oswego, N.Y.

Kegl, J., and D. Nash. 1976. Transcription and comments on a tape of Warlpiri Sign Language: Spoken and signed. Unpublished manuscript. MIT, Cambridge, Mass.

Kegl, J., and G. Nigrosh. 1975. Sign language and pictographs: A comparison of the signs and picture writing of the North American Plains Indians. Unpublished manuscript. Brown University, Providence, R.I.

Kegl, J., and R. Wilbur. 1976. When does structure stop and style begin? Syntax, morphology, and phonology vs. stylistic variation in American Sign Language. In S. Mufwene, C. Walker, and S. Steever (eds.), Papers from the Twelfth Regional Meeting, Chicago Linguistic Society. The University of Chicago Press, Chicago.

Kiernan, C. 1977. Alternatives to speech: A review of research on manual and other forms of communication with the mentally handicapped and other non-communicating populations. Br. J. Ment. Subnorm. 23:6–28.

Klima, E., and U. Bellugi. 1975. Wit and poetry in American Sign Language. Sign Lang. Stud. 8:203–224.

Klima, E., and U. Bellugi. 1979. The Signs of Language. Harvard University Press, Cambridge, Mass.

Klima, E., and U. Bellugi-Klima. 1966. Syntactic regularities in the speech of children. In J. Lyons and R. Wales (eds.), Psycholinguistics Papers. Edinburgh University Press, Edinburgh.

Konstantareas, M., J. Oxman, and C. Webster. 1978. Iconicity: Effects on the acquisition of sign language by autistic and other dysfunctional children. In P. Siple (ed.), Understanding Language through Sign Language Research. Academic Press, New York.

LaBerge, D. 1972. Beyond auditory coding. In J. Kavanagh and I. Mattingly (eds.), Language by Ear and by Eye: The Relationship between Speech and Reading. MIT Press, Cambridge, Mass.

Lacy, R. 1972a. Development of Pola's questions. Unpublished manuscript, Salk Institute for Biological Studies, La Jolla, Cal.

Lacy, R. 1972b. Development of Sonia's negations. Unpublished manuscript, Salk Institute for Biological Studies, La Jolla, Cal.

Lacy, R. 1973. Directional verb marking in the American Sign Language. Presented at the Summer Linguistic Institute, Linguistic Society of America, University of California, Santa Cruz.

Lacy, R. 1974. Putting some of the syntax back into semantics. Presented at the Linguistic Society of America Annual Meeting, New York.

Lane, H. 1976. The Wild Boy of Aveyron: A history of special education. Harvard University Press, Cambridge, Mass.

Lane, H., P. Boyes-Braem, and U. Bellugi. 1976. Preliminaries to a distinctive feature analysis of handshapes in American Sign Language. Cog. Psychol. 8:263–289.

Lane, H., and F. Grosjean. 1973. Perception of reading rate by speakers and listeners. J. Exp. Psychol. 97:141–147.

Langacker, R. 1972. Fundamentals of Linguistic Analysis. Harcourt Brace Jovanovich, New York.

Lenneberg, E. 1967. Biological Foundations of Language. John Wiley & Sons, New York.

Levitt, L. 1972. A method of communication for non-speaking severely subnormal children—trial results. Br. J. Disord. Commun. October.

Liddell, S. 1977. An investigation into the syntactic structure of American Sign Language. Unpublished doctoral dissertation. University of California, San Diego.

Liddell, S. 1978. An introduction to relative clauses in ASL. In P. Siple (ed.), Understanding Language through Sign Language Research. Academic Press, New York.

Lloyd, L. (ed.). 1976. Communication Assessment and Intervention Strategies. University Park Press, Baltimore.

Lloyd, L., and M. Fristoe. 1978. Iconicity of signs: Evidence for its predominance in vocabularies used with severely impaired individuals in contrast with American Sign Language in general. Presented at the Gatlinburg Conference on Research in Mental Retardation, Gatlinburg, Tenn.

Locke, J. 1970. Short-term memory encoding strategies in the deaf. Psychonom. Sci. 8:233–234.

Locke, J., and V. Locke. 1971. Deaf children's phonetic, visual, and dactylic coding in a grapheme recall task. J. Exp. Psychol. 89:142–146.

Long, J. 1918. The Sign Language: A Manual of Signs. Athens Press, Iowa City.

Lubert, B. 1975. The relation of brain asymmetry to visual processing of sign language, alphabetic and visual-spatial material in deaf and hearing subjects. Unpublished master's thesis. University of Western Ontario.

McCall, E. 1965. A generative grammar of Sign. Unpublished master's thesis. University of Iowa, Iowa City.

McCawley, J. 1970. Where do noun phrases come from? In R. Jacobs and P. Rosenbaum (eds.), Readings in English Transformational Grammar. Ginn and Co., Boston.

McIntire, M. 1974. A modified model for the description of language acquisition in a deaf child. Unpublished master's thesis. California State University, Northridge.

McIntire, M. 1977. The acquisition of American Sign Language hand configurations. Sign Lang. Stud. 16:247–266.

McIntire, M., and J. Yamada. 1976. Visual shadowing: Examining language processing in another mode. Presented at the Linguistic Society of American Annual Meeting, Philadelphia.

McKeever, W., H. Hoemann, V. Florian, and A. Van Deventer. 1976. Evidence of minimal cerebral asymmetries for the processing of English words and American Sign Language stimuli in the congenitally deaf. Neuropsychologia 14:413–423.

Madsen, W. 1972. Conversational Sign Language II. Gallaudet College, Washington, D.C.

Mandel, M. 1977. Iconic devices in American Sign Language. In L. Friedman (ed.), On the Other Hand: New Perspectives in American Sign Language. Academic Press, New York.

Manning, A., W. Goble, R. Markman, and T. LaBreche. 1977. Lateral cerebral differences in the deaf in response to linguistic and non-linguistic stimuli. Brain Lang. 4:309–321.

Markowicz, H. 1973. Aphasia and deafness. Sign Lang. Stud. 3:61–71.

Markowicz, H. 1976. L'Epée's Methodical Signs Revisited. In C. Williams (ed.), Proceedings of the Second Gallaudet Symposium on Research in Deafness: Language and Communication Research Problems. Gallaudet Press, Washington, D.C.

Markowicz, H., and J. Woodward. 1978. Language and the maintenance of the deaf community. In R. Wilbur (ed.), Sign Language Research. A special issue of Communication and Cognition.

Mayberry, R. 1974. Systems of manual communication and some clinical considerations for their use with normally hearing, non-communicative individuals. Unpublished manuscript. McGill University, Montreal.

Mayberry, R. 1976a. If a chimp can learn sign language, surely my nonverbal client can too. ASHA 18:223–228.

Mayberry, R. 1976b. An assessment of some oral and manual language skills of hearing children of deaf parents. Am. Ann. Deaf 121:507–512.

Mayberry, R. 1977. Facial expression, noise, and shadowing in American Sign Language. Doctoral proposal. McGill University, Montreal.

Mayberry, R. 1978. French-Canadian Sign Language: A study of inter-sign language comprehension. In P. Siple (ed.), Understanding Language through Sign Language Research. Academic Press, New York.

Meadow, K. 1966. The effects of early manual communication and family climate on the deaf child's early development. Unpublished doctoral dissertation. University of California, Berkeley.

Meadow, K. 1976. Personality and social development of deaf persons. In B. Bolton (ed.), Psychology of Deafness for Rehabilitation Counselors. University Park Press, Baltimore.

Meadow, K. 1977. Name signs as identity symbols in the deaf community. Sign Lang. Stud. 16:237–246.

Menn, L. 1976. Pattern, control, and contrast in beginning speech: A case study in the development of word form and word function. Unpublished doctoral dissertation. University of Illinois, Urbana-Champaign.

Menyuk, P. 1963. Syntactic structures in the language of children. Child Dev. 34:407–422.

Menyuk, P. 1964. Syntactic rules used by children from preschool through first grade. Child Dev. 35:533–546.

Menyuk, P. 1977. Language and Maturation. Academic Press, New York.

Miller, A., and E. Miller. 1973. Cognitive developmental training with elevated boards and sign language. J. Autism Child. Schizo. 3:65–85.

Miller, G., and S. Isard. 1963. Some perceptual consequences of linguistic rules. J. Verb. Learn. Behav. 2:227–228.

Miller, G., and P. Nicely. 1955. An analysis of perceptual confusions among some English consonants. J. Acoustic. Soc. Am. 27:339–352.

Moores, D. 1969. Cued Speech: Some practical and theoretical considerations. Am. Ann. Deaf 114:23–27.

Moores, D. 1971. Recent research on manual communication. Research, Development, and Demonstration Center in Education of the Handicapped, University of Minnesota, Minneapolis.

Moores, D. 1972. Communication: Some unanswered questions and some unquestioned answers. In T. O'Rourke (ed.), Psycholinguistics and Total Communication: The State of the Art. National Association of the Deaf, Silver Spring, Md.

Moores, D. 1974. Nonvocal systems of verbal behavior. In R. Schiefelbusch and L. Lloyd (eds.), Language Perspectives—Acquisition, Retardation, and Intervention. University Park Press, Baltimore.

Moores, D. 1977. Educating the Deaf: Psychology, Principles, and Practices. Houghton Mifflin Co., Boston.

Moores, D. Alternate communication modes: Visual-motor systems. In R. Schiefelbusch (ed.), Nonspeech Language and Communication: Analysis and Intervention. University Park Press, Baltimore. In press.

Moores, D., C. McIntyre, and K. Weiss. 1973. Evaluation of programs for hearing impaired children. Research report #39. Research, Development, and Demonstration Center in Education of the Handicapped, University of Minnesota, Minneapolis.

Moores, D., and P. O'Malley. 1976. Pronominal reference in American Sign Language. Research, Development, and Demonstration Center in Education of the Handicapped, University of Minnesota, Minneapolis.

Moores, D., K. Weiss, and M. Goodwin. 1977. Early intervention programs for hearing impaired children: A longitudinal assessment. Asha Monographs.

Morgan, A. 1975. The process of imitation in deaf children of deaf parents. Unpublished master's thesis. University of Minnesota, Minneapolis.

Moskowitz, A. 1970. The two-year-old stage in the acquisition of English phonology. Language 46:426-441.

Moulton, R., and D. Beasley. 1975. Verbal coding strategies used by hearing-impaired individuals. J. Speech Hear. Res. 18:559-570.

Myklebust, H. 1964. The Psychology of Deafness. Grune & Stratton, New York.

Myklebust, H. 1967. Development and Disorders of Written Language. Grune & Stratton, New York.

Neisser, U. 1967. Cognitive Psychology. Prentice-Hall, Englewood Cliffs, N.J.

Neville, H., and U. Bellugi. 1978. Patterns of cerebral specialization in congenitally deaf adults: A preliminary report. In P. Siple (ed.), Understanding Language through Sign Language Research. Academic Press, New York.

Newkirk, D. 1975. Outline for a proposed orthography for American Sign Language. Unpublished manuscript. Salk Institute for Biological Studies, La Jolla, Cal.

Norman, D. 1969. Memory and Attention. John Wiley & Sons, New York.

Norman, D. 1972. The role of memory in the understanding of language. In J. Kavanagh and I. Mattingly (eds.), Language by Ear and by Eye: The Relationship between Speech and Reading. MIT Press, Cambridge, Mass.

Obler, L. Right hemispheric participation in second language acquisition. In K. Diller (ed.), Individual Differences and Universals in Language Learning Aptitude. Newbury Press, Rowley, Mass. In press.

Odom, P., R. Blanton, and C. McIntyre. 1970. Coding medium and word recall by deaf and hearing subjects. J. Speech Hear. Res. 13:54-58.

Office of Demographic Studies. 1972. Academic achievement test results of a national testing program for hearing impaired students: United States. Gallaudet College, Washington, D.C.

Oleron, P. 1974. Eléments de repertoire du language gestuel des sourds-muets. Centre National de la Récherche Scientifique, Paris.

O'Malley, P. 1975. The grammatical function of indexic reference in American Sign Language. Unpublished manuscript. Research, Development and Demonstration Center in Education of the Handicapped, University of Minnesota, Minneapolis.

O'Rourke, T. 1972. Psycholinguistics and Total Communication: The State of the Art. National Association of the Deaf, Silver Spring, Md.

O'Rourke, T. 1973. A Basic Course in Manual Communication. National Association of the Deaf, Silver Spring, Md.

O'Rourke, T., T. Medina, A. Thames, and D. Sullivan. 1975. National Association of the Deaf Communicative Skills Program. Programs Hand. April:27-30.

Owens, M., and B. Harper. 1971. Sign Language: A Teaching Manual for Cottage Parents of Non-Verbal Retardates. Pinecrest State School, Pineville, La.

Paget, R. 1951. The New Sign Language. The Welcome Foundation, London.

Paget, R. 1971. An introduction to the Paget-Gorman sign system with examples. AEDE Publications Committee, Reading, England.

Paget, R., and P. Gorman. 1968. A Systematic Sign Language. National Institute for the Deaf, London.

Paget, R., and P. Gorman. 1971. An introduction to the Paget-Gorman sign system with examples. AEDE Publications Committee, % 13 Ashbury Dr., Tilehurst, Reading, Berkshire, England.

Paris, S., and A. Carter. 1973. Semantic and constructive aspects of sentence memory in children. Dev. Psychol. 9:109–113.

Pearl, E. 1978. Iconic representation in American Sign Language. Presented at the MIT Sign Language Symposium, Cambridge, Mass.

Phippard, D. 1977. Hemifield differences in visual perception in deaf and hearing subjects. Neuropsychologia 15:555–561.

Piaget, J. 1951. Play, Dreams, and Imitation in Childhood. W. W. Norton and Co., New York.

Piaget, J. 1952. The Origins of Intelligence in Children. International Universities Press, New York.

Piaget, J. 1964. Development and learning. J. Res. Sci. Technol. 2:176–186.

Poizner, H., R. Battison, and H. Lane. 1978. Cerebral asymmetry for perception of ASL: The effects of moving stimuli. Unpublished manuscript. Northeastern University, Boston.

Poizner, H., and H. Lane. 1977. Cerebral asymmetry in the perception of American Sign Language. Unpublished manuscript. Northeastern University, Boston.

Poole, J. A comparison of Martha's Vineyard sign language to ASL. Manuscript in preparation. Boston University.

Power, D. 1971. Deaf children's acquisition of passive voice. Unpublished doctoral dissertation. University of Illinois, Urbana-Champaign.

Power, D. 1974. Language development in deaf children: The use of manual supplements in oral education. Aust. Teach. Deaf 15.

Quigley, S. 1969. The influence of fingerspelling on the development of language, communication, and educational achievement in deaf children. Institute for Research on Exceptional Children, University of Illinois, Urbana-Champaign.

Quigley, S., and R. Frisina. 1961. Institutionalization and Psychoeducational Development in Deaf Children. Council on Exceptional Children, Washington, D.C.

Quigley, S., D. Montanelli, and R. Wilbur. 1976. Auxiliary verbs in the language of deaf students. J. Speech Hear. Res. 19:536–550.

Quigley, S., N. Smith, and R. Wilbur. 1974. Comprehension of relativized structures by deaf students. J. Speech Hear. Res. 17:325–341.

Quigley, S., R. Wilbur, and D. Montanelli. 1974. Question formation in the language of deaf students. J. Speech Hear. Res. 17:699–713.

Quigley, S., R. Wilbur, and D. Montanelli. 1976. Complement structures in the written language of deaf students. J. Speech Hear. Res. 19:448–457.

Quigley, S., R. Wilbur, D. Power, D. Montanelli, and M. Steinkamp. 1976. Syntactic Structures in the Language of Deaf Children. Institute for Child Behavior and Development, University of Illinois, Urbana-Champaign.

Rainer, J., K. Altshuler, and F. Kallmann (eds.). 1963. Family and Mental Health Problems in a Deaf Population. State Psychiatric Institute, Columbia, N.Y.

Richards, J. 1974. Error Analysis and Second Language Learning. Longman Publishing Co., New York.

Riekehof, L. 1963. Talk to the Deaf. Gospel Publishing House, Springfield, Mo.

Robbins, N. 1976. Selecting sign systems for multi-handicapped students. Presented at the American Speech and Hearing Association Conference, Houston.

Robbins, N., J. Cagan, C. Johnson, H. Kelleher, J. Record, and J. Vernacchia. 1975. Perkins Sign Language Dictionary. Perkins School for the Blind, Watertown, Mass.

Rogers, G. 1976. The effects of iconicity on the acquisition of signs in Down's syndrome children. Unpublished manuscript. Boston University.

Ross, J. 1967. Constraints on variables in syntax. Unpublished doctoral dissertation. MIT, Cambridge, Mass.

Rupert, J. 1969. Kindergarten program using Cued Speech at the Idaho State School for the Deaf. Report of the Proceedings of the 44th Meeting of the American Instructors of the Deaf, Berkeley.

Russell, W., D. Power, and S. Quigley. 1976. Linguistics and Deaf Children: Transformational syntax and its applications. Alexander Graham Bell Association, Washington, D.C.

Rutter, M. 1968. Concepts on autism: A review of research. J. Child Psychol. Psychiatry 9:1-25.

Sachs, J. 1967. Recognition memory for syntactic and semantic aspects of connected discourse. Percept. Psychophys. 2:437-442.

Sachs, J., and M. Johnson. 1976. Language development in a hearing child of deaf parents. In W. Von Raffler Engel and Y. Lebrun (eds.), Baby Talk and Infant Speech. Swets & Zeitlinger, Lisse, The Netherlands.

Sanders, J. (ed.). 1968. The ABC's of Sign Language. Manca Press, Tulsa, Okla.

Sapir, E. 1925. Sound patterns in language. Language 1:37-51.

Schaeffer, B. Spontaneous language through signed speech. In R. Schiefelbusch (ed.), Nonspeech Language and Communication: Analysis and Intervention. University Park Press, Baltimore. In press.

Schaeffer, B., G. Kollinzas, A. Musil, and P. McDowell. 1977. Spontaneous verbal language for autistic children through signed speech. Sign Lang. Stud. 17:287-328.

Schein, J., and T. Delk. 1974. The Deaf Population of the United States. The National Association of the Deaf, Washington, D.C.

Schiefelbusch, R. (ed.). 1978. Nonspeech Language and Communication: Analysis and Intervention. University Park Press, Baltimore. In press.

Schlesinger, H. 1972. Meaning and enjoyment: Language acquisition of deaf children. In T. O'Rourke (ed.), Psycholinguistics and Total Communication: The State of the Art. National Association of the Deaf, Silver Spring, Md.

Schlesinger, H., and K. Meadow. 1972. Sound and Sign: Childhood Deafness and Mental Health. University of California Press, Berkeley.

Schlesinger, I. 1970. The grammar of sign language and the problems of language universals. In J. Morton (ed.), Biological and Social Factors in Psycholinguistics. University of Illinois Press, Urbana-Champaign.

Schlesinger, I., B. Presser, E. Cohen, and T. Peled. 1970. Transfer of meaning in sign language. Working paper #12, The Hebrew University, Jerusalem.

Schmitt, P. 1968. Deaf children's comprehension and production of sentence transformations and verb tenses. Unpublished doctoral dissertation. University of Illinois, Urbana-Champaign.

Scouten, E. 1967. The Rochester method: An oral multi-sensory approach for instructing prelingual deaf children. Am. Ann. Deaf. 112:50–55.

Scouten, E. 1976. English acquisition as a requirement for job placement of deaf people. Audiol. Hear. Aug./Sept.:7,11.

Shaffer, T., and H. Goehl. 1974. The alinguistic child. Ment. Retard. 12:3–6.

Sheridan, C. 1978. Linguistic considerations of language in a visual mode. In R. Wilbur (ed.), Sign Language Research. A special issue of Communication and Cognition.

Siegel, J. 1969. The enlightment and a language of signs. J. Hist. Ideas 3:96–115.

Simmons, J., and C. Baltaxe. 1975. Language patterns of adolescent autistics. J. Autism Child. Schizo. 3:333–351.

Siple, P. 1973. Constraints for sign language from visual perception data. Unpublished manuscript. Salk Institute for Biological Studies, La Jolla, Cal.

Siple, P. (ed.). 1978. Understanding Language through Sign Language Research. Academic Press, New York.

Smeets, P., and S. Striefel. 1976. Acquisition of sign reading by transfer of stimulus control in a retarded deaf girl. J. Ment. Def. Res. 20:197–205.

Smith, N. 1973. The Acquisition of Phonology: A Case Study. Cambridge University Press, London.

Stevenson, E. 1964. A study of the educational achievement of deaf children of deaf parents. California News 80:143.

Stohr, P., and K. Van Hook. 1973. The development of manual communication in the severely and profoundly retarded. Paper presented at the American Speech and Hearing Association Convention, San Francisco.

Stokes, W., and P. Menyuk. 1975. A proposal for the investigation of the acquisition of American Sign Language and Signed English by deaf and hearing children enrolled in integrated nursery school programs. Unpublished manuscript. Boston University.

Stokoe, W. 1960. Sign language structure: An outline of the visual communication system of the American deaf. Stud. Ling. Occasional Papers No. 8.

Stokoe, W. 1970a. The study of Sign Language. ERIC Clearinghouse for Linguistics, Center for Applied Linguistics, Washington, D.C.

Stokoe, W. 1970b. Sign language diglossia. Stud. Ling. 21:27–41.

Stokoe, W. 1972. Classification and description of sign languages. In T. Sebeok (ed.), Current Trends in Linguistics 12. Mouton, The Hague.

Stokoe, W., D. Casterline, and C. Croneberg. 1965. Dictionary of American Sign Language. Gallaudet College, Washington, D.C. (Revised 1978. Linstock Press, Silver Spring, Md.)

Stremel-Campbell, K., D. Cantrell, and J. Halle. 1977. Manual signing as a language system and as a speech initiator for the non-verbal severely handicapped student. In E. Sontag, J. Smith, and N. Certo (eds.), Educational Programming for the Severely and Profoundly Handicapped. The Council for Exceptional Children, Reston, Va.

Stuckless, R., and J. Birch. 1966. The influence of early manual communication on the linguistic development of deaf children. Am. Ann. Deaf 106:436–480.

Supalla, T., and E. Newport. 1978. How many seats in a chair? The derivation of nouns and verbs in American Sign Language. In P. Siple (ed.), Understanding Language through Sign Language Research. Academic Press, New York.

Sutherland, G., and J. Becket. 1969. Teaching the mentally retarded sign language. J. Rehab. Deaf 2:56–60.

Sutton, V. 1976. Sutton Movement Shorthand: The Sign Language Key. The Movement Shorthand Society Press, Irvine, Cal.

Swadesh, M. 1934. The phonemic principle. Language 10:117–129.

Swadesh, M., and C. Vogelin. 1939. A problem in phonological alternation. Language 15:1–10.

Taylor, L. 1969. A language analysis of the writing of deaf children. Unpublished doctoral dissertation. Florida State University, Tallahassee.

Tervoort, B. 1961. Esoteric symbols in the communicative behavior of young deaf children. Am. Ann. Deaf 106:436–480.

Tervoort, B. 1968. You me downtown movie fun. Lingua 21:455–465.

Thompson, H. 1977. The lack of subordination in American Sign Language. In L. Friedman (ed.), On the Other Hand: New Perspectives in American Sign Language. Academic Press, New York.

Tjapkes, S. 1976. Distinctive feature analysis of American Sign Language: A theoretical model. Unpublished master's thesis. University of South Florida, Tampa.

Todd, P. 1971. A case of structural interference across sensory modalities in second-language learning. Word 27.

Todd, P. 1972. From sign language to speech: Delayed acquisition of English by a hearing child of deaf parents. Unpublished doctoral dissertation. University of California, Berkeley.

Twaddell, W. 1935. On defining the phoneme. Language Monograph No. 16.

Tweney, R., and G. Heiman. 1977. The effect of sign language grammatical structure on recall. Bull. Psychonom. Soc. 10:331–334.

Van Biervliet, A. 1977. Establishing words and objects as functionally equivalent through manual sign training. Am. J. Ment. Def. 82:178–186.

Vasishta, M., K. Wilson, and J. Woodward. 1978. Sign language in India: Regional variation within the deaf population. Presented at the Fifth International Congress of Applied Linguistics, Montreal.

Vernon, M., and S. Koh. 1970. Effects of early manual communication on achievement of deaf children. Am. Ann. Deaf. 115:527–536.

Wampler, D. 1971. Linguistics of Visual English. Early Childhood Education Department, Aurally Handicapped Program Santa Rosa City Schools, Santa Rosa, Cal.

Wampler, D. 1972. Linguistics of Visual English. 2322 Maher Dr. 35, Santa Rosa, Cal.

Washabaugh, W., J. Woodward, and S. DeSantis. 1976. Providence Island Sign: A context-dependent language. Presented at the Linguistic Society of American Annual Meeting, Philadelphia.

Washington State School for the Deaf. 1972. An Introduction to Manual English. The Washington State School for the Deaf, Vancouver.

Wasow, T. 1973. The innateness hypothesis and grammatical relations. Synthese 26:38–56.

Watson, D. 1964. Talk with your hands. George Banta, Menasha, Wisc. (Reprinted 1973.)

Watson, L. 1977. Conversational participation by language-deficient and normal children. Presented at the American Speech and Hearing Association Conference, Chicago.

Webster, C., M. Konstantareas, and J. Oxman. 1976. Simultaneous communication with severely dysfunctional non-verbal children: An alternative to speech training. Working paper, University of Victoria.

Webster, C., H. McPherson, L. Sloman, M. Evans, and E. Kaucher. 1973. Communicating with an autistic boy with gestures. J. Autism Child. Schizo. 3:337–346.

Wickelgren, W. 1965. Distinctive features and errors in short-term memory for English vowels. J. Acoust. Soc. Am. 38:583–588.

Wilbur, R. 1973a. The phonology of reduplication. Unpublished doctoral dissertation. University of Illinois, Urbana-Champaign.

Wilbur, R. 1973b. The identity constraint: An explanation of the irregular behavior of reduplicated forms. Stud. Linguist. Sci. 3:143–154.

Wilbur, R. 1974a. When is a phonological rule not a phonological rule? The morphology of Sierra Miwok. In A. Bruck, R. Fox, and M. LaGaly (eds.), Papers from the Parasession on Natural Phonology. Chicago Linguistic Society, Chicago.

Wilbur, R. 1974b. Deaf and hearing children's abilities to recognize word patterns: The development of morpheme structure constraints in children. Presented at the American Speech and Hearing Association Convention, Las Vegas.

Wilbur, R. 1974c. Reading and memory processes in deaf people who learned ASL as their first language. Unpublished manuscript. Institute for Research on Exceptional Children, University of Illinois, Urbana-Champaign.

Wilbur, R. 1975. Morphology and the rule ordering controversy. In C. Cogen, H. Thompson, G. Thurgood, and K. Wright (eds.), Proceedings of the First Annual Meeting of the Berkeley Linguistic Society. Berkeley Linguistic Society, Berkeley.

Wilbur, R. 1976. The linguistics of manual languages and manual systems. In L. Lloyd (ed.), Communication Assessment and Intervention Strategies. University Park Press, Baltimore.

Wilbur, R. 1977. An explanation of deaf children's difficulty with several syntactic structures of English. Volta Rev. 79:85–92.

Wilbur, R. 1978a. On the notion of derived segments in American Sign Language. In R. Wilbur (ed.), Sign Language Research. A special issue of Communication and Cognition.

Wilbur, R. (ed.), 1978b. Sign Language Research. A special issue of Communication and Cognition.

Wilbur, R. Theoretical phonology and child phonology: Argumentation and implications. In D. Goyvaerts (ed.), Phonology in the 1970's. Story-Scientia, Ghent. In press a.

Wilbur, R. Nonspeech symbol systems: Discussant's comments. In R. Schiefelbusch (ed.), Nonspeech Language and Communication: Analysis and Intervention. University Park Press, Baltimore. In press b.

Wilbur, R., M. Bernstein, and R. Kantor. 1978. The semantic domain of classifiers in ASL. Presented at the MIT Sign Language Symposium, Cambridge, Mass. and at the summer meeting, Linguistic Society of America, Urbana, Ill.

Wilbur, R., and J. Flood. 1977. Sign language and initial reading instruction: A comparison of methods. Presented at the American Speech and Hearing Association Convention, Chicago.

Wilbur, R., and M. Jones. 1974. Some aspects of the bilingual/bimodal acquisition of sign language and English by three hearing children of deaf parents. In M. LaGaly, R. Fox, and A. Bruck (eds.), Papers from the Tenth Regional Meeting, Chicago Linguistic Society. Chicago Linguistic Society, Chicago.

Wilbur, R., and L. Menn. 1975. Towards a redefinition of psychological reality: On the internal structure of the lexicon. San Jose State Occasional Papers 2:212-221.

Wilbur, R., D. Montanelli, and S. Quigley. 1976. Pronominalization in the language of deaf students. J. Speech Hear. Res. 19:120-141.

Wilbur, R., and S. Quigley. 1975. Syntactic structures in the language of deaf students. Volta Rev. 77:194-203.

Wilbur, R., S. Quigley, and D. Montanelli. 1975. Conjoined structures in the language of deaf students. J. Speech Hear. Res. 18:319-335.

Wilson, K. 1978. Syntactic features of sign languages in India. Presented at the MIT Sign Language Symposium, Cambridge, Mass.

Wilson, P. 1974. Sign language as a means of communication for the mentally retarded. Presented at the Eastern Psychological Association Conference, New York.

Wing, G. 1887. The theory and practice of grammatical methods. Am. Ann. Deaf 32:84-89.

Wolf, J., and M. McAlone. A multi-modality language program for retarded preschoolers. Educ. Train. Ment. Retard. In press.

Woodward, J. 1972. Implications for sociolinguistic research among the deaf. Sign Lang. Stud. 1:1-17.

Woodward, J. 1973a. Implicational lects on the deaf diglossic continuum. Unpublished doctoral dissertation. Georgetown University, Washington, D.C.

Woodward, J. 1973b. Some observations on sociolinguistic variation and American Sign Language. Kansas J. Sociol. 9:191-200.

Woodward, J. 1973c. Interrule implication in American Sign Language. Sign Lang. Stud. 3:47-56.

Woodward, J. 1973d. Some characteristics of Pidgin Sign English. Sign. Lang. Stud. 3:39-46.

Woodward, J. 1974a. Implicational variation in American Sign Language: Negative incorporation. Sign Lang. Stud. 5:20-30.

Woodward, J. 1974b. A report on Montana-Washington implicational research. Sign Lang. Stud. 4:77-101.

Woodward, J. 1974c. Variety is the spice of life. Presented at the First Annual Conference on Sign Language, Gallaudet College, Washington, D.C.

Woodward, J. 1975. Variation in American Sign Language syntax. Unpublished manuscript, Linguistics Research Laboratory, Gallaudet College, Washington, D.C.

Woodward, J. 1976a. Black Southern Signing. Lang. Soc. 5:211-218.

Woodward, J. 1976b. Signs of change: Historical variation in American Sign Language. Sign Lang. Stud. 10:81-94.

Woodward, J. 1976c. Signs of sexual behavior. Presented at the Annual Meeting of the National Registry of Interpreters for the Deaf, St. Petersburg.

Woodward, J. 1977a. Sex is definitely a problem: Interpreter's knowledge of signs for sexual behavior. Sign Lang. Stud. 14:73-88.

Woodward, J. 1977b. All in the family: Kinship lexicalization across sign languages. Presented at the Georgetown Roundtable on Language and Linguistics, Washington, D.C.

Woodward, J. 1978. Historical bases of American Sign Languages. In P. Siple (ed.), Understanding Language through Sign Language Research. Academic Press, New York.

Woodward, J., and S. DeSantis. 1977a. Two-to-one it happens: Dynamic phonology in two sign languages. Sign Lang. Stud. 17:329-346.

Woodward, J., and S. DeSantis. 1977b. Negative incorporation in French and American Sign Language. Lang. Soc. 6.

Woodward, J., and C. Erting. 1975. Variation and historical change in American Sign Language. Lang. Sci. 37:9-12.

Woodward, J., C. Erting, and S. Oliver. 1976. Facing and hand(l)ing variation in American Sign Language phonology. Sign Lang. Stud. 11:43-51.

Woodward, J., and H. Markowicz. 1975. Some handy new ideas on pidgins and creoles: Pidgin sign languages. Presented at the International Conference on Pidgin and Creole Languages, Honolulu.

Woodward, M. 1959. The behavior of idiots interpreted by Piaget's theory of sensori-motor development. Br. J. Educ. Psychol. 29:60-71.

Yoder, D. 1978. Non-speech communication. Presented at the Boston University Miniseminar on Non-speech Language Intervention.

Author Index

Subject Index

Transparency, 152–153, 182
Trial pronoun, 114, 116
Two-out-of-three principle, 210, 214,
    215

Unit phrase, 118
UP, *see* Unit phrase
Utterance, definition, 121

VC, *see* Verb complex
Verb
  classes of, 103, 160–161
  directionality, 103, 104, 136
  reduplication, 75, 82, 189–190
  reversibility, 103, 104, 161
  tense, 95–101
Verb agreement, 103–104
  acquisition of, 160–161
Verb complex
  formalization of, 132–136
  word order in, 132–136
Verb inflection
  acquisition of, 160
  by body shift, 93, 105–106, 117,
    128, 135
  location incorporation, 103, 104,
    139–140, 155, 160–161

for negation, 98–99
for plural, 93–94, 104
points in space and, 122, 127,
    130, 132
for time, 95–97
for unaccomplished aspect, 97–98
Verb phrase, 132–133
V handshape
  as classifier, 70, 86, 149
  in dual form, 94, 114
  functions, 85–86
Vocabulary, acquisition, stages of,
    157
Vocabulary Norms for Deaf Children,
    219
VP, *see* Verb phrase

Warlpiri Sign Language, 2
WH-complement, 142
WH-questions, 146
  in English, acquisition and, 233
WH-words, 85
Word order, 123–140
  early analyses of, 124–128
  flexibility condition, 131–132
  nonmanual cues and, 136–140
  point in space, role in, 128–131